Student Problem Manual

for use with

Ross/Westerfield/Jaffe

Corporate Finance

Second Edition

Prepared by

R. Bruce Swensen
Adelphi University
and
Bradford D. Jordan
University of Missouri—Columbia

Homewood, IL 60430
Boston, MA 02116

© Richard D. Irwin, Inc., 1988 and 1990

Printed in the United States of America.

ISBN 0-256-07918-8

1 2 3 4 5 6 7 8 9 0 ML 7 6 5 4 3 2 1 0

TABLE OF CONTENTS

PREFACE

With all the changes and innovations of recent years, studying and understanding corporate finance have never been more challenging or rewarding than they are today. In the second edition of <u>Corporate Finance</u>, Professors Stephen A. Ross, Randolph W. Westerfield and Jeffrey F. Jaffe have done a superb job of presenting the modern principles of financial management. This Student Problem Manual is intended to give you, the student, every advantage in mastering those principles as quickly and as easily as possible.

This Manual will be useful to you in several ways as you study and learn corporate finance. It will assist you in your reading and understanding of the text by providing concise, intuitive explanations, as well as detailed numerical examples illustrating essential concepts. It will provide assistance in your exam preparation by providing numerous concept questions, with answers, along with valuable practice in solving numerical problems; detailed solutions are provided for the problems.

Organization of the Student Problem Manual

The organization of this guide closely parallels that of the text, and it contains a comprehensive treatment of every chapter. For each chapter, this guide provides you with:

<u>Chapter Highlights</u>. Rather than just providing you with a simple outline, this Manual covers all the essential concepts and subjects in an easily understandable narrative. Extra discussion is provided for the more difficult subjects. Numerical examples are used throughout to illustrate important ideas.

<u>Concept Test</u>. This Manual contains approximately 15 to 20 concept questions for each chapter. These fill-in-the-blank questions are designed to allow you to test your understanding of the material and to identify your strengths and weaknesses by comparing your answers to those provided.

<u>Problems and Solutions</u>. Approximately 15 detailed problems and solutions are provided for each chapter. One of the most important features of this Manual is that each problem is followed by a **detailed** solution; you will be able to see immediately both the right answer and detailed discussion indicating **how** to solve the problem.

Tips for the User

Many of the problems build on each other in order to provide you with a step-by-step learning guide. As an aid in this process, a solution immediately follows each problem. You'll get a lot more out of the problems if you try to solve them yourself and then compare your results to our solutions. Also, many of the problems were solved using a financial calculator or a personal computer. If you use financial tables, don't be surprised if your answer is slightly different from ours. This is a result of rounding in the tables.

Preface

We've greatly enjoyed preparing this Study Guide for you. However you use it, we hope it makes your studies more fruitful and enjoyable--and a little easier.

Best wishes to you all.

R. Bruce Swensen
Adelphi University

Bradford D. Jordan
University of Missouri-Columbia

ACKNOWLEDGEMENTS

Completion of this project required invaluable assistance from many individuals. My gratitude goes to Mike Junior, of Richard D. Irwin, Inc., for having faith in my ability to prepare this Student Problem Manual; to Reuben Molloy, of the Adelphi University Computer Center, for his patient, informative assistance in Word Perfect; to Dave Hale, of the Adelphi University Computer Center, for his equally patient guidance in matters related to hardware, especially printing; and, to Glenn Duffy, an M.B.A. student at Adelphi University, for his important contributions, especially in proof-reading and preparing portions of the Concept Tests.

Brad Jordan's excellent Study Guide, which accompanied the first edition of <u>Corporate Finance</u>, was extremely well-prepared and was both the predecessor to, and the foundation for, this Student Problem Manual. The outstanding work of Stephen A. Ross, Randolph W. Westerfield and Jeffrey F. Jaffe on the second edition of <u>Corporate Finance</u> has made the preparation of this Manual both informative and satisfying. An excellent job of reviewing the manuscript for this Student Problem Manual was done by Tom Bankston, who made numerous corrections and valuable suggestions for improvement.

And, for inspiration, my thanks and my love to my daughter, Kristina.

R. Bruce Swensen

CHAPTER 1
INTRODUCTION TO CORPORATE FINANCE

CHAPTER HIGHLIGHTS

Chapter 1 covers essential background material. For students familiar with basic accounting and economics, much of this material is review. The most important concept introduced in the chapter concerns the goals of the corporate firm. Before discussing these goals, however, some preliminary material on the modern corporation is presented.

What is Corporate Finance?

The most important concern of financial managers is **value creation**. Suppose you were to purchase materials, buildings and equipment (assets) to be used in producing a product. To pay for these assets, you use some of your own money (equity) as well as funds obtained by borrowing (debts or liabilities). Having done this, so long as the value of the cash flows derived from the sale of the product exceeds the cost of the assets required to produce the product, you have created value. This value is reflected in the fact that you, as the owner of the firm, would be able to sell your ownership of the firm for a dollar amount which exceeds the amount you have invested in the firm.

The concept of value creation can be summarized by reference to the **balance sheet model** of the firm. The balance sheet is a summary, at a point in time, that indicates the value of a business. The left-hand side of the balance sheet lists the assets of the firm, which are classified as **current assets** or **fixed assets**. A fixed asset, such as a warehouse, has a relatively long life. A current asset has a shorter life, generally less than one year. Inventory, for example, would normally be purchased and sold within a year, and is thus classified as a current asset.

In order to acquire assets, a corporation must raise cash by issuing, or selling, **securities**. A security is a claim on the assets of the firm, either in the form of a debt (i.e., a loan agreement) or an equity share (i.e., a stock certificate). The liabilities and owners', or shareholders', equity are listed on the right-hand side of the balance sheet. A debt that must be repaid in a year or less is classified as a current liability, while other debts are categorized as long-term liabilities.

By definition, the difference between the value of the assets and the value of the liabilities (current plus long-term) is the shareholders' equity. For example, suppose the firm had current assets of $100, fixed assets of $500, short-term debt of $70, and long-term debt of $200. The total assets are ($100 + $500) = $600, the total liabilities are ($70 + $200) = $270, so the shareholders' equity is the difference: ($600 - $270) = $330. The balance sheet would thus look like:

Assets		Liabilities	
Current assets	$100	$ 70	Current liabilities
Fixed assets	500	200	Long-term debt
	___	330	Shareholder's equity
Total assets	$600	$600	Total liabilities and shareholders' equity

The difference between current assets and current liabilities ($30 in this example) is called the firm's **net working capital**.

The balance sheet model of the firm suggests that the study of corporate finance can be viewed in terms of the following three questions:

1. What fixed assets should the firm buy?
2. What is the best way to raise cash in order to finance the purchase of fixed assets?
3. How should the firm manage its short-term assets and liabilities?

The first question represents the **capital budgeting** decision. The process of making capital budgeting decisions is described in detail in Part Two of the text.

The second issue is the **capital structure** decision. Capital structure refers to the mix of long-term debt and equity which the firm chooses in order to finance its investment in fixed assets. Capital structure decisions are discussed in Part Four of the text.

The third question is the **short term finance** decision. Since cash inflows and outflows do not occur at the same time, gaps in cash flows must be managed by appropriate adjustments of current assets and current liabilities. The topic of short term finance is presented in Part Six.

In the most general sense, the job of the financial manager is to create value for the owners of the firm by acquiring assets whose value is greater than their cost, and by issuing securities whose selling price is greater than their value. These responsibilities are the capital budgeting decision and the capital structure decision, respectively. In capital budgeting, the financial manager must forecast the cash inflows associated with the acquisition of a fixed asset, determine the value of the asset based on the cash flow forecast, and then compare value and cost. For capital structure decisions, the financial manager forecasts the cash outflows associated with repayment of a debt security, for example, determines the value of these outflows, and compares the value and the selling price of the security.

It is important to avoid confusing cash flows with accounting income. For accounting purposes, a sale is recorded at the time of purchase, but the cash inflow obviously does not occur until payment is actually made. Similarly, a cost is recorded when the obligation to pay is incurred, not when the bill is actually paid.

The value of a fixed asset or security depends on the size, timing and risk of the associated cash flows. For the most part, **Generally Accepted Accounting Principles** (GAAP) ignore both the timing and the risk associated with cash flows. Financial managers must be concerned not only with how much cash the firm expects to receive, but also when, and how likely, the firm is to receive it. A significant portion of the text is devoted to developing an understanding of how these dimensions of cash flows affect value. The relationship between the timing of cash flows and value is presented in detail in Part Two of the text; the affect of risk on value is the primary focus of Part Three.

Corporate Securities as Contingent Claims on Total Firm Value

The primary difference between debt and equity is that debt represents a promise by the corporation to pay a fixed amount at a specified time, whereas equity is a residual claim; that is, equity represents a claim to the value that remains after the debtholders (or creditors) are paid. Suppose that the firm has promised to pay F dollars to its creditors in one year and that, at the end of the year, the firm is worth X dollars. If X is greater than F, then the creditors receive F, as promised, and the stockholders collect (X - F). However, if X is less than F, then the creditors receive X (which is the most that the firm can pay) and the stockholders have zero. Consequently, debt and equity securities are said to be **contingent claims** on the total firm value because the value of the securities is contingent upon the value of the firm.

The Corporate Firm

Businesses can be organized in three different legal forms. Each of the three has distinct advantages and disadvantages in terms of the life of the business, the ability of the business to obtain financing, and taxes.

Sole Proprietorship. A sole proprietorship is owned by one person. The owner keeps all the profits but has **unlimited liability** for business debts. There is no distinction between personal and business income, so that profits are taxed as individual income. The sole proprietorship is the simplest type of business to form and is the least regulated. However, the life of the business is limited to its owner's lifespan, and the amount of equity financing is limited to the proprietor's personal wealth. Ownership of a sole proprietorship cannot be easily transferred.

Partnership. A partnership is similar to a proprietorship except that there are two or more owners, or partners. In a **general partnership**, all the partners share in gains or losses and all have unlimited liability for partnership debts. In a **limited partnership**, one or more general partners run the business and have unlimited liability, while one or more limited partners do not actively participate in the business. A limited partner's liability for business debts is limited to the amount she contributes to the partnership.

The advantages and disadvantages of a partnership are basically the same as those for a proprietorship. The partnership terminates when a general partner dies, no corporate taxes are paid, and the amount of equity financing available is limited to the partners' combined wealth. Ownership is not easily transferred.

The Corporation. The corporation is the most important form of business organization. A corporation is a legal entity, separate and distinct from its owners. Forming a corporation involves preparing **articles of incorporation** and a set of **bylaws**. The articles of incorporation must contain information regarding the corporation's name, its intended life (which can be perpetual), its business purpose, and the number of shares that can be issued. The bylaws are rules describing how the corporation regulates its own existence.

The shareholders and the management of a corporation are usually separate groups. The shareholders elect the members of the board of directors, who then select the managers. Management is charged with running the corporation's affairs in the shareholders' interest.

As a result of the separation of ownership and management, the corporate form has several advantages. Ownership is represented by shares of stock and can be readily transferred, so that the life of the corporation is not limited. The shareholders have **limited liability** for corporate debts; that is, the most they can lose is the amount they have invested in the corporation.

The major disadvantage of the corporate form is **double taxation.** Corporate profits are subject to corporate income taxes and then dividends paid to shareholders are taxed as income to the shareholder.

Goals of the Corporate Firm

Corporate finance can be thought of as the study of the process of financial decision-making within the corporation. In general, decision-making requires knowledge of the objectives which the decision-maker attempts to achieve. Decision-making in the corporate setting is complicated by the fact that numerous constituencies are affected by a financial manager's decisions. Consequently, it is necessary to understand the relationships among the various constituencies in order to specify the appropriate goal for the financial decision-maker.

Agency Costs and the Set-of-Contracts Perspective. It is informative to view the corporation as a **set of contracts** among different groups with conflicting goals. Instead of managing the firm themselves, the **principals** (i.e., the shareholders) contract with **agents** (i.e., the management) to perform the task. An **agency problem** exists because management goals may differ from shareholder goals. From the owners' point of view, the goal of the corporation is the **maximization of shareholder wealth**; that is, maximizing the price per share of the firm's common stock. Shareholders can encourage managers to perform in a manner consistent with shareholders' interests by creating appropriate management incentive contracts and by monitoring management activity. The costs associated with these activities are called **agency costs**. Since agency problems are often costly to resolve, it is unlikely that every action taken by the corporation will be strictly in the best interests of the owners.

Managerial Goals. It is sometimes argued that, left to themselves, managers would tend to be motivated by considerations such as organizational survival, managerial independence, and corporate self-sufficiency. These factors are consistent with the maximization of the amount of resources over which managers have control or, more generally, the maximization of corporate wealth. Corporate wealth is closely related to corporate size or growth, but decisions that increase the size of the firm do not necessarily increase the price per share of the stock.

Separation of Ownership and Control. Some large corporations have millions of stockholders. This dispersion of ownership may prevent effective control of management behavior, thereby creating a separation of ownership and control.

Do Shareholders Control Managerial Behavior? Even in the largest corporations, mechanisms exist that tend to ensure that management will act in the shareholders' interest. First, shareholders elect corporate directors who hire (and fire) management. Second, management compensation is often based, at least in part, on stock value. Third, poorly managed firms may find themselves taken over by another firm, with the result that existing management is replaced. Finally, those managers who are successful in achieving shareholder goals will be in greater demand and command greater salaries in the labor market.

The available theory and evidence are consistent with the view that shareholders control the firm and that shareholder wealth maximization is the relevant goal of the corporation. Even so, there probably will be times when management goals are pursued at the expense of the shareholders, at least temporarily.

Financial Markets

The debt and equity securities issued by firms are bought and sold in the financial markets. Financial market transactions are often classified according to the maturity of the financial instruments bought and sold. Debt instruments requiring repayment in less than one year are said to trade in the **money market**; long-term debt and shares of stock trade in the **capital market**.

The money market is a loosely connected **dealer** market, consisting of large New York banks (i.e., money-market banks), government securities dealers, money brokers and dealers in other short-term debt instruments. A **dealer** continuously quotes prices at which it stands ready to buy and sell a particular financial instrument.

Commercial paper dealers

The Primary Market: New Issues. When a firm or government first sells, or issues, a security, the sale is said to take place in the **primary market**. Primary market transactions may be **public offerings** or **private placements**. A public offering is generally **underwritten** by a group of investment banking firms which purchase the securities from the issuing firm and then resell them to the public at a higher price.

Securities offered for sale to the public (i.e, a public offering) must be registered with the Securities and Exchange Commission (SEC). This registration requires full disclosure of all information relevant to the new issue. The costs of registration and compliance can be substantial; consequently, a firm may elect to sell a new issue privately, to large investors. A private placement need not be registered with the SEC.

Secondary Markets. After a security has been sold to the public, subsequent trades are said to take place in the **secondary markets**. Secondary markets are either **auction markets** or **dealer markets**. The common stock of most large U.S. corporations trades in organized auction markets, of which the New York Stock Exchange (NYSE) is the best known and largest. Most debt securities (i.e., bonds) trade in dealer markets. Some common stock trading takes place in the **over-the-counter (OTC)** market, which is a dealer market. The **National Association of Securities Dealers Automated Quotation System (NASDAQ)** is a telecommunications network linking dealers in OTC stocks.

85% + American & Midwest Stock Exchanges

Exchange Trading of Listed Stocks. An auction market, unlike a dealer market, has a physical location, generally referred to as an exchange, and trading in a specified stock takes place on the floor of the exchange at a particular location, called a **post**. **Specialists**, who are members of the exchange, **make a market** in specified stocks; that is, specialists are required to buy and sell, as needed, to ensure that there is a buyer for every seller and a seller for every buyer. The purpose of this arrangement is to make the market **liquid**. A liquid market is one in which assets can be sold quickly and at little expense.

→ & communicated immediately to public via computer

Listing. A stock that trades on the NYSE is said to be **listed** on the exchange. To be listed, a firm must apply to the exchange and meet certain minimum requirements regarding earnings, assets, market value, number of shares outstanding, and number of stockholders.

Outline of the Book

Both <u>Corporate Finance</u> by Ross, Westerfield and Jaffe, and this Student Problem Manual are organized into seven parts. The organization of the material reflects the three basic concerns of corporate finance: capital budgeting, capital structure, and short term finance. The first part is the overview presented in Chapters 1 and 2, which provides some background and describes the goal of the corporation. Part Two (Chapters 3 through 7) describes how assets are valued, develops the important concept of net present value and applies this concept to the capital budgeting problem. Part Three (Chapters 8 through 11) is about evaluating and measuring risk. The well-known Capital Asset Pricing Model (CAPM) and Arbitrage Pricing Theory (APT) are introduced. Part Four (Chapters 12 through 17) addresses the second basic issue of corporate finance: how should the firm obtain the financing required in order to pay for the acquisition of fixed assets? Closely related to this capital structure question is the issue of dividend policy, which is also examined in Part Four. Part Five (Chapters 18 through 23) is devoted to describing the alternative forms of long-term financing available. In Part Six (Chapters 24 through 27), the third basic question is explored; namely, how should the firm manage its short-term finances? Part Seven (Chapters 28 through 29) is devoted to two important special topics: mergers and acquisitions, and international finance.

CONCEPT TEST

1. Short-term assets are called _____ assets. Long-term assets are called _____ assets.

2. A _____ is a claim on the assets of a firm, either in the form of a debt or an equity share.

3. The mixture of debt and equity that a firm uses to finance its purchases of assets is called the firm's _____.

4. The decision regarding which fixed assets to buy is called the _____ decision.

5. A debt or obligation that must be repaid within a year is called a _____.

6. The difference between a firm's current assets and current liabilities is called the firm's _____.

7. Since the payments to the creditors and the owners of a firm depend on the value of the firm, bonds and stocks are said to be _____ on the value of the firm.

8. A business owned by a single person is a _____.

9. In a _____ partnership, all the partners have unlimited liability for partnership debts.

10. In a _____ partnership, there are two kinds of partners. The _____ partners have unlimited liability, whereas the _____ partners have limited liability.

11. The rules and procedures by which a corporation governs itself are contained in the corporate _____.

12. All corporations must prepare a document called the _____ describing the number of shares which may be issued, the business purpose, the intended life, and other details.

13. The primary disadvantage of the corporate form of organization is _____ of corporate income.

14. The primary goal of the corporation is maximization of _____.

15. Because management goals may conflict with shareholder goals, an _____ problem is said to exist.

16. A frequently cited **management** goal is maximization of _____.

17. The costs associated with aligning shareholder goals and management goals are called _____ costs.

18. When financial markets are classified according to the maturity of the financial instruments, the two types of markets are _____ markets and _____ markets.

19. The _____ market is the market for short-term debt instruments.

20. A market in which firms continuously stand ready to buy and sell is a _____ market.

21. The New York Stock Exchange is an example of a secondary market which functions as an _____ market.

22. A stock that trades on the NYSE is said to be _____ on the exchange.

23. All trading in a particular stock on the NYSE is handled by an individual known as a _____.

24. The dealer market for equities is called the _____ market.

25. When a security is first offered to the public, it is said to be trading in the _____ market. Later, it trades in the _____ market.

ANSWERS TO CONCEPT TEST

1. current; fixed
2. security
3. capital structure
4. capital budgeting
5. current liability
6. net working capital
7. contingent claims
8. sole proprietorship
9. general
10. limited; general; limited
11. bylaws
12. articles of incorporation
13. double taxation

14. shareholder wealth
15. agency
16. corporate wealth
17. agency
18. money; capital
19. money
20. dealer
21. auction
22. listed
23. specialist
24. over-the-counter
25. primary; secondary

PROBLEMS AND SOLUTIONS

Problem 1

Husky Corporation has fixed assets of $2000, current assets of $500, current liabilities of $200, and long-term debt of $1200. What is shareholders' equity for Husky? What is Husky's net working capital?

Solution 1

Shareholders' equity = Total assets - total liabilities = ($2500 - $1400) = $1100
Net working capital = Current assets - current liabilities = ($500 - $200) = $300

APPENDIX: TAX RATES

The Tax Reform Act of 1986 substantially changed the U.S. tax law. As of 1989, the maximum marginal tax rate is 34% for corporations and 33% for individuals. Capital gains realized when an asset is sold are taxed at the same rates as ordinary income, whereas prior law specified preferential tax rates for long-term capital gains. The investment tax credit has been eliminated, and procedures for calculating depreciation allowances have been changed; these are covered in detail in Chapter 7. Under previous law, 85% of the dividends received by one corporation from another were exempt from taxation. This exemption is now reduced to 80%.

Capital losses to offset gains are limited to $3000/yr

In making financial decisions, it is important to distinguish between marginal and average tax rates. An average tax rate is total taxes paid divided by total taxable income. A marginal tax rate is the tax rate applied to the last dollar earned.

CONCEPT TEST

1. Under current tax law, the maximum marginal tax rate for corporations is _34_ %.

2. When a corporation receives dividends from another corporation, _80_ % is exempt from federal taxes.

ANSWERS TO CONCEPT TEST

1. 34   2. 80

PROBLEMS AND SOLUTIONS

Problem 1

Suppose that the tax code requires you to pay taxes equal to 20% of your first $20,000 in income and 40% on income above $20,000. If you earn $30,000, what is your tax bill? Your average tax rate? Your marginal tax rate?

Solution 1

Your tax bill is [.20($20,000) + .40($30,000 - 20,000)] = $8000. Your average tax rate is thus ($8000/$30,000) = 26.67%. The tax rate on the last dollar earned is 40%, so 40% is your marginal tax rate.

CORP

Bd of Dir
↓
CEO
↓
COO
↓
VP-FIN ↙   ↘

[A] Treasurer
↓
[1] Cash Mgr   [2] Credit Mgr
                [4] Financial
[3] Capital   Planning
expenditures

[3] Controller
↓
[1] Tax Mgr   [2] Cost Acctg Mgr

[3] Financial   [4] Data Processing
Acctg Mgr   Mgr

Table 1A.1 p.23.

CHAPTER HIGHLIGHTS

This chapter delves more deeply into two topics introduced in Chapter 1: accounting statements and cash flow concepts. Those with a background in financial accounting will find that much of the material is review. The chapter emphasis is not on accounting per se, however. Instead, we recognize that financial statements are a key source of information for financial decisions; thus, the chapter emphasizes the **use** of accounting statements in corporate finance, rather than the preparation of the statements.

The Balance Sheet

As discussed in Chapter 1, the balance sheet is a snapshot of a firm's accounting value as of a particular date. The firm's **assets** are listed on the left-hand side, and the **liabilities** and **shareholders' equity** are shown on the right-hand side. By definition, the value of the firm's assets is equal to the sum of its liabilities and shareholders' equity:

$$\text{Assets} = \text{Liabilities} + \text{shareholders' equity}$$

This equality can also be thought of in terms of the definition of shareholders' equity, which is the difference between the value of the firm's assets and its liabilities.

The financial manager must be especially aware of the following three aspects of the balance sheet: **accounting liquidity, debt versus equity,** and **value versus cost.** Each of these items is related to one of the three basic issues of corporate finance introduced in Chapter 1.

Accounting Liquidity. Accounting liquidity refers to the speed and ease with which an asset can be converted to cash. Assets are listed on the balance sheet in order of decreasing liquidity. Current assets are relatively liquid and typically include cash, marketable securities (money-market instruments purchased by the firm), accounts receivable (money owed, but not yet paid, to the firm by customers), and inventory. Of these, cash and marketable securities are generally most liquid, while inventory is least liquid. Compared to current assets, fixed assets are relatively illiquid.

Liquidity is valuable because it increases the firm's ability to meet its short-term obligations. Unfortunately, liquid assets generally earn lower rates of return than do fixed assets. Thus there is a tradeoff between liquidity and foregone potential returns. This tradeoff is one of the key issues for financial managers to consider in managing short-term assets and liabilities.

Debt versus Equity. Liabilities are debts and therefore obligate the firm to repay principal and interest to creditors at a specified time. In contrast, equity holders are entitled only to residual cash flows and assets; that is, the portion which remains after creditors claims are satisfied. The differences between the claims of creditors and those of shareholders are important considerations for financial managers making capital structure decisions.

Value versus Cost. The values shown on the balance sheet for the firm's assets (sometimes called **book value** or **carry value**) generally do not indicate the assets current worth, or **market value**. Instead, asset values are based on **historical cost**. It would be purely a coincidence if the actual market value of an asset (that is, the price at which the asset could be sold) were equal to its book value. The financial manager must be especially aware of these distinctions when making capital budgeting decisions.

Two abbreviated balance sheets for Stowe Enterprises are shown below. If you are unfamiliar with the general form of a balance sheet, you should study these carefully.

Assets	1990	1991	Liabilities and owners' equity	1990	1991
Current assets			Current liabilities		
Cash	$ 200	$ 503	Accounts payable	$ 500	$ 530
Accounts			Notes payable	543	460
receivable	650	688	Other	214	183
Inventory	1045	700			
			Long-term debt	897	945
			Deferred taxes	200	239
Fixed assets			Stockholders' equity		
Net plant and			Common stock	190	240
equipment	1490	1689	Capital surplus	400	480
			Accumulated retained		
			earnings	441	503
Total assets	$3385	$3580	Total liabilities and owners' equity	$3385	$3580

The Income Statement

The income statement measures a firm's performance over a period of time. The income statement equation is:

$$\text{Revenues - Expenses = Income}$$

An income statement usually has several sections. The first section reports revenues and expenses from the firm's principal operations. The second contains nonoperating expenses, such as interest paid. Taxes paid are reported separately. The last item on the income statement is **net income** (i.e., 'the bottom line'). Net income is often expressed on a per share basis and called **earnings per share (EPS)**. A financial manager should keep the following concepts in mind when analyzing an income statement: GAAP, noncash items, time and costs.

Generally Accepted Accounting Principles. Generally Accepted Accounting Principles (GAAP) require that revenue is recorded on the income statement when it is earned, or **accrued**, even if the actual cash inflow from payment has not occurred. For example, if goods are sold on credit, then the revenue is recognized when the sale takes place, not when payment is made.

Noncash Items. A primary reason that accounting income differs from cash flow is that an income statement contains **noncash items**, as expenses deducted from income, which do not affect cash flow. The most important of these is **depreciation**. Suppose a firm purchases an asset for $5000, and pays for the asset in cash. Obviously, the firm has a $5000 cash outflow at the time of purchase. However, instead of deducting the $5000, as an expense, from the current year's revenues, an accountant might depreciate the asset over a five-year period. If the asset is depreciated on a straight-line basis, then each year ($5000/5) = $1000 would be deducted from revenues. The applicable accounting concept here is the 'matching principle,' which specifies that the expense of the asset is matched with the benefit produced by the asset. From the financial manager's point of view, the important concept to recognize is that the five annual $1000 deductions are noncash items; the actual cash outflow occurred when the asset was purchased.

Time and Costs. For financial decision-making, it is often useful to distinguish between variable costs and fixed costs. In the long run, all business costs are variable; given sufficient time, assets can be sold, debts can be paid, and so on. If our time horizon is relatively short, however, some costs are effectively fixed. Other costs, such as wages to laborers, are variable even in the short run. Even though the distinction between fixed and variable costs is important to the financial manager, accountants often do not make this distinction.

An abbreviated 1991 income statement for Stowe Enterprises is shown below:

Net sales		$1400
Cost of goods sold		700
Depreciation		200
Earnings before interest		
and taxes		$500
Interest paid		150
Taxable income		$350
Taxes		119
Current	80	
Deferred	39	
Net income		$231
Retained earnings	62	
Dividends	169	

Net Working Capital

The **statement of changes in net working capital** traces the changes in net working capital (NWC) over a period of time. The basic relationship is:

$$\text{Sources of NWC - Uses of NWC = Net Additions to NWC}$$

Sources of NWC are those transactions which bring in cash, such as increased borrowing, sale of additional stock, sale of fixed assets, and cash flow generated from operations. Uses of NWC are transactions which involve cash outflows. Examples include repayment of debt, purchase of assets, and payment of dividends.

Suppose that, during the course of the year, Stowe issued $128 of long-term debt and $219 of common stock, and sold fixed assets with a book value of $130. Given this information, along with the income statement and balance sheets, a statement of changes in net working capital can be completed for Stowe Enterprises as shown below:

Sources of Net Working Capital

After-tax cash flow	Net income	$ 231
	Depreciation	200
	Cash flow after interest and taxes	431
Decreases in fixed assets	Sales of fixed assets	130
Increases in long-term debt and equity	Deferred taxes	39
	Long-term debt financing	128
	Long-term equity financing	219
	Total sources	$ 947

Uses of Net Working Capital

Increases in fixed assets	Acquisition of fixed assets	$ 529
Decreases in long-term debt and equity	Retirement of of long-term debt	80
	Repurchase of equity	89
	Dividends	169
	Total uses	$ 867
	Additions to net working capital	$ 80
	Total	$947

Note that cash flow after interest and taxes is the sum of net income and depreciation; the notion that depreciation is a source of net working capital seems inconsistent with the fact that depreciation is an expense. The explanation for this apparent paradox lies in the fact that depreciation is a **noncash** deduction. Therefore, depreciation should not be deducted from revenues in computing cash flow, although it is deducted in calculating net income. In order to derive cash flow after interest and taxes from net income, depreciation must be added back. An equivalent calculation of cash flow after interest and taxes can be derived from the income statement by deducting taxes and all expenses, except depreciation, from revenues.

The uses of NWC include a fixed asset acquisition of $529. The 1990 balance sheet indicates that fixed assets were $1490 at the end of the year. The income statement shows that, during 1991, these assets depreciated by $200. Also, $130 in fixed assets were sold during the year. If no new assets were purchased, fixed assets would have been ($1490 - $200 - $130) = $1160. The 1991 balance sheet shows $1689 in fixed assets, so ($1689 - $1160) = $529 in fixed assets were acquired.

The retirement of long-term debt, as a use of net working capital, is equal to the year-end 1990 level of long-term debt ($897) plus new debt ($128) less the year-end 1991 amount ($945), or $80. Similarly, the equity repurchased is the beginning amount plus new equity plus retained earnings less the ending amount: ($1031 + $219 + $62 - $1223) = $89.

Cash Flow

The balance sheet equation indicates that the value of a firm's assets is equal to the value of its liabilities plus the value of its equity. Similarly, the cash flow from the firm generated by the use of its assets, CF(A), is equal to the sum of the cash flow to creditors, CF(B), and the cash flow to stockholders, CF(S):

$$CF(A) = CF(B) + CF(S)$$

Cash flow from the firm's assets has three components: **operating cash flow, changes in fixed assets**, and **additions to net working capital**.

The 1991 income statement shows that Stowe Enterprises has earnings before interest and taxes (EBIT) of $500. To this figure, we add the $200 in depreciation, since depreciation is a noncash deduction. Finally, current taxes are paid in cash, so we subtract the $80 in current taxes. The result is **operating cash flow**:

```
Earnings before interest and taxes      $500
Depreciation                             200
Current taxes                            (80)
   Operating cash flow                  $620
```

The change in fixed assets is equal to the difference between sales of fixed assets and the acquisition of fixed assets. The previous calculations indicate that Stowe Enterprises had a change in fixed assets of ($529 - $130) = $399.

Based on our sources and uses of NWC, additions to NWC were $80 in 1991. We can check this by noting that 1990 NWC was ($1895 - $1257) = $638 and for 1991, NWC was ($1891 - $1173) = $718. Thus the addition to NWC was ($718 - $638) = $80, as previously calculated.

Given these figures, the total cash flow from the firm's assets can be calculated as operating cash flow, less the change in fixed assets, less the net investment in working capital: ($620 - $399 - $80) = $141. Notice that the total cash flow to the firm does **not** equal the change in NWC.

The cash flow to investors in a firm consists of net payments to creditors and net payments to shareholders. The net payment to creditors is interest paid plus repayments of long-term debt, minus new long-term borrowing. Interest paid during 1991 was $150, and long-term debt increased by $128 less $80, or $48 net. So, the net cash flow to creditors is ($150 - $48) = $102.

Cash flow to shareholders consists of dividends paid plus shares of stock repurchased by the firm, minus the proceeds from the sale of new equity. In this example, cash flow to shareholders is ($169 + $89 - $219) = $39. Finally, total cash flow to creditors and stockholders is ($102 + $39) = $141, which equals the total cash flow from the firm's assets.

CONCEPT TEST

1. By definition, the value of a firm's assets is equal to _____ + _____.

2. An asset that can be converted to cash quickly and easily is said to be a _____ asset.

3. The fixed asset values shown on a firm's balance sheet are not current market values. Instead, they are shown at _____.

4. Net income divided by the number of shares outstanding is called _____.

5. For accounting purposes, revenue is shown on the income statement when it _____, not necessarily when payment is received.

6. The reason that net income is not the same as cash from operations is that some deductions are _____ deductions.

7. Of current assets and fixed assets, _____ are less liquid.

8. In the short run, rent is an example of a _____ cost.

9. The most common noncash expense is _____.

10. Operating cash flow is calculated as _____ + _____ - _____.

11. Total cash flow to the firm is calculated as _____ - _____ - _____.

12. Cash flow to creditors is calculated as _____ + _____ - _____.

13. Cash flow to stockholders is calculated as _____ + _____ - _____.

14. The firm's activities which bring in cash are called _____ of net working capital (NWC).

15. The firm's activities which use up cash are called _____ of net working capital (NWC).

For Questions 16-21, indicate whether the action is a source of net working capital or a use of net working capital.

16. Net fixed assets increase by $2000.

17. Inventory decreases by $150.

18. The firm repays a long-term debt early.

19. A cash dividend is paid.

20. Accounts receivable increase by $400.

21. A short-term bank loan is received.

For Questions 22-25, indicate whether the action results in an increase in net working capital, a decrease in net working capital, or no change.

22. Inventory is purchased with cash.

23. A warehouse is purchased with cash.

24. Proceeds from the sale of long-term debt are used to pay off a short-term loan.

25. A customer pays an overdue bill.

ANSWERS TO CONCEPT TEST

1. total liabilities;
     shareholders' equity
2. liquid
3. historical cost
4. earnings per share
5. accrues
6. noncash
7. fixed assets
8. fixed
9. depreciation
10. earnings before interest and taxes;
      depreciation; taxes
11. operating cash flow;
      capital spending;
      additions to net working capital

12. interest; repayments of long-term debt;
      proceeds from new long-term debt
13. dividends; stock repurchased;
      stock issued
14. sources
15. uses
16. use
17. source
18. use
19. use
20. use
21. source
22. no change
23. decrease
24. increase
25. no change

PROBLEMS AND SOLUTIONS

Problem 1

The Terri-Yung Company had sales of $1000, cost of goods sold of $400, depreciation of $100, and interest paid of $150. If the tax rate is 34% and all taxes are paid currently, what is net income?

Solution 1

Net income can be calculated as follows:

Net sales	$1000
Cost of goods sold	400
Depreciation	<u>100</u>
Earnings before interest	
and taxes	$500
Interest paid	<u>150</u>
Taxable income	$350
Current taxes	<u>119</u>
Net income	$<u>231</u>

Problem 2

Based on the information in Problem 1, what is Terri-Yung's operating cash flow?

Solution 2

Cash flow from operations is calculated as follows:

Earnings before interest	
and taxes	$500
+Depreciation	100
−Taxes	<u>119</u>
Cash flow from operations	$<u>481</u>

Problem 3

The asset side of the balance sheet for Terri-Yung is shown below. For each account, compute the change during the year, and classify each change as either a source or a use of net working capital.

Current Assets	1989	1991	Change	Source/Use
Cash	$ 800	$ 500	_____	_____
Marketable securities	400	300	_____	_____
Accounts receivable	900	800	_____	_____
Inventory	1,800	2,000	_____	_____
Fixed Assets				
Net plant	$ 6,000	$ 8,000	_____	_____
Total assets	$ 9,900	$11,600		

Solution 3

Current Assets	1990	1991	Change	Source/Use
Cash	$ 800	$ 500	−300	Source
Marketable securities	400	300	−100	Source
Accounts receivable	900	800	−100	Source
Inventory	1,800	2,000	200	Use
Fixed Assets				
Net plant	$ 6,000	$ 8,000	2000	Use
Total assets	$ 9,900	$11,600		

Problem 4

In 1990, Terri-Yung had notes payable of $1200, accounts payable of $2400, and long-term debt of $3000. The corresponding entries for 1991 are $1600, $2000, and $2800. Based on the assets in Problem 3, construct the right-hand side of the balance sheet for 1990 and 1991. (Hint: remember that shareholders' equity is the residual.)

Solution 4

Since total assets are $9,900 in 1990 and $11,600 in 1991, we can construct the liability side of the balance sheets:

Current Liabilities	1990	1991
Accounts payable	$2400	$2000
Notes payable	1200	1600
Total	$3600	$3600
Long-term Debt and Shareholders' Equity		
Long-term debt	$3000	$2800
Equity	3300	5200
Total	$6300	$8000
Total liabilities and equity	$9,900	$11,600

Problem 5

During the year, Terri-Yung sold $2400 worth of stock and used the entire proceeds to buy fixed assets. There was no new long-term borrowing, and dividends of $120 were paid. Based on this information and the financial statements for Terri-Yung, construct a statement of changes in net working capital for 1991.

Solution 5

We can prepare the statement as follows:

Sources of Net Working Capital

After-tax cash flow	Net income	$ 231
	Depreciation	100
	Cash flow after	
	interest and taxes	331
Decreases in fixed assets	Sales of fixed assets	300
Increases in long-term		
debt and equity	Deferred taxes	-
	Long-term debt	
	financing	-
	Long-term equity	
	financing	2400
	Total sources	$ 3031

Uses of Net Working Capital

Increases in fixed assets	Acquisition of	
	fixed assets	$ 2400
Decreases in long-term	Retirement of	
debt and equity	of long-term debt	200
	Repurchase of equity	611
	Dividends	120
	Total uses	$ 3331
	Additions to net	
	working capital	$ (300)

Solution notes: From the balance sheets, we see that net fixed assets increased by $2000, and we know that $2400 of new assets were purchased. The old assets depreciated by $100. Thus assets sold must be ($2400 - $2000 - $100) = $300. Also, net equity increased by $1900. Retained earnings were ($231 - $120) = $111. New equity was sold for $2400. So we must have repurchased ($2400 + $111 - $1900) = $611. The ($300) means a $300 **decrease.** This means the firm took $300 out of net working capital. This is a **source** of funds.

Problem 6

Based on the balance sheets for Terri-Yung, what was net working capital for 1990? For 1991? What must additions to net working capital have been? (Note that this is a good way to check your answer to Problem 5.)

Solution 6

Net working capital in 1990 was ($3900 - $3600) = $300. Net working capital in 1991 was ($3600 - $3600) = $0. So the addition to net working capital was ($0 - $300) = ($300), as previously calculated.

Problem 7

What was Terri-Yung's total cash flow to the firm in 1991?

Solution 7

Total cash flow to the firm can be calculated as:

```
        Operating cash flow                $ 481
        Net capital spending               (2100)
        Addition to net working capital      300
        Total                             ($1319)
```

Note from Problem 1 that Terri-Yung has a positive net income, but the cash flow is negative. A primary reason for this discrepancy is that the calculation of net income does not include capital spending. In general, net income is **not** equal to cash flow.

Solution notes: From Problem 5, we see that the firm invested $2400 in new assets and sold $300 of assets, so net capital spending was $2100. Also, the firm took $300 **out** of net working capital. Overall, the firm received $481 in cash from operations and $300 from liquidating working capital. The firm spent $2100 on new assets.

Problem 8

What was Terri-Yung's cash flow to long-term creditors in 1991?

Solution 8

Cash flow to creditors is interest paid ($150) plus repayment of long-term debt ($200), less new borrowing ($0), or $350 total.

Problem 9

What was Terri-Yung's cash flow to shareholders in 1991?

Solution 9

Cash flow to shareholders is dividends paid ($120) plus stock repurchased ($611) less new stock financing ($2400), or a total cash flow of negative $1669. Note that the total cash flow to creditors and to stockholders is ($350 - $1669) = -$1319, which is the answer to Problem 7.

Problem 10

Try this one on your own. Based on the following information for Pascucci Corp., calculate cash flow for the firm, cash flow to creditors, and cash flow to stockholders for 1991. (The tax rate is 34%.)

	1990	1991
Sales	$2230	$2890
Costs	1050	1437
Depreciation	418	418
Interest	225	276
Dividends	350	400
Current assets	1140	1335
Fixed assets	5670	5877
Current liabilities	884	1006
Long-term debt	2349	2666

Solution 10

```
Cash flow to long-term creditors (1991):   $( 41)
Cash flow to stockholders (1991):           $ 538
Cash flow to creditors and
    stockholders (1991):                    $ 497
```

APPENDIX: FINANCIAL STATEMENTS ANALYSIS

Financial managers, among others, use financial statements to evaluate various aspects of the firm's performance, including: short-term solvency, asset activity, financial leverage, profit margins, overall profitability, and value. In order to be able to make comparisons over time, or with similar businesses, the analysis of financial statements is often based on ratios of various balance sheet and income statement items, rather than dollar values. Accounting data for firms of vastly different size, or for a firm which grows over time, can not otherwise be reasonably compared.

Some ratios commonly used for financial statement analysis are described below. As you study them, keep in mind that most of them are based on accounting data, rather than cash flows and market values. As a result, they fail to capture many important dimensions of financial management. For example, these ratios generally ignore risk.

Short-term Solvency

This group of ratios is intended to measure the firm's short-term liquidity. The most common measures are the current ratio and the quick (or 'acid test') ratio.

Current Ratio. The current ratio compares the available current assets to current liabilities:

$$\text{Current ratio} = \frac{\text{Total current assets}}{\text{Total current liabilities}}$$

Deterioration of this ratio through time may indicate a worsening liquidity position.

Quick Ratio. The quick ratio is similar to the current ratio except that inventory is not included in the numerator:

$$\text{Quick ratio} = \frac{\text{(Total current assets - inventory)}}{\text{Total current liabilities}}$$

Inventory is subtracted from current assets in computing the quick ratio because inventory is usually the least liquid current asset.

Activity Ratios

These ratios are intended to measure how effectively the firm uses its assets. For any given category of assets, the appropriate level of investment is analyzed by comparison with the firm's sales. Three common measures which compare asset levels with sales are: the total asset turnover ratio, the receivables turnover ratio, and the inventory turnover ratio.

Total Asset Turnover. This ratio is designed to indicate how effectively the firm manages its total assets in generating revenues. It is defined as operating revenues (or sales) per dollar of assets:

$$\text{Total asset turnover} = \frac{\text{Total operating revenue}}{\text{Total assets (average)}}$$

A low value for this ratio, in comparison with that of other firms in the same industry, may indicate that assets are not being used as efficiently as possible; either the firm should be able to generate more sales revenue from the given level of assets, or the firm should reduce the level of assets for the given level of sales.

Receivables Turnover. The receivables turnover measures the firm's ability to manage collections of accounts from customers. The receivables turnover ratio is equal to operating revenue (or sales) per dollar in receivables:

$$\text{Receivables turnover} = \frac{\text{Total operating revenues}}{\text{Receivables (average net)}}$$

The average collection period (ACP) is a related measure, which is defined as the number of days (on average) that an account is outstanding:

$$\text{Average collection period} = \frac{\text{Days in period}}{\text{Receivables turnover}}$$

An ACP of 40 means that the firm, on average, collects payment 40 days after a sale. The relevant period is usually one year, so the numerator here is 365.

Inventory Turnover. Inventory turnover is comparable to receivables turnover in that it measures how quickly inventory is produced and sold. The inventory turnover ratio is calculated as follows:

$$\text{Inventory turnover} = \frac{\text{Cost of goods sold}}{\text{Inventory (average)}}$$

A high level of the inventory turnover ratio, relative to that of similar firms, may indicate that the firm is efficient in its inventory management. We can also compute the average number of days in inventory as follows:

$$\text{Days in inventory} = \frac{\text{Days in period}}{\text{Inventory turnover}}$$

Financial Leverage

Measures of financial leverage measure the extent to which a firm uses debt financing rather than equity financing. An increase in the level of debt increases the probability of default. On the other hand, the use of debt financing can provide value for shareholders; one of the advantages of moderate levels of debt-financing is the tax-deductibility of interest payments.

The two most common measures of financial leverage are the debt ratio and the interest coverage ratio. These ratios are intended to measure how heavily the firm relies on debt and the firm's ability to meet its debt obligations.

Debt Ratio. The debt ratio is given by:

$$\text{Debt ratio} = \frac{\text{Total debt}}{\text{Total assets}}$$

There are several other ways to examine the firm's use of debt. Two common variations are the debt-to-equity ratio and the equity multiplier:

$$\text{Debt-to-equity ratio} = \frac{\text{Total debt}}{\text{Total equity}}$$

$$\text{Equity multiplier} = \frac{\text{Total assets}}{\text{Total equity}}$$

Interest Coverage. This ratio measures the firm's ability to meet its interest obligations. It is calculated as follows:

$$\text{Interest coverage ratio} = \frac{\text{Earnings before interest and taxes}}{\text{Interest expense}}$$

Deterioration in this ratio through time can be a signal that the firm is heading for financial distress.

Profitability

Profitability ratios attempt to measure a firm's profitability using accounting statement data. However, since accounting data ignore both future profitability and risk, the profitability ratios may not provide an accurate indication of a firm's performance.

Profit Margin. Net profit margin and gross profit margin are computed as follows:

$$\text{Net profit margin} = \frac{\text{Net income}}{\text{Total operating revenue}}$$

$$\text{Gross profit margin} = \frac{\text{Earnings before interest and taxes}}{\text{Total operating revenue}}$$

Return on Assets. Net return on assets (ROA) and gross return on assets are commonly reported measures of performance. These ratios are defined as follows:

$$\text{ROA (net)} = \frac{\text{Net income}}{\text{Average total assets}}$$

$$\text{ROA (gross)} = \frac{\text{Earnings before interest and taxes}}{\text{Average total assets}}$$

The du Pont method of financial control relates return on assets to net profit margin and total asset turnover:

$$\text{ROA (net)} = \text{Net profit margin} \times \text{Asset turnover}$$

The point here is that return on assets can be increased by increasing either of its components. Furthermore, a firm can be profitable with a low profit margin, as long as low prices increase turnover, or with a high profit margin, even if high prices reduce turnover.

Return on Equity. The return on equity (ROE) is a measure of the return to the firm's stockholders; it is defined as:

$$\text{ROE} = \frac{\text{Net Income}}{\text{Shareholders' equity (average)}}$$

Return on equity can be thought of as follows:

$$\text{ROE} = \text{ROA} \times \text{Equity multiplier} =$$
$$\text{Profit margin} \times \text{Asset turnover} \times \text{Equity multiplier}$$

This last equation highlights the fact that the firm's return on equity depends on its efficiency of operations (as measured by profit margin), the effectiveness of its asset management, and its degree of leverage.

Payout Ratio. The payout ratio is the percentage of net income paid out as cash dividends:

$$\text{Payout ratio} = \frac{\text{Cash dividends}}{\text{Net income}}$$

The retention ratio is the percentage of net income that is retained in the firm; it can be computed as (1 - payout ratio).

Market Value Ratios

Financial statements do not tell us much about market values. Generally, market value information is combined with accounting information in the analysis of financial statements.

Market Price. The market price of a share of stock is the price that investors establish when they buy and sell the stock. The total market value of a firm's equity is the price per share multiplied by the number of shares. It is difficult to compare market values across firms because they are influenced by the number of shares outstanding and the size of the firm. Financial analysts frequently use ratios to make such comparisons.

Price-to-Earnings (P/E) Ratio. The P/E ratio is a widely quoted ratio in financial analysis. It is computed as current market price per share divided by annual earnings per share.

Dividend Yield. The dividend yield is calculated by dividing annualized dividends per share by current market price per share.

Market-to-Book (M/B) Value and the Q Ratio. The M/B ratio is the market price per share divided by the book value per share. A similar measure, called Tobin's Q, is defined as the total market value of the firm's debt and equity divided by the replacement cost of its assets. A firm with a Q ratio above 1 has a greater incentive to invest than does a firm with a Q ratio below 1.

CONCEPT TEST

1. The current ratio is defined as _____ divided by _____.

2. The quick ratio is similar to the current ratio except that _____ is deducted from current assets.

3. Total asset turnover is defined as _____ divided by _____.

4. The ACP is _____ divided by _____.

5. The days in inventory is calculated as _____ divided by _____.

6. Earnings before interest and taxes divided by interest expense is called the _____ ratio.

7. Three common measures of financial leverage are the _____ ratio, the _____ ratio, and the _____.

8. Net profit margin is _____ divided by _____.

9. Net return on assets is defined as _____ divided by _____.

10. Return on equity is defined as _____ divided by _____.

11. Return on equity can be written as the product of _____, _____, and the _____.

12. The _____ is calculated by dividing annualized dividends per share by current market price per share.

13. The _____ ratio is the market price per share divided by the book value per share.

14. The _____ is a measure of the return to the firm's stockholders.

15. The _____ measures the firm's ability to meet its interest obligations.

ANSWERS TO CONCEPT TEST

1. current assets; current liabilities
2. inventory
3. operating revenues; average total assets
4. days in period; receivables turnover
5. days in period; inventory turnover
6. coverage
7. debt; debt-to-equity; equity multiplier
8. net income; sales
9. net income; average total assets
10. net income; average shareholders' equity
11. profit margin; asset turnover; equity multiplier
12. dividend yield
13. market-to-book value
14. return on equity
15. interest coverage ratio

PROBLEMS AND SOLUTIONS

Problem 1

Use the 1991 financial statement information for Stowe Enterprises, on pages 13-14, to fill in the following table:

Financial Ratios for Stowe Enterprises

Short-term solvency ratios

Current ratio _____
Quick ratio _____

Activity ratios

Total asset turnover _____
Inventory turnover _____
Receivables turnover _____

Financial leverage ratios

Debt ratio _____
Debt-to-equity ratio _____
Equity multiplier _____
Interest coverage _____

```
              Profitability ratios

Net profit margin           _____
Return on assets            _____
Return on equity            _____
```

Solution 1

Financial Ratios for Stowe Enterprises

```
        Short-term solvency ratios

    Current ratio           1.61
    Quick ratio             1.02

            Activity ratios

    Total asset turnover     .40
    Inventory turnover       .80
    Receivables turnover    2.09

        Financial leverage ratios

    Debt ratio               .66
    Debt-to-equity ratio    1.93
    Equity multiplier       2.93
    Interest coverage       3.33

          Profitability ratios

    Profit margin          16.50%
    Return on assets        6.63%
    Return on equity       20.50%
```

Problem 2

Use the du Pont method to compute ROA and ROE for Stowe Enterprises.

Solution 2

Based on the du Pont method, ROA for Stowe is:

$$ROA = .1650(.40) = 6.6\%.$$

ROE is:

$$ROE = .1650(.40)(2.93) = .066(2.93) = 19.3\%.$$

This is not exactly the same as the 20.5% above because the equity multiplier is not based on average values for the year. If you calculate the equity multiplier using average values, you should get 3.1, and the du Pont method will indicate .1650(.40)(3.1) = 20.5%.

Problem 3

If the debt-to-equity ratio is .5, what is the total debt ratio? The equity multiplier?

Solution 3

If the debt-to-equity ratio is .5, the firm has $.50 in debt for every $1 in equity. This means the firm has $.50 in debt for every $1.50 in value, so the total debt ratio is .3333. The firm also has $1 in equity for every $1.50 in value, so the equity multiplier is 1.5.

Problem 4

If ROE is 16% and the debt ratio is .5, what is ROA?

Solution 4

The firm has $.50 in equity for every $1 in value, so the equity multiplier is 2. From the du Pont method, ROA(2) = ROE = .16, so ROA is 8%.

Problem 5

Suppose that beginning inventory is $1000 and ending inventory is $1200. Sales for the year are $14,000. Cost of goods sold is 70% of sales. Compute days in inventory.

Solution 5

Average inventory is $1100, so the inventory turnover is [.70($14,000/1100)] = 8.91. The days in inventory is (365/8.91) = 40.97 days.

CHAPTER 3
FINANCIAL MARKETS AND NET PRESENT VALUE: FIRST PRINCIPLES OF FINANCE

CHAPTER HIGHLIGHTS

The purpose of this chapter is to describe the way in which financial markets come to exist and how information obtained from financial markets is used to evaluate investment opportunities. This chapter also develops what is probably the single most important and useful concept in corporate finance: **net present value.** Net present value (NPV) is central to an understanding of virtually all of corporate finance. In order to focus on the net present value concept, discussion of the problems encountered in evaluating risk is deferred to later chapters. Therefore, we assume here that investments are free of risk.

Throughout this chapter, when we speak of investment decisions, we are referring to investments in **capital**, that is, investments which would appear as fixed assets on a corporate balance sheet.

The Financial Market Economy

Financial markets exist because individuals have different preferences for current consumption vs. future consumption. Consider two individuals, one of whom wishes to save some current income for the future (Susan) while the other wishes to spend more than his current income (Susan's husband, Brad). In a free enterprise economy, these two individuals can 'make a market.' Brad can borrow money from Susan and promise to repay the loan, with interest, at a later date. A financial instrument may come into being as a by-product of this transaction. Brad can give Susan an IOU indicating that he will pay, at a specified time, the borrowed amount, plus interest, to whomever holds the IOU. In this case, the IOU is a **bearer** instrument because Brad promises to 'pay the bearer.' Thus, if Susan wanted her money early, she could sell the IOU to someone else, although she would not receive the full interest payment. Susan is indifferent as to where the money comes from, as long as she gets paid, while Brad is indifferent with regard to whom he ultimately pays. It is important to note that Brad really does not care from whom he borrows, and Susan does not care to whom she lends. (Note that the risk of default on the loan is being ignored here; that is, we assume that there is no possibility that the borrower will fail to repay the loan when due.)

Anonymous Markets. In a large economy, a great number of transactions such as the one described above take place. Because it is costly and inefficient for lenders and borrowers to actually locate each other, institutions that specialize in matching borrowers and lenders (e.g., commercial banks, savings banks, mutual funds, credit unions) come into being. Such institutions are called **financial intermediaries**. Because intermediaries exist, the market is **anonymous** in the sense that borrowers and lenders never actually meet.

Market Clearing. In an economy with anonymous markets, there are many borrowers and lenders. If the amount of money that borrowers wish to borrow is equal to the amount that lenders wish to lend, then the market **clears**. If the market does not clear, it is because the interest rate is too high or too low. Suppose that the demand for borrowing exceeds the amount that lenders wish to lend. In this case, the interest rate is too low. If the rate were to rise, then some borrowers would borrow less (because of the higher rate) and some lenders would lend more. The rate that causes the market to clear is called the **equilibrium rate of interest**, which we denote as r.

Making Consumption Choices

In this section, we consider alternative consumption patterns for an individual whose consumption preferences differ from his income pattern. Suppose, for example, that you have income of $110 this year and $200 next year, and the opportunity to borrow or lend in the financial market. If you were to spend nothing at all this year, how much can you spend next year? The answer depends on r, the interest rate. If r is 10%, then you can lend $110 today in exchange for a promise to repay principal and interest next year. One year from now, the $110 principal would be repaid and you would also receive ($110)(10%) = $11 in interest, for a total of $121. In general, if you lend $110 for one year, you will receive [$110(1 + r)] next year. Thus, the most you could spend next year is next year's $200 income plus the proceeds from the $110 loan, or $321 in all.

Now consider another alternative consumption pattern: if you were to spend nothing at all next year, how much could you spend this year? Since you only have $200 income next year, this is the most you can repay on a loan. So the amount you can borrow is the value of B (borrowing) in the following equation:

$$B \times (1 + r) = \$200$$

Solving for B:

$$B = \frac{\$200}{(1.10)} = \$181.82$$

Thus you can spend a maximum of $291.82 this year ($110 income plus $181.82 borrowed).

This discussion indicates that there is an unlimited number of spending patterns, as long as individuals can borrow and lend freely. Using the data from the previous example, the following are a few of the possibilities (check for yourself that these are possible):

This Year's Consumption	Next Year's Consumption
$ 0	$321
50	266
100	211
200	101
292	0

Figure 3.1 represents the various consumption possibilities, which are represented by a straight line with slope -(1+.10). The slope reflects the fact that for every dollar you borrow, you will have 1.10 fewer dollars to spend next year. In Figure 3.1, the original income pattern of ($110, $200) is shown as point B. Point A corresponds to zero consumption this year and $321 next year. Point C corresponds to consuming everything today ($292), leaving nothing for next year. All the points between A and B involve lending money, while the points between B and C involve borrowing.

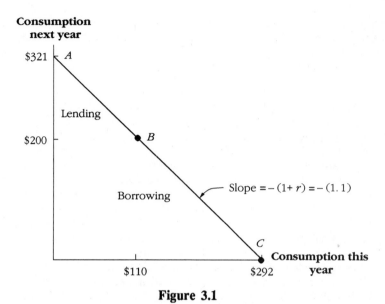

Figure 3.1

This simple illustration demonstrates the value of financial markets. Different individuals have different time preferences for consumption and different income patterns. The existence of a financial market allows everyone to adjust his or her consumption patterns, and everyone is better off as a result.

The Competitive Market

The financial market we have been describing has the characteristics of a **perfectly competitive financial market** (perfect market, for short). All borrowers and lenders are 'price takers;' that is, the equilibrium interest rate in the market is unaffected by the actions of any one individual or small group of individuals. In general, such a market exists when:

1.   All market participants have costless access to the financial market.
2.   All market participants have information about borrowing and lending opportunities in the financial market.
3.   There are many market participants, no one of which has a significant impact on prices or rates.

In a one-year, perfectly competitive financial market with no default risk, only one market interest rate can exist.

In order to understand this conclusion, suppose there were two rates, say 9% and 10%. What would happen? Everyone would rush to borrow at 9% and immediately lend at 10%, thereby earning a guaranteed profit with no net investment. Even if you had no money at all, you could borrow $10 million at 9% and lend it at 10%. At the end of the year, you would receive $11 million and only have to repay $10.9 million, for a guaranteed $100,000 profit. This situation is a pure 'money machine,' and it exists so long as there is more than one interest rate. Simultaneous buying and selling (or borrowing and lending) activities that earn certain profits with no net investment are called **arbitrage** opportunities. In the above example, the different rates could not continue to exist simultaneously. All borrowers would seek to borrow at the lower rate while all lenders would lend at the higher rate; this is, of course, impossible, because there would be no lenders at the lower rate and no borrowers at the higher rate. Consequently, such arbitrage opportunities are extremely rare in a perfectly competitive market.

The Basic Principle

Borrowing and lending opportunities in the financial markets allow individuals to modify their consumption patterns in accordance with their preferences. The aggregate of all financial market transactions determines the equilibrium rate of interest. In turn, this market determined interest rate provides the criterion against which investment opportunities are measured; that is, the **first principle of investment decision-making** specifies that an investment is acceptable only if it is superior to financial market opportunities, as indicated by the market interest rate.

Practicing the Principle

Consider an investor who has the opportunity to invest $1,000 today to acquire an asset which can be sold for $1,200 one year from today. According to the first principle of investment decision-making, the only additional information required in order to determine whether this is an acceptable investment is the interest rate in the financial markets. As noted earlier, the assumption that all financial transactions are riskless implies that there is only one equilibrium interest rate. If this interest rate, r, is 8%, then the investor compares the investment opportunity described above with the 8% interest rate available in the financial markets. The investor can make this comparison on the basis of either: (1) future value; (2) present value; or (3) rate of return calculations. The first two approaches are presented in this section; the third is discussed in Chapter 4.

The two alternatives which the investor must consider are: first, he can lend $1,000 at the market rate of interest or, second, he can invest $1,000 today in return for $1,200 one year from today. If he selects the first alternative, then, one year from today, he will receive:

$$\$1000 \ (1 + .08) = \$1080$$

Clearly, the second alternative is preferable since the investor will have $1,200, rather than $1,080, one year from today.

This analysis of the investment opportunity is based on a comparison between the return from the purchase of the asset (i.e., $1,200) and the **future value** of the market alternative (i.e., $1,080). In general, a future value is the amount to which an initial dollar amount will grow when interest is compounded at a specified interest rate for a specified number of years. Since the relevant time period here is one year, the above future value calculation can be summarized algebraically as:

$$FV = C_0 \times (1 + r)$$

where FV is the future value, C_0 is the initial investment and r is the market interest rate. The investor can also evaluate the given investment opportunity using present value analysis. This analysis requires that the investor answer the following question: At the market rate of interest, what deposit would the investor have to make today in order to receive a return (i.e., future value) of $1,200 one year from today? This question can be answered algebraically by substituting the relevant values into the above future value equation: FV = $1200, r = 8% and C_0 is unknown.

$$\$1,200 = C_0 \times (1 + .08)$$

Solving for C_0:

$$C_0 = \frac{\$1200}{(1.08)} = \$1,111.11$$

At the market rate of interest, the investor would have to deposit $1,111.11 today in order to receive a return of $1,200 one year from now. Consequently, the investor would select the investment providing the opportunity to purchase an asset for only $1,000, returning $1,200 one year from today.

In the above calculation, $1,111.11 is referred to as **the present value** of $1,200, to be received one year from today, when the relevant market interest rate is 8%. It is important to note here that the present value is dependent on the amount of the future payment (i.e., the future value), the time period and the market rate of interest. Algebraically, the present value calculation for a one-year time period can be written as:

$$PV = C_0 = \frac{FV}{(1+r)}$$

where PV can be used in place of C_0 to represent the initial investment.

The present value approach to investment decision-making can also be described in terms of the difference between the present value of the investment (i.e., $1,111.11 in the above example) and the cost of the investment ($1,000). The difference ($111.11 in this example) is called the **net present value**, which can be thought of as the net gain to the investor who chooses to first purchase the asset for $1,000 and then immediately sell the asset. The price at which he would be able to sell the asset is $1,111.11; the above calculations indicate that a second investor who purchased the asset for $1,111.11, and who would subsequently receive $1,200 one year from today, would be earning the 8% market rate of interest over the one-year time period. Consequently, the ability of the first investor to purchase the asset for $1,000, and then sell it at a price which provides the second investor with the market rate of interest, yields a net gain to the first investor; this net gain is equal to the net present value of the asset.

An alternative interpretation of the net present value can be appreciated by supposing that the investor purchasing the asset for $1,000 must borrow money at the market rate of interest in order to finance the purchase of the asset. Further, suppose that the investor determines the amount of money he will borrow by answering the following question: What is the maximum amount that can be borrowed today if the proceeds from the sale of the asset next year (i.e., $1,200) will be used to repay the loan? Given that the market rate of interest is 8%, then the answer is $1,111.11, as indicated earlier. Therefore, the investor can borrow $1,111.11 today, purchase the asset for $1,000, and use the proceeds from the sale of the asset next year to repay $1,200 principal plus interest. This provides the investor with $111.11 which he can spend today, thereby increasing his wealth by an amount equal to the net present value of the investment opportunity.

The above discussion implies two important conclusions for financial decision-making. The first is the fact that investment decisions are independent of the investor's income pattern and consumption preferences; this result is demonstrated in the above example by the fact that the investment opportunity was found to be acceptable solely on the basis of the comparison with the market rate of interest. This **separation theorem** is not only an important result for investment decisions made by individual investors, but it is, as demonstrated in the next section, essential to the corporate investment decision-making process. The second major conclusion is that the net present value not only provides a criterion for determining whether an investment is acceptable, but it is also an unambiguous measure of the value of the investment. An investment with a positive net present value provides a net benefit to the investor equal to the net present value; an investment with a negative net present value is unacceptable and should be rejected by the investor. These concepts are the basis for corporate investment decision-making.

Corporate Investment Decision-Making

In order to understand the role of the separation theorem and the net present value criterion in corporate investment decision-making, consider the following simplified example. Suppose you are considering the formation of a corporation with a one year life, in order to acquire an asset which costs $100,000 and which, you are certain, can be sold one year from now for $120,000. You would like to convince each of 100 investors (including yourself) to purchase a share in this corporation for $1,000. Since each investor is a 1% owner, each investor would then receive 1% of $120,000, or $1,200, one year from now. Assume that the market rate of interest is 8%. The issue here is whether this investment opportunity is attractive to potential investors.

As noted earlier, this problem can be analyzed from either a future value or a present value perspective. In order to focus on the significance of the net present value criterion, consider the net gain to investors who are not willing to wait one year for their $1,200 share of the selling price of the asset. If the corporation purchases this asset today, the present value of the $120,000 to be received next year is:

$$PV = \frac{\$120,000}{(1.08)} = \$111,111.11$$

Since the entire corporation consists of this one asset, this present value is the value of the corporation once the asset is purchased. An investor who purchases one share for $1,000 and then wishes to immediately sell the share in the financial market will be able to sell for $1,111.11. This figure can be viewed as 1% of the value of the firm, or as the present value of 1% of the $120,000 future value of the asset:

$$PV = \frac{\$1200}{(1.08)} = \$1,111.11$$

Similarly, the net present value of an investor's share is $111.11. This can be thought of as 1% of the net present value of the firm (i.e., 1% of the difference between $111,111.11 and $100,000) or as the difference between the present value of one share ($1,111.11) and the cost of a share ($1,000). Consequently, an investor who chooses to sell his share will realize a net gain equal to 1% of the net present value of the corporation.

The above example demonstrates the following points. First, a corporate investment with a positive net present value provides a net benefit to the shareholder equal to his proportionate share of the net present value of the corporate investment. Second, the management of the firm can determine whether an investment is acceptable to the stockholders without regard for the income patterns or consumption preferences of the stockholders. Management must simply accept investments with positive net present value, since such investments provide value to the stockholders. Consequently, the net present value criterion and the separation theorem together indicate that corporate financial managers should seek to maximize the current value of the shares of the firm by adopting investments with positive net present value.

CONCEPT TEST

1. A financial instrument that is a promise to pay the owner as it comes due is called a _____ instrument.

2. When total funds demanded by borrowers equals the amount that lenders wish to loan, then the market is said to _____.

3. If the amount borrowers wish to borrow is greater than the amount lenders wish to loan out, then the interest rate will _____.

4. An institution that matches buyers and sellers of money (borrowers and lenders) is called a _____.

5. A financial market in which borrowers and lenders do not actually meet is called an _____ market.

6. The interest rate that clears the market is called the _____.

7. If no individual in a market can have an impact on the market price, then market participants are called _____.

8. A financial market in which trading is costless, information is freely available, and no trader has a significant impact on price is called a _____.

9. Simultaneous buying and selling activities that earn guaranteed profits and require no net investment are called _____ opportunities.

10. The idea that investment decisions can be made without reference to an individual's consumption preferences or income pattern is called the _____.

11. A _____ is the amount to which an initial dollar amount will grow when interest is compounded at a specified interest rate for a specified number of years.

12. The difference between the current worth of an investment and its cost is called the _____ of the investment.

13. The value that the financial market would place on a future cash flow is called the _____ of that cash flow.

14. "An investment is acceptable only if it is superior to alternatives in the financial market" is a statement of the _____.

15. The financial manager acts in the best interests of the shareholders by choosing investments to _____.

ANSWERS TO CONCEPT TEST

1. bearer
2. clear
3. rise
4. financial intermediary
5. anonymous
6. equilibrium rate of interest
7. price takers
8. perfectly competitive
   financial market

9. arbitrage
10. separation theorem
11. future value
12. net present value
    (NPV)
13. present value (PV)
14. first principle of
    investment decision making
15. maximize NPV

PROBLEMS AND SOLUTIONS

Problem 1

An investor's income is $100,000 this year and $120,000 next year. She plans to consume $80,000 this year and $143,200 next year. If this difference between her income and consumption patterns results from a financial market transaction, what is the market interest rate?

Solution 1

The solution is the value of r in the following equation:

$$\$100,000 + \frac{\$120,000}{(1+r)} = \$80,000 + \frac{\$143,200}{(1+r)}$$

$$\$20,000 = \frac{\$23,000}{(1+r)}$$

$$1 + r = 1.16$$

$$r = 16\%$$

Problem 2

An individual has an income of $5000 this year and $8000 next year. If the market rate of interest is 15%, what is the most he can consume this year? Next year?

Solution 2

The maximum he can consume this year is [$5000 + ($8000/1.15)] = $11,956.52. The maximum possible consumption next year is [$5000(1.15) + 8000] = $13,750. Notice that each dollar received one year from now is worth ($1/1.15) = $.87 today, so [$13,750 × (1/1.15)] = $11,956.52. This is a good way to check your answer.

Problem 3

Given the data in Problem 2, complete the following table:

This Year's Consumption	Next Year's Consumption
$ 0	
5,000	
8,000	
10,000	
12,000	

Solution 3

This Year's Consumption	Next Year's Consumption
$ 0	$13,750
5,000	8,000
8,000	4,550
10,000	2,250
12,000	not possible

The information provided indicates that the maximum that can be consumed today is $11,956.52 (see Problem 1). If, however, it were possible to borrow against income in later years, this individual could borrow ($12,000 - $11,956.52) = $43.48 this year, and repay the loan plus interest in two years. The payment at that time would be $57.50. (The compounding of interest over a period of more than one year is covered in Chapter 4.)

Problem 4

An investment in real assets requires an initial outlay of $2 million. It promises to pay $2.18 million in one year. The market interest rate is 10%. Is this a good investment? What is the rate of return on this investment?

Solution 4

If you invest $2 million at the 10% market rate of interest, you will have ($2,000,000)×(1.10) = $2.2 million in one year. By the first principle of investment decision making, the investment in real assets is not a good investment.

The rate of return for the investment is [($2.18 million - $2 million)/$2 million] = 9%, which is less than the market interest rate.

Problem 5

In Problem 4, what is the present value of the future cash flow? What is the net present value (NPV) of the investment?

Solution 5

Each future dollar is worth ($1/1.10) = $.909 today, so the present value is [$2.18 million × (1/1.10)] = $1.982 million. The net present value is:

$$($1.982 \text{ million} - $2 \text{ million}) = -$.0182 \text{ million} = -$18,181.82$$

Problem 6

Calculate the present value for each of the following cash flows to be received one year hence:

Future cash flow	Interest rate	Present value
$ 10,000	10%	
153,200	13%	
153,200	10%	
2,567,450	5%	
(120,600)	9%	

Solution 6

Future cash flow	Interest rate	Present value
$ 10,000	10%	$ 9,090.91
153,200	13%	135,575.22
153,200	10%	139,272.73
2,567,450	5%	2,445,190.48
(120,600)	9%	(110,642.20)

In the second and third cases, notice that the future cash flow is the same, but the present value is greater when the market interest rate is 10% than for a market interest rate of 13%. This result illustrates the fact that present value and interest rates are inversely related.

Problem 7

As a newly-coined MBA embarking on a career in investment banking, you naturally must own a BMW 325is immediately. The car costs $28,320. You also have to spend $3,248 on blue pin-stripe suits. Your salary this year is $42,000, and next year it will be $46,000. Your routine living expenses this year will be $34,000. You plan to make up the difference between current income and current consumption by borrowing. How much will you have left to spend next year if the market interest rate is 14%?

Solution 7

This year you need a total of ($28,320 + $3248 + $34,000) = $65,568. So, you must borrow ($65,568 - $42,000) = $23,568 this year. Next year, you will have to repay [$23,568(1.14)] = $26,867.52, leaving you with $19,132.48 of next year's income.

Problem 8

Ajay does not believe in saving and is interested only in maximizing current consumption. His income is $49,000 this year and $50,000 next year. He has three investment opportunities, each of which costs $5,000. One will pay $6000, one will pay $7000, and one will pay $8000. The market interest rate is 25%. What is the net present value of each of the investments? How much can Ajay spend today?

Solution 8

The net present values of the three investments are -$200, $600, and $1,400, respectively. Ajay will not accept the first one since it has a negative net present value, but he will accept the other two.

Ajay can spend his current income of $49,000, less the $10,000 investment, plus the present value of next year's income, which is ($65,000/1.25) = $52,000. Thus Ajay can spend $91,000 today. To check this, notice that Ajay can borrow $52,000 against the future income of $65,000 (i.e., $50,000 plus $15,000 investment income). He will thus have to repay [$52,000(1.25)] = $65,000, which will leave him with exactly zero for next year's consumption, as planned.

Problem 9

If you deposit $10,000 today in a bank account paying 10.38%, how much will you have in one year; that is, what is the future value of your investment? If you need $12,000 in one year, how much do you have to deposit today?

Solution 9

If you deposit $10,000, you will have ($10,000)(1.1038) = $11,038 at the end of the year. If you need $12,000, you will have to deposit ($12,000/1.1038) = $10,871.53 today.

Problem 10

Sam has current income of $60 and his income next year is zero. Given this income pattern, he prefers to consume $20 this year. Sam has an investment opportunity. If he accepts this investment opportunity, he would be able to increase his current consumption to $80 (with no consumption next year), or increase next year's consumption to $100 (with no consumption this year). If he accepts the investment, he would then choose to consume $60 next period.

What is the net present value of the investment? What is the market interest rate? Ignoring the investment, what would Sam choose to consume next period? What is the most Sam could consume next period if he ignores the investment opportunity? If Sam accepts the investment opportunity, what will he consume this period?

Solution 10

The net present value of the investment is ($80 - $60) = $20. The interest rate is found by solving for r in the following equation:

$$\$100/(1 + r) = \$80$$

The interest rate is therefore 25%. If Sam ignores the investment opportunity, he would consume ($60 - $20)(1.25) = $50 next year. Without the investment, the most Sam could consume next period is ($60)(1.25) = $75. With the investment, Sam will consume [($100 - $60)/1.25] = $32 this period.

Problem 11

An individual has the opportunity to invest $1000 today to acquire an asset which will generate $300 in income one year from today and which can be sold for $900 at that time. Use the first principle of investment decision-making to determine the minimum level of the market interest rate for which the investment would be attractive.

Solution 11

Substitute the relevant values (PV = $1000; FV = $1200) into either the future value formula or the present value formula, and then solve for the interest rate r. Using the future value formula:

$$FV = C_0 \times (1 + r)$$

$$\$1200 = \$1000 \times (1 + r)$$

$$1 + r = 1.20$$

$$r = .20 = 20\%$$

For values of r greater than 20%, the investment in the asset described above is inferior to the market opportunity; for values of r less than 20%, the investment in the asset is superior to the market opportunity.

Problem 12

Investor Melissa expects her income to be: $40,000 in the current year (year 0), then $44,000 and $49,000 over the subsequent two years (year 1 and year 2). Her consumption is $30,000 for the current year and $52,000 next year. The market rate of interest is 10% for the coming year, but it will increase to 12% beginning one year from now. One year from now, Melissa will have an investment opportunity which will require an outlay of $26,400 and which will provide her a rate of return of 15%. How much can Melissa spend two years from now?

Solution 12

Total income available next year (year 1), without borrowing:

$$\$10,000(1.10) + \$44,000 = \$55,000$$

Cash required for consumption and investment next year:

$$\$52,000 + \$26,400 = \$78,400$$

Deficit in year 1 to be financed from year 2 income, by borrowing at 12%:

$$\$78,400 - \$55,000 = \$23,400$$

Repayment of loan in year 2:

$$\$23,400 \ (1.12) = \$26,208$$

Proceeds of investment in year 2:

$$\$26,400 \ (1.15) = \$30,360$$

Cash available for consumption in year 2:

$$\$49,000 - \$26,208 + \$30,360 = \$53,152$$

Problem 13

Suppose that, in the above example, the investor elects to consume the maximum amount possible in year 1, with no consumption in either the current year or in year 2. What is the maximum consumption possible?

Solution 13

Cash available from current year's income for year 1 consumption:

$$\$40,000 \ (1.10) = \$44,000$$

Cash available from year 2 income for year 1 consumption, by borrowing:

$$(\$49,000 + \$30,360)/1.12 = \$70,857.14$$

Maximum total consumption for year 1:

$$\$44,000 + \$70,857.14 = \$110,857.14$$

Problem 14

An investment requires an initial outlay of $195. The cash inflow from this investment will be $114 one year from today (year 1) and $144 two years from today (year 2). The market rate of interest is 20%. Find the net present value of the investment.

Solution 14

Consider the $144 received two years from today. In order to find its value as of year 1, calculate the following present value:

$$PV = \frac{\$144}{(1.20)} = \$120$$

Consider the $120 as a year 1 cash flow, so that the total year 1 cash flow is ($120 + $114) = $234. Find the present value of $234:

$$PV = \frac{\$234}{(1.20)} = \$195$$

The net present value for the investment is the present value ($195) less the cost ($195), or zero. The fact that the net present value is zero indicates that an investor would be indifferent between the investment opportunity described here and an investment at the market rate of interest.

Consequently, the above calculation also demonstrates the fact that the rate of return for the investment described above is the same as the market rate of interest, 20%.

Problem 15

An entrepreneur has purchased an asset for $2,000,000 which will produce a cash inflow of $3,000,000 one year from today. He plans to issue 1,000 shares of common stock to himself and sell 9,000 shares of stock to the general public. His business, which consists entirely of this one asset, will cease to exist after one year. The market rate of interest is 20%, and the future cash inflow to the firm is guaranteed. At what price per share should the entrepreneur sell the common stock? What gain will the entrepreneur realize?

Solution 15

The present value of the future cash inflow is $2,500,000. Therefore, each of the 10,000 shares is worth $250; that is, an investor who purchases a share for $250 today will receive $300 one year from today. This investment provides a rate of return equal to the 20% market rate of interest. If the entrepreneur chose to issue all 10,000 shares to the general public, he would realize a gain of $500,000, which is equal to the net present value of the investment in the asset. By selling 9,000 shares, he has realized a gain of $450,000; the remaining $50,000 is an unrealized gain, unless he also chooses to sell the additional 1,000 shares.

CHAPTER 4
NET PRESENT VALUE

CHAPTER HIGHLIGHTS

The emphasis of this chapter is on the application of the net present value criterion to investments whose cash flows take place over a period longer than one year. The chapter begins with a review of the one-period model developed in the previous chapter; this includes a discussion of both future value and present value calculations. These concepts are then extended to the multi-period case. The last section of the chapter describes simplifying formulas for present value calculations involving specific cash-flow patterns commonly encountered in financial decision-making.

While the mathematical concepts presented in this chapter are not especially complicated, the mechanics of the calculations often require the use of tables or a financial calculator. The tables provided in the Appendix are sufficient for most problems in the chapter, but a financial calculator, such as the Sharp EL-733 Business/Financial calculator, can be a valuable time-saving aide. The calculator tips provided in this chapter are based primarily on the Sharp EL-733, although other financial calculators use mathematical and financial functions similar to those of the Sharp calculator.

The One-Period Case

Future-value analysis and present-value analysis are alternative, but equivalent, frameworks for investment decision-making. The net present value criterion is, in one sense, simply a different perspective from which to view present-value analysis, but the net present value is also a measure of the net gain derived from an investment.

Suppose that an investor is considering the purchase of an antique automobile. The automobile can be purchased for $60,000 today; the investor expects that it can be sold for $70,000 one year from today. Assume that the expected selling price is known with certainty and that the market rate of interest is 12%.

If the investor uses future-value analysis to evaluate this investment, he calculates the future value of $60,000, at an interest rate of 12%, for one year:

$$FV = C_0 \times (1 + r) =$$

$$\$60,000 \times (1.12) = \$67,200$$

Since the investment in the automobile provides a return of $70,000, while the opportunity to invest at 12% in the financial markets provides a return of only $67,200, the investor will choose to purchase the automobile.

Present-value analysis requires that the investor determine the amount which he would have to invest today, at the market rate of interest, in order to obtain a return of $70,000 one year from today; that is, he would calculate the present value of $70,000 to be received one year from today, using a 12% interest rate. Algebraically, the present value is determined by solving the following for C_0:

$$FV = C_0 \times (1 + r)$$

$$\$70,000 = C_0 \times (1.12)$$

$$C_0 = \frac{\$70,000}{(1.12)} = \$62,500$$

In order to obtain a return of $70,000 one year from now, the required investment in the financial markets is $62,500. Consequently, the investor can obtain a $70,000 return with a smaller initial investment by purchasing the automobile for $60,000.

Since the investor is able to purchase the automobile for $60,000, and would then be able to sell it immediately for $62,500, he would realize a current gain of $2,500. The net present value measures this net benefit to the investor:

Net present value =

(present value of next year's selling price) - (cost of asset today) =

$62,500 - $60,000 = $2,500

Algebraically, this definition of net present value can be represented as:

$$NPV = -C_0 + \frac{C_1}{(1+r)}$$

where C_0 is the initial investment and C_1 is the return at the end of one year.

Note that the above example refers to cash flows which occur today or one year from today; in the next section, cash flows are assumed to occur several years into the future. In reality, it is often the case that investment returns occur throughout the year. For simplicity and clarity in the discussion of multi-period investment decisions, we continue to assume that cash flows occur only at discrete intervals (e.g., today, one year from today, 5 years from today, n years from today, etc.) and we refer to these dates in time as date 0, date 1, date 5 and date n. Alternative terminology sometimes encountered refers to year 0, year 1, year 5 and year n, respectively.

The Multi-Period Case

An investor who makes a deposit in a bank account generally earns compound interest on the deposit. Consider, for example, a bank account which pays 10% interest per year. An investor who deposits $100 in an account will receive $10 interest at the end of the first year. If he withdraws the $10 interest, but leaves the original $100 on deposit for a second year, he will receive another $10 interest payment the second year, for a total of $20 interest over the two-year period. However, if he leaves the first year's interest on deposit during the second year, he will earn not only $10 interest on the original $100 deposit, but also 10% interest on the first year's interest, or an additional $1 interest. This interest on interest is called **compound interest.**

In general, the future value of an investment which earns compound interest is given by:

$$FV = C_0 \times (1 + r)^T$$

where C_0 is the initial deposit, r is the annual interest rate and T is the number of time periods during which interest is compounded. In the above example, the future value is:

$$FV = \$100 \times (1.10) \times (1.10) = \$100 \times (1.10)^2 = \$121$$

Although this future value can be determined easily with any calculator, or even with pencil and paper, compounding over long periods of time generally requires the use of tables or a financial calculator. Table A.3 provides values of $(1+r)^T$ for various combinations of interest rates and time periods; these values are referred to as **future value factors.** For example, in Table A.3, the second row of the column labeled '10%' indicates that $(1.10)^2$ is equal to 1.2100. Therefore, in the above example, it would only be necessary to multiply this future value factor times $100 in order to determine the future value. Clearly, the table is more useful when it is necessary to determine future value factors over long periods of time.

Values of $(1+r)^T$ can also be easily determined using a calculator with an exponent function key, usually indicated as [y^x]. For the above example, $(1.10)^2$ could be calculated using the following sequence on the Sharp EL-733:

$$1.10 \ [y^x] \ 2 \ [=]$$

It is sometimes helpful to be able to use the future value concepts developed above in order to calculate the interest rate for a particular investment or loan. For example, if you were to borrow $5,000 today (i.e., date 0) in exchange for a promise to repay $7,500 in principal plus interest six years from today (i.e., date 6) what is the annual interest rate you are paying for this loan? The answer can be determined by using the basic future value formula developed earlier, along with either Table A.3 or a financial calculator.

Substitute FV=$7500, C_0=$5000, T=6 in the future value formula:

$$FV = C_0 \times (1 + r)^T$$

$$\$7500 = \$5000 \times (1 + r)^6$$

$$1.500 = (1 + r)^6$$

An approximate value for r can now be determined from Table A.3. (As indicated below, a precise value can be easily obtained with a financial calculator.) The above equation is solved by locating, in Table A.3, the future value factor for a six-year period which is closest to 1.500. The future value factor 1.5007 under the 7% column indicates that $(1.07)^6$=1.5007, so that r is approximately 7%.

The alternative approach to solving for r is to take the sixth root of both sides of the above equation. The right hand side of the equation becomes (1+r). In order to find the sixth root of 1.500 (i.e., to raise 1.5 to the one-sixth power), use the following sequence with the EL-733 calculator:

$$1.5 \; [y^x] \; 6 \; [1/x] \; [=]$$

The sixth root is 1.069913, so that:

$$1.069913 = (1 + r)$$

and, subtracting 1.0 from both sides of the equation, r = 0.069913 or 6.9913%

A multi-period present value calculation can be represented, mathematically, as the reciprocal of a future value calculation. Therefore, it may be helpful to conceptualize the present value problem in terms of the above future value formula. For example, suppose that an individual would like to invest an amount today which would be sufficient to provide $250,000 for retirement; the investor intends to retire in 30 years and can earn 9% interest on his investment. Substitute FV=$250,000, r=0.09, T=30 in the future value formula:

$$FV = C_0 \times (1 + r)^T$$

$$\$250,000 = C_0 \times (1.09)^{30}$$

$$C_0 = PV = \frac{\$250,000}{(1.09)^{30}} = \frac{\$250,000}{13.26768} = \$18,842.78$$

An investment of $18,842.78 today, at 9% interest, will provide $250,000 30 years from now.

The above present value calculation can be presented in two alternative forms. First, rather than substituting into the future value formula and solving for the present value, the future value formula can be rewritten as a present value formula by solving for PV (or C_0). Second, the resulting present value formula can be restated in a form which treats present value calculations as multiplication, rather than division, problems.

$$FV = C_0 \times (1 + r)^T$$

$$C_0 = PV = \frac{FV}{(1+r)^T}$$

$$C_0 = PV = FV \times \frac{1}{(1+r)^T}$$

The factor $[1/(1+r)^T]$ is commonly referred to as a **present value factor**. Present value factors are given in Table A.1. To solve the above problem using Table A.1:

$$PV = FV \times \frac{1}{(1+r)^T} = \$250,000 \times \frac{1}{(1.09)^{30}}$$

$$= \$250,000 \times .0754 = \$18,850$$

The present value factor $[1/(1.09)^{30}] = .0754$ is given in Table A.1. Since this factor is rounded to four decimal places, it provides a somewhat less accurate result than that obtained earlier.

The preceding example indicates the procedure for determining the present value of a payment to take place one or more years into the future. Financial decision-making often requires that an investor calculate present value for an investment providing several payments over a period of years. Consequently, it is necessary to calculate the sum of the present values for the individual payments. For example, suppose that you are offered the opportunity to lend $10,000 today to a borrower who will repay the loan as follows: $5,000 to be paid at date 1 and $8,000 to be paid at date 2. This opportunity must be compared to the market interest rate, which is assumed to be 12%.

Although it is possible to use future-value analysis to evaluate this opportunity, the more commonly accepted approach is present-value analysis. The present value of each payment is determined; then the sum of these present values is compared to the initial $10,000 outlay.

$$PV = \frac{\$5000}{(1.12)^1} = \frac{\$5000}{1.12} = \$4,464.29$$

$$PV = \frac{\$8000}{(1.12)^2} = \frac{\$8000}{1.2544} = \$6,377.55$$

The sum of these present values is $10,841.84; this represents the investment required, at the 12% market interest rate, in order for the investor to receive payments of $5,000 at date 1 and $8,000 at date 2. Since the investor has the opportunity to lend only $10,000 in order to receive payments of $5,000 at date 1 and $8,000 at date 2, this latter alternative is clearly preferable to the market alternative.

As noted earlier, the difference between the present value calculated above (i.e., $10,841.84) and the $10,000 outlay is the net present value (i.e., $841.84). Algebraically, the net present value calculation for this example can be summarized as follows:

$$NPV = -C_0 + \frac{C_1}{(1+r)^1} + \frac{C_2}{(1+r)^2}$$

where C_0 is the initial $10,000 outlay, C_1 is the $5,000 payment one year from now, C_2 is the $8,000 payment two years from now and r is the 12% market interest rate. The more general formula for net present value is:

$$NPV = -C_0 + \frac{C_1}{(1+r)^1} + \frac{C_2}{(1+r)^2} + \cdots + \frac{C_T}{(1+r)^T}$$

where T represents the last period during which a payment is received.

Net present value can be easily determined using the Sharp EL-733. However, there are three preliminary steps which must be followed prior to using the financial functions of the calculator. First, the calculator must be set to 'financial' mode by repeating the sequence [2ndF] [Mode] until 'FIN' appears in the calculator display. Second, the financial mode memories of the calculator must be cleared as follows: [2nd F] [CA]. Third, if 'BGN' appears in the calculator display, then [BGN] must be used to cancel the 'begin' mode. The 'begin' mode assumes that cash inflows start immediately; most problems encountered in this chapter assume that the first inflow occurs at date 1, one year from now. Therefore, the 'begin' mode must be turned off by using the [BGN] function key. Now, the following sequence is used to calculate the net present value for the above problem:

$$10000 \ [+/-] \ [CF_i]$$
$$5000 \ [CF_i]$$
$$8000 \ [CF_i]$$
$$12 \ [i]$$
$$[COMP] \ [NPV]$$

The first step enters the $10,000 loan as a negative number, representing an outlay, at date 0. The second and third steps represent the date 1 and date 2 cash inflows, respectively. Next, the 12% interest rate is entered, and then the net present value is computed.

Compounding Periods

The preceding discussion of future-value and present-value analysis has been based on the assumption that interest rates are compounded annually. However, banks and other financial institutions often compound interest on deposits more frequently. For example, a bank might advertise that it pays 12% interest per year, compounded quarterly, which is equivalent to 3% interest each quarter. In other words, with quarterly compounding, the depositor begins to receive interest on interest during the second quarter, rather than after the first year, as in the case of annual compounding. In order to calculate the future value for a deposit in the account described above, it is only necessary to determine the quarterly interest rate (i.e., 3% in this example) and to treat the quarter, rather than the year, as the relevant time period. Therefore, the future value, after one year, of a $1,000 deposit is:

$$FV = \$1,000 \times (1.03)^4 = \$1,000 \times 1.12551 = \$1,125.51$$

If the account paid 12% interest per year, compounded annually, the future value would be $1,120, so that the additional $5.51 is the interest on interest during the second, third and fourth quarters of the year. If the bank paid 12.551% interest per year, compounded annually, the future value for a $1,000 deposit over a one-year period would also be $1,125.51:

$$FV = \$1,000 \times (1.12551)^1 = \$1,000 \times 1.12551 = \$1,125.51$$

Therefore, a **stated annual interest rate** of 12%, compounded quarterly, is equivalent to an **effective annual interest rate** of 12.551%. This can be seen directly in the example by noting that:

$$(1.03)^4 = (1.12551)^1$$

so that the effective annual interest rate is simply

$$(1.12551)^1 - 1.0 = .12551 = 12.551\%$$

In general, this result is presented algebraically as follows:

$$\text{effective annual interest rate} = (1 + \frac{r}{m})^m - 1$$

where m is the number of times per year interest is compounded. For compounding m times per year over a period of T years, the future value is given by:

$$FV = C_0 \times \left(1 + \frac{r}{m}\right)^{mT}$$

Quarterly, monthly and daily compounding are often used by banks and other financial institutions, and it is even possible to compound interest hourly or each minute or second. While these latter compounding periods are not common, continuous compounding, which is equivalent to compounding over the smallest possible period of time, is frequently used in financial calculations. Suppose that in the above example, the bank pays 12% interest per year, compounded continuously. The future value is determined according to the following formula:

$$FV = C_0 \times (e^{rT})$$

where e is a constant whose value is approximately 2.718. Therefore, if a $1,000 deposit is compounded for 3 years, the future value is:

$$FV = C_0 \times (e^{rT}) = \$1000 \times [e^{(.12 \times (3))}] = \$1000 \times e^{.36}$$

The value of $e^{.36}$ is 1.43333, which can be determined from Table A.5, or with the use of a financial calculator. In Table A.5, the value of $e^{.36}$ is given in the third row of the column headed '12%,' so that using Table A.5 for continuous compounding is analogous to using Table A.3 for annual compounding. The calculation can also be performed using the Sharp EL-733 as follows:

.36 [2nd F] [e^x]

The future value for the above example is $1,433.33.

Simplifications

The formulas and procedures presented in this chapter can be used to determine the present value (or net present value) for any series of cash flows. However, the calculations can be simplified in certain circumstances, depending on the pattern of the cash flows involved in any particular problem. The simplifying formulas presented in this section can be applied to the following cash-flow patterns: perpetuity, growing perpetuity, annuity, growing annuity. In all cases, the simplifying formulas are derived algebraically from the basic present value formula described earlier.

A perpetuity (or perpetual annuity) is a constant series of cash flows, occurring at regular intervals, which continues perpetually. The series of dividend payments for a share of preferred stock is often thought of as a perpetuity. Applying the techniques described earlier, the present value of a perpetuity would be given by:

$$PV = \frac{C}{(1+r)^1} + \frac{C}{(1+r)^2} + \frac{C}{(1+r)^3} + \cdots$$

where C is the constant payment or cash flow. However, the simplifying formula for the present value of a perpetuity can be derived by considering the following example: Suppose that a share of preferred stock pays an annual dividend of $8 and the market interest rate is 5%. What is the present value of the $8 perpetuity? In other words, what would an investor be willing to pay to purchase the share of preferred stock? The answer is that he would pay whatever price (PV) would equate the $8 payments to a 5% interest rate or, algebraically:

$$PV \times .05 = \$8$$

$$PV = \frac{\$8}{.05} = \$160$$

In general, this simplifying formula becomes:

$$PV = \frac{C}{r}$$

A growing perpetuity is a series of cash flows, occurring at regular intervals, which grows perpetually at a constant rate. In certain circumstances, the series of dividend payments for a share of common stock can be considered a growing perpetuity, as long as the size of the dividend payment increases at the same rate each year. Consider, for example, an investor who intends to purchase a share of common stock which is expected to pay a $2 dividend one year from now, with dividends increasing at 5% per year indefinitely. If the market rate of interest is 12%, the present value calculation is:

$$PV = \frac{\$2}{(1.12)^1} + \frac{\$2(1.05)}{(1.12)^2} + \frac{\$2(1.05)^2}{(1.12)^3} + \cdots$$

In general, this formula is:

$$PV = \frac{C}{(1+r)^1} + \frac{C(1+g)}{(1+r)^2} + \frac{C(1+g)^2}{(1+r)^3} + \cdots$$

where g is the growth rate in the annual cash flows. Algebraically, the above formula is equivalent to:

$$PV = \frac{C}{r-g}$$

which is the simplifying formula for the present value of a growing perpetuity. Applying this result to the example above, the present value is:

$$PV = \frac{\$2}{.12-.05} = \$28.57$$

It is important to note here that this result is the exact present value of the growing perpetuity; that is, this simplifying formula, as well as the others in this section, is not an approximation to the present value.

An annuity is a constant series of cash flows, occurring at regular intervals, which continues for a fixed number of time periods. The present value of an annuity can be determined according to the procedures described earlier:

$$PV = \frac{C}{(1+r)^1} + \frac{C}{(1+r)^2} + \frac{C}{(1+r)^3} + \cdots + \frac{C}{(1+r)^T}$$

where T is the time period of the last payment of the annuity. The simplifying formula for the present value of an annuity is:

$$PV = C \left[\frac{1}{r} - \frac{1}{r(1+r)^T} \right]$$

The last term in the above equation is called an **annuity factor**, and is sometimes represented by the notation A^T_r, so that the formula can be written:

$$PV = C \times A^T_r$$

To find the present value of a ten-year annuity paying $500 per year, when the market rate of interest is 12%:

$$PV = \$500 \left[\frac{1}{.12} - \frac{1}{.12(1.12)^{10}} \right] = \$500 \times 5.65022 = \$2825.11$$

The value of $A^{10}_{.12}$ is also given in Table A.2, which is used in a manner analogous to the procedures for the tables discussed earlier.

The present value of an annuity can be easily determined using the Sharp EL-733, as follows:

> 10 [n]
> 12 [i]
> 500 [PMT]
> [COMP] [PV]

The first three steps enter the time period, interest rate and annual payment, respectively. The fourth step computes the present value, which is displayed as -2,825.11. The negative sign indicates that if you were to purchase this annuity, you would pay out $2,825.11 in order to receive an inflow of $500 per year. The receipts are entered as positive numbers and the present value, which in this case would be an outlay, is displayed as a negative number. If the annual payments were entered as negative numbers (e.g., to indicate annual payments on a loan), then the present value would display as a positive number, to indicate the proceeds of the loan.

The fourth simplifying formula of this section applies to a growing annuity, which is analogous to a growing perpetuity except that the payments occur for a fixed number of time periods. The formula for the present value of a growing annuity is:

$$PV = C \left[\frac{1}{(r-g)} - \frac{1}{(r-g)} \times \left(\frac{1+g}{1+r} \right)^T \right]$$

CONCEPT TEST

1. When money is invested in the financial markets for multiple time periods and the interest is reinvested, the money is said to earn _____ or _____.

2. An interest rate is quoted as '10% compounded daily;' the 10% interest rate is an example of a _____ interest rate.

3. If 10% compounded daily is equivalent to 10.5156% compounded annually, then 10.5156% is the _____ interest rate. Are these rates equivalent?

4. The expression $(1 + r)^T$ is called a _____.

5. The expression $[1/(1 + r)^T]$ is called a _____.

6. For a given stated rate, the effective rate is _____ (higher/lower) the more often the rate is compounded during the year.

7. If an interest rate is compounded an infinite number of times during the year, this is called _____ compounding.

8. A _____ is a constant series of cash flows, occurring at regular intervals, which continues perpetually.

9. An _____ is a constant series of cash flows, occurring at regular intervals, which continues for a fixed number of periods.

10. The expression $PV = [C/(r-g)]$ is used to find the present value of a _____.

ANSWERS TO CONCEPT TEST

1. interest on interest; compound interest
2. stated annual
3. effective annual; yes
4. future value factor
5. present value factor

6. higher
7. continuous
8. perpetuity
9. annuity
10. growing perpetuity

PROBLEMS AND SOLUTIONS

Problem 1

What is the present value of $145 to be received in 5 years if the market interest rate is 8%?

Solution 1

The answer is $[\$145/(1.08)^5] = \$98.685$.

Problem 2

What is the future value of $235 dollars invested at 12% for 4 years?

Solution 2

The answer is $[\$235(1.12)^4] = \$369.777$.

Problem 3

For each of the following, compute the present value.

Future value	Years	Interest rate	Present value
$ 498	7	13%	
1,033	13	6	
14,784	23	4	
898,156	4	31	

Solution 3

Future value	Years	Interest rate	Present value
$ 498	7	13%	$ 211.680
1,033	13	6	484.311
14,784	23	4	5,998.258
898,156	4	31	304,976.653

Problem 4

For each of the following, compute the future value.

Present value	Years	Interest rate	Future value
$ 123	13	13%	
4,555	8	8	
74,484	5	10	
167,332	9	1	

Solution 4

Present value	Years	Interest rate	Future value
$ 123	13	13%	$ 602.455
4,555	8	8	8,430.987
74,484	5	10	119,957.227
167,332	9	1	183,008.544

Problem 5

An investment offers cash flows of (-$1243, $400, $889, $432). The market interest rate is 12%. Is this a good investment?

Solution 5

Compute the net present value for the investment as follows:

$$NPV = -\$1243 + (\$400/1.12) + (\$889/1.12^2) + (\$432/1.12^3) = \$130.337$$

Since the net present value is positive, the investment is acceptable.

Problem 6

An investment offers cash flows of ($300, -$200, -$100). Is this a good investment if the market rate of interest is 15%?

Solution 6

The net present value is:

$$\$300 - (\$200/1.15) - (\$100/1.15^2) = \$50.473$$

Since the NPV is positive, this is an acceptable investment.

Solution note: in this case, the first cash flow is positive, while the subsequent cash flows are negative. This fact does not affect the calculation of the net present value, although it would affect the application of the internal rate of return criterion. These cash flows should be thought of as a loan. This is an acceptable 'investment' because the money we receive today ($300) is greater than the present value of the future cash outflows.

Problem 7

A local bank is offering 9% interest, compounded monthly, on savings accounts. If you deposit $700 today, how much will you have in 2 years? How much will you have in 2.5 years?

Solution 7

The interest rate is actually $(.09/12) = .0075 = .75\%$ per month. Since there are 24 months in two years, the future value factor is:

$$(1.0075)^{24} = 1.1964$$

Multiply the future value factor times the $700 deposit; you will have $837.489 after 2 years. Alternatively, the effective annual rate is:

$$[1 + (.09/12)]^{12} - 1 = 9.38069\% \text{ per year}$$

After 2 years, you will have:

$$\$700(1.0938069)^2 = \$837.489$$

After 2.5 years (or 30 months), you will have:

$$\$700(1.0075)^{30} = \$700(1.0938069)^{2.5} = \$875.890$$

Problem 8

For each of the following, calculate the effective annual rate:

Stated rate	Number of times compounded	Effective rate
5%	semiannually	
11%	quarterly	
16%	daily	
20%	infinite	

Solution 8

Stated rate	Number of times compounded	Effective rate
5%	semiannually	5.063%
11%	quarterly	11.462%
16%	daily	17.347%
20%	infinite	22.140%

Problem 9

You have just joined the investment banking firm of Knot, Wirthem, et al. They have offered you two different salary arrangements. You can have $50,000 per year for the next 3 years or $25,000 per year for the next 3 years, along with a $50,000 signing bonus today. If the market interest rate is 16%, compounded quarterly, which salary arrangement do you prefer?

Solution 9

The effective annual rate is 16.986%. The present value of $50,000 for 3 years is $110,504.57. The present value of $25,000 for 3 years is half as much, or $55,252.29. The total value of this option is $105,252.29. You should select the $50,000 per year option.

Problem 10

Suppose the effective annual rate for a loan is 8% and the loan requires monthly payments. What is the stated rate?

Solution 10

We need to solve the following equation for r:

$$[1 + (r/12)]^{12} - 1 = .08$$

$$[1 + (r/12)]^{12} = 1.08$$

Find the twelfth root of 1.08:

$$(1.08)^{1/12} = 1.006434$$

Thus, $r/12 = 1.006434 - 1 = .006434$ and $r = 7.7208\%$.

Calculator tip: Find the value of $(1.08)^{(1/12)}$ as follows:

$$1.08 \; [y^x] \; 12 \; [1/x] =$$

Problem 11

A local loan shark offers 'four for five on payday;' this means you borrow $4 today and you must repay $5, 6 days from now, when you get your next paycheck. What is the effective annual interest rate for this loan?

Solution 11

The interest rate is $[(5/4) - 1] = 25\%$ for 6 days. There are about $(365/6) = 60.8333$ such periods in a year. The effective rate is thus 1.25 raised to the power 60.8333, minus 1. This works out to be a nice round 78.59 **million** percent. This is high, but it beats having your legs broken.

Problem 12

A local bank is offering an account that has an effective annual interest rate of 12.75%. If the bank is using continuous compounding, what is the stated rate?

Solution 12

We need to solve for r in the following equation:

$$e^r - 1 = .1275$$

$$e^r = 1.1275$$

where e is the constant 2.7183. The solution requires finding the natural logarithm of both sides of the above equation. The natural logarithm of e^r is r. The natural logarithm of 1.1275 is determined by using the following sequence on a financial calculator: 1.1275 [ln]. Thus, $r = .12 = 12\%$.

If logarithms make you nervous, then it may help to know that compounding about 5000 times per year is nearly the same as continuous compounding. With this in mind, you can solve this problem the same way that Problem 10 was solved. The five thousandth root of 1.1275 is 1.000024, and 5000(.000024) is about .12.

Problem 13

Solve for the unknown time period in each of the following:

Present value	Future value	Interest rate	Time (years)
$ 100	$ 350	12%	
123	$ 351	10%	
4,100	$ 8,523	5%	
10,543	$26,783	6%	

Solution 13

Present value	Future value	Interest rate	Time (years)
$ 100	$ 350	12%	11.05
123	$ 351	10%	11.00
4,100	$ 8,523	5%	15.00
10,543	$26,783	6%	16.00

Problem 14

Solve for the unknown interest rate in each of the following:

Present value	Future value	Interest rate	Time (years)
$ 100	$ 305		5
123	$ 218		6
4,100	$ 8,523		7
10,543	$21,215		12

Solution 14

Present value	Future value	Interest rate	Time (years)
$ 100	$ 305	25%	5
123	$ 218	10%	6
4,100	$ 8,523	11%	7
10,543	$21,215	6%	12

Problem 15

Suppose you are offered an investment that pays 13.98% continuously compounded. How long will it take your money to double?

Solution 15

There are two ways to solve this problem. First, calculate the effective annual rate and then find out how long it would take to double your money at that rate. The effective annual rate is 15%, so it will take just under 5 years (4.96 years) to double your money. Alternatively, solve the following equation for t:

$$\$1(e^{.1398\,t}) = \$2$$

Solve for t by taking the natural log of 2 and dividing by .1398; the solution is 4.96 years.

Problem 16

You expect to receive an annuity of $1000 per year for the next five years (that is, date 1 to date 5). The market rate of interest is 12%. Assuming that you do not spend any of the income at any other time, what is the maximum you can spend from these payments at date 5? At date 0? At date 3?

Solution 16

The first question requires that you find the future value of the annuity. This can be done as follows:

$$FV = \$1000 \times (1.12^4 + 1.12^3 + 1.12^2 + 1.12^1 + 1.12^0)$$

$$= \$1000 \times (6.35285) = \$6{,}352.85$$

Note that the term in parentheses is a future value annuity factor, which can be found in Table A.4 of the appendix. This calculation indicates that you could invest your first $1000 payment, to be received at date 1, for a period of four years, at a 12% rate; the second payment could be invested for four years, and so on; the proceeds of these investments could then be spent at date 5.

The second question requires that you find the present value of the annuity. This can be done as follows:

$$PV = \$1000 \left[\frac{1}{(1.12)^1} + \frac{1}{(1.12)^2} + \frac{1}{(1.12)^3} + \frac{1}{(1.12)^4} + \frac{1}{(1.12)^5} \right]$$

$$= \$1000 \times (3.60478) = \$3{,}604.78$$

The term in parentheses is a present value annuity factor, which can be found in Table A.2. This calculation indicates that you could borrow $3,604.78 today, at a 12% interest rate, and repay the loan in five annual installments of $1000 each.

The third question requires that you invest the first two payments and borrow against the last two payments in order to spend the maximum possible at date 3. The maximum possible consumption at date 3 is $5,064.45.

Problem 17

An investment will increase in value by 270% over the next 17 years. What is the annual interest rate which, when compounded quarterly, provides this return?

Solution 17

Solve the following equation for r (where C is the beginning amount):

$$C \left(1 + \frac{r}{4}\right)^{68} = C (1 + 2.70) = 3.70C$$

$$\left(1 + \frac{r}{4}\right)^{68} = 3.70$$

$$\frac{r}{4} = (3.70)^{1/68} - 1 = .019426$$

Therefore, r = .07770 = 7.770%.

Problem 18

Consider a perpetuity which pays $100 per year; the market rate of interest is 10%. What is the present value of the perpetuity? What is the present value of the perpetuity at date 3? What is the present value at date n? Under what circumstances does the value of a perpetuity change?

Solution 18

The present value of the perpetuity is given by the following formula:

$$PV = \frac{C}{r} = \frac{\$100}{.10} = \$1000$$

Three years from now (or n years from now) the value of the perpetuity is still $1000. An investor who purchases the perpetuity at any subsequent date is purchasing a perpetual series of payments, regardless of the date. The value of the perpetuity changes only if the market rate of interest changes.

Problem 19

A firm invests $3 million in a project which will yield a perpetuity of $1 million per year. What is the discount rate r for which this project's net present value is $1.5 million?

Solution 19

Solve the following equation for r:

$$-\$3,000,000 + \frac{\$1,000,000}{r} = \$1,500,000$$

The solution is r = .22 = 22%. For values of r less than 22%, the NPV of the project is greater than $1,500,000.

CHAPTER 5
HOW TO VALUE STOCKS AND BONDS

CHAPTER HIGHLIGHTS

This chapter extends present value concepts to the valuation of financial instruments such as bonds and stocks. In order to value financial instruments, it is necessary to understand the basic features of the securities; these features are introduced in this chapter, although further details are provided in later chapters.

How To Value Bonds

Bonds are long-term debt securities issued by corporations as well as governmental units, including the U. S. Treasury and state and local governments. Although bonds can take many different forms, the three basic varieties discussed in this section are: pure discount bonds, level coupon bonds and consols. The valuation of these securities is based on the present value concepts developed in the two preceding chapters.

In general, the value of a security (or of any asset) is the present value of the future cash payments to the holder of the security. Consequently, the valuation of a security is a process of first determining the relevant payments and appropriate market rate of interest, and then applying present value concepts in calculating the instrument's value. The present value thus determined indicates the amount an individual would have to invest today, at the market rate of interest, in order to duplicate the security's cash flows. Since the investor can receive these future payments by investing at the market rate of interest, the present value is the highest price which an investor would pay for a given security. All investors are presumed to perform the same evaluation, so that the present value is the price at which the security would sell in the financial markets.

A **pure discount bond** promises a single payment, from the issuer to the holder of the bond, at a specified future date. The payment is referred to as the face value of the bond and the date on which the payment is made is the maturity date. The general equation for the value of a pure discount bond is:

$$PV = \frac{F}{(1+r)^T}$$

where F is the face value of the bond, T is the number of years to the maturity date and r is the market rate of interest. This is simply the present value formula of the previous chapter; it indicates that an investor who purchases the bond for the price given by PV will earn the market rate of interest r.

The value of a **level coupon bond** is determined according to the same present value principles. A level coupon bond promises regular interest payments (either annually or semi-annually), as well as a specified principal payment, or face value, at the maturity date. For example, suppose that today is January 1, 1990 and that an investor is considering the purchase of a corporate bond which promises a 9% coupon interest rate and a $1,000 face value, payable on January 1, 2010. The 9% coupon interest rate indicates that the issuer of the bond will pay (9% × $1000) = $90 interest per year for the next twenty years, and the $1,000 face value on January 1, 2010. The $90 interest payment is often referred to as the coupon payment, or simply the 'coupon,' and is generally paid in the form of two semi-annual payments of $45. For the bond described above, the first payment would be made on July 1, 1990 and subsequent payments would be made on January 1 and July 1 of each year. The fortieth, and last, coupon payment would be made on January 1, 2010, at which time the bondholder would also receive the $1,000 principal payment. Assuming a market interest rate of 12%, the value of the bond described above is given by:

$$PV = \frac{\$45}{(1.06)^1} + \frac{\$45}{(1.06)^2} + \cdots + \frac{\$45}{(1.06)^{40}} + \frac{\$1000}{(1.06)^{40}} = \$774.31$$

$$r \qquad (semi-annual)\ r = \frac{annual\ mkt\ int\ rate}{2}$$

In general, the above calculation can be represented as follows:

$$PV = \frac{C}{(1+r)^1} + \frac{C}{(1+r)^2} + \cdots + \frac{C}{(1+r)^T} + \frac{\$1000}{(1+r)^T}$$

$$C = coupon\ interest\ rate(\%)\ \times\ face\ value$$

where C is the semi-annual coupon payment, T is the number of time periods to the maturity date and $1,000 is the principal payment at maturity. Since the coupon payments are in the form of an annuity, the above equation can be rewritten as:

$$PV = (C \times A^T_r) + \frac{\$1000}{(1+r)^T}$$

where A^T_r is the annuity factor for T periods at an interest rate r per period. Using Table A.2 to determine the annuity factor, the present value of the bond is calculated as follows:

$$PV = (\$45 \times A^{40}_{.06}) + \frac{\$1000}{(1.06)^{40}}$$

$$= (\$45 \times 15.046) + (\$1000 \times .0972) = \$774.27$$

Note that the difference between this solution and that obtained earlier results from the rounding in the tables. The more accurate answer above is obtained with the use of a financial calculator, following the sequence:

```
0 [CFi]
39 [2ndF] [Ni] 45 [CFi]
1045 [CFi]
6 [i]
[COMP] [NPV]
```

The first step enters $0 as the year 0 cash flow; this is necessary in order to use the NPV function to calculate present value. The second step enters 39 semi-annual coupon payments of $45 each; the last coupon payment is combined with the $1,000 principal payment as the fortieth payment. The interest rate is 6% every six months, and the present value is computed using the [NPV] function.

The third type of bond considered in this section is a **consol**, which is a bond paying a constant, perpetual coupon payment; that is, a consol is a perpetuity. While consols are rare, preferred stock is often regarded as equivalent to a consol. The valuation of consols or preferred stock is based on the formula for the present value of a perpetuity from the preceding chapter:

$$\text{—}\!* \qquad PV = \frac{C}{r}$$

where C is the annual coupon payment.

Further discussion of the level-coupon bond described above can provide insight regarding two additional aspects of bond valuation: the relationship between interest rates and bond prices, and the concept of a bond's yield to maturity, which is the rate of return for a bond. In order to simplify the mathematics of this section, it is assumed that coupon payments are made annually rather than semi-annually, so that the holder of the 9% coupon bond will receive twenty annual payments of $90, beginning January 1, 1991.

If the market interest rate is 12%, the value of the bond is:

$$PV = (\$90 \times A^{20}_{.12}) + \frac{\$1000}{(1.12)^{20}}$$

$$= (\$90 \times 7.4694) + (\$1000 \times .1037) = \$775.95$$

(Note that this result differs somewhat from that obtained earlier because the assumption of annual, as opposed to semi-annual, compounding changes the effective annual rate and, consequently, the present value. Also, the result here is obtained with the use of the tables in Appendix A; a financial calculator provides the more accurate figure of $775.92.)

A change in the market interest rate changes the value of the bond. The nature of the relationship between interest rates and bond prices can be understood from both an intuitive perspective and a strictly mathematical perspective. Suppose an investor purchases the bond for the price indicated above and then finds that shortly thereafter, the market interest rate increases to 14%. If the investor then chooses to sell the bond, he will find that the value of the bond has changed. Previously, an investor who paid $775.95 for the bond would be earning a 12% rate of return; however, when investments at the market interest rate are paying 14%, investors will no longer be willing to accept a 12% rate of return, and consequently will no longer be willing to pay as much as $775.95 for the bond. The new price of the bond, assuming that it still has 20 years to maturity, is:

$$PV = (\$90 \times A^{20}_{.14}) + \frac{\$1000}{(1.14)^{20}}$$

$$= (\$90 \times 6.6231) + (\$1000 \times .0728) = \$668.88$$

Mathematically, it is clear that the value of the bond decreases when the market rate of interest increases because the interest rate is in the denominator of the present value formula; an increase in the denominator reduces the present value.

A decrease in the market rate of interest increases the value of the bond. For example, if r=8%, then the value of the bond is:

$$PV = (\$90 \times A^{20}_{.08}) + \frac{\$1000}{(1.08)^{20}}$$

$$= (\$90 \times 9.8181) + (\$1000 \times .2145) = \$1,098.13$$

When the bond value is greater than its $1,000 face value, the bond is said to be selling at a **premium**; a bond which sells for less than face value is selling at a **discount**. When the market rate of interest is equal to the bond's coupon rate (i.e., 9% in this case), the bond value is $1,000; an investor who pays $1,000 for a bond and receives annual coupon payments of $90 is earning a 9% rate of return on the investment.

An understanding of the relationship between interest rates and bond values is essential in determining the rate of return, or **yield to maturity**, for a given bond. For example, suppose that the bond described above is known to be selling for $915; what yield to maturity will an investor earn who purchases the bond for this price? The answer to this question is the value of r which solves the equation:

$$PV = (C \times A^{T}_{r}) + \frac{\$1000}{(1+r)^{T}}$$

$$\$915 = (\$90 \times A^{20}_{r}) + \frac{\$1000}{(1+r)^{20}}$$

The solution can be obtained in two ways: trial-and-error, using the tables in Appendix A; or, with the use of a financial calculator. The calculations presented earlier indicate that: for r=8%, PV=$1,098.13; for r=12%, PV=$775.95. Furthermore, when r is equal to the coupon rate (i.e., 9% for this bond), PV=$1,000. Given the inverse relationship between interest rates and bond prices, it is clear that the yield to maturity for the bond selling at a price of $915 is between 9% and 12%. At this point, one might 'guess' that r is approximately 10% or 11%; for r=11%, PV=$840.73. Since a decrease in r increases PV, the next 'trial' or 'guess' should be 10%, resulting in PV=$914.86. (Note: these last two PV calculations are obtained with a financial calculator.) Therefore, for a purchase price of $915, the yield to maturity is approximately 10%.

The precise yield to maturity (9.9983%) can be obtained with the Sharp financial calculator as follows:

915 [+/-] [CF$_i$]
19 [2ndF] [N$_i$] 90 [CF$_i$]
1090 [CF$_i$]
[COMP] [IRR]

The first step enters $915 as a negative number, representing an outflow. The use of the [IRR] function key reflects the fact that the yield to maturity is mathematically equivalent to the Internal Rate of Return, which is discussed in the next chapter.

The Present Value of Common Stocks

The valuation of common stocks is based on the same present value principles applied earlier to the valuation of bonds. However, numerous problems become apparent when analyzing common stock because of the uncertainty associated with the cash flows paid to the common stock investor. The discussion of bond valuation is based on the assumption of previous chapters that future payments are guaranteed so that the appropriate interest rate in present value calculations is the market interest rate for no-risk investments (i.e., the risk-free rate). While this assumption is not entirely realistic even for bonds, it is reasonable to retain this assumption in order to focus on the essential valuation concepts presented in the previous section. However, in evaluating common stock, the assumption of one risk-free market rate of interest is completely inappropriate.

It is important to realize that the discount rate for common stock valuation is not the risk-free rate. The specification of the appropriate rate is covered in detail later in the text; it is sufficient for now to realize that the discount rate in this section must be adjusted for the risk inherent in any particular common stock investment. In general, this means that an investor must evaluate the riskiness of an investment and then determine the market rate of return for investments of comparable risk. Clearly, such a rate for risky investments must be higher than the market rate of interest for risk-free investments; if it were not, investors would not invest in the risky asset.

Although the relevant interest rate is still identified as r in this section, we must be aware of the fact that the discount rate for common stock valuation is adjusted, according to the procedure described above, for the riskiness of the particular common stock investment under consideration. Furthermore, since it is no longer appropriate to refer to the market rate of interest in this context, alternative terminology is required. The most general term applied is the **discount rate**, although this language is sometimes confusing because it does not make clear the reason why a particular rate is relevant. Alternative, more descriptive, terminology includes phrases such as 'opportunity cost,' 'opportunity cost of capital,' 'required rate of return' or 'risk-adjusted rate of return.'

The second issue encountered in attempting to evaluate common stock is the identification of the relevant cash flows. Although investors purchase common stock expecting returns in the form of dividends and/or future price appreciation, it is not immediately apparent which of these cash flows are relevant. For example, an investor who plans to hold a share of stock for one year might determine the value of a share as follows:

$$P_0 = PV = \frac{Div_1}{(1+r)} + \frac{P_1}{(1+r)}$$

where P_0 and P_1 are the price of the stock today and one year from today, respectively, and Div_1 is next year's dividend. In order to determine the price at which the stock can be sold next year (i.e., P_1), the investor must determine the present value, as of next year, of dividends and future selling price to be realized subsequent to next year. However, any future selling price is the present value of all subsequent dividend payments, so that regardless of any particular investor's time horizon, the present value of a share of common stock is the present value of all future dividends.

Since it is virtually impossible to accurately forecast dividend payments far into the future, some simplifying assumption is generally made regarding the pattern of dividend payments. Three assumptions considered in this section are: (1) zero growth, or constant dividends; (2) constant growth in dividends; and, (3) differential growth in dividends.

A stock with constant dividends is a perpetuity. Therefore, the value is given by:

$$P_0 = PV = \frac{Div}{r}$$

where Div is the annual dividend.

Dividends which grow at a constant rate are equivalent to a growing perpetuity. The value of a stock whose dividends grow at the constant rate g is:

$$P_0 = PV = \frac{Div}{r-g}$$

where Div is next year's dividend payment.

The assumption of differential growth is most clearly illustrated with an example. Suppose that Husky Corporation's dividend this year is $1.20 per share and that dividends will grow at 10% per year for the next three years, followed by 6% annual growth. The appropriate discount rate for Husky common stock is 12%. To value this stock, first compute the present value of the first three dividend payments as follows:

Future year	Growth rate	Expected dividend	Present value
1	0.10	$1.3200	$1.1786 = ($1.20 × 1.10) PVF$_{1, 12\%}$
2	0.10	$1.4520	$1.1575 = ($1.20 × 1.10^2) PVF$_{2, 12\%}$
3	0.10	$1.5972	$1.1369 = ($1.20 × 1.10^3) PVF$_{3, 12\%}$

$PV_{div_{1,2,3}}$ Present value of dividends = $3.4730 ←

Next, compute the dividend for year 4:

$$Div_4 = \$1.20 \times (1.10)^3 \times (1.06) = \$1.6930$$

The price as of year 3 can be determined by using the formula for the present value of a stock whose dividends grow at a constant rate:

$$\textit{Price} \quad P_3 = \frac{Div_4}{r-g} = \frac{\$1.6930}{.12-.06} = \$28.2167$$

Note that the above formula values the stock as of year 3, using the year 4 dividend in the numerator. To find the present value, as of year 0, of this year 3 price:

$$PV = \frac{\$28.2167}{(1.12)^3} = \$20.0841$$

Div_{1to3} $Price_3$
Therefore, $P_0 = (\$3.4730 + \$20.0841) = \$23.5571$ or $23.56.

Growth Opportunities

A firm which pays out all its earnings as dividends is sometimes referred to as a 'cash cow.' Such a firm may be foregoing opportunities for growth, a policy which is detrimental to the stockholders.

For the sake of simplicity, it is assumed in this section that a firm acting as a cash cow also expects constant earnings for the foreseeable future. For example, a firm with 1,000,000 shares outstanding expects earnings of $5,000,000 per year; that is earnings per share (EPS) and dividends per share are each $5. If the appropriate discount rate is 20%, then the value of a share is:

$$P_0 = PV = \frac{Div}{r} = \frac{EPS}{r} = \frac{\$5}{.20} = \$25$$

If the firm chooses to retain this year's earnings in order to invest in a project which will yield a perpetuity of $1,500,000 per year (i.e., a return of 30%), the net present value of this project is:

5000000 (.3) =
C_0 = initial investment
C = return after 1 yr
r = rate

$$NPV = -C_0 + \frac{C}{r}$$

$$= -\$5,000,000 + \frac{\$1,500,000}{.20} = \$2,500,000$$

(5000000 + 1500000)

Total earnings for the firm become $6,500,000, or $6.50 per share. If the firm reverts to paying all earnings out as dividends, then the value of a share will be:

CASH COW $$P_0 = PV = \frac{Div}{r} = \frac{EPS}{r} = \frac{\$6.50}{.20} = \$32.50$$

However, since each shareholder had to forfeit $5 of current income, the net increase in value to each shareholder resulting from the firm's adopting the new project is: ($32.50 - $25.00 - $5.00) = $2.50 per share. This is the **net present value (per share) of the growth opportunity** (NPVGO). NPVGO can also be determined directly from the net present value of the project by simply dividing the net present value ($2,500,000) by the number of shares outstanding (1,000,000).

APPENDIX: THE TERM STRUCTURE OF INTEREST RATES

The presentation of this and the preceding chapters has been based on the assumption that the market rate of interest is constant for all future time periods. In reality, however, interest rates vary, depending on the maturity of the investment under consideration. For example, the interest rates for a one-year zero-coupon bond (Bond 1) and a two-year zero-coupon bond (Bond 2) might be 7% and 9%, respectively, even if both bonds are risk free. If each bond has a $1,000 face value, the present values are determined by discounting $1,000, using interest rates of 7% for Bond 1 and 9% for Bond 2:

$$PV_1 = \frac{\$1,000}{(1.07)} = \$934.58$$

$$PV_2 = \frac{\$1,000}{(1.09)^2} = \$841.68$$

where PV_1 and PV_2 are the present values of Bond 1 and Bond 2, respectively. If the two zero-coupon bonds are selling for the prices indicated here, then the yields to maturity are 7% and 9%, respectively. These interest rates on zero-coupon bonds are referred to as the one-year and two-year **spot rates**, respectively, and are indicated r_1 and r_2. Given these spot rates, the value of a two-year level-coupon bond, paying a 10% coupon, is determined by discounting future cash flows by the relevant spot rate, as indicated below:

(handwritten margin notes, left): level = payments are for life · same for life · (\$1000) = \$100 · 10% (\$1000) = \$100 · yr 1 = \$100 · yr 2 =

(handwritten margin notes, top right): yr 1 · yr 2 · yr 2 matures · $\frac{\$100}{(1.07)^1} + \frac{\$100}{(1.09)^2} + \frac{\$1000}{(1.09)^2}$

Chapter 5

$$PV = \frac{\$100}{(1+r_1)^1} + \frac{\$1,100}{(1+r_2)^2}$$

$$= \frac{\$100}{(1.07)^1} + \frac{\$1,100}{(1.09)^2} = \$1,019.31$$

The yield to maturity for the level-coupon bond is a weighted average of the two spot rates, and is determined by solving the following equation for r:

$$\$1,019.31 = \frac{\$100}{(1+r)^1} + \frac{\$1,100}{(1+r)^2}$$

As noted earlier, this equation can be solved using trial-and-error or a financial calculator; the latter approach shows that the yield to maturity is 8.9037%.

The relationship between spot rates and maturity is called the **term structure of interest rates.** As the above calculations demonstrate, spot rates can be directly observed only from zero-coupon bonds; however, in practice it is often necessary to approximate spot rates from the yields on level-coupon bonds, due to the lack of a sufficient number of zero-coupon bonds in the financial markets.

In order to understand the term structure of interest rates, it is necessary to first develop the concept of a forward rate. Using the spot rates from the previous example, the **forward rate** over the second year (f_2) is the solution to the following equation:

$$\$1 \times (1.09)^2 = \$1 \times (1.07) \times (1 + f_2)$$

In this example, f_2 is 11.037%. To understand the concept of this forward rate, suppose that when an investor purchases a two-year zero-coupon bond paying 9%, he thinks of this investment as equivalent to two consecutive investments in one-year zero-coupon bonds; the first of these one-year bonds pays the current one-year spot rate of 7%, and the second one-year bond would have to pay 11.037% to provide a return over the two-year period equivalent to that provided by purchasing the two-year zero-coupon bond. The forward rate f_2 is not currently observable in the financial markets; it is the one-year rate which would have to prevail one year from now in order to make the two one-year investments equivalent to the current two-year spot rate.

In general, given spot rates r_1 and r_2, the forward rate f_2 can be determined from:

$$(1+r_2)^2 = (1+r_1) \times (1 + f_2)$$

Solving for f_2:

$$f_2 = \frac{(1+r_2)^2}{(1+r_1)} - 1$$

A forward rate for any future year (f_n) can be determined as follows:

$$f_n = \frac{(1+r_n)^n}{(1+r_{n-1})^{n-1}} - 1$$

where r_n and r_{n-1} are spot rates for n years and (n-1) years, respectively.

Theories explaining the term structure of interest rates are described in terms of the relationship between a forward rate and the corresponding expected spot rate. The expectations hypothesis states that investors expect next year's one-year spot rate (i.e., the one-year spot rate expected over year 2) to be equal to the forward rate over year 2 (i.e., f_2). Note that f_2 is determined today based on today's spot rates (r_1 and r_2) but next years's one-year spot rate is not observable today. The expectations hypothesis describes investor's expectations regarding next year's rates as equal to the forward rate. Since this is an hypothesis, it may be true or false in reality. If the hypothesis is true, then it implies that an investor expects to receive the same return, over a one-year period, from either of the following investments: invest $1 today in a one-year zero-coupon bond, or; invest $1 today in a two-year zero-coupon bond and sell the bond one year from now. Using the above example, the return on the first investment is:

$$\$1 \times (1+r_1) = \$1 \times (1.07) = \$1.07$$

The return on the second investment is:

$$\frac{\$1 \times (1+r_2)^2}{(1+f_2)} = \frac{\$1 \times (1.09)^2}{(1.11037)} = \$1.07$$

The numerator is the return from the investment after two years. After one year, the price at which this investment can be sold is the present value of the numerator, discounted at the one-year spot rate which prevails one year from now; if this spot rate is the same as the forward rate (i.e., 11.037%) then the return on the second investment is the same as the return on the first investment (i.e., $1.07 in both cases).

Most financial economists do not believe that the expectations hypothesis accurately describes investors' expectations. The first investment described above is riskless, while the return on the second investment depends on the spot rate which prevails one year from now. Since this rate is not known, the second investment is risky. The typical risk-averse investor would not make the second investment unless he expected a return greater than that available on the riskless investment.

The alternative to the expectations hypothesis is the liquidity preference hypothesis, which states that:

$$f_2 > \text{spot rate expected over year two}$$

If this hypothesis is true, then the second investment above has a higher expected return than the first, so that some risk-averse investors are willing to accept the risk inherent in the second investment in order to have the opportunity for a higher rate of return.

CONCEPT TEST

1. A bond that promises a single payment at a future date is called a _____ bond or _____ bond.

2.   A _____ promises regular coupon interest payments, as well as a specified principal payment at the maturity date.

3.   Bonds that are outstanding forever are called _____ or _____.

4.   The regular cash payments for a level-coupon bond are called _____.

5.   A financial instrument that promises a fixed payment every period for a set number of periods is called an _____.

6.   The amount that a bond pays when it matures is called the bond's _____ and is typically $_____.

7.   Bond prices and bond yields are _____ related. This means that bond prices _____ when interest rates rise.

8.   A bond pays a coupon of $120. If the market interest rate is 10%, then the bond will sell at a _____. If the market interest rate is 15%, then the bond will sell at a _____.

9.   The value of a share of common stock is equal to the _____ of all future dividends.

10. The _____ hypothesis states that investors expect next year's one-year spot rate to be equal to the forward rate over year 2.

11. The interest rate appropriate for discounting a cash flow to be received in year 5 is called the 5-year _____.

12. The relationship between spot interest rates and time is called the _____ of interest rates.

13. The discount rate used in present value calculations when the cash flows are risky is variously called the _____, _____, or _____.

ANSWERS TO CONCEPT TEST

1. pure discount; zero-coupon
2. level-coupon bond
3. consols; perpetuities
4. coupon payments or 'coupons'
5. annuity
6. face value; 1000
7. inversely; fall

8. premium; discount
9. present value
10. expectations
11. spot rate
12. term structure
13. opportunity cost of capital; cost of capital; required rate of return

PROBLEMS AND SOLUTIONS

Problem 1

The Akella Corporation has issued a 10-year pure discount bond with a face value of $1000; the market rate of interest is 11%. Calculate the bond's current value.

Solution 1

Since the bond pays a single lump sum of $1000, in 10 years, and the interest rate is 11%, the value is [$1000/(1.11^{10})] = $352.18.

Problem 2

What is the value of a consol that pays $100 every 6 months when the market interest rate is 18%?

Solution 2

The relevant interest rate is 9% every 6 months, so the value is ($100/.09) = $1,111.11.

Problem 3

Verbrugge Company has a level-coupon bond outstanding (face value = $1000) that pays $120 per year and has 10 years to maturity. If the yield for similar bonds is currently 14%, what is the bond's value?

Solution 3

The bond's value is the present value of the coupon payments plus the present value of the $1000 face amount:

$$PV = \frac{\$120}{(1.14)^1} + \frac{\$120}{(1.14)^2} + \ldots + \frac{\$120}{(1.14)^{10}} + \frac{\$1000}{(1.14)^{10}}$$

$$= (\$120 \times 5.216116) + (\$1000 \times .269744) = \$895.68$$

Problem 4

Suppose the Verbrugge Co. bond made semiannual coupon interest payments. What would its value be?

Solution 4

The coupon payments are now $60 per period for 20 time periods; the relevant discount rate is 7%. The present value is:

$$PV = \frac{\$60}{(1.07)^1} + \frac{\$60}{(1.07)^2} + \ldots + \frac{\$60}{(1.07)^{20}} + \frac{\$1000}{(1.07)^{20}}$$

$$= (\$60 \times 10.594014) + (\$1000 \times .258419) = \$894.06$$

Problem 5

Hilliard, Inc., has just paid a $2 annual dividend on its common stock. The dividend is expected to increase at a constant 8% per year indefinitely. If the required rate of return on Hilliard's stock is 16%, what is its current value?

Solution 5

Since the growth rate in dividends is constant, the value of the stock is $[D_1/(r - g)]$. The next dividend is expected to be [$2(1 + .08)] = $2.16, so the value is [$2.16/(.16 - .08)] = $27.00.

Problem 6

Pettway Corporation's next annual dividend is expected to be $4. The growth rate in dividends over the following three years is forecasted at 15%. After that, Pettway's growth rate is anticipated to be equal to the industry average of 5%. If the required rate of return is 18%, what is the current value of the stock?

Solution 6

The current value of the stock is equal to the present value of the dividends from the high growth phase plus the present value of the stock price when the high growth phase ends. Notice that the **next** dividend (D_1) is forecasted at $4. To calculate the stock price at date 4, we must first determine the date 5 dividend (D_5):

$$D_5 = D_1 \times (1.15)^3 \times (1.05) = \$6.39$$

The price at date 4 is thus [$6.39/(.18 - .05)] = $49.16. The present value of this amount is [$49.16/(1.18^4)] = $25.34. We can calculate the PV of the first four dividend payments as follows:

Year	Growth Rate (g)	Expected Dividend	Present Value
1	15%	$4.000	$3.3898
2	15%	$4.600	$3.3036
3	15%	$5.290	$3.2197
4	15%	$6.084	$3.1381

The total present value for the first four dividend payments is $13.0512. The share value is thus ($25.34 + $13.05) = $38.39.

Problem 7

Sasha Co. has a level-coupon bond outstanding with a $90 coupon interest payment, payable annually. The bond has 20 years to maturity, and similar bonds currently yield 7%. By prior agreement the company will skip the coupon payments in years 8, 9, and 10. These coupons will be repaid without interest at maturity. What is the bond's value?

Solution 7

This problem can be solved by calculating the present value of each coupon payment, plus the present value of the face value. An easier approach is to calculate the present value under the assumption that all the coupons are paid; then deduct the present value of the coupons that are skipped and add the present value of the coupons paid at maturity. The value of the bond (ignoring the skipped and repaid coupons) is $1,211.88 (check this for practice). The present value of the skipped coupons is:

$$PV = \frac{\$\ 90}{(1.07)^8} + \frac{\$\ 90}{(1.07)^9} + \frac{\$\ 90}{(1.07)^{10}} = \$147.09$$

At maturity, an extra (3)($90) = $270 will be paid. The present value of this $270 is $69.77. Thus the value of the bond is ($1,211.88 - $147.09 + $69.77) = $1,134.56.

Problem 8

The dividend paid this year (date 0) on a share of common stock is $10. Assuming dividends grow at a 5% rate for the foreseeable future, and that the required rate of return is 10%, what is the value of the stock today? Last year (date -1)? Next year (date 1)?

Solution 8

The value today is:

$$P_0 = \frac{D_1}{r\text{-}g} = \frac{\$10(1.05)}{.10\text{-}.05} = \$210$$

The value last year was:

$$P_{-1} = \frac{D_0}{r\text{-}g} = \frac{\$10}{.10\text{-}.05} = \$200$$

The value next year will be:

$$P_1 = \frac{D_2}{r\text{-}g} = \frac{\$10(1.05)^2}{.10\text{-}.05} = \$220.50$$

Problem 9

The current year's dividend for a share of common stock is $2 and the current price of the stock is $30. Dividends are expected to grow at a 5% rate for the foreseeable future. What is the current rate of return for this stock? What is the capital gain (or loss) on the stock over the past year if the required rate of return was 10% last year?

Solution 9

Substitute P_0=$30, D_0=2, g=.05 into the following equation and solve for r:

$$P_0 = \frac{D_1}{r\text{-}g} = \frac{\$\ 2(1.05)}{r\ \text{-}\ .05} = \$30$$

The rate of return is r = .12 = 12%. In order to determine the capital gain (or loss) find the value of the stock last year (P_{-1}):

$$P_{-1} = \frac{D_0}{r\text{-}g} = \frac{\$2}{.10 - .05} = \$40$$

Therefore, the capital loss is $10.

Problem 10

A company pays a current dividend of $1.20 per share on its common stock. The annual dividend will increase by 3%, 4% and 5%, respectively, over the next three years, and then by 6% per year thereafter. The appropriate discount rate is 12%. What is the current price of the stock? What is the capital gain (or loss) on the stock over the past year?

Solution 10

Dividends for the next three years are determined as follows:

$$D_1 = \$1.20 \times (1.03) = \$1.24$$

$$D_2 = \$1.20 \times (1.03) \times (1.04) = \$1.29$$

$$D_3 = \$1.20 \ (1.03) \times (1.04) \times (1.05) = \$1.35$$

The year 3 price is:

$$P_3 = \frac{D_4}{r\text{-}g} = \frac{\$1.35(1.06)}{.12 - .06} = \$23.83$$

The current price (P_0) is the present value of the next three year's dividends plus the present value of P_3, discounted at 12%; P_0 is $20.06. In order to find the capital gain, we must determine last year's price (P_{-1}), by finding the present value of the dividends D_0 to D_3, discounted to last year, plus the present value of P_3, also discounted to last year; P_{-1} is equal to $18.98, so that the capital gain is ($20.06 - $ 18.98) = $1.08.

Problem 11

The current price of a stock (P_0) is $20 and last year's price (P_{-1}) was $18.87. The current year's dividend (D_0) is $2. Assume a constant growth rate (g) in dividends and stock price. What is the stock's rate of return for the coming year?

Solution 11

This problem can be solved by finding the solution for r in the following equation:

$$P_0 = \frac{D_1}{r\text{-}g}$$

$$r = \frac{D_1}{P_0} + g$$

We know that P_0 = $20. We can determine the values of both g and D_1 from the information given. The growth rate for dividends is the same as the growth rate for stock price; since the price increased from $18.87 to $20, g is 6%. Applying the growth rate to dividends, we see that D_1 = [$2(1.06)] = $2.12. Substituting these values, we find that r = .166 = 16.6%.

Problem 12

A corporation issues a bond today with a $1000 face value, an 8% coupon interest rate, and maturity in 25 years. An investor purchases the bond for $1000. What is the yield to maturity?

Solution 12

The yield to maturity is the value of r in the following equation:

$$PV = (C \times A^T_r) + \frac{\$1000}{(1+r)^T}$$

$$\$1000 = (\$80 \times A^{25}_r) + \frac{\$1000}{(1+r)^{25}}$$

Trial-and-error indicates that the solution is r = .08 = 8%; that is, when r = .08, the present value of the future payments is exactly $1000. However, this problem can be solved directly by realizing that the $80 coupon payment is 8% of the face value of the bond. Consider an investor who deposits $1000 in an account which pays $80 interest each year; the investor withdraws each interest payment but leaves the principal on deposit for 25 years, at which time he withdraws the $1000. Clearly, the investor has earned 8% interest on his principal and, since he has not left any interest on deposit to accumulate compound interest, 8% is the rate of return for the deposit. Similarly, the yield to maturity for the bond is 8%, the same as the coupon interest rate. The result is true regardless of the time period; that is, an investor who buys a bond for its $1000 face value receives a yield to maturity equal to the coupon interest rate.

Problem 13

Suppose that the investor bought the bond described in the previous problem for $900. What is the yield to maturity?

Solution 13

The yield to maturity is the value of r in the following equation:

$$PV = (C \times A^T_r) + \frac{\$1000}{(1+r)^T}$$

$$\$ 900 = (\$80 \times A^{25}_r) + \frac{\$1000}{(1+r)^{25}}$$

We determined in the previous problem that the yield to maturity is 8% when the price of the bond is $1000. Now, the purchase price is less than $1000, so that the yield to maturity must be greater than 8%. Therefore, using trial-and-error, we 'guess' that the yield to maturity is 10%, and calculate the present value:

$$PV = (\$80 \times A^{25}{}_{.10}) + \frac{\$1000}{(1.10)^{25}} = \$818.46$$

Since a price of $818.46 implies a yield to maturity of 10%, the yield to maturity for the $900 price is less than 10%. If we now 'guess' that the yield is 9%, we find that the present value is $901.77. Therefore, the yield to maturity is slightly greater than 9%. The precise value of the yield to maturity is 9.01969%, as determined using a financial calculator.

Problem 14

Suppose that the bond described in the previous two problems has a price of $1,100 five years after it is issued. What is the yield to maturity at that time?

Solution 14

The yield to maturity is the value of r in the following equation:

$$PV = (C \times A^{T}{}_{r}) + \frac{\$1000}{(1+r)^{T}}$$

$$\$1100 = (\$80 \times A^{20}{}_{r}) + \frac{\$1000}{(1+r)^{20}}$$

We know that the yield to maturity is less than the coupon rate because the bond is selling at a premium. Therefore, we will 'guess' that r = 6%, and calculate PV = $1,229.40. Our second 'guess' is that r = 7%, and PV = $1,105.94. Therefore, the yield to maturity is slightly greater than 7%; the exact value is 7.05224%.

Problem 15

A pure discount bond is selling for $400; it has a face value of $1000 and the maturity date is 14 years from today. What is the rate of return, or yield to maturity, for the bond?

Solution 15

Substitute PV=$400, F=$1000 and T=14 into the following equation and solve for r:

$$PV = \frac{F}{(1+r)^{T}}$$

$$\$400 = \frac{\$1000}{(1+r)^{14}}$$

$$(1+r)^{14} = 2.50$$

$$(1+r) = (2.50)^{(1/14)} = 1.0676387$$

Therefore, r = .0676387 = 6.76387%.

Problem 16

A share of preferred stock with a $12 annual dividend is selling for $75. What is the rate of return for the preferred stock?

Solution 16

Substitute C=$12 and PV=$75 into the following equation and solve for r:

$$PV = \frac{C}{r}$$

$$\$75 = \frac{\$12}{r}$$

Therefore, r = .16 = 16%.

CHAPTER 6
SOME ALTERNATIVE INVESTMENT RULES

CHAPTER HIGHLIGHTS

In the three preceding chapters, we have concluded that the net present value is the appropriate criterion for corporate investment decision-making, and we have discussed the application of the criterion to capital budgeting problems. In this chapter, we consider alternatives to the NPV criterion and analyze the advantages and disadvantages of these alternatives. The criteria evaluated in this chapter are: the payback period, the discounted payback period, the average accounting rate of return, the internal rate of return, and the profitability index.

The Payback Period Rule

The **payback period rule** specifies that an investment is acceptable if the sum of its undiscounted cash flows equals the initial investment before some specified cutoff time period (for example, two years). Consider an investment with the following cash flows:

$$(-\$10{,}000, \$2000, \$5000, \$3000, \$6000)$$

The initial investment is $10,000. After three years, the sum of the cash flows equals $10,000, so the payback period for this investment is three years. Consequently, this investment would be rejected if the cutoff time period were, for example, two years.

The deficiencies of the payback rule, in comparison to the net present value criterion, are:

1. The timing of cash flows within the payback period is ignored, thereby treating these cash flows equally; in contrast, the net present value properly discounts these cash flows.
2. All cash flows after the cutoff time period are ignored, while the net present value discounts all cash flows.
3. There is no objective criterion for choosing the cutoff time period, while the net present value criterion is based on the market interest rate.

The primary advantage of the payback rule is its simplicity; it is both easy to compute and easy to understand. It is often used in practice for making low-level, relatively small investment decisions. Any project that pays back in two years, for example, and lasts longer than that probably has a positive NPV. Another advantage of the payback period rule is related to the issue of evaluating a manager's decision-making ability. A manager may have determined, for instance, that the payback for a particular investment is two years. It would require only two years to determine whether this analysis is correct. This factor may be important in the evaluation of managerial decisions.

The Discounted Payback Period Rule

The **discounted payback period** rule indicates that a project is acceptable if the sum of the discounted cash flows equals the initial investment before a specified cutoff time period. This rule is identical to the payback period rule except that the time value of money is considered since the cash flows are discounted.

Suppose a company requires a discounted payback period of three years. Using the data from the previous example and a 10% discount rate, the sum of the discounted cash flows for the first three years is $8,204.36, and for the first four years is $12,302.44. Therefore, this project has a discounted payback period between three and four years, so that it would be rejected according to the discounted payback period rule. Notice that the net present value is $2,302.44, indicating that the investment should be accepted.

The discounted payback period rule may appear preferable to the payback period rule because cash flows are discounted. However, two of the three deficiencies of the payback period criterion also apply to the discounted payback period; that is, cash flows after the cutoff time period are ignored and there is no objective criterion for choosing the cutoff time period. Consequently, the discounted payback period lacks the simplicity of the payback period without being as meaningful as the net present value.

The Average Accounting Return

The **average accounting return** (AAR) is defined as average net income attributed to an investment divided by average book value of the asset. Suppose that the data above represent accounting net income rather than cash flows. The average net income would be:

$$(\$2000 + \$5000 + \$3000 + \$6000)/4 = \$4000$$

If the $10,000 investment is depreciated to a value of zero, on a straight-line basis, over a four-year period, then the book value decreases by ($10,000/4) = $2500 per year. The average book value is:

$$(\$10,000 + \$7500 + \$5000 + \$2500 + \$0)/5 = \$5000$$

(Note that even though the asset is depreciated over a four-year period, the average book value is the average of five observations, beginning with the year 0 book value, and ending with the year 4 book value.) The AAR for this investment is ($4000/$5000) = 80%. The project is acceptable if the firm's target AAR is less than 80%.

The AAR rule has several serious flaws. First, the AAR method uses accounting income and book value data, which generally are not closely related to cash flows, the relevant data for financial decision-making. Second, as is true for the payback period, the AAR ignores the time value of money; income received in three years is treated as equivalent to income received in one year. Third, the target AAR must be arbitrarily specified because it is not a rate of return in the financial market sense.

The Internal Rate of Return

The **internal rate of return** (IRR) criterion is the most significant alternative to the net present value criterion. For any investment, the IRR is the rate of return (or discount rate) which equates the present value of the cash inflows with the cash outlay, or cost, of the investment; alternatively, the

IRR is defined as the rate of return for an investment. Algebraically, the IRR is the solution for the discount rate r in the following equation:

$$C_0 = \frac{C_1}{(1+r)} + \frac{C_2}{(1+r)^2} + \cdots + \frac{C_T}{(1+r)^T}$$

where C_i is the cash flow at date i.

Consider the investment described earlier, with the following cash flows:

$$(-\$10000, \$2000, \$5000, \$3000, \$6000)$$

To calculate the internal rate of return, substitute into the above equation:

$$\$10,000 = \frac{\$2000}{(1+r)} + \frac{\$5000}{(1+r)^2} + \frac{\$3000}{(1+r)^3} + \frac{\$6000}{(1+r)^4}$$

Solving this equation for r is equivalent to solving for the yield to maturity of a level coupon bond, as discussed in the preceding chapter. Therefore, the value of r can be determined by using either trial-and-error or a financial calculator; for either approach, the solution technique is analogous to the corresponding solution of the yield to maturity problem.

Using trial-and-error, one might 'guess' that r is 5%; since this is purely a guess, two different individuals solving the same problem could very well make different first 'guesses.' To determine whether the guess is correct, find the present value of the cash inflows, discounted at 5%:

$$\frac{\$2000}{(1.05)} + \frac{\$5000}{(1.05)^2} + \frac{\$3000}{(1.05)^3} + \frac{\$6000}{(1.05)^4} = \$13,967.64$$

This present value is greater than C_0, which is $10,000; consequently, r = 5% is not the solution to the above equation. The next 'guess' at a solution must be a value of r greater than 5%, since a larger denominator in the above equation reduces the present value. Therefore, a reasonable second guess might be 10%. (Note that a student might wonder why 10% would be a more reasonable guess than, say, 6% or 60%. The answer is that none of these guesses is more or less reasonable than another; at this point it is not yet determined which of these rates is closest to the correct value for r.) Substituting r = 10% in the above equation:

$$\frac{\$2000}{(1.10)} + \frac{\$5000}{(1.10)^2} + \frac{\$3000}{(1.10)^3} + \frac{\$6000}{(1.10)^4} = \$12,302.44$$

(Note that this present value was calculated earlier, in the section on the discounted payback period; that result could have been used in this section to save the time required to perform the above calculations.) Again, the value of r must be increased, because the present value exceeds C_0. Extrapolating the above results indicates that the IRR must be substantially greater than 10%, so that a reasonable guess would be that r is approximately 20%:

$$\frac{\$2000}{(1.20)} + \frac{\$5000}{(1.20)^2} + \frac{\$3000}{(1.20)^3} + \frac{\$6000}{(1.20)^4} = \$9,768.52$$

Now it is clear that the internal rate of return is between 10% and 20%, although substantially closer to 20%. Subsequent trials reveal that for values of r equal to 18% and 19%, the present values are $10,206.46 and $9,983.76, respectively, so that the internal rate of return is between 18% and 19%. A reasonable next guess would be r=18.5%, which results in a present value of $10,094.16; therefore, r is between 18.5% and 19%.

The above procedure can be continued until the desired degree of accuracy is reached, but it is apparent that the trial-and-error process is both tedious and time consuming. An accurate solution can be reached quickly with a financial calculator, using the following sequence:

$$10000 \ [+/-] \ [CF_i]$$
$$2000 \ [CF_i]$$
$$5000 \ [CF_i]$$
$$3000 \ [CF_i]$$
$$6000 \ [CF_i]$$
$$[COMP] \ [IRR]$$

The internal rate of return is 18.9259%. (Note: Since a similar procedure was used to calculate the yield to maturity in the previous chapter, this calculator solution will not be described in further detail here.)

The trial-and-error procedure requires finding the solution for r which equates the present value of the future cash flows with the cash outlay C_0. When the present value and the cash outlay are equal, the net present value is zero. Therefore, the above solution technique can also be described as the process of finding the value of r which equates the net present value to zero.

Before proceeding to discuss the application of the IRR criterion to investment decision-making, it is essential to clarify the interpretation of the internal rate of return calculated above. Recall that the IRR is the discount rate which equates the present value of the cash inflows with the cost of the asset. Also, as presented in Chapter 4, the present value of a specified future cash flow is the outlay required, at a designated interest rate, in order to receive a future dollar return equal to the specified cash flow. Therefore, the above IRR indicates that an individual who invests $10,000 in the asset described earlier receives a rate of return equal to 18.9259%. In other words, an individual would have to invest $10,000 at 18.9259% in order to receive returns of $2000, $5000, $3000 and $6000 at dates 1, 2, 3 and 4, respectively, so that the rate of return for the above investment is the IRR calculated here.

In part, the appeal of the internal rate of return is the simplicity in applying and understanding the criterion. An investment project is acceptable if the IRR is greater than the rate of return which could be earned in the financial markets on investments of equal risk; an investment project is unacceptable if the IRR is less than the relevant rate of return in the financial markets.

If the investment under consideration is free of risk, then the relevant comparison in applying the above criterion is between the IRR and the riskless rate of return in the financial markets. On the other hand, since most investments are risky to some extent, then the comparison must be between the IRR and the rate available in the financial markets for investments with risk level equal to that of the investment under consideration. As noted in the preceding chapter, this rate is often referred to as the 'discount rate,' although alternative terminology is also used, including 'opportunity cost' or 'required rate of return.'

Figure 6.1 is a **net present value profile** for the investment described earlier. The NPV profile summarizes the relationship between the discount rate (r) and the NPV of the investment. Clearly, as the discount rate increases, the NPV decreases. The IRR is indicated as the value of r for which the NPV is zero.

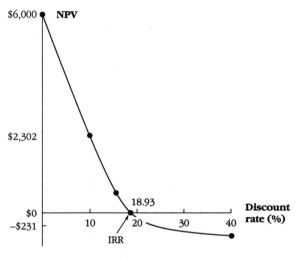

Figure 6.1

The NPV profile illustrates the reason why, under certain circumstances, the IRR and the NPV criteria lead to identical decisions regarding the acceptability of an investment. If the IRR for a particular investment is greater than the required rate of return, then the following conclusions apply: first, according to the IRR criterion, the investment is acceptable; second, the NPV discounted at the required rate of return is positive (that is, on the NPV profile, the NPV is positive for any discount rate less than the IRR); and, third, since the NPV is positive, the investment is also acceptable according to the NPV criterion. Consequently, both criteria lead to the same decision. (The same conclusion applies when the IRR is less than the required rate of return; that is, both criteria indicate that the investment is unacceptable.)

The above discussion seems to imply that the IRR criterion is equivalent to the NPV criterion in its ability to identify acceptable investments. However, under certain circumstances, the IRR criterion does not correctly indicate whether an investment is acceptable. These problems with the IRR criterion are presented in the next section.

Problems with the IRR Approach

Definition of Independent and Mutually Exclusive Projects. In order to understand the difficulties which may arise in applying the IRR criterion, it is first necessary to distinguish between independent and mutually exclusive investment projects. An **independent investment project** is an investment whose acceptance or rejection does not affect, and is not affected by, the acceptance or rejection of any other projects. A set of **mutually exclusive investment projects** requires that the acceptance of any one project implies the rejection of all other projects in the set. For example, a company which is considering the purchase of a delivery truck may have under consideration numerous models produced by several manufacturers; since only one truck will be purchased, the alternatives under consideration comprise a set of mutually exclusive investments.

Two General Problems Affecting Both Independent and Mutually Exclusive Projects. The first of these problems occurs when the cash flows from a particular project begin with an inflow which is then followed by an outflow. For example, consider a project with a $10,000 inflow followed by a $12,000 outflow. Using the procedures of the previous section, it can be shown that the IRR for this project is 20%. However, in contrast to the example of the previous section, the NPV for this project increases as the discount rate increases, thereby requiring that the IRR criterion be restated for such situations; that is, when a project's initial cash flow is positive and subsequent cash flows are negative, the project is acceptable when the IRR is less than the required rate. The reason for this paradoxical conclusion is most readily understood by realizing that the project described above is equivalent to a loan, rather than an investment. Consequently, the project (i.e., the 'loan') is acceptable when its IRR (i.e., the 'interest rate' on the 'loan') is less than the rate at which loans are available in the financial markets.

The second problem arises when the cash flows change sign (from negative to positive, or positive to negative) more than once. Consider the following cash flows:

$$(-\$60, \$155, -\$100)$$

The NPV is zero when the discount rate is 25% and is also zero when the discount rate is 33.33%, so that there are two internal rates of return. This situation is an example of the **multiple rates of return problem.** Since there is no basis for choosing one of these rates as the IRR, it is impossible to apply the IRR criterion when cash flows change sign more than once.

Problems Specific to Mutually Exclusive Projects. The difficulties encountered in applying the IRR criterion to mutually exclusive projects are referred to as the **scale problem** and the **timing problem.** Since these problems are similar in some respects, only the scale problem is discussed in detail here.

Suppose we have two mutually exclusive investments, X and Y, with the following respective cash flows:

$$X: (-\$200, \$100, \$300, \$400)$$
$$Y: (-\$5000, \$4000, \$1000, \$2000)$$

These investments are said to differ in scale because the cash flows for Y are substantially larger than those for X. Further, suppose that the appropriate discount rate is 10%. Since these investments are mutually exclusive, we must determine, first, whether each investment is acceptable and, second, if both are acceptable, which is preferable. At the 10% discount rate, the net present values are $439.37 and $965.44 for X and Y, respectively, indicating that both investments are acceptable. The internal rates of return are 87.20% and 22.81%, respectively, for X and Y. Note that X has the higher IRR while Y has the higher NPV, so that it is not immediately apparent which is the preferable alternative.

It is important to remember here the discussion of Chapters 3 and 4, establishing the validity of the NPV criterion for investment decision-making. Given those conclusions, it is clear that Y is the preferable alternative. Although this decision is correct, it often seems inappropriate to those encountering this result for the first time. In order to understand why the IRR criterion can, under certain circumstances, mislead a decision-maker, it is helpful to think of the choice between X and Y in terms of the **incremental IRR.**

In order to apply the incremental IRR criterion, we first define an incremental investment (Y-X); this is an investment which, when implemented along with investment X, will have the same cost and will generate the same cash flows as investment Y. Therefore, (Y-X) can be thought of as the incremental cash flows which would result if Y were accepted in place of X. (Y-X) requires that an additional $4800 ($5000 - $200) be invested in order to receive incremental cash flows of $3900, $700, and $1600.

Next, decide whether investment X (the investment with the smaller outlay and cash inflows), treated as an independent investment, would be acceptable; both the NPV and IRR criteria indicate that X is acceptable. Finally, determine whether the incremental investment (Y-X) is acceptable. (Y-X) has an IRR of 17.70% and an NPV (at 10%) of $526.07, so it is a good investment. We have determined that X is acceptable and that (Y-X) is acceptable; viewed in this way, accepting project Y amounts to accepting project X plus another acceptable investment (Y-X). Therefore, Y is the preferable alternative.

The timing problem arises when two investments requiring the same initial outlay differ substantially in terms of the timing of the cash inflows; that is, the larger cash inflows for one investment occur early in the life of the asset, while the larger inflows for the other occur later. As is the case for the scale problem, it is possible that the IRR criterion will mislead the decision-maker into selecting the less desirable alternative. As described above, this can be avoided by: (1) applying the NPV criterion; (2) comparing the incremental IRR with the required rate of return; or, (3) applying the NPV criterion to the incremental cash flows.

The Profitability Index

The **profitability index** (PI) is defined as the present value of the future cash flows divided by the initial investment. In one sense, the profitability index is comparable to the NPV criterion, because it provides an indication of whether the present value of the future cash flows exceeds the initial investment. If this ratio is greater than one, then the investment is desirable, because the present value of the future cash flows is greater than the initial outlay. Any independent investment shown to be acceptable according to the PI criterion is also acceptable according to the NPV criterion. However, as in the case of the IRR, problems may arise in applying the PI to mutually exclusive investment projects. For example, a smaller project may have a higher PI, but a lower NPV, than a larger project. Incorrect decisions are avoided by: (1) applying the NPV criterion; (2) applying the PI criterion to the incremental cash flows; or, (3) applying the NPV criterion to the incremental cash flows.

The profitability index is useful when a firm is subject to **capital rationing** during the current time period. Capital rationing occurs when, for whatever reason, the amount of investable funds is limited and a firm has more positive NPV projects than can currently be undertaken. In this case, an often proposed solution is to rank the projects by profitability index, and accept those with the highest values.

The Practice of Capital Budgeting

In surveys of large corporations, discounted cash flow approaches (i.e., NPV, IRR, PI) are the most commonly used capital budgeting techniques. It appears that 80% or more use discounted cash flow, but not necessarily to the exclusion of other procedures.

CONCEPT TEST

1. The length of time until the sum of a project's cash flows equals the initial investment is called the _____.

2. The length of time until the sum of a project's discounted cash flows equals the initial investment is called the _____.

3. Since the payback period criterion requires simply adding a project's cash flows, it ignores the _____.

4. A deficiency common to both the payback period and discounted payback period rules is that the _____ must be arbitrarily selected.

5. The major advantage of the payback period rule is its _____.

6. The average accounting return (AAR) is defined as _____ divided by _____.

7. The AAR requires that the _____ be arbitrarily specified.

8. A deficiency common to both the AAR criterion and the payback period criterion is that both ignore the _____.

9. The internal rate of return (IRR) is the discount rate at which the NPV is _____.

10. The profitability index is the ratio of the _____ to the _____.

11. When a firm is considering two or more potential investments, of which only one can be accepted, then the investments are said to be _____.

12. An _____ is an investment whose acceptance or rejection does not affect, and is not affected by, the acceptance or rejection of any other projects.

13. If the cash flows for a project change signs more than once, then the IRR criterion may fail to identify an acceptable project because of the _____ problem.

14. If a project is acceptable according to the discounted payback period criterion, is it necessarily acceptable by the net present value criterion?

15. The internal rate of return is the rate of return (or discount rate) which equates the present value of the _____ with the _____ of the investment.

16. If a project is acceptable according to the payback period criterion, then it is necessarily acceptable by the NPV criterion only if the required rate of return is _____.

17. If a project is acceptable according to the profitability index rule, is it necessarily acceptable according to the net present value criterion?

18. Suppose a project's cash flows are a level perpetuity. In this case, the payback period is the same as one divided by _____.

19. Solving for the internal rate of return is equivalent to solving for the yield to maturity of a
    _____.

20. If the first cash flow for an investment is positive and all the remaining cash flows are negative,
    then the internal rate of return criterion becomes: "Accept the investment if the IRR is
    _____ the required return."

21. If, due to limited funds availability, a firm has more profitable investments than it can accept,
    then _____ is said to exist.

22. If funds are limited in the current period, then the _____ criterion may be useful
    for choosing among positive NPV investments.

23. If we are comparing two investments, does the one with the higher internal rate of return
    necessarily have the higher net present value?

24. In practice, the most commonly used capital budgeting techniques are _____
    techniques.

25. The profitability index criterion states that a project is acceptable if the index value is greater
    than _____.

ANSWERS TO CONCEPT TEST

1. payback period
2. discounted payback period
3. time value of money
4. cutoff period
5. simplicity
6. average net income;
     average book value
7. target AAR
8. time value of money
9. zero
10. PV of future cash flows;
     initial investment
11. mutually exclusive
12. independent investment project

13. multiple rates of return
14. yes
15. cash inflows; cash outlay or cost
16. zero
17. yes
18. the IRR
19. level coupon bond
20. less than
21. capital rationing
22. profitability index
23. no
24. discounted cash flow
25. one

PROBLEMS AND SOLUTIONS

For Problems 1-5, use the following cash flows for projects A and B:

A: (-$2000, $500, $600, $700, $800)
B: (-$2000, $950, $850, $400, $300)

Problem 1

Calculate the payback period for projects A and B.

Solution 1

The sum of the first three cash flows for project A is $1800, and the sum of the first four cash flows is $2600, so the payback period for A is between three and four years. After three years, A is within $200 of paying back the initial cost. The cash flow in the fourth year is $800. The fractional year is thus ($200/$800) = .25, so we could say the payback period is 3.25 years.

The payback period for project B is 2.5 years.

Problem 2

If the discount rate is 12%, what is the discounted payback period for project A? For project B?

Solution 2

The sum of the four discounted cash flows for project A is $1931.41, so A does not pay back its initial cost. For B, the sum of the four discounted cash flows is $2001.20, so the payback period is almost exactly four years.

Problem 3

Calculate (by trial-and-error) the internal rate of return for projects A and B.

Solution 3

The solution to problem 2 provides some useful information for solving this problem. For project B, the discounted payback period is almost exactly equal to the life of the project, so the internal rate of return must be slightly greater than 12%. The exact value of the IRR is 12.0351%. For project A, the NPV is -$68.59 at a 12% discount rate, so the IRR is somewhat less than 12%. At discount rates of 10% and 11%, the NPV is $22.74 and -$23.76, respectively. Therefore, the IRR must be between 10% and 11%. The exact value is 10.4845%.

Problem 4

If A and B are mutually exclusive and the required rate of return is 5%, which project should be accepted?

Solution 4

Using a discount rate of 5%, the NPV for A is $283.26 and the NPV for B is $268.08. Therefore, A is preferred even though it has the lower IRR.

Problem 5

If the discount rate is 12%, and A and B are mutually exclusive, which project should be accepted? At what discount rate will we be indifferent between A and B?

Solution 5

From Problem 3, A has a negative NPV at a 12% discount rate (-$68.59). B has an NPV of $1.20, so it is acceptable and preferred.

To solve for the rate at which we are indifferent between A and B, we need to compute the discount rate such that A and B have the same net present value:

$$NPV_A = NPV_B$$

This is equivalent to finding the discount rate such that:

$$NPV_A - NPV_B = 0$$

This is solved by finding the internal rate of return for the incremental cash flows for an investment (A - B): ($0, -$450, -$250, $300, $500). This rate is found by trial and error or with the use of a financial calculator; the latter approach indicates that the rate is 6.0654%. At this discount rate, both A and B have an NPV of $223.51.

Problem 6

Compute the internal rate of return for the following investments:

(-$60, $155, -$100) and ($60, -$155, $100)

How do you interpret the results in terms of the IRR rule?

Solution 6

Since the cash flows for each of these investments change sign more than once, each investment has more than one internal rate of return. These can be determined by trial and error, but since these cash flows extend over only three time periods, it is possible to solve algebraically for the two IRR values. Consider, for example, the first of the two investments. The IRR is the rate r which is a solution to the following equation:

$$\$60 = \frac{\$155}{(1+r)} - \frac{\$100}{(1+r)^2}$$

Algebraically, this is a quadratic equation; in general, a quadratic equation has two solutions, which can be determined directly by using the quadratic formula. The two solutions here are $r_1 = .25 = 25\%$ and $r_2 = .3333 = 33.33\%$. These same values are the two solutions for the second investment above.

To interpret these results, we can compute the net present value at a rate between the two IRRs. At a discount rate of 30%, for example, the NPV is +$.06 for the first investment and -$.06 for the second. We should accept the first investment only if our required rate of return is between 25% and 33.33%, and we should accept the second one only if our required return is outside the range 25% to 33.33%. This conclusion derives from the fact that a quadratic equation, when graphed, has the shape of a parabola, so that the net present value must be either exclusively negative or exclusively positive between the two solutions identified here, and has the opposite sign outside the range of the two solutions.

Problem 7

You have been asked to analyze the investment (-$51, $100, -$50). Compute the internal rate of return for this investment. Is the investment acceptable? The required return is unknown.

Solution 7

This is a problem designed to keep graduate students out of trouble by keeping them busy. There is no IRR! All this means is that there is no real number for which the NPV is zero. At any discount rate, the NPV is negative, so the required return is irrelevant. This result can also be demonstrated algebraically because the IRR is the solution to a quadratic equation, as discussed in the solution to Problem 6. For this problem, however, the quadratic equation does not have a solution.

Problem 8

Consider the following abbreviated financial statements for a proposed investment:

Year	0	1	2	3	4
Gross book value	$160	$160	$160	$160	$160
less: Accumulated depreciation		40	80	120	160
Net book value	160	120	80	40	0
Sales		$95	$90	$97	$80
Costs		33	30	25	10
Depreciation		40	40	40	40
Taxes (50%)		11	10	16	15
Net Income		$11	$10	$16	$15

What is the average accounting return? What is the internal rate of return?

Solution 8

The average net income is [($11 + $10 + $16 + $15)/4] = $13. The average book value is $80, so the AAR is 16.25%.

To compute the internal rate of return, the cash flows must first be tabulated. As indicated in Chapter 2, operating cash flow can be derived by adding depreciation to net income, so that cash flows are $51, $50, $56, and $55, respectively over the four year period. (Note: the calculation of cash flows is discussed in greater detail in Chapter 7.) The initial investment is $160. Using trial and error, it can be shown that the IRR is approximately 12%; the exact value is 12.0608%.

Problem 9

Calculate the internal rate of return for an investment with the following cash flows: ($792, -$1780, $1000).

Solution 9

Since the sign of the cash flows changes twice, there are two IRRs for this problem. These can be determined using trial and error, and they can also be determined algebraically since the problem can be formulated as a quadratic equation. (Note that a financial calculator will not provide both solutions. Furthermore, a computer spreadsheet program will generally provide one solution at a time; in order to determine the second solution, you must be aware of the fact that a second solution exists in order to derive the second solution.) The two values of the internal rate of return are 11.1111% and 13.6364%.

Problem 10

For the investment identified in Problem 9, determine the acceptability of the investment when the required rate of return is 10%; when the required rate of return is 12%; when the required rate of return is 14%.

Solution 10

This problem can be solved using the net present value criterion by simply calculating the NPV for the investment at each value of the required rate of return. The net present values are $.26, -$.09, and $.06, respectively for the three required rates. These results indicate that the investment is acceptable if the required rate of return is either 10% or 14%, but it is unacceptable if the required rate of return is 12%. These results can be understood algebraically by noting that the quadratic equation in this problem has negative net present value for values of r between the two solutions derived in Problem 9 and positive net present value for values of r outside the range of the two solutions. Therefore, the investment is unacceptable if the required rate of return is any value between 11.1111% and 13.6364%, and is acceptable otherwise.

Problem 11

You have the opportunity to borrow $8000, to be repaid in yearly installments of $2,200 at the end of each of the next five years. Use the IRR criterion to determine whether this loan is preferable to borrowing at the market rate of 11.5%.

Solution 11

We can use the trial and error process or a financial calculator to find the interest rate for this loan. Since the loan payments are in the form of an annuity, however, it is more efficient to take advantage of this fact and solve for the interest rate directly, either using the present value annuity factors in Table A.2 or the annuity functions of a financial calculator. The interest rate is the value of r which is the solution to the following equation:

$$\$2200 \times A_r^5 = \$8000$$

The value of the annuity factor in the above equation is 3.6364. Referring to the fifth row of Table A.2, we find that the present value annuity factor is 3.6048 for r = 12%; therefore, the interest rate on the loan is somewhat less than 12%. The exact value can be determined using the annuity functions of a financial calculator as follows:

8000 [+/-] [PV]
5 [n]
2200 [PMT]
[COMP] [i]

The interest rate is 11.6488%. It is clear that borrowing at the market rate of 11.5% is preferable to borrowing at the higher rate indicated in this example. This is consistent with the IRR criterion for financial opportunities which begin with an inflow; that is, for such opportunities, the opportunity is acceptable only if the internal rate of return (i.e., the interest rate for the loan) is less than the market rate of interest.

Problem 12

A firm is considering the following mutually exclusive investment projects:

Project A requires an initial outlay of $500 and will return $120 per year for the next seven years. Project B requires an initial outlay of $5,000 and will return $1,350 per year for the next five years.

The required rate of return is 10%. Use the net present value criterion to determine which investment is preferable.

Solution 12

Since the returns for each investment are in the form of an annuity, we can use the present value annuity factors in Table A.2 to determine the net present values. For project A:

$$PV = \$120 \times A^7_{.10} = \$120 \times 4.8684 = \$584.21$$

Therefore, the net present value for project A is $84.20. Similarly, the net present value for project B is $117.58. The net present value criterion indicates that B is the preferred alternative. (Note that there may be an additional problem here arising from the difference in the life of the two assets; if the assets perform a comparable task, the shorter life of project A may imply that a new investment in a replacement is required sooner for A than for B. This possibility is addressed in Chapter 7.)

Problem 13

Calculate the internal rate of return for each of the investment projects described in Problem 12.

Solution 13

Since the returns for each project are in the form of an annuity, we can estimate the IRRs using Table A.2 and the solution technique of Problem 11, or we can determine the exact values using the annuity functions of a financial calculator. The latter approach indicates that the internal rates of return are 14.9500% and 10.9162% for projects A and B, respectively. In spite of the fact that project A has the higher IRR, the solution to Problem 12 indicates that project B is preferable. This is an example of the scale problem discussed in the chapter.

Problem 14

Calculate the profitability index for each of the investment projects described in Problem 12.

Solution 14

The profitability index is defined as the ratio of the present value of the future cash flows divided by the initial investment. For project A, the profitability index is ($584.21/$500) = 1.1684. For project B, the profitability index is ($5117.58/$5000) = 1.0235. If these two projects were independent of each other, both would be acceptable according to the profitability index criterion because each of the above values is greater than 1. This conclusion is consistent with that implied by the net present value and internal rate of return criteria for independent projects. However, since the projects are in fact mutually exclusive, the profitability index criterion can not be used to select the preferred alternative.

Problem 15

Again, refer to the two investments identified in Problem 12; calculate the internal rate of return, the profitability index and the net present value for the incremental investment (B-A).

Solution 15

The cash flows for the incremental investment (B-A) are:

(-$4500, $1230, $1230, $1230, $1230, $1230, -$120, -$120)

The internal rate of return for (B-A) is 10.3009%, the present value is $4533.35, the profitability index is 1.0074 and the net present value is $33.35. All three criteria indicate that the incremental investment (B-A) is acceptable; it is always true that the three criteria applied to the incremental investment result in the same decision. Consequently, since project A is acceptable and the incremental investment (B-A) is acceptable, then project B is preferred. We have demonstrated that the internal rate of return and profitability index criteria, when applied to the incremental investment, result in the same decision derived by applying the NPV criterion in Problem 12.

CHAPTER 7
PRACTICAL APPLICATION OF
CAPITAL BUDGETING TECHNIQUES

CHAPTER HIGHLIGHTS

In the preceding chapters, we have provided a detailed discussion of the application of the net present value criterion to capital budgeting problems. Thus far, however, we have not examined some of the important complications which arise when the NPV approach is applied to 'real-world' problems. These complications are the focus of the current chapter. The major concept discussed in this chapter is the identification of the relevant cash flows for a net present value analysis of a capital budgeting problem. Other topics include: the effect of inflation on capital budgeting; the evaluation of mutually exclusive investments with unequal useful lives; and, the assessment of risk in capital budgeting, using techniques such as decision trees and sensitivity analysis.

Incremental Cash Flows

Although financial managers use accounting income data in their decision-making, financial decisions must be based on cash flows rather than income. Furthermore, the relevant cash flows for any particular capital budgeting decision are the cash flows which are incremental to the project under consideration. Therefore, even though we use accounting data, we must be able to interpret the data in such a way as to identify the incremental cash flows. Numerous problems arise in the course of such an analysis. Some of the most common occur in the interpretation of the following concepts: **sunk costs, opportunity costs,** and **side effects.**

Sunk Costs. A sunk cost is money the firm has already spent, or is committed to spend, regardless of whether it accepts the project under consideration. The cost of a feasibility study undertaken before the accept/reject decision is made is a sunk cost, because it must be paid regardless of the decision. This cost is not incremental to the project, and therefore is not relevant to the capital budgeting decision.

Opportunity Costs. Suppose we are considering a project that involves building a new factory on land we already own. The price paid for the land, at some time in the past, is a sunk cost and is therefore not relevant to the current decision. However, by building a factory on the land, we lose the opportunity to use the land for some alternative project. One alternative to building the factory would simply be to sell the property. Thus, by using the property, we forego the proceeds from a sale; hence, the market value of the property is an opportunity cost which is an incremental cost to the project.

Side Effects. Capital budgeting projects often have side effects which must be taken into consideration. An example of a side effect is **erosion**. When a consumer products manufacturer introduces a new product, some portion of the new product's sales come at the expense of reduced sales of the company's other products. The resulting reduction in cash flow to other product lines is a direct consequence of introducing the new product; that reduction is an incremental cost to the project.

Incremental Cash Flows: An Example

In this section, we consider an example of a proposed capital budgeting project, for which we must first determine the relevant incremental cash flows. We will suppose that the KMS Corporation is a profitable, successful eight-year old company which manufactures bicycles and is considering the purchase of new, more efficient manufacturing equipment. KMS expects that the new equipment will allow the firm to produce a better quality product at lower cost, so that sales revenue will increase by $30,000 and operating costs will be reduced by $20,000. The cost of the equipment is $100,000, it is expected to have a useful economic life of five years and a market value of $10,000 at the end of the five years. The asset will be depreciated according to the 1986 Tax Reform Act. For an asset in the five-year category, the following depreciation percentages apply over a six-year time period: 20%, 32%, 19.2%, 11.52%. 11.52% and 5.76% for each of the six years, respectively. We assume a 40% tax rate for both ordinary income and capital gains. In addition to the outlay for the purchase of the asset, KMS projects an investment of $15,000 in working capital; this investment will remain constant for the life of the asset and is then completely recovered at the end of year five.

The investment outlays for the project consist of the $100,000 outlay for the purchase of the equipment plus the $15,000 outlay for the investment in working capital. Therefore, the total outlay at year 0 is $115,000.

Cash inflows for each of the five years of the asset's life are determined as follows:

	Year 1	Year 2	Year 3	Year 4	Year 5
Sales Revenue	$30,000	$30,000	$30,000	$30,000	$30,000
Operating Costs	-20,000	-20,000	-20,000	-20,000	-20,000
Depreciation	20,000	32,000	19,200	11,520	11,520
Income Before Taxes	30,000	18,000	30,800	38,480	38,480
Tax (at 40%)	12,000	7,200	12,320	15,392	15,392
Net Income	18,000	10,800	18,480	23,088	23,088
Cash Flow from Operations	$38,000	$42,800	$37,680	$34,608	$57,912

Notice that the decrease in operating costs results in an increase in income. For years 1 through 4, the cash flow from operations is equal to sales revenue minus operating costs and taxes; for example, the year 1 cash flow from operations is [$30,000 - (-$20,000) - $12,000] = $38,000. For year 5, we have additional cash flows from the sale of the asset and the recovery of working capital. When the asset is sold at the end of year 5, it has a book value of $5,760, because total depreciation expense for the first five years is $94,240. Therefore, the sale of the asset for $10,000 results in a capital gains tax equal to [($10,000 - $5,760)(.40)] = $1,696. The additional cash flow in year 5 is equal to the $10,000 market value of the asset, less the capital gains tax, plus the recovery of the working capital investment: ($10,000 - $1,696 + $15,000) = $23,304. The year 5 cash flow from operations is ($23,304 + $23,088 + $11,520) = $57,912.

In order to determine the acceptability of the investment, we now determine the net present value of the cash flows. For simplicity, we assume that all cash flows occur at the end of the year. If the opportunity cost for this investment is 16%, then the present value of the cash inflows for years 1 through 5 is $135,392.32 and the net present value of the investment is $20,392.32. Clearly, the NPV criterion indicates that the investment in new equipment is acceptable to KMS.

Inflation and Capital Budgeting

In order to correctly incorporate the effects of inflation on capital budgeting decisions, the relationship between interest rates and inflation must be understood.

Interest Rates and Inflation. Suppose that the market rate of interest is 10% and that the rate of inflation is 5%. If an individual deposits $1 in a bank account, he will have $1.10 at the end of one year; this is a nominal amount, because it is measured in actual dollars, but it does not reflect the change in the individual's purchasing power. If an item costs $1 at the beginning of the year, then $1 will buy one item. At the end of the year, the cost of the item increases by 5%, due to inflation, so that the $1.10 will buy ($1.10/$1.05) = 1.048 units of the same item. Consequently, the individual's purchasing power has increased by 4.8%, rather than by the 10% earned on the deposit. The **nominal interest rate** is 10% but the **real interest rate** is only 4.8%, indicating the actual increase in the consumer's purchasing power. In this example, the real interest rate is determined from the following equation:

$$(1 + \text{Real interest rate}) = \frac{\$1 \times (1 + \text{Nominal interest rate})}{\$1 \times (1 + \text{Inflation rate})}$$

Therefore, the real interest rate is given by:

$$\text{Real interest rate} = \frac{(1 + \text{Nominal interest rate})}{(1 + \text{Inflation rate})} - 1$$

Cash Flow and Inflation. Financial managers must realize that cash flows, as well as interest rates, can be expressed in either nominal or real quantities. In the above example, the year-end cash flow is $1.10 in nominal terms and $1.048 in real terms.

Discounting: Nominal or Real? Both interest rates and cash flows are typically identified in nominal terms. However, for capital budgeting problems, it is sometimes convenient to express cash flows in real terms. The question then arises as to whether cash flows should be discounted at the nominal interest rate or the real interest rate. The answer is that the cash flows and the discount rate must be expressed in the same terms; that is, if the cash flows are nominal, then the discount rate must be the nominal interest rate, and if the cash flows are real cash flows, then the discount rate must be the real interest rate.

To illustrate the importance of consistency, suppose we are trying to value a mobile home park. Cash flow for the year just ended is $2 million. You expect no change in the operating characteristics of this project, so the cash flow is perpetual. The expected inflation rate is 10%, and you have determined that investments of similar risk have a required nominal return of 20%. What is the value of the mobile home park?

It may seem that the correct answer is that the park is worth ($2 million/.20) = $10 million. However, this result is incorrect because the $2 million cash flow is in current (that is, real) dollars, but the discount rate is quoted in nominal terms. To find the correct answer, we can either state the cash flows in nominal terms or state the discount rate in real terms.

The real interest rate is $[(1.20/1.10) - 1] = 9.09\%$, so that the value of the park is ($2 million/.0909) = $22 million. (Note that the result here is slightly inaccurate due to rounding in the calculation of the real interest rate.) Alternatively, the cash flow at the end of the first year, assuming it grows at the rate of inflation, is expected to be $[\$2\ million(1.10)] = \$2.2$ million. If it grows at this rate forever, then we can calculate the value of the park by using the formula for a growing perpetuity:

$$\frac{\$2,200,000}{(.20 - .10)} = \$22,000,000$$

A Capital Budgeting Simplification

In the earlier example of the KMS Corporation, we calculated each year's operating cash flow after taxes as follows: Revenues - Expenses - Taxes. Under certain circumstances, it is preferable to determine operating cash flows as:

$$(\text{Revenues}) \times (1 - T_c) - (\text{Expenses}) \times (1 - T_c) + (T_c) \times (\text{Depreciation})$$

We refer to the three terms above as after-tax revenues, after-tax expenses and the depreciation tax-shield, respectively. Consider, for example, the year 1 operating cash flows for KMS. Using this approach, we have:

$$(\$30,000)(1 - .40) - (-\$20,000)(1 - .40) + (.40)(\$20,000)$$

which is equal to $38,000, the same figure we determined in the earlier example. There are several advantages to deriving the cash flow as we have demonstrated in this section.

The first advantage of this approach is that it enables us to determine the marginal contribution to the cash flow which comes from each of the three sources. For example, a $1.00 increase in revenue, or a $1.00 decrease in expenses, increases cash flow by $.60. Similarly, cash flow increases by $.40 for each dollar increase in depreciation.

The second benefit of the above approach is that, in general, it makes the analysis of a capital budgeting problem more efficient. One example of this increased efficiency is the possibility that simplifying formulas can be used in the present value calculations. For example, if revenues and/or expenses are constant throughout the life of the project, this portion of the firm's cash flows can be treated as an annuity for the purpose of determining present values. In addition, it is also possible to discount the different contributions to the cash flow at different rates to reflect different levels of risk. For example, the depreciation tax shield is less subject to risk than are the after-tax revenues, so the depreciation tax-shield should be discounted at a lower rate. Also, the approach of this section makes it possible to treat nominal and real cash flows more easily.

Investments of Unequal Lives:
The Equivalent Annual Cost Method

A special problem may arise when we compare two different machines that provide the same service, but differ with respect to purchase price and operating costs. If the machines have the same operating life, this choice between mutually exclusive alternatives is resolved by choosing the machine with the lower present value of operating costs; in this situation, the present value criterion is equivalent to the net present value criterion. However, if the two machines have different operating lives **and** if we will be replacing the selected machine at the end of its useful life, then some allowance for the different lives must be made. This problem is resolved by the use of either matching replacement cycles in the present value comparison or the **equivalent annual cost (EAC)** method.

For example, suppose we are considering the purchase of either machine X or machine Y. The lives and annual costs for each are:

Date	Machine X	Machine Y
0	$ 100	$ 70
1	$ 10	$ 15
2	$ 10	$ 15
3	$ 10	

At a 10% discount rate, the present values of the costs for X and Y are $124.87 and $96.03, respectively. If we ignore the fact that machine Y would have to be replaced earlier than machine X, we would select Y because the present value of the costs is less. However, we can correctly acknowledge the difference in operating life by analyzing 'replacement chains' for the two machines over a common six-year period, so that the annual costs are:

Date	Machine X	Machine Y
0	100	70
1	10	15
2	10	85
3	110	15
4	10	85
5	10	15
6	10	15

Now, the present values are $218.68 and $240.99, respectively, indicating that Machine X is the preferable alternative.

The equivalent annual cost is the answer to the following question: what constant dollar amount, paid each year, has exactly the same present value as the machine's purchase price plus operating costs? For Machine X, this value is determined by solving for C in the following annuity formula:

$$PV = C \times A^T_r$$

$$\$124.87 = C \times A^3_{.10}$$

$$\$124.87 = C \times 2.48685$$

The equivalent annual cost for Machine X is therefore $50.21; the EAC for Machine Y is $55.33. The EAC for X is less than the EAC for Y, so that X has the lower cost.

Since the EAC and the replacement chain approach are mathematically equivalent techniques, the conclusion in both cases is that X is the preferable alternative. However, the replacement chain approach must be used when the relevant planning horizon differs significantly from the common time period (six years in this example), or a multiple of the common time period.

The EAC is also a valuable tool for analyzing equipment replacement problems. In order to determine whether existing equipment should be replaced, compare the EAC of the new equipment, assuming the replacement is made today, with the cost of maintaining the existing equipment for an additional year. If the EAC is less than the cost of maintaining the existing equipment, then the replacement should be made.

Decision Trees

Decisions trees are useful for evaluating uncertain cash flows. An example of a situation for which a decision tree might prove helpful would be an analysis of whether a manufacturer should test market a new consumer product. Assume that if the new product is successful, the cash inflow will be $200 per year forever. The total investment required to produce the new product is $1900. At a 10% discount rate, the NPV is [($200/.10) - $1900] = $100, if the product is successful.

An alternative to immediately beginning production is to do a pilot run and test market the product. The pilot run and test marketing would take one year and cost $30. If we do the test marketing, one of two outcomes will occur next year. If the product is successful, we have an NPV of $100; if it is unsuccessful, we do not proceed with production and the NPV is zero. We assume that there is a 50% chance of each outcome, so our expected NPV next year is [.50($100) + .50($0)] = $50. Thus we can invest $30 today for an expected NPV of $50 at date 1. The NPV of this investment is [($50/1.10) - $30] = $15.45, so we should proceed with the test marketing. Note that the conclusion here is that we should proceed with the test marketing, not the production of the product; this latter decision will be made next year, when we have the data from the test.

You might wonder whether we should bother test marketing at all. If we do not, then our expected cash flow is [.50($200) + .50($0)] = $100 forever. Therefore, the NPV of this alternative is [($100/.10) - $1900] = -$900, so that the test marketing is a good idea.

Sensitivity Analysis, Scenario Analysis
and Break-even Analysis

Whenever we do capital budgeting, we are dealing with the uncertain future. To the extent that our assumptions about future cash flows are incorrect, our estimates of NPV will be incorrect as well. **Sensitivity analysis, scenario analysis** and **break-even analysis** are commonly used techniques for evaluating the critical assumptions of our net present value calculations.

<u>Sensitivity Analysis and Scenario Analysis</u>. Revenue and cost projections are required before a firm can forecast future cash flows and determine the net present value for a particular capital budgeting project. Sensitivity analysis is a procedure for first identifying the critical assumptions used in deriving revenue and cost forecasts, and then examining the sensitivity of the net present value calculations to modifications in the critical assumptions.

Revenue projections may depend on assumptions regarding market share, size of the total market and selling price of a product. The financial manager analyzes the extent to which varying forecasts of future market share, for example, affect the net present value of the capital budgeting project. If the NPV is positive for the most optimistic forecast of market share, but significantly negative for the most pessimistic forecast, the appropriate course of action would be to gather more information regarding the likely value of the market share variable.

Similar analysis of cost projections must also be undertaken. Generally, costs are classified as **variable costs** or **fixed costs**. Variable costs are costs that vary with production, and they are frequently assumed to be proportional to the level of production. Direct labor cost is an example. Variable costs are equal to the cost per unit of output multiplied by the number of units of output. Variable costs are generally incremental in any decision. Fixed costs do not change over a specified time interval and must be paid regardless of production levels. Rent is an example of a fixed cost. For the purposes of sensitivity analysis, variable costs and fixed costs are treated as two separate variables in determining the sensitivity of NPV to costs.

Scenario analysis is a modification of sensitivity analysis. For the latter approach, we analyze the sensitivity of NPV to each of the critical assumptions individually, holding all other projections at their most likely levels. Scenario analysis examines the effect on all variables, and hence on NPV, of a hypothetical sequence of events. For example, if a new product proves unsuccessful, both market share and price will be adversely affected; therefore, it is reasonable to examine the effect of this scenario on NPV by evaluating the consequences of the most pessimistic outcomes for both variables simultaneously.

Break-even Analysis. The objective of **break-even analysis** is to determine the sales level at which a project becomes profitable. The accounting and financial interpretations of break-even differ. Accounting break-even occurs when accounting profit is equal to zero; financial break-even occurs when the NPV is zero.

Heggestad, Inc. has forecast sales of a new product at 3000 units per year forever, with a selling price of $5.95 per unit. Variable costs are $3.50 per unit. Fixed costs will be $3000 per year, and an initial investment of $25,000 is required. Depreciation will be $3000 annually, the corporate tax rate is 34%, and Heggestad requires a 15% rate of return on new products.

We can calculate accounting break-even by setting accounting profit (net income) equal to zero and solving for the unknown quantity:

$$\text{Net income} = [(\text{Sales - variable costs}) - 3000 - 3000](1 - .34) = 0$$

$$[(\text{Sales - variable costs}) - 6{,}000 =$$

$$[(\$5.95 - \$3.50) \times \text{Units sold}] - 6{,}000 = 0$$

Thus, break-even occurs when unit sales are ($6000/$2.45) = 2449. The cash flow is $3000 per year at this sales level.

In general, the accounting break-even occurs when the number of units, Q, is equal to:

$$Q = \frac{(\text{Total fixed costs + Depreciation})}{(\text{Unit price - Unit variable cost})}$$

To determine the financial break-even point, we must first calculate the equivalent annual cost (EAC) for the initial investment. The initial investment for the Heggestad project is $25,000, and the project is a perpetuity. At 15%, $3750 per year forever has a present value of $25,000. Thus this project breaks even when the cash flow is $3750 per year. The accounting break-even point substantially understates the financial break-even point.

CONCEPT TEST

1. The difference in the firm's cash flows with and without a project is called the _____ for that project.

2. Relevant project cash flows consist of two parts: _____ and _____.

3. A cost that the firm will incur regardless of whether it accepts or rejects a particular project is called a _____.

4. A cost that is associated with using an asset which could be used in a different way is called an _____.

5. Suppose one project has the effect of increasing the cash flow to another project. This increase is an incremental cash flow and is an example of a _____.

6. Cash revenues in a particular year are equal to sales less the change in _____.

7. Cash costs in a particular year are equal to operating costs and taxes less the change in _____.

8. Suppose we are considering two machines which are mutually exclusive and which have different useful lives; if the machine chosen will be replaced at the end of its life, then we use the _____ method to evaluate the decision.

9. Costs that change as the quantity of output changes are called _____.

10. Costs that do not change when output changes are called _____.

11. Interest rates that have not been adjusted for the effect of inflation are called _____ interest rates.

12. Interest rates that have been adjusted for the effect of inflation are called _____ interest rates.

13. The discount rate used in capital budgeting is normally stated in _____ terms.

14. One device for identifying uncertain future cash flows is a _____.

15. A _____ is useful for determining the impact of assumptions made about critical variables in calculating NPV.

16. The sales level at which net income is zero is called the _____ sales level.

17. The sales level at which NPV is zero is called the _____ break-even level.

For Questions 18-22, answer 'yes' if the cash flow is incremental and 'no' if it is not.

18. The cost of an environmental impact study before the study is commissioned.

19. The cost of an environmental impact study after the study has been completed.

20. A change in credit terms that results in more credit sales.

21. A new project's share of total corporate fixed overhead that existed before accepting the project.

22. The change in total fixed corporate overhead that results from a new project.

ANSWERS TO CONCEPT TEST

1. incremental cash flow
2. operating cash flows;
     capital requirements
3. sunk cost
4. opportunity cost
5. side effect
6. accounts receivable
7. accounts payable
8. equivalent annual cost (EAC)
9. variable costs
10. fixed costs

11. nominal
12. real
13. nominal
14. decision tree
15. sensitivity analysis
16. accounting break-even
17. financial
18. yes
19. no
20. yes
21. no
22. yes

PROBLEMS AND SOLUTIONS

Use the following information to solve Problems 1-7:

Klaatu Co. has recently completed a $400,000, two-year marketing study. Based on the results of the study, Klaatu has estimated that 10,000 of its new RUR-class robots could be sold annually over the next 8 years, at a price of $9500 each. Variable costs per robot are $7400, and fixed costs total $12 million per year.

Start-up costs include $40 million to build production facilities, $2.4 million for land, and $8 million in net working capital. The $40 million facility will be depreciated on a straight-line basis to a value of zero over the eight-year life of the project. At the end of the project's life, the facilities (including the land) will be sold for an estimated $8.4 million. The value of the land is not expected to change during the eight year period.

Finally, start-up would also entail tax-deductible expenses of $1.4 million at year zero. Klaatu is an ongoing, profitable business and pays taxes at a 34% rate on all income and capital gains. Klaatu has a 10% opportunity cost for projects such as this one.

Problem 1

What is the cash flow for the RUR project for years 1 through 7?

Solution 1

Revenues, expenses and depreciation are expected to be constant for years 1 through 7. In addition, there are no capital requirements in any of these years, so the cash flows will be identical for these years. Annual revenue will be [($9500)(10,000)] = $95 million. Annual depreciation is ($40,000,000/8) = $5 million. Annual variable costs will be [($7400)(10,000)] = $74 million and total operating costs equal ($74,000,000 + $12,000,000) = $86 million. Taxable income is ($95,000,000 - $86,000,000 - $5,000,000) = $4 million and taxes are [(.34)($4,000,000)] = $1.36 million, so that net income is $2.64 million. Operating cash flow is equal to revenues minus operating costs minus taxes, or $7.64 million.

Problem 2

Express the operating cash flows from Problem 1 in terms of after-tax revenues, after-tax expenses and the depreciation tax shield. What is the marginal contribution to cash flow of each of the three components?

Solution 2

Operating cash flow can be written as:

$$\text{Revenues } (1 - T_c) - \text{Expenses } (1 - T_c) + (T_c) \text{ Depreciation} =$$

$$(\$95 \text{ million})(.66) - (\$86 \text{ million})(.66) + (.34)(\$5 \text{ million}) =$$

$$\$62.70 \text{ million} - \$56.76 \text{ million} + \$1.70 \text{ million}$$

The three terms above are, respectively, the after-tax revenues, after-tax expenses and the depreciation tax-shield. The marginal contributions of each term to operating cash flows are, respectively, $.66 per dollar of increase in revenues, $.66 per dollar of decrease in expenses and $.34 per dollar of increase in depreciation.

Problem 3

What is the year 0 cash flow?

Solution 3

The year 0 cash outflows are: $40 million to build production facilities, $2.4 million for land, $8 million in working capital and the after-tax cost of the tax-deductible $1.4 million in expenses, or [($1,400,000)(.66)] = $.924 million. The total of these outflows is $51.324 million. Note that the test market expense is a sunk cost, so it is excluded from this calculation.

Problem 4

What is the year 8 cash flow?

Solution 4

The year 8 operating cash flow will be $7.64 million, as determined in Problem 1. Additional calculations are necessary in order to determine the capital requirements. First, the company will sell the land for $2.4 million. Second, the plant and equipment will be sold for ($8,400,000 - $2,400,000) = $6 million. The plant and equipment will be depreciated to a book value of zero. The difference between the book value and the sale proceeds is taxable as a recapture of excess depreciation, so the firm will net [($6,000,000)(.66)] = $3.96 million from the sale. The land cannot be depreciated, so its book value is $2.4 million.

Finally, the $8 million in working capital will be recovered. This happens as, among other things, accounts are paid, inventory is sold off, and working cash balances are freed up. The total year 8 cash inflow is $22 million.

Solution note: in reality, some portion of the working capital would not be recovered because of bad debts, inventory losses ('shrinkage'), and so forth.

Problem 5

Should Klaatu proceed with the RUR project?

Solution 5

The cash flows for this project consist of -$51.324 million in year 0, $7.64 million in years 1 through 7, and $22 million in year 8. The present value of the cash inflows for years 1 through 8, discounted at 10%, equals $47.458 million, so that the net present value is -$3.866 million. Therefore, Klaatu should not proceed with the project.

Problem 6

Elijah Bailey, a recent Yale grad, has objected to your recommendation that the RUR project be rejected, and has stated: "At 10,000 units per year, we are way above the break-even point on this project." What is the accounting break-even unit volume? Is he correct?

Solution 6

The accounting break-even is the ratio of fixed costs plus depreciation to unit price less unit variable cost, or (in millions) [(12 + 5)/(.0021)] = 8095 units. The RUR project is projected to more than breakeven on an accounting basis, so the above statement is correct, but misleading. The project will still lose money when we consider time value (see Problem 7).

Problem 7

What is the financial break-even operating cash flow?

Solution 7

To calculate the financial break-even cash flow, we must first calculate the equivalent annual cost for the capital investment. In this case, the capital requirements occur at different points in time. The capital requirements consist of -$51.324 million in year zero and ($8 + $2.4 + $3.96) million =

$14.36 million in year 8. The present value of the year 8 capital requirement is $6.70 million, so the effective capital investment is (-$51.324 + $6.70) million = -$44.625 million.

The annuity factor for 8 years at a 10% discount rate is 5.3349. The financial break-even operating cash flow is [($44,625,000)/5.3349] = $8.365 million, which is substantially greater than the projected cash flow.

Problem 8

Olivaw is a leading manufacturer of positronic brains, a key component in robots. The company is considering two alternative production methods. The costs and lives associated with each are:

Year	Method 1	Method 2
0	$900	$800
1	$ 20	$ 80
2	$ 20	$ 80
3	$ 20	$ 80
4		$ 80

The relevant opportunity cost of capital is 10%. Assuming that Olivaw will **not** replace the equipment when it wears out, which production method should the firm buy?

Solution 8

The present value of the operating costs for Methods 1 and 2 are $949.74 and $1053.59, respectively. If the equipment is not to be replaced, then Method 1 should be selected because it has the lower present value of costs.

Problem 9

Consider the data from Problem 8 and assume that Olivaw is going to replace the equipment when it wears out. Which method should the firm purchase?

Solution 9

If the equipment will be replaced, then we need to calculate the equivalent annual cost (EAC) for each method. For Method 1, an annuity of $381.90 per year has a present value of $949.74, so that the costs associated with this method are equivalent to paying $381.90 each year for three years. For Method 2, the EAC is $332.38. The firm should select Method 2 because it has the lower EAC.

Problem 10

You have been asked to value orange groves belonging to the Roll Corporation. The groves produce 1.6 billion oranges per year. Oranges currently sell for $.10 per 100. With normal maintenance, this level of production can be sustained indefinitely. Variable costs (primarily upkeep and harvesting) are $1.2 million per year. Fixed costs are negligible. The nominal discount rate is 18%, and the inflation rate is 10%. Assuming that orange prices and the variable costs change with inflation, what is the value of the groves? (Ignore taxes and depreciation.)

Solution 10

Revenues from sales of 1.6 billion oranges, at $.001 apiece, are equal to $1.6 million. Since we are ignoring both taxes and depreciation, operating cash flow is equal to revenues minus expenses or ($1.6 million - $1.2 million) = $.4 million per year. At this point, it's tempting to treat the $.4 million as a perpetuity, and divide by .18 to calculate the present value. This would not be correct. The $.4 million annual cash flow is in current dollars and therefore does not reflect future inflation. The 18% discount rate does reflect future inflation, so we are being inconsistent by dividing a real cash flow by a nominal discount rate.

To be consistent, we must modify the above calculation by using either the nominal cash flows or the real discount rate. We will demonstrate that the approaches are equivalent by using both procedures. The real discount rate is [(1.18/1.10) - 1] = 7.2727%. The present value of the perpetuity is ($400,000/.072727) = $5.5 million. Alternatively, we could use the formula for a growing perpetuity to determine the present value. The nominal cash flow grows by 10% per year. The year 1 cash flow is thus ($400,000)(1.1) = $440,000. To find the present value of a growing perpetuity, divide the year 1 cash flow by the discount rate less the growth rate; therefore, the present value is [($440,000)/(.18 - .10)] = $5.5 million.

Problem 11

Suppose that, for the data in Problem 10, costs only increase at half the inflation rate. What is the value of the groves?

Solution 11

If the costs increase by only 5% per year, then in real terms, the costs are decreasing. As a result, it is easier to solve this problem using nominal cash flows.

Next year's revenues are expected to be [($1,600,000)(1.10)] = $1.76 million. The present value of the future revenues is [($1,760,000)/(.18 - .10)] = $22 million. Next year's costs are expected to be [($1,200,000)(1.05)] = $1.26 million. The present value of the future costs is [($1,260,000)/(.18 - .05)] = $9.692 million. The value of the groves is ($22 - $9.692) million = $12.308 million.

Problem 12

Tralfamador, Inc., is considering replacing its four old cronosynclastic infundibula devices (CIDs) with a single new model. The old CIDs are worth $100 apiece today, each costs $30 per year to operate, and each will be worth $5 when it wears out in four years. All CIDs are replaced when they wear out. A new CID costs $1000 to buy and install, costs $20 per year to operate, lasts eight years, and can be sold for $100 when it wears out. The relevant opportunity cost is 12%. Should Tralfamador replace now or later?

Solution 12

If we decide to keep the four old CIDs, then we forgo the $100 each that we could receive by selling; this is an opportunity cost. The present value of the costs of keeping the old equipment is [4($100 + $30(3.03735) - $5(.6355))] = [4($187.94)] = $751.77. The present value of the costs for the new equipment is $1058.96. However, the old equipment has a shorter life than the new equipment. The decision here can be regarded as a choice between two mutually exclusive alternatives with unequal lives. The alternatives are to 'purchase' the old machines (that is, we do not sell the old machines) or to purchase the new one. In other words, we compute the EAC for each alternative. The EAC of keeping the old equipment is [$61.88(4)] = $247.51. The EAC for the new equipment is $213.17. Therefore, Tralfamador should replace the existing equipment now.

Problem 13

The Trout Corporation is deciding whether or not to introduce a new form of aluminum siding. Projected sales, total NWC requirements, and capital investments are:

Year	Sales	NWC	Capital
0	$ 0	$400	$20,000
1	$ 5,000	$500	
2	$ 6,000	$500	
3	$ 9,000	$700	
4-6	$10,000	$700	

Variable costs are 60% of sales, and fixed costs are negligible. The $20,000 in production equipment will be depreciated on a straight-line basis, to a value of zero, over a five-year period. The equipment will actually be worth $10,000 in six years. The required rate of return is 10% and the firm's tax rate is 34%. Should Trout proceed with the project?

Solution 13

We can calculate the cash flows as follows:

Year:	0	1	2	3	4-5	6
Revenues		$5000	$6000	$9000	$10000	$10000
Operating Costs		3000	3600	5400	6000	6000
Depreciation		4000	4000	4000	4000	0
Operating Cash Flow		$2680	$2944	$3736	$4000	$2640
Working Capital	$ 400	$ 100	$ 0	$ 200	$ 0	-$ 700
Capital Investments	$20000					-$6600
Capital Requirements	$20400	$ 100	$ 0	$ 200	$ 0	-$7300
Cash Flow	-$20400	$2580	$2944	$3536	$4000	$9940

The present value of the future cash flows, discounted at the 10% required rate of return, is $18,261.77, and the net present value is ($18,261.77 - $20,400) = -$2138.23. The project should be rejected.

Problem 14

For Problem 13, assume that the inflation rate is 8% and that all the data in the problem (including the discount rate) are in real terms. Should the aluminum siding project be accepted? Why do we get a different answer?

Solution 14

The nominal cash flows for years 1 through 6 are indicated below; the year 0 cash flows are identical to those in Problem 13. Notice that depreciation is not adjusted for inflation because the depreciation charge is based on cost and is therefore unaffected by inflation.

Year:	1	2	3	4	5	6
Revenues	$5400	$6998	$11337	$13605	$14693	$15869
Operating Costs	3240	4199	6802	8163	8816	9521
Depreciation	4000	4000	4000	4000	4000	0
Operating Cash Flow	$2786	$3207	$4353	$4952	$5239	$4190
Working Capital	$ 108	$ 0	$ 252	$ 0	$ 0	-$1111
Capital Investments						-$10473
Capital Requirements	$ 108	$ 0	$ 252	$ 0	$ 0	-$11584
Cash Flow	$2678	$3207	$4101	$4952	$5239	$15774

The nominal discount rate is $[(1.10)(1.08) - 1] = 18.8\%$. Using this discount rate, the present value of the cash flows is $17,283.48 and the net present value of the investment is -$3116.52.

This result differs from that in Problem 13 because the depreciation deduction is not adjusted for inflation. As a result, the real depreciation tax shield declines in value and real taxes increase. The net present value decreases by the present value of the increase in taxes.

APPENDIX 1: OPTIONS

Our capital budgeting analysis has been static in the sense that we have ignored the managerial options implicit in any new investment. Two particularly important managerial options in capital budgeting are the option to expand a successful project and the option to reduce the scale of a project, or even abandon a project, if it is unsuccessful. Since these options have value to the firm, they must be considered in capital budgeting analysis.

The Option to Expand. If the demand for a particular product were to exceed expectations, then the firm might have the option to increase production by expansion or to increase cash flow by raising the price of the product. Consequently, the potential cash flow is greater than we have previously indicated, because we have implicitly assumed that no expansion or price increase is possible.

The Option to Abandon. If demand were significantly below expectations, it might be less expensive to abandon the project than to proceed with it. In other words, we may be underestimating a project's NPV if we assume that the project must last for some fixed number of years.

In general, the value of a project is equal to the net present value of the project, ignoring the options to expand or contract, plus the value of these managerial options.

PROBLEMS AND SOLUTIONS

Problem 1

We are considering a project that is expected to produce annual sales of 100 units at $1 cash flow per unit for the foreseeable future. After one year, the expected demand will be revised to either 50 units or 150 units, depending on the success of the project. Success and failure are equally likely. The cost of the project is $550, and the discount rate is 20%. The project can be dismantled and sold in one year for $400. Should the project be accepted?

Solution 1

The expected cash flow is a perpetuity of $100 per year and the discount rate is 20%. The present value of the cash flows is ($100/.20) = $500, so the net present value is ($500 - $550) = -$50. Therefore, it appears that the project should not be accepted. However, this analysis is static.

One year from now, the opportunity cost of staying in business is $400. If the expected cash flows are revised to $50 at that time, then the present value of the cash flows, as of year one, is ($50/.20) = $250, and the net present value is ($250 - $400) = -$150. Thus, if we accept the project now, we will abandon it in one year if it is unsuccessful. Our cash flow at year one is then ($400 + $50) = $450 in this case. On the other hand, if the demand is revised upward, then the present value of the future cash flows at year 1 is ($150/.20) = $750, and the year 1 value is ($750 + $150) = $900. Thus, at year 1, we have either $450 in cash or $150 in cash plus future cash flows worth $750. The expected value is therefore [.5($450) + .5($900)] = $675. The present value of this year 1 expected value is $562.50, so the net present value is $12.50.

Recognizing the value of the option to abandon the unsuccessful project has increased the NPV by $62.50. Where did this increase in value come from? Our original analysis assumed we would continue the project even if it was a failure. At year 1, the NPV of the project was -$150 in the event of a failure. The option to abandon saves us this $150. There is a 50% probability of this outcome, so the expected saving is $75. The present value of this expected saving (the value of the option to abandon) is ($75/1.20) = $62.50.

APPENDIX 2: A NOTE ON DEPRECIATION

The 1986 Tax Reform Act specifies seven classes of depreciable assets, according to the life of the asset; these range from the three-year class for certain specialized short-lived assets, to 27.5 and 31.5 years for residential and non-residential property, respectively. Assets in the three-year, five-year, and seven-year classes are initially depreciated using 200% declining balance, with a change to straight-line depreciation at a time during the life of the asset specified in the Tax Reform Act. Assets in the fifteen-year and twenty-year classes use 150% declining balance with a change to straight-line, and real estate is depreciated on a straight-line basis. The actual depreciation deductions use a half-year convention which is based on the assumption that an asset is put into service at midyear. Therefore, depreciation deductions for an asset in the five-year class, for example, are taken over a six-year period. The depreciation percentages for each category of assets are specified in the IRS publication Depreciation. The table below indicates the depreciation deductions for three classes of assets.

Year	Three-year class	Five-year class	Seven-year class
1	33.34%	20.00%	14.28%
2	44.44	32.00	24.49
3	14.81	19.20	17.49
4	7.41	11.52	12.50
5		11.52	8.92
6		5.76	8.92
7			8.92
8			4.48

PROBLEMS AND SOLUTIONS

Problem 1

You have an investment that has a depreciable basis of $50,000. Calculate the depreciation for each year, assuming that the asset is in the three-year class, the five-year class or the seven-year class.

Solution 1

Year	Three-year class	Five-year class	Seven-year class
1	$ 16,670	$ 10,000	$ 7,140
2	22,220	16,000	12,245
3	7,405	9,600	8,745
4	3,705	5,760	6,250
5		5,760	4,460
6		2,880	4,460
7			4,460
8			2,240

CHAPTER 8
CAPITAL MARKETS: AN OVERVIEW

CHAPTER HIGHLIGHTS

The capital budgeting concepts presented in the preceding chapters have, for the most part, ignored the issue of risk. It has been assumed throughout much of this discussion that future cash flows are riskless, so that the risk-free interest rate is the appropriate discount rate for present value analysis. However, since capital budgeting projects generally involve risky cash flows, a risk-adjusted discount rate is required in place of the risk-free rate. This chapter and the subsequent three chapters describe procedures for determining the appropriate risk-adjusted discount rate.

Returns

Dollar Returns. When you buy a share of common stock, your return on the investment comes in two forms: **dividends** and **capital gains**. Dividends, which represent the income component of your return, are cash payments by a corporation to its shareholders. Capital gains (or losses) for an investment in common stock result from increases (or decreases) in the value of the stock; a decrease in the value of a share of common stock can also be thought of as a negative capital gain.

Suppose you buy 100 shares of Ahlers Corporation common stock for $25 per share. Over the course of a year, Ahlers pays a cash dividend of $2 per share and the value of the stock rises to $30. At the end of the year, you have received $200 in dividends and you own 100 shares of stock worth $30 per share, so that the total value of your position is $3200. The total investment is $2500, so the total return is $700.

$$\left(\$30/s\right)\left(100\ s.\right) + \left(\$200\ div\right)$$

Percentage Returns. For financial decision-making, it is often inconvenient to think of returns in dollars; percentage returns are easier to work with because the results apply regardless of the amount invested in a particular asset. In the case of the investment in Ahlers common stock, you received $700 on a $2500 investment, so your **total percentage return** is [($3200 - $2500)/$2500] = .28 = 28%. This 28% is comprised of a **dividend yield** plus the **percentage capital gain** (or **capital gains yield**). The dividend yield is given by:

$$\frac{Div_1}{P_0} = \frac{\$2}{\$25} = .08 = 8\%$$

where Div_1 is the dividend paid at date 1 and P_0 is the price of the stock at date 0. The capital gains yield is:

$$\frac{\$30 - \$25}{\text{}}$$

$$\frac{P_1 - P_0}{P_0} = \frac{\$5}{\$25} = .20 = 20\%$$

where P_1 is the price at date 1. The total percentage return (R_1) is the sum of the dividend yield and the capital gains yield: $R_1 = (8\% + 20\%) = 28\%$.

Holding Period Returns

If you invest in, say, a portfolio of bonds, and, over a three-year period, your percentage returns are 12%, -7%, and 20%, respectively, how much will you have at the end of the three years? For every dollar you invest, you will have $1.12 at the end of the first year. At the end of the second year, you will have 7% less or (.93)($1.12) = $1.0416. This amount will grow by 20% in the last year, so you will have $1.25 at the end of three years. The three-year period is called your **holding period**, and 25% is the three-year **holding period return.**

In general, the T-period holding period return can be calculated as:

$$[(1 + R_1) \times (1 + R_2) \times \ldots \times (1 + R_T)] - 1$$

where R_1 is the return in the first period, R_2 is the return in the second period, and so on. For the above example, the 25% holding period return could have been computed directly as follows:

$$[(1.12)(.93)(1.20) - 1] = .25 = 25\%.$$

Return Statistics

In order to be able to use the history of stock market rates of return for financial decision-making purposes, it is necessary to summarize percentage return data for an individual stock or for the stock market as a whole. For example, we may find it appropriate to use historical returns data to estimate returns for a given future time period. For this purpose, it may be appropriate to calculate the **average return** or **mean return**, which is simply the ordinary average: total the returns and divide by the number of observations. The calculation of the mean return is summarized algebraically as follows:

$$\text{Mean} = \bar{R} = E(R) = \frac{R_1 + R_2 + \ldots + R_T}{T}$$

where $\bar{R}$ and $E(R)$ are alternative notations for the mean return, and T is the number of time periods Consider an investment which has a guaranteed 100% return the first year and a guaranteed 60% loss the second. The average return is [100% + (-60%)]/2 = 20%. Financial managers are often interested in the answer to the question: "What rate can I expect to earn next year?" In this case, the best forecast of this expected return may be the average return for some historical period.

When we discuss an average return projected over a future time period, we often refer to the **expected return**. This terminology does not indicate that we actually expect the average return to be precisely realized next year; rather, the use of the term 'expected' has statistical connotations related to the concept of expected value. An expected value is an average or mean of possible future outcomes, although we often use historical data as our most reliable indicator of future outcomes. As noted above, the notation $E(R)$ is often used to denote the expected return for an asset.

Average Stock Returns and Risk-Free Returns

A common benchmark used in comparing returns is the return on securities issued by the U.S. government. One form of government security is the **Treasury bill** or **T-bill**, which is a pure discount security, sold by the government, and maturing in less than one year. Because the government can always raise taxes in order to repay its debts, and because the maturities of these securities are relatively short, T-bills are considered virtually risk-free; hence, we refer to the T-bill rate as the **risk-free rate of return**.

From 1926 to 1988, the average return on T-bills was 3.6% per year. The difference between the 12.1% rate of return for the S&P 500 and the 3.6% earned on T-bills is called the **excess return on the risky asset**. Since the excess return is a reflection of the greater riskiness of stock investments, the excess return is also called the **risk premium**. The historical risk premium for the S&P 500 is (.121 - .036) = .085 = 8.5%.

Risk Statistics

Since riskiness affects returns, we must be able to measure the degree of risk associated with an investment in order to understand the relationship between risk and return. The most common measures are the **variance** and its square root, the **standard deviation**. We denote variance using the notation Var or σ^2, and we use SD and σ to indicate standard deviation.

Variance. Suppose that a particular investment returned 10%, 12%, 3%, and -9% over the last 4 years. The mean return is [(.10 + .12 + .03 - .09)/4] = .04 = 4%. As noted above, the mean return here might also be referred to as the expected return in either of the following situations: first, the calculation of the mean may be based on historical data, but if we believe that the historical data provide the best available forecast of possible future returns, we can consider the mean to be an average of possible future outcomes; and, second, the calculation may be based on forecasts of possible future outcomes, derived from a forecasting model which relies on data other than strictly historical observations. Since we are most often interested in mean returns and risk for decisions regarding future outcomes, it is common to refer to the mean return as the expected return. Note that, technically, the phrase 'expected return' refers to the 'expected value of future returns,' and should be thought of as an average.

Financial economists equate risk with the statistical concept of variability. The most commonly used statistical measures of variability are the variance and the standard deviation. In the financial context, we use the variance to measure the variability of rate of return from the mean rate of return; the greater the deviations from the mean, the more variable the rate of return and the higher the level of risk.

The variance measures the average of the squared deviations from the mean of a set of data. In the above example, the deviations from the average are (.10-.04), (.12-.04), etc. To compute the variance, we square and then sum these deviations, and divide the sum of the squared deviations by T, the number of observations. The variance is therefore the mean, or expected value, of the squared deviations from mean return. We can summarize the above calculations as follows:

$$Var(R) = \sigma_R^2 = \text{Expected value of } (R - \bar{R})^2 = \text{Expected value of } [R - E(R)]^2$$

Consider the following alternative perspective for the data described above. Suppose that a financial analyst believes that there are four equally likely states of the economy next year, and that the rate of return for a given common stock depends on the state of the economy as indicated in the table below. The calculation of the variance is summarized in this table:

State of the Economy	R Rate of Return	(R − R̄) Deviation from Expected Return	(R − R̄)² Squared value of deviation
Boom	.10	.06	.0036
Normal	.12	.08	.0064
Recession	.03	−.01	.0001
Depression	−.09	−.13	.0169

The variance is the average squared deviation: $\sigma^2 = (.027/4) = .00675$. The standard deviation is the square root of .00675: $\sigma = .08216$.

Normal Distribution And Its Implications For Standard Deviation. For many random events, the **normal distribution** (or 'bell-shaped curve') is useful for deriving the probability that the value of a variable falls within a certain range. For example, if stock returns have a normal distribution, then the probability that the rate of return in a given year is within one standard deviation of the mean is about 68%, or approximately 2/3. The probability that the return is within two standard deviations of the mean is about 95%. Figure 8.1 illustrates a normal distribution.

A Normal Distribution

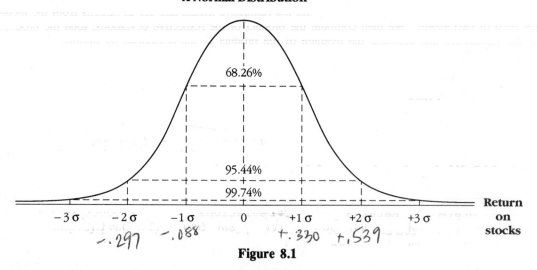

Figure 8.1

For the S&P 500, the standard deviation of returns for the period 1926 to 1988, is approximately 20.9%. As described above, the mean rate of return during this period was 12.1%. The probability that the rate of return in a given year is in the range -.088 to .330 (.121 plus or minus .209) is approximately 2/3. Put another way, there is one chance in three that the rate of return would fall outside this range. This result illustrates that the stock market can be quite volatile. However, there is only a 5% chance (approximately) that the mean rate of return would be outside the range -.297 to .539 [.121 plus or minus (2 × .209)]. Assuming that the return on the S&P 500 is normally distributed, these points are illustrated in Figure 8.1.

(S&P)

(T-Bills)

Risk premium = return on risky asset − risk free return

A Note On The Discount Rate For Risky Projects

Suppose we are interested in evaluating a nonfinancial investment that is about as risky as the S&P 500. What discount rate should we use for out present value analysis? Recall that the difference between the return on a risky asset and the risk-free return is the risk premium, so that the appropriate discount rate for evaluating a risky investment is the sum of the risk-free rate plus a risk premium. The historic risk premium on the S&P 500 is 8.5%. If T-bills are currently yielding 7%, then the appropriate rate to use in evaluating this investment would be (7% + 8.5%) = 15.5%.

Clearly, not all risky investments have the same risk level as the S&P 500; therefore, we can not use the above procedure for evaluating all risky investments. It is therefore necessary to determine the appropriate measure of risk, and the relationship between risk and return in the financial markets. This objective requires that we understand statistical measures of the relationship among returns for various assets.

Covariance and Correlation

Covariance is a measure of the tendency for two variables to vary together. The covariance of returns for two stocks A and B is indicated by the notation $Cov(R_A, R_B)$ or σ_{AB}. If the prices of two stocks, say GM and Ford, tend to move up and down together, then we say they have positive covariance. If the prices of two stocks tend to move in opposite directions, then they have negative covariance. If there is no particular relationship between the prices, then the covariance is zero.

To compute the covariance, we first compute the respective means and the deviations from the mean for each of two assets. We then compute the product of the respective deviations, total the product of the deviations, and compute the average of the product of the deviations by dividing by T, the number of observations. These calculations are summarized by the following formula:

$$ \text{COVARIANCE} = \left[\sum (A - \bar{A})(B - \bar{B}) \right] \div n $$

$$ Cov(R_A, R_B) = \sigma_{AB} = \text{Expected value of } [(R_A - \bar{R_A}) \times (R_B - \bar{R_B})] $$

Suppose we were interested in studying the way in which General Motors (GM) stock moves with the overall market. Our measure of the return for the market is the S&P 500 index. We believe that there are five equally likely states of the economy next year, and that the rates of return for GM and for the S&P 500 depend on the state of the economy, as indicated in the table below. The table demonstrates how the covariance is calculated:

(−.06) (−.07)   *(GM) × (S&P)*

State	Returns		Deviations		Product of
	GM	S&P 500	GM	S&P 500	the Deviations
1	.10	.12	.04	.05	.0020
2	.04	.06	−.02	−.01	.0002
3	−.09	−.10	−.15	−.17	.0255
4	.20	.22	.14	.15	.0210
5	.05	.05	−.01	−.02	.0002
Totals	.30	.35	.00	.00	.0489

÷ 5 = 6%   ÷ 5 = 7%   ÷ 5   *= covariance*

The average return for GM is 6% and for the S&P 500, 7%. The covariance between them is: $Cov(R_{GM}, R_M) = \sigma_{GM,M} = (.0489/5) = .00978$, where M represents the overall market. The returns for GM and for the S&P 500 tend to be above their respective means for the same states of the economy

(all deviations) above

(i.e., states 1 and 4) and to be below their respective means for the same states (i.e., states 2, 3 and 5), so that the products of the deviations are positive; consequently, the covariance here is positive.

Although the interpretation of the sign of the covariance is rather straightforward, it is difficult to understand the significance of the relative size of different covariances for different pairs of assets. This problem is resolved by calculating the **correlation**. The correlation between the return for two assets A and B is represented by ρ_{AB} or $\text{Corr}(R_A,R_B)$. The correlation between two assets is equal to the covariance divided by the product of the respective standard deviations:

$$ \text{CORRELATION} \quad \rho_{AB} = \text{Corr}(R_A,R_B) = \frac{\text{Cov}(R_A,R_B)}{\sigma_A \times \sigma_B} $$

In the table below, we compute the standard deviations for GM and for the S&P 500:

State	Returns		Deviations		Squared deviations	
	GM	S&P 500	GM	S&P 500	GM	S&P 500
1	.10	.12	.04	.05	.0016	.0025
2	.04	.06	-.02	-.01	.0004	.0001
3	-.09	-.10	-.15	-.17	.0225	.0289
4	.20	.22	.14	.15	.0196	.0225
5	.05	.05	-.01	-.02	.0001	.0004
Totals	.30	.35	.00	.00	.0442	.0544

The variance for GM is: $\sigma_{GM}^2 = (.0442/5) = .00884$. The standard deviation is: $\sigma_{GM} = .09402$. For the S&P 500, the variance and standard deviation are: $\sigma_M^2 = .01088$ and $\sigma_M = .10431$. Thus the correlation between GM and the S&P is:

$$ \rho_{GM,M} = \text{Corr}(R_{GM},R_M) = \frac{\text{Cov}(R_{GM},R_M)}{\sigma_{GM} \times \sigma_M} = \frac{.00978}{(.09402)(.10431)} = .99722 $$

The important property of the correlation which makes it easier to interpret than the covariance is the fact that it is always between +1 and -1. If the correlation between two assets is +1, then we say they have perfect positive correlation. If x and y have perfect positive correlation, then y is equal to [a(x) + b], where a is a positive number. Thus, if x increases by 2, then y increases by exactly (a)×(2). In the case of GM and the S&P, the correlation is very close to +1, indicating that the increases (or decreases) in the value of one asset are always almost directly proportional with increases (or decreases) in the value of the other asset. In reality, these two assets would have positive correlation, but not as high as in this example.

If the correlation is -1, the two assets have perfect negative correlation and move in exactly opposite directions. In this case, x and y have perfect negative correlation if y = [a(x) + b], where a is a negative number.

For risky assets such as stocks, correlations have historically been positive, and, for annual returns, values in the range .40 to .60 are fairly typical.

CONCEPT TEST

1. The cash or income component from owning a share of stock is called the _____.

2. The portion of an investor's return that comes from changes in value is called the _____ component of the return.

3. You own a share of stock which has a total return of 26% for the last four years. The 26% return is your four-year _____.

4. If you add the returns for an asset during the four previous years and then divide the total by four, you have computed the _____ return.

5. The Treasury bill rate is commonly referred to as the _____.

6. The excess above the T-bill return earned on a share of stock is called the _____ on the stock's return.

7. The return on a share of stock or other risky asset is composed of two parts, the _____ and the _____.

8. The most common measures of risk for assets such as stocks and bonds are the _____ and the _____.

9. The 'bell-shaped curve' is called the _____.

10. If an asset's return is normally distributed, the probability that a given return will be within one standard deviation of the mean is _____. The probability that a given return is within two standard deviations of the mean is _____.

11. The commonly used measures of the tendency for the prices of two assets to move up and down together are the _____ and the _____.

12. If the returns on two assets change in the same direction and are directly proportional, then the returns have _____.

13. If the returns on two assets change in the opposite direction and are directly proportional, then the returns have _____.

14. If there is no relationship between the returns on two risky assets, then their returns have _____.

15. In general, the returns on risky assets are _____ correlated.

ANSWERS TO CONCEPT TEST

1. dividend
2. capital gains
3. holding-period return
4. mean or average
5. risk-free rate
6. risk premium
7. risk-free return; risk premium
8. variance; standard deviation
9. normal distribution
10. 68%; 95%
11. covariance; correlation
12. perfect positive correlation
13. perfect negative correlation
14. zero correlation
15. positively

PROBLEMS AND SOLUTIONS

Problem 1

Suppose that, one year ago, you bought 100 shares of Bradley Corporation common stock for $32 per share. During the year, you have received total dividends of $250. Bradley common stock is currently selling for $33.50 per share. How much did you earn in capital gains? What was your total dollar return? Calculate your capital gains yield, dividend yield and total percentage return.

Solution 1

Capital gains are equal to [($33.50 - $32)(100)] = $150 and total dollar return is ($150 + $250) = $400. Capital gains yield is [$150/($32)(100)] = .0469 = 4.69%. Dividend yield is [$250/($32)(100)] = .0781 = 7.81%. Total percentage return is [($150 + $250)/($32)(100)] = .1250 = 12.50% = (4.69% + 7.81%).

Problem 2

Suppose that, one year from today, you expect the Bradley Corporation common stock described in Problem 1 to be selling for $33 per share, and that during the coming year, you expect to receive dividends of $2 per share. Calculate your expected capital gains yield, dividend yield and total percentage return for the coming year. Calculate your holding period return for the two year period.

Solution 2

The capital gains yield for the coming year is [(-$.50)(100)/($33.50)(100)] = -.0149 = -1.49%. The dividend yield is [($2)(100)/($33.50)(100)] = .0597 = 5.97%. The total percentage return is (-.0149 + .0597) = .0448 = 4.48%. The holding period return can be determined from the general formula for the T-period holding period return:

$$[(1 + R_1) \times (1 + R_2) \times \ldots \times (1 + R_T)] - 1$$

Therefore, we can calculate the two-year holding period return as follows:

$$[(1.1250)(1.0448)] - 1 = .1754 = 17.54\%$$

Note that the holding period return can also be determined directly from the capital gains and dividend payments for each of the two years. Capital gains are [$150 + (-$50)] = $100 for the two-year period. Dividends are ($250 + $200) = $450. However, the calculation of the holding period return is based on the assumption that dividends received during the first year are reinvested in Bradley common stock during the second year; that is, we assume that the $250 dividend received at the end of year 1 is invested at a 4.48% rate during year 2. Therefore, for the purposes of calculating the holding period return, we assume returns from dividends at the end of the two-year period equal to [($250)(1.0448) + ($200)] = $461.20. The two-year holding period return is:

$$[(\$100 + \$461.20)/\$3200] = .1754 = 17.54\%$$

Use the following information to solve Problems 3-10:

Year	Returns	
	X	Y
1	15%	18%
2	4	-3
3	-9	-10
4	8	12
5	9	5

Problem 3

What is the mean return for asset X? For asset Y?

Solution 3

Year	Returns	
	X	Y
1	.15	.18
2	.04	-.03
3	-.09	-.10
4	.08	.12
5	.09	.05
Totals:	.27	.22

Thus the mean returns are: $\bar{R}_x = E(R_x) = (.27/5) = .054 = 5.4\%$ and $\bar{R}_y = E(R_y) = (.22/5) = .044 = 4.4\%$ for Y.

Problem 4

What is the five-year holding period return for asset X? For asset Y?

Solution 4

In general, the T-period holding period return can be calculated as:

$$[(1 + R_1) \times (1 + R_2) \times \ldots \times (1 + R_T)] - 1$$

Therefore, for asset X, we can calculate the five-year holding period return as follows:

$$[(1.15)(1.04)(.91)(1.08)(1.09)] - 1 = .2812 = 28.12\%$$

Similarly, the five-year holding period return for asset Y is 21.14%.

Problem 5

What is the variance of the return for asset X? For asset Y?

Solution 5

Year	Returns		Deviations		Squared deviations	
	X	Y	X	Y	X	Y
1	.15	.18	.096	.136	.009216	.018496
2	.04	-.03	-.014	-.074	.000196	.005476
3	-.09	-.10	-.144	-.144	.020736	.020736
4	.08	.12	.026	.076	.000676	.005776
5	.09	.05	.036	.006	.001296	.000036
Totals	.27	.22	.000	.000	.032120	.050520

Thus $Var(X) = \sigma_X^2 = (.032120/5) = .006424$ and $Var(Y) = \sigma_Y^2 = .010104$.

Problem 6

What is the standard deviation of the return for asset X? For asset Y?

Solution 6

The standard deviation is the square root of the variance. Therefore, the standard deviation for asset X is $SD(X) = \sigma_X = (.006424)^{.5} = .080150 = 8.0150\%$, and $SD(Y) = \sigma_Y = (.010104)^{.5} = .100519 = 10.0519\%$.

Problem 7

Suppose that the returns for assets X and Y each have a normal distribution with the mean returns and standard deviations calculated in Problems 3 and 6, respectively. For each asset, determine the range of returns within one standard deviation of the mean and the range of returns within two standard deviations of the mean. Interpret these results.

Solution 7

For asset X, the range of returns within one standard deviation of the mean is from [.054 - (1)(.080150)] to [.054 + (1)(.080150)], or -2.6150% to 13.4150%. The range of returns within two standard deviations of the mean is from [.054 - (2)(.080150)] to [.054 + (2)(.080150)], or -10.6300% to 21.4300%. These results indicate that there is approximately a 68% probability that, in any given year, the return for asset X will be between -2.6150% and 13.4510%, and approximately a 95% probability that the return will be between -10.6300% and 21.4300%. For asset Y, the probability is approximately 68% that the return will be between -5.6519% and 14.4519%, and approximately 95% that the return will be between -15.7038% and 24.5038%.

Problem 8

Given the data from Problems 3, 6 and 7, what is the probability that, in any given year, the return for asset X will be negative? What is the probability that the return for asset Y will be negative?

Solution 8

To solve this problem, we must determine the relevant value of z, and use Table A.5 to determine the probability. For asset X, z = [(0 - .054)/.080150] = -.674. Rounding this result to .67, the cumulative probability given in Table A.5 is .2486. This represents the probability that a value of z is between 0 (i.e., the mean of a distribution) and -.67. Since the probability of a z value less than 0 is .50, then the probability of a z value less than -.67 is (.50 - .2486) = .2514 or 25.14%. Therefore, the probability is 25.14% that the return for asset X is negative.

For asset Y, z = [(0 - .044)/.100519] = -.438 or approximately -.44. Therefore, the probability that the return for asset Y is negative is equal to (.50 - .1700) = .3300 = 33.00%.

Problem 9

What is the covariance between the returns for assets X and Y?

Solution 9

Year	Returns X	Returns Y	Deviations X	Deviations Y	Product of Deviations
1	.15	.18	.096	.136	.013056
2	.04	-.03	-.014	-.074	.001036
3	-.09	-.10	-.144	-.144	.020736
4	.08	.12	.026	.076	.001976
5	.09	.05	.036	.006	.000216
Totals	.27	.22	.000	.000	.037020

Thus, $Cov(R_X,R_Y) = \sigma_{XY} = (.030720/5) = .007404$.

Problem 10

What is the correlation between the returns for assets X and Y?

Solution 10

The correlation is equal to the covariance divided by the product of the standard deviations:

$$\rho_{XY} = Corr(R_X,R_Y) = \frac{Cov(R_X,R_Y)}{\sigma_X \times \sigma_Y} = \frac{.007404}{(.080150)(.100519)} = .9190$$

Problem 11

The probability that the economy will experience a recession next year is .3, while the probabilities of moderate growth or rapid expansion are .5 and .2, respectively. The common stock of Firm A is expected to return 5%, 15% or 20%, depending on whether the economy experiences a recession, moderate growth or rapid expansion, respectively. The rates of return for Firm B are expected to be 0%, 16% or 30%, respectively. Calculate the expected rate of return for each firm's common stock.

Solution 11

The expected rates of return for Firms A and B common stock are:

$$\bar{R}_A = E(R_A) = (.30)(.05) + (.50)(.15) + (.20)(.20) = .13 = 13\%$$

$$\bar{R}_B = E(R_B) = (.30)(.00) + (.50)(.16) + (.20)(.30) = .14 = 14\%$$

Problem 12

What is the variance of the rate of return for Firm A common stock? For Firm B common stock?

Solution 12

The variance for Firm A is calculated from the results in the following table, where Pr is the probability of each state of the economy and R_A is the rate of return under each state of the economy.

State of the Economy	Pr	R_A	$(R_A-\bar{R}_A)$	$(R_A-\bar{R}_A)^2$	$[(Pr)(R_A-\bar{R}_A)^2]$
Recession	.30	.05	-.08	.0064	.00192
Moderate Growth	.50	.15	.02	.0004	.00020
Rapid Expansion	.20	.20	.07	.0049	.00098

The variance is determined by first calculating the deviation from the expected return for each state; these deviations are then squared and multiplied by the respective probabilities of each state. The sum of the weighted squared deviations is the variance. Therefore, Var(A) = σ_A^2 = .00310. The comparable calculations for Firm B indicate that Var(B) = σ_B^2 = .01120.

Problem 13

What is the standard deviation of the rate of return for Firm A common stock? For Firm B common stock?

Solution 13

The standard deviation is the square root of the variance. The standard deviation for Firm A common stock is SD(A) = σ_A = $(.00310)^{.5}$ = .05568 = 5.568%, and SD(B) = σ_B = $(.01120)^{.5}$ = .10583 = 10.583%.

Problem 14

What is the covariance between the returns for Firm A stock and Firm B stock?

Solution 14

The covariance is determined from the data in the following table, where Pr is the probability of each state of the economy and R_A and R_B are the rates of return, under each state of the economy, for Firm A and Firm B stock, respectively.

Pr	$(R_A-\bar{R}_A)$	$(R_B-\bar{R}_B)$	$(R_A-\bar{R}_A) \times (R_B-\bar{R}_B)$	$[(Pr)(R_A-\bar{R}_A) \times (R_B-\bar{R}_B)]$
.30	-.08	-.14	.0112	.00336
.50	.02	.02	.0004	.00020
.20	.07	.16	.0112	.00224

The covariance is determined by first calculating the deviation from the expected return for each stock under each state of the economy; next, the deviations for the two stocks in each state are multiplied, and these products are then multiplied by the respective probabilities of each state. The sum of the weighted squared products is the covariance. Therefore, $Cov(R_A,R_B) = \sigma_{AB} = .00580$.

Problem 15

What is the correlation between the returns for Firm A stock and Firm B stock?

Solution 15

The correlation is equal to the covariance divided by the product of the standard deviations:

$$\rho_{AB} = Corr(R_A,R_B) = \frac{Cov(R_A,R_B)}{\sigma_A \times \sigma_B} = \frac{.00580}{(.05568)(.10583)} = .9843$$

CHAPTER HIGHLIGHTS

In the previous chapter, we introduced some of the basic concepts in the measurement of risk. Our emphasis in Chapter 8 was on the measurement of risk for individual securities. Our goal in Chapters 9, 10 and 11 is to derive the appropriate discount rate for risky capital budgeting projects. In order to accomplish this task, we must first develop the concepts of risk measurement for portfolios, and the contribution to the risk of a portfolio which is made by any given asset in the portfolio.

Portfolios versus Individual Securities

The basic characteristics of individual securities discussed in the previous chapter are the concepts of expected return [E(R)], variance (σ^2) and standard deviation (σ). The relationship between returns for two different securities (e.g., A and B) is measured by covariance (σ_{AB}) and correlation (ρ_{AB}). In this section, we discuss: how the expected return for a portfolio is determined by the expected returns for the individual securities which comprise that portfolio; and, how the standard deviation for a portfolio is determined by the standard deviations of the individual securities which comprise that portfolio as well as the correlations between these securities.

In order to illustrate these concepts, we will use an example which combines data from the previous chapter with additional information presented here. We will consider the example of GM stock, as presented in Chapter 8, along with data for Exxon stock. This information is summarized in the table below:

State	Returns		Deviations		Squared deviations	
	GM	Exxon	GM	Exxon	GM	Exxon
1	.10	.03	.04	−.04	.0016	.0016
2	.04	−.08	−.02	−.15	.0004	.0225
3	−.09	.07	−.15	.00	.0225	.0000
4	.20	.12	.14	.05	.0196	.0025
5	.05	.21	−.01	.14	.0001	.0196
Totals	.30	.35	.00	.00	.0442	.0462

The expected return for GM is (.30/5) = .06 = 6% and the expected return for Exxon is (.35/5) = .07 = 7%. The variance (σ_{GM}^2) and standard deviation (σ_{GM}) for GM are (.0442/5) = .00884 and [(.00884)$^{.5}$] = .09402, respectively. The variance (σ_{EX}^2) and standard deviation (σ_{EX}) for Exxon are (.0462/5) = .00924 and [(.00924)$^{.5}$] = .09613, respectively. The covariance ($\sigma_{GM,EX}$) is calculated by finding the product of the deviations for the two stocks for each state of the economy, then summing these products and dividing by 5; the resulting covariance is (.00700/5) = .00140. The correlation is equal to the covariance divided by the product of the standard deviations:

$$\rho_{GM,EX} = Corr(R_{GM},R_{EX}) = \frac{Cov(R_{GM},R_{EX})}{\sigma_{GM} \times \sigma_{EX}} = \frac{.00140}{(.09402)(.09613)} = .1549$$

Now consider the case of an individual who elects to invest 60% of his money in GM stock and 40% in Exxon stock. For each of the states of the economy indicated above, the investor's return on his investment will be equal to a weighted average of the returns in that state for the respective stocks. For example, in state 1, the investor's return would be:

$$(.60)(.10) + (.40)(.03) = .072 = 7.2\%$$

Similarly, the returns for this portfolio can be determined for each of the remaining possible states of the economy. The table below indicates the returns for the portfolio in each of the five states of the economy, as well as the calculations required to determine the expected return, variance and standard deviation for the portfolio:

State		Returns		Deviations	Squared Deviations
	GM	Exxon	Portfolio		
1	.10	.03	.072	.008	.000064
2	.04	-.08	-.008	-.072	.005184
3	-.09	.07	-.026	-.090	.008100
4	.20	.12	.168	.104	.010816
5	.05	.21	.114	.050	.002500
Totals	.30	.35	.320	.000	.026664

The expected return for the portfolio [E(R_P)] is (.320/5) = .064 = 6.4%. The variance for the portfolio [Var(P) or σ_p^2] is (.026664/5) = .0053328 and the standard deviation (σ_p) is [(.0053328)$^{.5}$] = .07303. Before we discuss the significance of these results, we first consider alternative, and generally simpler, procedures for calculating the expected return and variance for a portfolio.

The expected return for a portfolio is equal to a weighted average of the expected returns of the securities which comprise the portfolio. This conclusion can be easily deduced from the procedure used in the table above to determine the expected return for the portfolio. In the example here, the expected return is:

$$X_{GM}\bar{R}_{GM} + X_{EX}\bar{R}_{EX} = (.60)(.06) + (.40)(.07) = .064$$

where X_{GM} and X_{EX} are the proportions of the investor's portfolio invested in GM and Exxon, respectively. In general:

$$\text{Expected return on portfolio} = X_A\bar{R}_A + X_B\bar{R}_B$$

Although the expected return for a portfolio is a weighted average of the expected returns of the individual securities, the variance of a portfolio is not equal to a weighted average of individual variances. The variance of a portfolio is given by the following equation:

$$\text{Var(portfolio)} = X_A^2 \sigma_A^2 + 2X_A X_B \sigma_{A,B} + X_B^2 \sigma_B^2$$

For the portfolio of GM and Exxon stock described above:

$$\text{Var(portfolio)} = (.6)^2(.00884) + 2(.6)(.4)(.00140) + (.4)^2(.00924)$$

Therefore, Var(portfolio) = .0053328. The standard deviation for the portfolio [SD(portfolio) or σ_P] is equal to the square root of the variance, or .07303.

We noted earlier in this section that the expected return for a portfolio is a weighted average of the returns for the individual securities in the portfolio. Clearly, the variance and standard deviation for the portfolio are not weighted averages of the corresponding characteristics of the individual securities. In fact, the variance and standard deviation for the portfolio of GM and Exxon stock are each less than the corresponding individual characteristics for GM and Exxon stock. Although this latter result is not always true for a portfolio of two stocks, it does provide some indication of the benefits derived from diversification. The more general result can be stated as follows: As long as the correlation between two securities is less than 1, then the standard deviation of a portfolio comprised of the two securities is less than the weighted average of the standard deviations of the two securities. Furthermore, the lower the correlation, the greater the benefit of diversification, in the sense that the portfolio standard deviation is further reduced below the weighted average of the standard deviations.

The Efficient Set for Two Assets

An infinite number of portfolios can be created by combining GM and Exxon stock in varying proportions. The curved line in Figure 9.1 demonstrates the possibilities. The point on the graph labeled 'Exxon' represents the expected return and standard deviation for Exxon stock. This point can also be thought of as a portfolio comprised of 100% Exxon stock and 0% GM stock. Similarly, the point labeled 'GM' represents the expected return and standard deviation for GM stock. The portfolio described in the previous section (i.e., $X_{GM} = 60\%$ and $X_{EX} = 40\%$) is also indicated on the graph. Portfolios with X_{GM} greater than 60% are located on the portion of the curve below and to the right of the portfolio noted above, while portfolios with X_{GM} less than 60% are on the remainder of the curve. As X_{GM} increases, the portfolios are closer to the point labeled GM and as X_{EX} increases, the portfolios are closer to the point labeled Exxon.

The straight line in Figure 9.1 represents the portfolios which would be possible if the correlation between GM and Exxon were +1. The effect of diversification is indicated by comparing the straight line with the curved line. Remember that the curve represents portfolios which are possible given a correlation between GM and Exxon equal to .1549, as calculated in the previous section. Consider, for example, the portfolio indicated on the curved line. If the correlation between the two stocks were +1, then the portfolio with $X_{GM} = 60\%$ and $X_{EX} = 40\%$ would lie on the straight line at the point labeled P. This portfolio has the same expected return as the portfolio on the curve (i.e., 6.4%) but it has a substantially higher standard deviation. Consequently, we see that the lower correlation results in the reduction of the portfolio standard deviation below the weighted average of the individual security standard deviations. Furthermore, the lower the correlation between the two stocks, the lower the standard deviation for any given portfolio proportions.

The point in Figure 9.1 identified as MV is the **minimum variance portfolio**. This is the portfolio with the lowest variance, and, consequently, with the lowest standard deviation. Note that even though the graph is presented in terms of standard deviation, it is common usage to refer to this portfolio as the minimum variance portfolio.

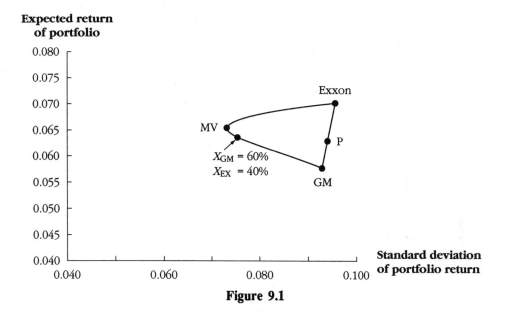

Figure 9.1

The curved line in Figure 9.1 is referred to as the **opportunity set** or the **feasible set** of portfolios. An investor can achieve any point on the curve by selecting the appropriate values of X_{GM} and X_{EX}. The portion of the curve between MV and Exxon is the **efficient set**. Investors are able to achieve results on the opportunity set below the minimum variance portfolio, but would not choose to do so. Note that these portfolios, compared to the minimum variance portfolio, have both higher standard deviation and lower expected return. Consequently, it is only choices on the efficient set which are selected by investors.

The selection of a portfolio from among those in the efficient set is a subjective choice which depends on the individual investor's personal attitudes towards risk. For example, an investor who is relatively tolerant of risk would be likely to select a portfolio which is invested more heavily in Exxon stock. A portfolio with $X_{GM} = 10\%$ and $X_{EX} = 90\%$ would be on the portion of the efficient set close to the point representing Exxon stock. Such a portfolio has a higher expected return and higher standard deviation than does the minimum variance portfolio, but an investor who is relatively tolerant of risk might find this an acceptable tradeoff. On the other hand, an investor who is more highly averse to risk might select the minimum variance portfolio; such an investor is not willing to accept the higher risk level which must be tolerated in order to achieve the higher level of expected return.

The Efficient Set for Many Securities

In the previous section, we developed the concepts of the opportunity set and the efficient set for a portfolio of two securities. The opportunity set of all portfolios formed from a universe of several hundred securities would have the appearance of the shaded area in Figure 9.2. Each of the infinite number of points in the opportunity set represents a portfolio with different proportions of each stock in the universe of securities. Since the proportion for any given security can be zero, the points in the opportunity set do not each contain the same number of securities. Some points represent portfolios with one security, for example, while others represent portfolios containing all securities in the universe. For the latter portfolios, the variations in the proportions result in different expected return and standard deviation for the portfolio; this result is a generalization of the conclusion in the preceding section for portfolios of two securities. Note that every point in the shaded region represents a feasible portfolio and that every feasible portfolio is in the shaded region.

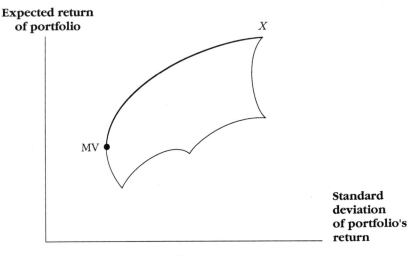

Figure 9.2

The opportunity set in Figure 9.2 has a different appearance from the opportunity set of Figure 9.1. That is, the opportunity set for a universe of hundreds of securities is an entire region in Figure 9.2, while the opportunity set for a portfolio of two securities is represented by the points on a curve in Figure 9.1. However, the shape of the efficient set is very similar in both cases. In Figure 9.2, the efficient set is the curve from the minimum variance portfolio (MV) to the portfolio indicated by X. As we noted in the previous section, no investor would choose that part of the opportunity set which lies on the curve below and to the right of MV, because any portfolio on that portion of the curve has both lower expected return and higher standard deviation than does MV. Similar reasoning leads us to conclude that no investor would choose a portfolio in that portion of the opportunity set which lies below the curve from MV to X. Consider any portfolio in the portion of the opportunity set below the curve; an investor can find a portfolio on the efficient set which has the same standard deviation and higher expected return, so that only portfolios on the curve would be considered.

Variance and Standard Deviation in a Portfolio of Many Assets. In the first section of this chapter we presented the formula for the variance of a two-asset portfolio; the formula is repeated here:

$$\text{Var(portfolio)} = X_1^2\sigma_1^2 + 2X_1X_2\sigma_{1,2} + X_2^2\sigma_2^2$$

(Note that we have changed the designation of the assets in the portfolio from securities A and B to securities 1 and 2.) We now extend this formula to a portfolio of three or more securities.

In order to understand this generalization, note that there are two kinds of terms in the equation above. The first category is comprised of variance terms; the first and third terms above are variance terms and there is one variance term for each security in the portfolio. The second category consists of covariance terms; there is one covariance term for each pair of assets in the portfolio. Since there are only two assets in the portfolio there is only one covariance term in the above expression.

However, for a portfolio of three securities there would be three pairs of assets and three covariance terms. The pairs of assets are securities 1 and 2, securities 1 and 3, and securities 2 and 3. Therefore, the formula for the variance of a three-asset portfolio has three variance terms and three covariance terms, as indicated below:

$$Var(portfolio) = X_1^2\sigma_1^2 + X_2^2\sigma_2^2 + X_3^2\sigma_3^2 +$$

$$2X_1X_2\sigma_{1,2} + 2X_1X_3\sigma_{1,3} + 2X_2X_3\sigma_{2,3}$$

The three variance terms are in the first row of the above expression and the three covariance terms are in the second row. For a four-asset portfolio, there are four variance terms and six covariance terms:

$$Var(portfolio) = X_1^2\sigma_1^2 + X_2^2\sigma_2^2 + X_3^2\sigma_3^2 + X_4^2\sigma_4^2$$

$$+ 2X_1X_2\sigma_{1,2} + 2X_1X_3\sigma_{1,3} + 2X_1X_4\sigma_{1,4}$$

$$+ 2X_2X_3\sigma_{2,3} + 2X_2X_4\sigma_{2,4} + 2X_3X_4\sigma_{3,4}$$

Diversification: An Example

The effects of diversification for portfolios with many securities can be illustrated by making the following assumptions:

1. All securities have the same variance, represented by var.
2. All covariances are equal, and are represented by cov.
3. All securities are equally weighted in the portfolio, with weight $X_i = 1/N$, where N is the number of securities in the portfolio.

In this case, it can be shown that, as the number of securities, N, increases, the variance of the portfolio approaches cov, the average covariance. In other words, the variances of the individual securities are diversified away; however, the covariances can not be diversified away.

In the example described here, it must be true that the security variance is greater than the security covariance, and that:

Total risk of		Unsystematic or
individual security	= Portfolio risk +	diversifiable risk
(var)	= (cov) +	(var - cov)

An individual who holds only one security in his portfolio has risk equal to var. An individual who holds a diversified portfolio has risk equal to cov; this portfolio risk is also referred to as systematic or market risk. The risk which can be diversified away in a large portfolio is the unsystematic or diversifiable risk. For an investor with a diversified portfolio, only the portfolio risk is of consequence; such an investor can eliminate diversifiable risk and consequently is unconcerned with this source of risk.

Riskless Borrowing and Lending

Consider the case of an individual who intends to invest $10,000 in a portfolio which consists of a risk-free asset and Exxon stock. The risk-free asset has a return of 5% and a standard deviation of zero, while Exxon stock has an expected return of 7% and a standard deviation of .10. (Note that we have rounded σ_{BX} for the purposes of this example.) If the individual invests 25% of his portfolio in the risk-free asset and 75% in Exxon stock, then the expected return for the portfolio is:

$$(.25)(.05) + (.75)(.07) = .065 = 6.5\%$$

The variance for the portfolio is given by:

$$\text{Var(portfolio)} = X_A^2\sigma_A^2 + 2X_A X_B \sigma_{A,B} + X_B^2\sigma_B^2$$

where the subscript A applies to the risk-free asset and the subscript B applies to Exxon stock. However, since the risk-free asset has zero variance, and zero covariance with all other assets, the above expression simplifies to:

$$X_B^2\sigma_B^2 = (.75)^2(.10)^2 = .005625$$

The standard deviation is .075.

Suppose that, alternatively, the investor described above is able to borrow $3,000 at the risk-free rate and decides to invest his original $10,000 plus the borrowed $3,000 in Exxon stock. He will be investing 130% of the original $10,000 in Exxon stock, but he will be paying interest on an amount equal to 30% of his portfolio. Consequently, his expected rate of return is:

$$(-.30)(.05) + (1.30)(.07) = .076 = 7.6\%$$

Note that the expected return for the portfolio is greater than the expected return for Exxon stock; that is, the investor increases his expected return by borrowing money, at a 5% interest rate, which he then invests at an expected rate of 7%.

The variance for this portfolio is:

$$X_B^2\sigma_B^2 = (1.30)^2(.10)^2 = .0169$$

and the standard deviation is .130.

The discussion of this section indicates four points on the opportunity set of portfolios formed by combining the risk-free asset and Exxon stock. It can be shown, both algebraically and graphically, that these portfolios, and all portfolios formed from these two assets, lie on a straight line; that is, the opportunity set for portfolios constructed from the risk-free asset and a risky asset lie on the straight line whose y-intercept is the risk-free asset and which includes the point representing the expected return and standard deviation of the risky asset. For example, suppose that the point X in Figure 9.3 represents Exxon stock. Then the opportunity set is the line from the y-intercept at R_F through the point X. The portfolio with 75% invested in Exxon lies between R_F and X, while the portfolio with 130% invested in Exxon lies to the right of X.

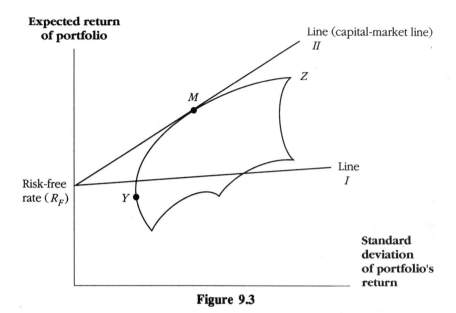

Figure 9.3

The Optimal Portfolio. An investor can form portfolios by combining the risk-free asset with any single security or with any portfolio of securities. In either case, the resulting opportunity set is a straight line between R_F and the risky asset or portfolio. Figure 9.3 indicates two such opportunity sets, Line I, combining the risk-free asset with X, and Line II, combining the risk-free asset with M. Since all portfolios on Line II have higher expected return for a given level of risk than do portfolios on Line I, any investor would choose portfolios on Line II. In fact, Line II is the efficient set for all assets because it provides the investor with the best possible opportunities. Line II is called the **capital market line**. Points between R_F and M represent portfolios comprised of investing in the portfolio of risky assets, M, and the risk-free asset. Points to the right of M are formed by borrowing at the rate R_F and investing in portfolio M.

The capital market line in Figure 9.3 implies the **separation principle** of investment decision-making. According to this principle, an investor can identify his preferred portfolio in two steps. First, he can identify the efficient set represented by the curve YMZ based on objective data regarding expected returns and variances for individual securities and covariances between pairs of securities. Second, he can select his own preferred portfolio on the capital market line based on his personal attitudes towards risk. The point of the separation principle is that the first step does not require any information regarding an individual investor's preferences; given the same information, all investors would arrive at the same efficient set. Personal preferences enter the process only in the second step.

Market Equilibrium

Definition of the Market-Equilibrium Portfolio. Financial economists often use the simplifying assumption of **homogeneous expectations** in order to develop a model of security market equilibrium. According to this assumption, all investors have the same information, or expectations, regarding security returns, variances and covariances. While this assumption is not literally consistent with reality, it may be sufficiently accurate to allow us to derive useful conclusions regarding investor behavior and risk in the securities markets.

With homogeneous expectations, all investors perceive the same capital market line, such as Line II in Figure 9.3. Consequently, all investors will select portfolios on the capital market line and all investors who hold portfolios of risky assets will hold portfolio M, combined with the risk-free asset. Therefore, portfolio M must have an important characteristic; that is, portfolio M is the **market portfolio**.

In order to demonstrate the meaning of the market portfolio, imagine that there are 100 investors in the world, that the investors have homogeneous expectations, and that each investor owns a portfolio of assets whose value is equal to 1% of the total value of the securities in the market. Each investor must then hold 1% of the shares of each stock in the market. If, for example, one investor held less than 1% of Stock X, then another investor would have to hold more than 1% of Stock X so that 100% of the outstanding shares of Stock X are owned by investors. But, given homogeneous expectations, all investors must hold the same portfolio M, so that each must hold the same percentage of each stock. Consequently, the portfolio of risky assets which each investor holds must be the market portfolio; in other words, each investor holds a proportion of each security equal to his proportion of the total market wealth.

Definition of Risk When Investors Hold the Market Portfolio. Based on the formula for the variance of a portfolio, it can be shown that the contribution of a particular stock (e.g., Stock 2) to the risk of the market portfolio of N stocks is given by:

$$X_1\sigma_{2,1} + X_2\sigma_{2,2} + X_3\sigma_{2,3} + ... + X_N\sigma_{2,N}$$

(Note that $\sigma_{2,2}$ is the same as σ_2^2, the variance of stock 2.) The above expression is equal to $\sigma_{2,M}$, the covariance between the return for security 2 and the return for the market portfolio. In general, the contribution of security i to the risk of the market portfolio is given by $\sigma_{i,M}$, the covariance between the return for security i and the return for the market portfolio. For ease of interpretation and calculation, this result is often standardized by dividing the covariance by the variance of the market portfolio. The resulting value is referred to as the beta for security i (β_i), which is defined as follows:

$$\beta_i = \frac{\sigma_{i,M}}{\sigma_M^2}$$

Since the variance of the market portfolio is a constant for all securities in the portfolio, dividing the covariance by σ_M^2 does not change the significance of the conclusions of this section.

Beta as a Measure of Responsiveness. One of the advantages of using beta as a measure of a security's contribution to the risk of the market portfolio is the fact that there is an intuitive explanation of beta which makes it easier to interpret than the covariance. Beta indicates the average responsiveness of the return for a security to changes in the return for the market portfolio. Suppose that stock X has a beta value equal to 2. If the expected return for the market increases by 1%, then the expected return for stock X increases by (2)(1%) = 2%. Similarly, if the expected return for the market decreases by 1%, then the expected return for stock X decreases by 2%. In practice, the value of beta is often calculated as the slope of a **characteristic line**, which is a statistically determined line relating the expected return for the market portfolio to the expected return for the security. The statistical procedure used to determine the value of beta is referred to as regression analysis.

Relationship between Risk and Return

We conclude from the information developed in the preceding sections of this chapter that beta is the appropriate measure of risk for a security and that, therefore, the expected return for a security is positively related to its beta. This conclusion is illustrated by the upward-sloping straight line in Figure 9.4. This line is referred to as the **security market line** (SML).

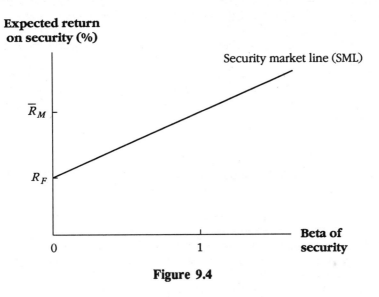

Figure 9.4

The security market line indicates that the expected return for a security with beta equal to zero is the risk-free rate. The value of beta for the market portfolio is 1, and the expected return for any security with beta equal to 1 is the same as the expected return for the market portfolio.

The security market line is a straight line. This results from the fact that combinations of assets on the SML must also lie on the SML. Therefore, any asset which is not on the SML is not in equilibrium. Consider, for example, a stock Z which lies below the SML. Since some combination of securities on the SML can be created with beta value equal to the beta for Z, this combination is preferable to Z. No one would invest in Z when there is an investment with the same risk and a higher expected return. Therefore, the price of Z must decline, and its expected return must increase, until Z is on the security market line. Analogous results occur for an asset above the SML. In this case, the price of the asset would increase, and its expected return would decrease, until it fell on the security market line.

The algebraic representation of the security market line is called the **capital-asset-pricing model** (CAPM). The SML is a straight line with an intercept equal to R_F and slope equal to:

$$(R_M - R_F)/(1 - 0) = (R_M - R_F)$$

The equation for the CAPM is:

$$R = R_F + \beta (R_M - R_F)$$

CONCEPT TEST

1. The expected return on a portfolio is computed as a _____ of the individual security expected returns.

2. If the correlation between two securities is less than 1, then the portfolio standard deviation is less than the _____ of the individual security standard deviations.

3. The set of all feasible portfolios which can be formed by combining risky securities is called the _____ set or the _____ set.

4. The portfolio in the opportunity set which has the lowest standard deviation is called the _____ portfolio.

5. The formula for the variance of a portfolio has two kinds of terms: _____ terms and _____ terms.

6. The formula for the variance of a portfolio has as many _____ terms as there are securities in the portfolio.

7. The formula for the variance of a portfolio has as many _____ terms as there are pairs of securities in the portfolio.

8. For a very highly diversified portfolio, the portfolio variance approaches the _____ as the number of assets grows large.

9. The opportunity set for a portfolio comprised of the risk-free asset and a risky asset is a _____ line, whereas the opportunity set for a portfolio comprised of two risky assets is a _____ line.

10. The _____ is the efficient set for all assets.

11. The _____ principle refers to the fact that the portfolio selection process can be thought of as two steps, one involving objective data and the other involving personal preferences.

12. The assumption of _____ states that all investors have the same information regarding security returns, variances and covariances.

13. The contribution of a security to the risk of the portfolio is measured by the _____ between the return for the security and the market portfolio.

14. The algebraic representation of the security market line is called the _____.

15. The y-intercept, corresponding to a zero beta, of the SML is _____.

16. The slope of the SML is equal to the _____.

17. The beta of the market portfolio is _____.

18. The y-axis of the SML measures _____.

19. The x-axis of the SML measures _____.

ANSWERS TO CONCEPT TEST

1. weighted average
2. weighted average
3. opportunity; feasible
4. minimum variance
5. variance; covariance
6. variance
7. covariance
8. average covariance
9. straight; curved
10. capital market line

11. separation
12. homogeneous expectations
13. covariance
14. capital asset pricing
   model (CAPM)
15. the risk-free rate
16. market risk premium
17. one
18. expected return
19. beta

PROBLEMS AND SOLUTIONS

Use the following information for Stock A and for the market portfolio (M) to solve Problems 1-6.

State of Economy	Probability of State	Rate of Return of A	Rate of Return of M
Boom	.10	.25	.18
Growth	.20	.10	.20
Normal	.50	.15	.04
Recession	.20	−.12	.00

Problem 1

What is the expected return for Stock A? For the market?

Solution 1

State of Economy	Probability of State (Pr)	Rate of Return of A (R_A)	$(Pr) \times (R_A)$
Boom	.10	.25	.025
Growth	.20	.10	.020
Normal	.50	.15	.075
Recession	.20	−.12	−.024
			.096

Thus the expected returns are $E(R_A) = \bar{R}_A = 9.6\%$ and $E(R_M) = \bar{R}_M = 7.8\%$.

Problem 2

What is the standard deviation for Stock A? For the market?

Solution 2

State of the Economy	Pr	$(R_A-\bar{R}_A)$	$(R_A-\bar{R}_A)^2$	$[(Pr)(R_A-\bar{R}_A)^2]$
Boom	.10	.25	.023716	.0023716
Growth	.20	.10	.000016	.0000032
Normal	.50	.15	.002916	.0014580
Recession	.20	-.12	.046656	.0093312
	1.00			.0131640

The variance for Stock A is: $\sigma_A^2 = .013164$. The standard deviation is the square root of .013164: $\sigma_A = .11473 = 11.473\%$. The variance and standard deviation for the market are $\sigma_M^2 = .005956$ and $\sigma_M = .07718 = 7.718\%$.

Problem 3

What is the covariance between Stock A and the market? What is the correlation?

Solution 3

State of Economy	Pr	$(R_A-\bar{R}_A)$	$(R_B-\bar{R}_B)$	$(Pr) \times (R_A-\bar{R}_A) \times (R_B-\bar{R}_B)$
Boom	.10	.154	.102	.0015708
Growth	.20	.004	.122	.0000976
Normal	.50	.054	-.038	-.0010260
Recession	.20	-.216	-.078	.0033696
	1.00			.0040120

The covariance between Stock A and the market is $Cov(R_A,R_M) = \sigma_{AM} = .004012$. The correlation is calculated as follows:

$$\rho_{AB} = Corr(R_A,R_B) = \frac{Cov(R_A,R_B)}{\sigma_A \times \sigma_B} = \frac{.004012}{(.11473)(.07718)} = .45308$$

Problem 4

Calculate the value of β for Stock A.

Solution 4

Beta is calculated as follows:

$$\beta_A = \frac{\sigma_{A,M}}{\sigma_M^2} = \frac{.004012}{.005956} = .6736$$

Problem 5

What is the expected return for a portfolio of Stock A and the market portfolio that is invested 20% in Stock A?

Solution 5

The expected return is:

$$.20(.096) + .80(.078) = .0816 = 8.16\%$$

Problem 6

What is the variance of a portfolio that is invested 60% in Stock A and 40% in the market portfolio?

Solution 6

The portfolio variance can be determined as follows:

$$Var(\text{portfolio}) = \sigma_p^2 = X_A^2\sigma_A^2 + 2X_AX_M\sigma_{A,M} + X_M^2\sigma_M^2$$

$$= .6^2(.013164) + .4^2(.005956) + 2(.6)(.4)(.004012) = .00761776$$

Problem 7

An individual plans to invest in Stock A and/or Stock B. The expected returns are 9% and 10% for Stocks A and B, respectively. The standard deviations are 4% and 5% for Stocks A and B, respectively. The correlation between A and B is .5. Find the expected return and the standard deviation of the portfolio if he invests 75% of his funds in Stock A.

Solution 7

The expected return for the portfolio is 9.25% and the variance is: $Var(R_p) = \sigma_p^2 = .0014313$. The standard deviation is the square root of the variance: $\sigma_p = .037832 = 3.7832\%$. Note that in calculating the variance, we must determine the covariance between A and B. The covariance is equal to the correlation times the product of the standard deviations:

$$Cov(R_A,R_B) = \sigma_{AB} = \rho_{AB} \times \sigma_A \times \sigma_B = [(.5)(.04)(.05)] = .001$$

Problem 8

Suppose that the investor in Problem 7 wants to construct a portfolio with expected return equal to 9.5%. What proportion of the investor's portfolio should be invested in each asset? What is the standard deviation for the portfolio?

Solution 8

In order to form a portfolio with expected return equal to 9.5%, the investor must solve the following equation for x:

$$.09x + (.10)(1-x) = .095$$

where x is the proportion of the portfolio invested in Stock A and (1-x) is the proportion invested in Stock B. The solution for x is .50, so that the portfolio will be invested 50% in each asset. The variance for this portfolio is .001525 and the standard deviation is .03905 = 3.905%.

Problem 9

Suppose that the investor described in Problem 7 decides to form a portfolio consisting of three assets, as follows: 10% invested in Stock A, 30% invested in Stock B and 60% invested in a risk-free asset with a return of 6%. What is the expected return for this portfolio? What is the standard deviation of return?

Solution 9

The expected return for the portfolio is:

$$(.10)(.09) + (.30)(.10) + (.60)(.06) = .075 = 7.5\%$$

For a portfolio comprised of three assets, the variance of the portfolio is found as follows:

$$\text{Var(portfolio)} = X_1^2\sigma_1^2 + X_2^2\sigma_2^2 + X_3^2\sigma_3^2 +$$

$$2X_1X_2\sigma_{1,2} + 2X_1X_3\sigma_{1,3} + 2X_2X_3\sigma_{2,3}$$

Let Stock A be represented by security 1, Stock B by security 2 and the risk-free asset by security 3. Since the risk-free asset pays a guaranteed return, the third, fifth and sixth terms above are zero. Therefore, the variance of the portfolio is equal to:

$$(.1)^2(.04)^2 + (.3)^2(.05)^2 + (2)(.1)(.3)(.001) = .000301$$

and the standard deviation is .017349 = 1.7349%. Note that the covariance is .001, as indicated in Problem 7.

Problem 10

Try this one on your own. Stocks A and B have perfect negative correlation. Define x as the percentage invested in Stock A and (1 - x) as the percentage invested in Stock B. The standard deviations for A and B are .40 and .20, respectively. If a portfolio of A and B has zero variance, what is x?

Solution 10

The percentage invested in A, x, must be one-third.

Use the following CAPM to answer Problems 11-14.

$$R_i = 6\% + 8\%\beta_i$$

Problem 11

Speiss Corporation has a beta of 2. What is its expected return?

Solution 11

The expected return is $6\% + 8\%(2) = 22\%$.

Problem 12

If we form a portfolio that is invested 70% in Speiss stock and 30% in the risk-free asset, what is the expected return for the portfolio? The beta for the portfolio?

Solution 12

The expected return is $.70(22\%) + .30(6\%) = 17.2\%$. The beta is $.70(2) + .30(0) = 1.4$. Notice that if we substitute this portfolio beta of 1.4 into the SML equation, we get the same expected return of 17.2%.

Problem 13

Dorigan Corporation has a beta of 1.5 and an expected return of 15%. Is Dorigan common stock a good buy?

Solution 13

From the SML, the expected return for Dorigan, given its beta of 1.5, should be 18%; therefore, it is not a good buy.

Problem 14

Construct a portfolio of Speiss common stock and the risk-free asset which has beta equal to 1.5. What is the expected return for this portfolio?

Solution 14

Let x represent the proportion of the portfolio invested in Speiss stock. Then the required portfolio is determined by solving the following equation for x:

$$1.5 = 2x + (0)(1 - x)$$

$$x = .75$$

Since the portfolio has the same beta as the Dorigan stock, the expected return is 18%. Thus, if we short sell Dorigan Corporation stock and invest the proceeds in a portfolio composed of 75% Speiss Corporation and 25% risk-free lending, we have created a risk-free arbitrage opportunity.

Problem 15

Assume that the three stocks listed below plot on the SML. The standard deviation for the market is 22%. What is the equation for the SML? Fill in the missing numbers in the table.

Security	$E(R_i)$	$Var(R_i)$	$Corr(R_i, R_M)$	β_i
1	.07	.0225		
2	.14	.0400		.8
3	.10	.1225	.6	
4	.07	.0000		

Solution 15

Stock 4 has a 7% expected return and zero variance; thus the risk-free rate is 7%. The correlation of Security 4 with the market is zero since the return for Security 4 does not vary. The beta for Security 4 is also zero. Security 1 has the same 7% return, so Security 1 must have a zero beta and thus zero correlation with the market. Security 2 has a beta of .8. A portfolio invested 80% in the market and 20% in the risk-free asset also has a beta of .8 and must have a return of 14%. This implies a market return of $.8[E(R_m)] + .2(7\%) = 14\%$, so the market expected return must be 15.75%. Based on these numbers, the SML equation is:

$$E(R_i) = 7\% + 8.75\%\beta_i$$

Security 3 has an expected return of 10%, so its beta must be $[(.10 - .07)/.0875] = .343$. For Security 2, the beta is .8. Since the market standard deviation is .22, the covariance of Security 2 with the market $[Cov(R_2, R_m)]$ must satisfy the following equation:

$$.8 = [Cov(R_2, R_M)]/(.0484)$$

Therefore, $Cov(R_2, R_M) = .03872$. The correlation is $[.03872/(.20 \times .22)] = .88$.

CHAPTER 10
AN ALTERNATIVE VIEW OF RISK AND RETURN:
THE ARBITRAGE-PRICING THEORY

CHAPTER HIGHLIGHTS

In the previous chapter, we developed the capital-asset-pricing model (CAPM), which establishes a positive, linear relationship between an asset's beta and its expected return. The arbitrage pricing theory (APT) is an alternative explanation of the relationship between risk and return.

Factor Models: Announcements, Surprises, and Expected Returns

The development of the APT requires a more detailed understanding of the factors which affect the behavior of the returns on individual securities. The actual return (R) on a security consists of two parts: the expected return plus a 'surprise,' or unexpected, part. The expected return is based on a large number of factors that may influence a given company. The risk for a particular asset comes from the unexpected part of the return. For a given stock, we can write:

$$R = \bar{R} + U$$

where R is the actual return, $\bar{R}$ is the expected part of the return and U is the unexpected part of the return. Consider the example of Texxon, a large oil company. The expected return on Texxon common stock is partially determined by the expected price of oil. Suppose the price of oil is currently $12 per barrel and that the price is completely controlled by the OPEC cartel. It is generally expected that the cartel will raise the price to $20 per barrel. Subsequently, however, the cartel announces that the price will be $22. The price changes by $10 per barrel, but $8 of this change was expected and was reflected in Texxon's expected return. It is the $2 deviation from the expected price that is the 'surprise' portion of the announcement.

In general, an announcement has two components: the expected part and the surprise part. In the Texxon example, if a price hike to $20 had actually been announced, there would have been no surprise. In the language of Wall Street, the market has already 'discounted' the news of a price increase to $20, which means that the value of the Texxon shares already reflects this information because it is anticipated by market participants.

Risk: Systematic and Unsystematic

The risk of owning an asset, such as common stock, results from unexpected events. After all, if events always occurred exactly as expected, there would be no risk. Given this risk of unexpected or surprise events, there is an important distinction to be made between systematic and unsystematic risk. A **systematic** risk tends to affect a large number of assets to a greater or lesser degree. An **unsystematic** risk affects only a single asset or a small group of assets. Systematic risks arise from uncertainty about economy-wide factors, such as GNP and interest rates, whereas the possibility of a labor strike or lawsuit involving a single company is an unsystematic, or 'idiosyncratic,' risk. Systematic risks are also called **market risks.** We must note here, however, that the distinction between systematic and unsystematic risks is not always entirely clear.

With the two types of risk in mind, we can rewrite the return, R, for a particular security as:

$$R = \bar{R} + m + \varepsilon$$

where m represents the part of the return that is market-related (i.e., the systematic part) and epsilon (ε) represents the idiosyncratic, or unsystematic, part. Since the unsystematic risk is particular to an individual asset, then the unsystematic risk for, say, General Motors is unrelated to the unsystematic risk for Sears. In other words, the correlation between the unsystematic risk for GM and for Sears is zero.

Systematic Risk and Betas

Because systematic risks affect almost all assets to some degree, the systematic risks for two different assets are related. Consider the case of Texxon, an oil supplier, and Engulf Power, which buys oil. Whenever oil prices are higher than expected, Texxon stock price increases while Engulf Power stock price decreases. In this case, we say that Texxon stock price is positively related to oil prices, while Engulf stock price has a negative relationship with oil prices.

The sensitivity of an asset to a systematic risk is measured by the **beta coefficient.** In the above example, Texxon would have a positive oil-price beta and Engulf Power would have a negative oil-price beta.

If we wish to focus on a particular set of systematic risks, such as those associated with uncertainty about Gross National Product (GNP) and interest rates (I), then we write the return for a particular security as:

$$R = \bar{R} + U = R + m + \varepsilon$$

$$R = \bar{R} + \beta_{GNP}(F_{GNP}) + \beta_I(F_I) + \varepsilon$$

The GNP beta (β_{GNP}) measures the sensitivity of the stock's return to unexpected changes in GNP (F_{GNP}) and the interest rate beta (β_I) measures the sensitivity of the return to unexpected changes in interest rates (F_I).

Suppose a particular company has an expected return of 12% for the coming year, a GNP beta of 2 and an interest rate beta of 1.5. The expected growth in GNP for the year is 3% and interest rates are expected to remain constant during the year. At the end of the year, GNP has actually increased by 2% and interest rates have increased by 3%; also, this company loses a significant lawsuit and, as a result, experiences a 4% decrease in rate of return ($\varepsilon = -4\%$). This information implies an unexpected change in GNP of -1% and an unexpected change in interest rates of 3%. The actual return for the year would be:

$$R = \bar{R} + \beta_{GNP}(F_{GNP}) + \beta_I(F_I) + \varepsilon$$

$$= 12\% + [(2)(-1\%)] + [(1.5)(3\%)] - 4\% = 10.5\%$$

Models such as the one described here are called **factor models**. Factors are sources of systematic risk, designated by F. A 'k-factor model,' where k is the number of factors, is written:

$$R = \bar{R} + \beta_1(F_1) + \beta_2(F_2) + ... + \beta_k(F_k) + \varepsilon$$

The appropriate set of factors to use in a k-factor model is a subject of much debate and research; there is no consensus regarding this issue. In practice, a single-factor model is often used, where the single factor is a broad market index, such as the S&P 500. These single factor models are called **market models** because the factor represents the unexpected change in the value of the overall market index.

Portfolios and Factor Models

In this section, we examine the characteristics of an N-stock portfolio composed of stocks which each follow the one-factor model. For stock i, we can express returns for the coming month as:

$$R_i = \bar{R}_i + \beta_i F + \varepsilon_i$$

The return for the N-stock portfolio (R_P) is a weighted average of the returns on the individual stocks in the portfolio:

$$R_P = X_1 R_1 + X_2 R_2 + X_3 R_3 + ... + X_N R_N$$

where X_i is the proportion of the portfolio invested in security i and:

$$X_1 + X_2 + X_3 + ... + X_N = 1$$

Therefore, R_P can be written as:

$$R_P = X_1(\bar{R}_1 + \beta_1 F + \varepsilon_1) + X_2(\bar{R}_2 + \beta_2 F + \varepsilon_2)$$
$$+ X_3(\bar{R}_3 + \beta_3 F + \varepsilon_3) + ... + X_N(\bar{R}_N + \beta_N F + \varepsilon_N)$$

Rearranging these terms, we can demonstrate that the return on the portfolio is determined by three sets of parameters:

$$R_P = X_1\bar{R}_1 + X_2\bar{R}_2 + X_3\bar{R}_3 + ... + X_N\bar{R}_N$$
$$+ (X_1\beta_1 + X_2\beta_2 + X_3\beta_3 + ... + X_N\beta_N)F$$
$$+ X_1\varepsilon_1 + X_2\varepsilon_2 + X_3\varepsilon_3 + ... + X_N\varepsilon_N$$

The three sets of parameters are: first, the weighted average of each security's expected return; second, the weighted average of the individual betas multiplied by the factor F; and, third, the weighted average of the unsystematic risks. The first row of the above expression is the expected return on the portfolio. The term in parentheses in the second row is the portfolio beta. The third row is the unsystematic risk of the portfolio.

The uncertainty associated with the portfolio return arises from the factor F in the second row of the above equation and from the unsystematic risk for each security in the third row. Diversification of a portfolio can eliminate the unsystematic risk, but not the systematic risk. Since the unsystematic risks are independent of each other, the larger the number of assets in the portfolio, the smaller the unsystematic risk. In a portfolio with a large number of assets, some assets will have idiosyncratic events that are beneficial while others will have events that are detrimental. For the portfolio, the unsystematic risk will be diversified away. Therefore, the return for a well-diversified portfolio is given by the first two rows of the above equation. The importance of this result is in the fact that the risk of a well-diversified portfolio does not depend on the unsystematic risks of the individual assets in that portfolio.

Betas and Expected Returns

We have noted that the riskiness of a well-diversified portfolio depends entirely on its systematic risk. Consequently, the unsystematic risk associated with a particular asset is not important to an investor with a diversified portfolio. Since the beta of a portfolio is a weighted average of the betas of the individual securities in that portfolio, it is the beta coefficient of an individual security that concerns a diversified investor.

A consequence of these observations is the fact that the expected return for a security depends only on its beta coefficient. Its unsystematic risk is irrelevant in the formulation of expected returns. Consider what would happen if an asset offered an extra return because of its unsystematic risk. Investors with diversified portfolios would seek to buy the asset because adding this asset to a diversified portfolio does not add unsystematic risk to the portfolio, but does provide extra return; therefore, investors would receive an extra return with no extra risk.

It will be useful to consider portfolios that consist of a risky asset and the risk-free asset. Let asset A be an individual security with beta equal to 1.2 and an expected return of 16%. Assume the risk-free rate (R_F) is 5%. Note that beta for the risk-free asset is zero. If x is the percentage of the portfolio invested in asset A, then (1 - x) is the percentage invested in the risk-free asset.

Given the information above, the expected return for a portfolio consisting of asset A and the risk-free asset is:

$$R_P = (x)(16\%) + (1 - x)(5\%)$$

Beta for this portfolio is:

$$\beta_P = (x)(1.2) + (1 - x)(0) = 1.2x$$

If we plot expected returns and beta (see Figure 10.1) for different values of x, we have a straight line through the expected return on A and the risk-free rate.

Assume that we have identified asset B, with beta equal to .6 and an expected return of 10%. Should we consider purchasing this asset? Consider a portfolio (P), comprised of A and the risk-free asset, with β_P equal to .6. Since the beta of this portfolio is 1.2x, x must be .5. The expected return for this portfolio is [(.5)(16%) + (.5)(5%)] = 10.5%. So, for the same risk, portfolio P has a greater expected return than does asset B, so that P is preferable to B. These results are illustrated in Figure 10.1.

Every investor who owned asset B would wish to sell it and to purchase portfolio P. This would lead to a decrease in the price of asset B and thus an increase in its expected return. Consequently, in equilibrium, asset B, and all assets, must fall directly on a straight line. This line is called the security market line (SML) and it is central to our understanding of risk and return. A security market line is drawn in Figure 10.2.

Expected Returns vs. Beta

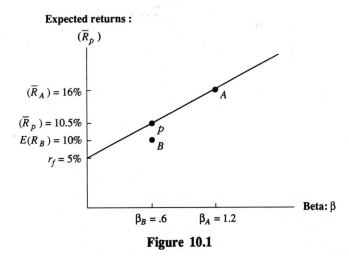

Figure 10.1

The market portfolio itself is an asset, so it too must plot on the security market line. In our single-factor model, beta measures the sensitivity of an asset's return to the unexpected return on the market portfolio. What then is the beta of the market portfolio? Clearly, the beta of the market portfolio must be exactly one. The beta of the market portfolio, β_M, and its expected return, R_M, are plotted on the SML in Figure 10.2.

The Security Market Line

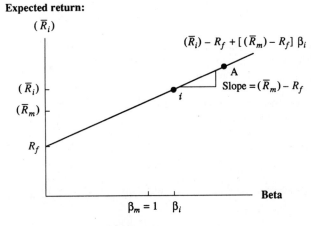

Figure 10.2

The equation of a straight line is $y = a + bx$, where a is the y-intercept and b is the slope. The dependent variable (i.e., the y variable) on the SML is expected return and the independent variable (i.e., the x variable) is beta. The y-intercept is the risk-free rate. The slope of the security market line is $[(R_M - R_F)/1] = (R_M - R_F)$. Since this slope is the excess return on the market over the risk-free rate, it is often called the market risk premium. The equation for the SML is thus:

$$R_F = \text{risk-free rate} \qquad\qquad R = R_F + \beta(R_M - R_F)$$

This result is identical to the CAPM, and it indicates the expected return for any asset for a given level of systematic risk.

The Capital Asset Pricing Model and the Arbitrage Pricing Theory

With k factors, the arbitrage pricing theory specifying the relationship between expected return and risk can be written as:

$$R = R_F + (R_1 - R_F)\beta_1 + (R_2 - R_F)\beta_2 + \ldots + (R_K - R_F)\beta_K$$

Notice that the only change from the SML specified in the previous section is that here we have multiple beta coefficients and multiple risk premiums. Each of the factors represents a systematic risk which is not diversified away, even for large portfolios. Since these risks are not diversifiable, the expected return for a security compensates for these risks; the greater the systematic risk, as indicated by the value of β, the higher the expected return for the security.

The primary advantage of the CAPM is that it has a single, explicitly defined factor. The primary advantage of the APT is that it allows for multiple sources of systematic risk. However, the primary disadvantage of the APT is that the appropriate factors are not specified.

CONCEPT TEST

1. The actual return for a risky security has two parts: the _____ return and the _____ return.

2. Security prices sometimes change following announcements, while other times, they do not. This is because an announcement has two parts: the _____ component and the _____ component.

3. Of the two components described in Question 2, security prices react only to the _____ component.

4. A new discovery that affects only a single company, or a small group of companies, is an example of an _____ or an _____ risk.

5. Risks that affect all companies to some degree are called _____ or _____ risks.

6. The covariance between the unsystematic risks of two companies is, by definition, equal to _____.

7. A _____ indicates the response of a stock's return to a systematic risk.

8. Security returns are often written as:

$$R = \bar{R} + \beta_1(F_1) + \beta_2(F_2) + ... + \beta_k(F_k) + \varepsilon$$

This model is called a _____.

9. If security returns are written as:

$$R = \bar{R} + \beta_{GNP}(F_{GNP}) + \beta_I(F_I) + \varepsilon$$

then F_{GNP} is the _____.

10. If security returns are written as:

$$R = \bar{R} + \beta_{GNP}(F_{GNP}) + \beta_I(F_I) + \varepsilon$$

then the expected value of F_{GNP} is _____.

11. If security returns are written as:

$$R = \bar{R} + \beta_{GNP}(F_{GNP}) + \beta_I(F_I) + \varepsilon$$

then ε is the _____.

12. A factor model which has an index such as the S&P 500 as the only factor is often called a _____.

13. Individual securities have both unsystematic and systematic risk. In a large, well-diversified portfolio, the _____ risks are diversified away.

14. The riskiness of a large, well-diversified portfolio depends on only its _____.

15. The total return for a security has three components: the _____, the _____, and the _____.

16. Expected return depends only on _____.

17. For the market model, the line that relates expected returns to betas for the single factor is called the _____.

18 Suppose that, for a market model, the expected market return is 14% and the risk-free rate is 5%. What is the return for an asset with a beta of 2?

19. For the model described in Question 18, what is the expected return for an asset with a beta of 0? An asset with a beta of 1?

20. For all practical purposes, the CAPM is indistinguishable from the _____.

ANSWERS TO CONCEPT TEST

1. expected; unexpected or surprise
2. expected; unexpected
3. unexpected
4. unsystematic; idiosyncratic
5. systematic; market
6. zero
7. beta coefficient
8. k-factor model
9. unexpected change in GNP
10. zero
11. unsystematic return

12. market model
13. unsystematic
14. beta coefficient(s)
15. expected return; systematic return; unsystematic return
16. systematic risk
17. security market line (SML)
18. 23%
19. 5%; 14%
20. one-factor APT

PROBLEMS AND SOLUTIONS

Use the information below to solve Problems 1-3.

Suppose a three-factor model is appropriate to describe the returns for a stock. The relevant data regarding these factors are presented here:

Factor	Beta of factor	Expected value	Actual value
Inflation	−1.0	7%	8.5%
Change in interest rates	−0.5	2%	−1.0%
Change in GNP	2.0	3%	4.5%
Stock return		12%	

Problem 1

What is the effect of the systematic risk on the stock return?

Solution 1

The effect of the systematic risk (m) on the stock return is given by:

$$m = \beta_I(F_I) + \beta_r(F_r) + \beta_{GNP}(F_{GNP})$$

where the subscripts I, r and GNP refer to inflation, interest rates and GNP, respectively.

The value of m is:

$$[(-1)(.085 - .07)] + [(-.5)(-.01 - .02)] + [(2)(.045 - .03)]$$

which is equal to .03.

Problem 2

Suppose that an unanticipated development contributes 3.5% to the return for the stock. What is the total effect of risk on the return for the stock?

Solution 2

The unanticipated surprise represents an unsystematic risk. Therefore, $\varepsilon = 5\%$ and the total effect of risk is:

$$m + \varepsilon = .03 + .05 = .08 = 8\%$$

where m is calculated in Problem 1.

Problem 3

What is the total return for the stock?

Solution 3

Total return is expected return plus the risky portion of the return, as calculated in Problem 2:

$$R = .12 + .03 + .05 = .17$$

Use the information below to solve Problems 4-6.

You are working with a two-factor model that is based on the growth rate in GNP and interest rates. For Ketcher Corporation, a major producer of zucchini, the GNP beta is 2 and the interest rate beta is .65. The expected return on Ketcher stock is 16%, the expected growth in GNP is 2%, and interest rates are expected to be 8%. One year later, GNP growth turns out to have been 4% and interest rates, 7%. Also, the company experienced a 3% increase in share value as the result of a patented cost-saving technology.

Problem 4

What is the effect of the systematic risk on the return for Ketcher stock?

Solution 4

The effect of the systematic risk (m) is given by:

$$(2)(.04 - .02) + (.65)(.07 - .08) = .0335 = 3.35\%$$

Problem 5

What is the total effect of risk on the return for Ketcher stock?

Solution 5

The total effect of risk is:

$$m + \varepsilon = .0335 + .03 = .0665 = 6.65\%$$

Problem 6

What is the actual return on the Ketcher stock?

Solution 6

The actual return is R = .16 + .0335 + .03 = .2235 = 22.35%.

Use the information below to solve Problems 7-10.

Assume the one-factor market model and the following information for Stocks X, Y and Z, and the market portfolio:

	Expected return	Beta
Stock A	9.5%	0.90
Stock B	13.0%	1.15
Stock C	11.0%	1.20
Market	12.0%	1.00

Problem 7

Write the market model equation for each stock.

Solution 7

For Stock A, the market model equation is:

$$R_A = .095 + [.90(R_M - .12)] + \varepsilon_A$$

The market model equations for B and C, respectively, are:

$$R_B = .130 + [1.15(R_M - .12)] + \varepsilon_B$$

$$R_C = .110 + [1.20(R_M - .12)] + \varepsilon_C$$

Problem 8

Write the market model equation for a portfolio with the following proportions: $X_A = .20$, $X_B = .30$, and $X_C = .50$.

Solution 8

Portfolio returns can be written as:

$$R_P = X_A[R_A + \beta_A(R_M - .12) + \varepsilon_A]$$

$$+ X_B[R_B + \beta_B(R_M - .12) + \varepsilon_B] + X_C[R_C + \beta_C(R_M - .12) + \varepsilon_C]$$

$$= (.20)[.095 + (.90)(R_M - .12) + \varepsilon_A] +$$

$$(.30)[.130 + (1.15)(R_M - .12) + \varepsilon_B] +$$

$$(.50)[.110 + (1.20)(R_M - .12) + \varepsilon_C]$$

Rearranging these terms, we can express the return on the portfolio as follows:

$$R_P = X_A R_A + X_B R_B + X_C R_C +$$

$$(X_A \beta_A + X_B \beta_B + X_C \beta_C)(R_M - .12) +$$

$$X_A \varepsilon_A + X_B \varepsilon_B + X_C \varepsilon_C$$

$$= (.20)(.095) + (.30)(.130) + (.50)(.110) +$$

$$[(.20)(.90) + (.30)(1.15) + (.50)(1.20)](R_M - .12) +$$

$$(.20)\varepsilon_A + (.30)\varepsilon_B + (.50)\varepsilon_C$$

$$= .113 + 1.125(R_M - .12) + (.20)\varepsilon_A + (.30)\varepsilon_B + (.50)\varepsilon_C$$

In this last expression, .113 is the expected return for the portfolio and 1.125 is the beta for the portfolio. Each of these portfolio characteristics is a weighted average of the corresponding characteristics for the individual securities.

Problem 9

Suppose the actual return for the market is 11% and there are no unsystematic surprises in the returns for each stock. Calculate the return for each stock.

Solution 9

The return for Stock A is:

$$R_A = .095 + [.90(R_M - .12)] + \varepsilon_A$$

$$= .095 + [.90(.11 - .12)] + 0 = .086 = 8.60\%$$

The return for Stock B is:

$$R_B = .130 + [1.15(.11 - .12)] + 0 = .1185 = 11.85\%$$

The return for Stock C is:

$$R_C = .110 + [1.20(.11 - .12] + 0 = .098 = 9.8\%$$

Problem 10

Given the information in Problem 9, calculate the return for the portfolio described in Problem 8.

Solution 10

The return for the portfolio can be determined as follows:

$$R_P = .113 + 1.125(R_M - .12) + (.20)\varepsilon_A + (.30)\varepsilon_B + (.50)\varepsilon_C$$

$$= .113 + (1.125)(.11 - .12) + 0 = .10175 = 10.175\%$$

Note that this result is equal to the weighted average of the security returns from Problem 9:

$$(.20)(.086) + (.30)(.1185) + (.50)(.098) = .10175$$

Problem 11

Consider the following two models:

$$R_A = E(R_A) + \beta_A(F_M) + \varepsilon_A$$

$$R_A = \alpha_A + \beta_A(R_M) + \varepsilon_A$$

where R_M is the total return (expected plus unexpected) on a market index, F_M is the unexpected return on the same index, and α_A is a constant. Both of these equations are referred to as market models. What is α_A if the two models are equivalent?

Solution 11

The unexpected return on the market index is the actual return, R_M minus the expected return, $E(R_M)$. If we substitute $[R_M - E(R_M)]$ for F_M, we get:

$$R_A = E(R_A) + \beta_A[R_M - E(R_M)] + \varepsilon_A$$

$$= E(R_A) + \beta_A(R_M) - \beta_A[E(R_M)] + \varepsilon_A$$

$$= [E(R_A) - \beta_A E(R_M)] + \beta_A(R_M) + \varepsilon_A$$

Thus α_A must be equal to $[E(R_A) - \beta_A E(R_M)]$, which is a constant.

CHAPTER HIGHLIGHTS

In earlier chapters, we have discussed in detail the application of the net present value criterion to capital budgeting problems under the assumption that cash flows are known with certainty. Now that we have established the basics of risk measurement, and examined the relationship between risk and return, we can apply these concepts to the evaluation of capital budgeting problems with risky cash flows.

In general, a firm with extra cash available has two alternatives: pay the cash to stockholders in the form of dividends; or, invest in a project now, paying out future cash flows as dividends. Assume that stockholders can reinvest dividends received in a financial asset with risk comparable to that of a capital budgeting project under consideration by the firm; then the project should be undertaken only if its expected return exceeds that of the comparable-risk financial asset. Therefore, the appropriate discount rate for capital budgeting projects with risky cash flows is the expected return for financial assets, typically common stock, with risk level comparable to that of the project under consideration.

The Beta of a Stock

We argued in Chapter 9 that the relevant risk for a financial asset is its beta value. In addition, we noted that beta for a security is equal to the slope of the characteristic line relating the security's expected return with that of the market. For practical applications, beta is determined using the statistical technique called **regression analysis**. Since not all points relating expected return for a security with expected return for the market fall on a straight line, regression analysis is required in order to determine the slope of the so-called **line of best fit** for any given stock.

The relevant beta for our purposes is the beta a stock will have in the future. However, historical data must be used for regression analysis; the resulting beta is an estimate, based on past data, of the value of beta in the future. Typically, financial economists use five years of monthly data in estimating beta.

Beta values are often determined using computer programs and, in some cases, statistical-function calculators. These procedures also provide values of a statistic called R^2, which measures the proportion of a stock's total risk that is systematic risk. R^2 values vary from zero to one. A value of zero indicates that none of a stock's risk is systematic (i.e., all of the risk is nonsystematic), whereas a value of one means that all of the stock's risk is systematic. Although the value of R^2 is often significant for other statistical applications of regression analysis, our discussion of risk demonstrates that only systematic risk is relevant for financial decisions; consequently, we are concerned only with beta, the measure of systematic risk for a security, not with R^2.

The Actual Calculation

Beta is equal to the covariance of a security with the market, divided by the variance of the market. For a particular security i, the beta value (β_i) is given by:

$$\beta_i = \frac{Cov(R_i, R_M)}{Var(R_M)} = \frac{\sigma_{i,M}}{\sigma_M^2}$$

(handwritten: $\beta = \frac{.00978}{.01088} = .8989$)

Recall that, in Chapter 8, we discussed the calculation of covariance and variance using data for General Motors stock and the S&P 500 index. We repeat the data here:

State	Returns		Deviations			Product of
	GM	S&P 500	GM	S&P 500	(S&P)	the Deviations
1	.10	.12	.04	.05	.0025	.0020
2	.04	.06	−.02	−.01	.0001	.0002
3	−.09	−.10	−.15	−.17	.0289	.0255
4	.20	.22	.14	.15	.0225	.0210
5	.05	.05	−.01	−.02	.0004	.0002
Totals	.30	.35	.00	.00	.0544	.0489

(handwritten above table: −.06, −.07; below: ÷5 = .06, ÷5 = .07, ÷5 = .01088, ÷5 = .00978 covariance)

In order to compute the covariance, we first compute the respective means for each of two assets, in this case, GM common stock and the S&P 500. The average return for GM is (.30/5) = .06 = 6% and for the S&P 500, (.35/5) = .07 = 7%. Next, we determine, for each asset, the deviation of each possible rate of return from the asset's mean return, as indicated in the above table. We then compute the product of the respective deviations, total the product of the deviations, and compute the average of the product of the deviations by dividing by T, the number of observations. [Note that it is not necessary here to actually compute the covariance by dividing by T. In other words, we could use the total of the product of the deviations (.0489) in the numerator of our beta calculation, as long as we also use the product of the squared deviations for the market, rather than the variance, in the denominator.] The covariance is: $\sigma_{GM,M}$ = (.0489/5) = .00978. In Chapter 8, we determined that the sum of the squared deviations for the S&P 500 is:

(handwritten left margin: $\frac{.0489}{.0544}$)

$$(.0025 + .0001 + .0289 + .0225 + .0004) = .0544$$

and the variance is: σ_M^2 = (.0544/5) = .01088. Therefore, the value of beta is: β_{GM} = (.00978/.01088) = .8989. Alternatively, as noted above, beta can be calculated as (.0489/.0544) = .8989.

The Discount Rate

Assume that General Motors is evaluating a proposed capital budgeting project and that: (1) the beta risk of the new project is the same as for the firm as a whole; and, (2) the firm is financed entirely with equity. Under these assumptions, the appropriate discount rate for capital budgeting projects is the expected return indicated by the capital-asset-pricing model. Suppose that the risk-free rate is 6.5% and that the market risk-premium is 8.5%. Then the cost of equity capital is given by the CAPM as follows:

(handwritten: $Rm = 15\%$, $Rm - Rf = 8.5\%$)

$$\bar{R} = .065 + (.085)\beta_{GM} = .065 + (.085)(.8989) = 14.14\%$$

(handwritten: $Rf = 6.5\%$, $\beta = .8989$, $R = Rf + \beta(Rm - Rf)$)

Extensions to the Basic Model

Risk of

The Firm versus the Project. The procedure described in the previous section is based on the assumption that the project under consideration has the same risk as does the firm as a whole. If, however, this assumption is not consistent with reality, then the appropriate value for beta in the above calculation is the beta for the project, not the beta for the firm. For example, if General Motors were to consider a project in the chemical industry, the relevant beta is the beta for the chemical industry project. In addition, if the project involves development of a new product, the risk of the project may be higher than that for the chemical industry as a whole. Consequently, numerous difficulties may develop in attempting to determine the value of beta for any given project.

Levered Firms. It is clearly inappropriate to assume that a firm such as General Motors is financed entirely with equity; in fact, most firms are **levered firms**, which means that they are financed with both equity and debt. The existence of debt in a firm's capital structure increases the riskiness of the firm's common stock. A firm financed entirely with equity is said to be subject to **business risk**, while the stockholders of a levered firm are also subject to **financial risk**. Consequently, beta for the common stock of a levered firm is greater than beta for an otherwise identical unlevered firm. The two techniques for determining the discount rate for capital budgeting projects of a levered firm are discussed in a subsequent chapter.

Determinants of Beta

Three factors which determine beta are: revenues, operating leverage and financial leverage.

Revenues. The revenues of some firms are highly sensitive to the phases of the business cycle, while those of other firms are relatively independent of the business cycle. Highly cyclical stocks, such as stocks of high-tech and automotive firms, have high beta values. Firms in the utilities and food industries are less cyclical and, consequently, have lower betas.

Operating Leverage. Suppose that two firms produce the same product using different technology. Firm A uses technology which is labor intensive, so that fixed costs are relatively low and variable cost per unit is relatively high. In contrast, Firm B uses an automated technology which has a high fixed cost but a relatively low variable cost. The two firms sell an identical product for $100 per unit; variable costs are $70 and $60 per unit for Firms A and B, respectively. Therefore, the contribution margins are ($100 - $70) = $30 for Firm A and ($100 - $60) = $40 for Firm B. Firm B is said to have higher operating leverage because an additional unit of sales increases profit by $40; for Firm A, an additional unit of sales increases profit by $30. Similarly, profits decrease by $40 and $30, respectively, if sales decrease by one unit. Since Firm B's profits are more sensitive to changes in sales, Firm B would tend to have a higher value of beta.

Financial Leverage. Financial leverage is analogous to operating leverage in that interest payments on debt are regarded as fixed costs which increase the sensitivity of a firm's profits to changes in sales.

CONCEPT TEST

1. A firm with extra cash available has two alternatives: pay the cash to stockholders in the form of _____, or _____.

2. The appropriate discount rate for capital budgeting projects with risky cash flows is the
_____ for financial assets with risk level comparable to that of the project under
consideration.

3. _____ for a security is equal to the slope of the characteristic line relating the
security's expected return with that of the market.

4. Beta is determined using the statistical technique called _____.

5. Regression analysis is required in order to determine the slope of the so-called _____
for a given stock.

6. _____ data must be used for regression analysis; the resulting beta is an estimate,
based on past data, of the value of beta in the future.

7. The statistic _____ measures the proportion of a stock's total risk that is systematic
risk.

8. If the project's risk is different from that of the firm as a whole, the appropriate value for beta
is the beta for the _____, not the beta for the _____.

9. Beta is equal to the _____ of a security with the market, divided by the
_____ of the market.

10. If a company is developing a new product, the risk of the project will generally be
_____ than for the industry as a whole.

11. Firms that are financed with both equity and debt are termed _____.

12. The existence of debt in a firm's capital structure _____ the riskiness of the firm's
common stock.

13. A firm financed entirely with equity is said to be subject to _____, while the
stockholders of a levered firm are also subject to _____.

14. Beta for the common stock of a levered firm is _____ than beta for an otherwise
identical unlevered firm.

15. Three factors which determine beta are: _____, _____, and
_____.

16. Cyclical stocks have _____ beta values.

17. A firm with a high degree of operating leverage tends to have a _____ value of beta.

18. A firm with a high degree of financial leverage tends to have a _____ value of beta.

ANSWERS TO CONCEPT TEST

1. dividends; invest in a project
2. expected return
3. beta
4. regression analysis
5. line of best fit
6. historical
7. R^2
8. project; firm
9. covariance; variance
10. higher

11. levered firms
12. increases
13. business risk; financial risk
14. greater
15. revenues; operating leverage; financial leverage
16. high
17. high
18. high

PROBLEMS AND SOLUTIONS

Use the following information to solve Problems 1-5.

The returns for the TTK Corporation and the New York Stock Exchange Composite Index (NYSE) during the past five years are listed below:

Year	TTK	NYSE
1	.12	.06
2	.15	.14
3	.04	.07
4	-.05	.00
5	.09	.13

Problem 1

Calculate the average return and standard deviation for TTK and for the NYSE.

Solution 1

The required calculations are summarized in the table below:

Year	Returns TTK	Returns NYSE	Deviations TTK	Deviations NYSE	Squared deviations TTK	Squared deviations NYSE
1	.12	.06	.05	-.02	.0025	.0004
2	.15	.14	.08	.06	.0064	.0036
3	.04	.07	-.03	-.01	.0009	.0001
4	-.05	.00	-.12	-.08	.0144	.0064
5	.09	.13	.02	.05	.0004	.0025
Totals	.35	.40	.00	.00	.0246	.0130

The average returns for TTK and for the NYSE are $(.35/5) = .07 = 7\%$ and $(.40/5) = .08 = 8\%$, respectively. The variances are: $\sigma_{TTK}^2 = (.0246/5) = .00492$ and $\sigma_M^2 = (.0130/5) = .00260$. The standard deviations are: $\sigma_{TTK} = [(.00492)^{.5}] = .07014$ and $\sigma_M = [(.00260)^{.5}] = .05099$.

Problem 2

Calculate the value of $\sigma_{i,M}$, the covariance between the returns for TTK and the returns for the NYSE.

Solution 2

The required calculations are summarized in the following table:

Year	Returns		Deviations		Product of the Deviations
	TTK	NYSE	TTK	NYSE	
1	.12	.06	.05	-.02	-.0010
2	.15	.14	.08	.06	.0048
3	.04	.07	-.03	-.01	.0003
4	-.05	.00	-.12	-.08	.0096
5	.09	.13	.02	.05	.0010
Totals	.35	.40	.00	.00	.0147

The covariance between TTK and the NYSE is (.0147/5) = .00294.

Problem 3

Calculate the value of β for TTK.

Solution 3

β is equal to the covariance between returns for TTK and the returns for the market, divided by the variance of the market returns:

$$\beta_{TTK} = \frac{Cov(R_i,R_M)}{Var(R_M)} = \frac{\sigma_{i,M}}{\sigma_M^2} = \frac{.00294}{.00260} = 1.1308$$

Problem 4

The risk-free rate is 6% and the market risk-premium is 8.5%. Assume that TTK is an all-equity firm. What is the appropriate discount rate for new projects which have risk level equal to that of the firm?

Solution 4

The appropriate discount rate is determined from the capital-asset pricing model as follows:

$$\bar{R} = .06 + (.085)\beta_{TTK} = .06 + (.085)(1.1308) = 15.61\%$$

Problem 5

The value of R^2 is equal to the correlation squared. Calculate and interpret the value of R^2 for TTK.

Solution 5

The correlation is equal to the covariance divided by the product of the standard deviations:

$$[.00294/(.07014)(.05099)] = .82205$$

Therefore, R^2 is equal to $[(.82205)^2] = .67577$. This result indicates that 67.577% of the total risk of TTK stock is systematic risk and 32.423% is unsystematic risk.

Use the following information to solve Problems 6-10.

The possible rates of return for assets K and M for five possible states of the economy are listed in the table below, along with the probability (Pr) of occurrence:

State	Pr	K	M
1	.20	.01	.06
2	.20	.15	.14
3	.30	.26	.07
4	.20	.03	.00
5	.10	-.06	.13

Problem 6

Calculate the expected return for asset K. Calculate the expected return for asset M.

Solution 6

State of Economy	Probability of State (Pr)	Rate of Return of K (R_K)	(Pr) x (R_K)
1	.20	.01	.002
2	.20	.15	.030
3	.30	.26	.078
4	.20	.03	.006
5	.10	-.06	-.006
			.110

The expected return for K is 11%. The expected return for M is also 11%.

Problem 7

What is the standard deviation for asset K? For asset M?

Solution 7

State of Economy	Pr	R_K	$(R_K-\bar{R}_K)^2$	$(Pr) \times (R_K-\bar{R}_K)^2$
1	.20	.01	.01000	.00200
2	.20	.15	.00160	.00032
3	.30	.26	.02250	.00675
4	.20	.03	.00640	.00128
5	.10	-.06	.02890	.00289
	1.00			.01324

The variance for asset K is: $\sigma_K^2 = .01324$. The standard deviation is the square root of .01324: $\sigma_K = .11507 = 11.507\%$. The variance and standard deviation for asset M are: $\sigma_M^2 = .00456$ and $\sigma_M = .15748 = 15.748\%$.

Problem 8

What is the covariance between the returns for asset K and the returns for asset M?

Solution 8

State of Economy	Pr	$(R_K-\bar{R}_K)$	$(R_M-\bar{R}_M)$	$(Pr) \times (R_K-\bar{R}_K) \times (R_M-\bar{R}_M)$
1	.20	-.10	-.03	.000600
2	.20	.04	.01	.000080
3	.30	.15	.09	.004050
4	.20	-.08	-.06	.000960
5	.10	-.17	-.11	.001870
	1.00			.007560

The covariance between the returns for K and the returns for M is: $\sigma_{K,M} = .007560$.

Problem 9

Assume that M is the market portfolio. Calculate the value of β for asset K.

Solution 9

β_K is equal to $(\sigma_{K,M}/\sigma_M^2) = (.007560/.004560) = 1.6579$.

Problem 10

Assume that K is an all-equity firm. Use the information regarding the risk-free rate and the market risk-premium from Problem 4 to determine the appropriate discount rate for new projects which have risk level equal to that of the firm.

Solution 10

The appropriate discount rate is determined from the capital-asset pricing model as follows:

$$\overline{R} = .06 + (.085)\beta_K = .06 + (.085)(1.6579) = 20.09\%$$

Problem 11

Consider a firm which can use either Technology X or Technology Y when producing a particular product. The characteristics of the two technologies are indicated in the following table:

		Technology X	Technology Y
Fixed Cost	(per year)	$100,000	$150,000
Variable Cost	(per unit)	$180	$170
Selling Price	(per unit)	$200	$200

Technology X has lower fixed costs than Technology Y, but it has higher variable costs because X is more labor intensive while Y is more highly automated. Calculate the contribution margin for each technology.

Solution 11

The contribution margin is the difference between selling price and variable cost per unit. For Technology X, the contribution margin is ($200 - $180) = $20. For Technology Y, the contribution margin is $30.

Problem 12

Calculate Earnings before Interest and Taxes (EBIT) for each technology at sales levels of 4000 units, 5000 units, 6000 units, 10,000 units and 20,000 units. Interpret the results in terms of operating leverage and beta.

Solution 12

For sales equal to 4000 units, revenues are [(4000)($200)] = $800,000 for each technology. For Technology X, total variable costs are [(4000)($180)] = $720,000 and EBIT is equal to:

$$\$800,000 - \$100,000 - \$720,000 = -\$20,000$$

For Technology Y, EBIT is -$30,000 for sales of 4000 units. At sales of 5000 units, EBIT is zero for each technology. The remaining results are summarized in the table below:

Sales (units)	EBIT Technology X	EBIT Technology Y
4000	($ 20,000)	($ 30,000)
5000	$ 0	$ 0
6000	$ 20,000	$ 30,000
10000	$100,000	$150,000
20000	$300,000	$450,000

Note that the technology with the higher contribution margin (i.e., Technology Y) has the larger changes in EBIT for a given change in sales. As a result, for Technology Y, EBIT increases more quickly as sales increase. In other words, operating leverage is greater for Technology Y than for Technology X. We would expect that the beta value for Technology Y would be greater than for Technology X. (Note that a firm choosing between these two technologies would not have a very difficult choice to make since Technology Y provides greater profitability for all sales levels above the break-even level of 5000 units.)

Problem 13

Suppose that Technology Y in Problem 12 had fixed costs of $200,000. Calculate EBIT for Technology Y at the sales levels indicated in Problem 12. Interpret the results in terms of operating leverage and beta.

Solution 13

EBIT is now $50,000 lower at each sales level for Technology Y. The results are summarized below:

Sales (units)	EBIT Technology X	EBIT Technology Y
4000	($ 20,000)	($ 80,000)
5000	$ 0	($ 50,000)
6000	$ 20,000	($ 20,000)
10000	$100,000	$100,000
20000	$300,000	$400,000

The conclusions regarding operating leverage and beta are essentially the same as described in Problem 12. That is, Technology Y still has the higher operating leverage because EBIT increases more quickly for any given increase in sales. In addition, we would still expect that Technology Y has the higher beta value. However, the choice between the two technologies is not as clear as in the previous problem. For sales levels below 10,000 units, Technology X has the higher level of EBIT; at sales levels above 10,000 units, Technology Y has the higher EBIT because the larger contribution margin has compensated for the higher fixed costs at these sales levels.

CHAPTER 12
CORPORATE FINANCING DECISIONS AND
EFFICIENT CAPITAL MARKETS

CHAPTER HIGHLIGHTS

To this point, we have focused our attention primarily on the question of which fixed assets a firm should purchase. This chapter and the next several chapters concern the second of the three main issues of corporate finance: what is the best way for the firm to finance the purchase of fixed assets? This is the capital structure question. Since the concept of efficient capital markets has important implications for the capital structure decision, the chapter begins with a discussion of market efficiency.

Can Financing Decisions Create Value?

When a firm identifies investment opportunities with positive net present value, it must also make several related financing decisions. First, how much debt and equity should be sold? (That is, how much financing should be obtained?) Second, what types of debt and equity securities should be issued? Finally, when should securities be issued? The appropriate criterion for making these financing decisions is the same as that for investment decisions: add value by identifying opportunities with positive net present value. However, such opportunities are likely to be quite rare for corporate financing decisions.

Financing opportunities with positive NPV are difficult to find because the financial markets in the United States have very low trading costs, and many buyers and sellers, all of whom have ready access to relevant information. These characteristics imply that it is difficult for a firm to create financial assets that are worth more to an investor than they cost the firm. In such a market, all transactions have exactly zero NPV; that is, assets are worth exactly what they cost.

Although the number of valuable financing opportunities is limited, those which do exist appear to fall in to three general categories. First, management might try to 'fool' investors into purchasing a security for a price which exceeds its value. An example of such an approach would be the issuing of a complex security which investors might mistakenly overvalue. The efficient markets hypothesis described below would lead one to conclude that such a strategy is unlikely to succeed, however.

The second approach to creating valuable financing opportunities is to reduce costs or increase subsidies available to the firm. For example, one form of financing might have a cost advantage over another, in terms of its effect on taxes or the costs of issuing the securities. Transactions of this kind may have value for the firm, even in an efficient market.

The third possibility is the creation of a new security which meets the needs of certain investors. These investors might then be willing to pay a price for the security which is greater than its value, or cost to the firm.

A Description of Efficient Capital Markets

An **efficient capital market** is a market in which all transactions have net present value equal to zero. Alternatively, it can be said that the price of any asset is always equal to its present value, so that the rate of return for an investment is equal to the equilibrium rate of return for a given level of risk. All that is required for a market to be efficient is that current market prices reflect available information. If a market is efficient with respect to some piece of information, then that piece of information can not be used to find a positive NPV investment.

The **efficient markets hypothesis** (EMH) asserts that prices for assets in U.S. capital markets are efficient with respect to available information. The hypothesis implies that no investment strategy based on current or historical information produces extraordinarily large profits. With thousands of investment advisory services, mountains of information, and millions of investors (all of whom have the same goals), the adjustment of prices to new information is almost instantaneous.

There are two important implications of market efficiency for investors and firms. First, investors buying stocks and bonds should expect to earn an equilibrium rate of return. Second, firms issuing securities should expect to receive from investors a price equal to the present value of the securities.

The Different Types of Efficiency

Financial economists generally identify three forms of market efficiency, based on the kinds of information which might be expected to influence stock prices.

The Weak-form. A market satisfies **weak-form efficiency** if current security prices completely incorporate the information contained in past prices. This means that it is pointless to analyze past prices in an attempt to find 'patterns' that would enable us to predict future prices. Such an evaluation procedure is called **technical analysis** (or 'charting'). Weak-form efficiency implies that technical analysis can not be used successfully to forecast future prices and therefore that technical analysts do not earn extraordinary profits. There is a great deal of evidence indicating that financial markets are weak-form efficient. Furthermore, economic analysis suggests that even if patterns in past stock prices could be used to forecast future prices, the resulting success of technical analysis would immediately eliminate the patterns, thus rendering technical analysis useless. There are, of course, those who would argue otherwise.

The Semistrong And Strong Forms. A market is said to be **semistrong-form efficient** if current prices incorporate all **publicly** available information. Semistrong-form efficiency implies that the analysis of published financial statements, for example, as a technique for making common stock investment decisions, does not result in earning excess profits. Notice that a semistrong efficient market is also weak-form efficient since past prices are a form of publicly available information.

At the extreme, a market is **strong-form efficient** if current prices reflect **all** information, including **inside information**; inside information is information about a firm which is available only to 'insiders,' including corporate executives and major stockholders. There seems to be little reason to believe that markets are strong-form efficient; that is, available evidence seems to indicate that valuable inside information does exist. At the other extreme, there are compelling reasons for believing that markets are weak-form efficient. There is a great deal of debate, however, over semistrong-form efficiency. A reasonable compromise view might be summarized as follows: some prices, some of the time, might not reflect all publicly available information, but most assets, most of the time, do reflect this information.

Some Common Misconceptions About the Efficient Markets Hypothesis. Two objections to the efficient markets hypothesis are frequently raised. The first of these is based on the observation that security prices fluctuate every day. However, this observation is not inconsistent with market efficiency. On the contrary, since new information arrives every day, the efficient markets hypothesis predicts that prices adjust rapidly to the new information. The second criticism is based on the argument that the market cannot be efficient because only a fraction of the outstanding shares change hands every day. Once again, however, this result is actually consistent with the hypothesis. Investors trade only when they expect to benefit from doing so. In a market with transaction costs, such as brokerage fees, there is little incentive for trades to take place if securities are correctly valued.

The efficient market hypothesis does not suggest that the determinants of price changes are unknown. Prices depend on expected future cash flows. It is the expectations of these future cash flows that change when new information arrives. The hypothesis also does not imply that we should select stocks randomly. The result could be an undiversified portfolio of securities with an undesirable level of risk. Finally, the EMH does not imply that investors are uninformed. To the contrary, the hypothesis is based on the assumption that investors are quite rational, and are not easily fooled or manipulated.

The Evidence

There is extensive evidence relating to market efficiency, and, to a great extent, it is supportive of the efficient markets hypothesis. There are three broad classes of studies: studies which have investigated whether stock price changes are random, event studies, and studies based on the performance of professionally managed portfolios.

The Weak Form. A stock price is said to follow a **random walk** if day-to-day price changes are independent of each other: that is, tomorrow's price change cannot be predicted from today's price change, because both are random changes resulting from the arrival of new information. A series of coin tosses is a random walk in that the probability of a head or tail is always the same, and the outcome of the next toss is independent of the outcomes in previous tosses. If a market follows a random walk, then it is also weak-form efficient.

Financial economists evaluate the random walk hypothesis by calculating the coefficient of **serial correlation** for common stock prices. The serial correlation coefficient indicates whether the price change in a security on a given day is related to the price change on a subsequent day. A positive coefficient of serial correlation indicates that an above average return today is likely to be followed by an above average return in the future, and that a below average return is likely to be followed by a below average return. A negative serial correlation indicates that an above average return is likely to be followed by a below average return, and vice versa. A zero correlation implies no relationship between price changes on successive days, and is consistent with the random walk hypothesis and the efficient markets hypothesis. As noted in Chapter 8, correlations range from -1 to +1. Data for numerous stock markets have shown serial correlation coefficients very close to zero. These and other studies of weak-form efficiency are generally consistent with the conclusion that it is not possible to forecast future prices from data about past prices. This evidence is consistent with a random walk in stock prices and with weak-form efficiency.

The Semistrong Form. The efficient markets hypothesis implies that stock prices react quickly to new information. An **event study** examines the reaction of stock prices when specific new information becomes available. Event studies have been used to evaluate the semistrong-form of the efficient markets hypothesis.

The **abnormal return** for a given stock on a given day, is the difference between the stock's return and the market's return on that date. The **cumulative abnormal return** is the sum of abnormal returns over some period of time. Event studies are statistical investigations of abnormal returns designed to test whether a stock's price reacts in the manner suggested by the efficient markets hypothesis, namely, an immediate adjustment to any new information and no significant subsequent reaction. Events which have been analyzed using this procedure include announcements of stock splits, stock dividends, mergers and new common stock issues. In general, the results of these studies are consistent with the semistrong-form of the efficient markets hypothesis. That is, positive abnormal returns are observed around the time of the announcement of the event, but cumulative abnormal returns show no further tendency to increase subsequent to the announcement.

The track record of professional money managers has been extensively examined as a test of the semistrong-form of the efficient markets hypothesis. Since mutual fund portfolio managers have access to any publicly available information, then their performance, in comparison to the average performance of the market, can be considered a valid test of the hypothesis. The conclusions of those who have analyzed the record of mutual fund managers are generally consistent with the hypothesis that securities markets are semistrong-form efficient; that is, these managers do not outperform the market.

Not all the available evidence supports the EMH. Some have argued that the kinds of tests that have been performed are not sufficiently sophisticated to detect inefficiencies. Furthermore, there is evidence that the volatility of stock prices exceeds that which can be explained by information arrival. Some studies have shown that stock prices display definite calendar-related, or 'seasonal,' patterns. These inefficiencies are frequently small, but their existence casts some doubt on the conclusions noted earlier. In addition, the stock market crash of October 19, 1987 is inconsistent with the EMH.

The Strong Form. Since insiders have access to information which is not available to the general public, examination of the profits earned by insiders on their common stock investments is considered a test of the strong form of the EMH. Insiders are required to report their trading activities to the SEC; analysis of these reports has suggested that insiders earn abnormal profits, contrary to the hypothesis of strong-form efficiency.

Implications for Corporate Finance

Three important implications for financial managers are derived from the efficient markets hypothesis. These concern accounting information, the timing of stock and bond issues, and the amount of financing that can be raised.

Accounting and Efficient Markets. The efficient markets hypothesis implies that accounting information affects stock price only if it reveals new information about the firm's future cash flows. The available evidence suggests that earnings announcements convey new information and that the market adjusts quickly and correctly to that information.

Because the market reacts to earnings announcements, it might be thought that firms could increase earnings artificially and thus 'fool' the market. However, the evidence on this issue seems relatively clear: changes in accounting procedures which increase reported earnings, without affecting cash flows, do not affect stock prices. It appears that attempts to 'cook the books' are largely unsuccessful.

Timing of Issuance of Financing. Year-to-year variation occurs in the amount of financing obtained by corporations. Some evidence suggests that financial managers attempt to 'time' issues by selling new common stock when the market price of outstanding shares is high, and by issuing bonds when interest rates are low. In an efficient market, however, it is impossible for the firm to benefit from these attempts to time new issues.

Financial managers may have inside information which could affect stock price and, in this case, they might sell stock when they perceive that it is overvalued or delay an issue if it is undervalued. This situation is inconsistent with strong-form efficiency, but not with semistrong-form efficiency.

Price Pressure Effects. How large a block of stock can a firm sell without depressing the price of the stock? When a large amount of stock is offered for sale at once, the supply is temporarily increased, thus putting downward pressure on the stock price. Some studies have found that price pressure does not exist, while others have found an effect which is generally small and short-lived (measured in minutes). This latter result may be significant for a firm which is issuing new securities.

CONCEPT TEST

1. A market in which prices reflect available information is called an _____

2. In an efficient market, all sales or purchases of assets are _____ transactions.

3. The _____ asserts that the prices of widely traded stocks and bonds reflect their true values.

4. If the past history of stock prices is not useful in earning abnormal returns, then the market is at least _____ efficient.

5. If publicly available information is not useful in earning abnormal returns, then the market is at least _____ efficient.

6. If no information of any kind is useful in earning abnormal returns, then the market is _____ efficient.

7. Stock price changes have very low serial correlations. This fact is consistent with the _____ form of the efficient markets hypothesis.

8. Professional money managers, as a group, cannot outperform market indexes. This fact is consistent with the _____ form of the efficient markets hypothesis.

9. The difference between a security's actual return in a given period and the return on a market index is called the _____ for that period.

10. The _____ is the sum of the abnormal returns over a given period of time.

11. In the absence of any new information, the cumulative abnormal return for a stock should be _____.

12. If stock price changes are independent and come from the same probability distribution, then stock price changes are said to follow a _____.

13. Does the efficient markets hypothesis imply that stock prices are random?

14. Does the efficient markets hypothesis suggest that all stocks have the same expected return?

15. Does the efficient markets hypothesis imply that stock prices do not have an upward trend?

16. If you are a firm believer in the EMH, should you select your stock portfolio by throwing darts at the Wall Street Journal stock listings?

17. Investors who examine the past history of stock prices in order to identify patterns are called _____ or _____.

18. An examination of the behavior of security returns following an announcement of new information is called an _____.

19. If financial managers have private information about the value of their stock, then they may try to sell stock when it is _____. As a result, announcements of new stock sales may lead to stock price _____.

For Questions 20 through 24, answer using one of the responses A through D below. In evaluating the hypothetical scenarios, pay particular attention to the word 'necessary' in response D.

A. Strong-form efficiency is violated.
B. Semistrong-form and strong-form efficiency are violated.
C. All forms are violated.
D. There is no **necessary** violation of any form.

20. You look up insider trading activities in SEC publications at your local law library. You are consistently able to beat the market by basing your trades on this information.

21. The Panzai mutual fund has outperformed the market for five consecutive years.

22. Your uncle Joe got extremely rich in a short period of time buying stocks based on his charting of their historical price movements and buying whenever the pattern looked like Richard Nixon's nose.

23. Whenever a stock reaches a 52-week high, its subsequent performance is abnormally poor.

24. A finance professor can predict with greater than 60% accuracy whether the market will be up or down in a given month.

ANSWERS TO CONCEPT TEST

1. efficient market
2. zero NPV
3. efficient markets hypothesis
4. weak-form
5. semistrong-form
6. strong-form
7. weak
8. semistrong
9. abnormal return
10. cumulative abnormal return
11. zero
12. random walk
13. no

14. no
15. no
16. no
17. technical analysts; chartists
18. event study
19. overvalued; decreases
20. B; it's public information
21. D; after the fact,
    some funds will have done this
22. D; some will get rich
    in spite of themselves
23. C
24. D

PROBLEMS AND SOLUTIONS

Use the following information to solve Problems 1-3:

The Gallowglass Company common stock has a daily standard deviation of return of 80 basis points (.80%). The expected return on the market is 2 basis points (.02%) per day. On a particular day, designated day 0, Gallowglass announced a major new product.

You have been asked to perform an event study. An abnormal return (AR) is considered statistically significant if it is larger than 2 standard deviations [2(.80%) = 1.60%] in absolute value.

Problem 1

The returns on Gallowglass around the announcement are shown below. Interpret the results in terms of the market's opinion of the new product. Are the observed returns consistent with market efficiency?

Day relative to announcement	Actual return
-3	1.1%
-2	.5
-1	-.6
0	3.0
1	1.0
2	-.8
3	-.4

Solution 1

The abnormal returns are calculated as the actual returns minus the expected market return:

Day relative to announcement	Actual return	Abnormal return
-3	1.1%	1.08%
-2	.5	.48
-1	-.6	-.62
0	3.0	2.98
1	1.0	.98
2	-.8	-.82
3	-.4	-.42

Inspecting the abnormal returns, we see that only the AR on day 0 is significant. This result is consistent with market efficiency because the price adjusts quickly to the new information. Apparently, the market views the new product as a good investment because the price increased significantly following the announcement.

Problem 2

A different set of returns is shown below. Answer the question posed in Problem 1 based on these returns.

Day relative to announcement	Actual return
-3	1.1%
-2	.5
-1	2.0
0	3.0
1	1.0
2	-.8
3	-.4

Solution 2

The abnormal returns are:

Day relative to announcement	Actual return	Abnormal return
-3	1.1%	1.08%
-2	.5	.48
-1	2.0	1.98
0	3.0	2.98
1	1.0	.98
2	-.8	-.82
3	-.4	-.42

In this case, the abnormal return on day -1 is significant. This suggests that the information was 'leaked.' If the information was not public knowledge until day 0, then this result is not inconsistent with semistrong-form efficiency. However, since the abnormal return is positive for day 0, strong-form efficiency appears to have been violated. If the market were strong-form efficient, all of the adjustment should occur on day -1.

Problem 3

A third set of returns is given below. Answer the question posed in Problem 1 based on these returns.

Day relative to announcement	Actual return
-3	1.1%
-2	.5
-1	-.6
0	-3.0
1	-2.0
2	-3.8
3	-2.4

Solution 3

The abnormal returns are:

Day relative to announcement	Actual return	Abnormal return
-3	1.1%	1.08%
-2	.5	.48
-1	-.6	-.62
0	-3.0	-3.02
1	-2.0	-2.02
2	-3.8	-3.82
3	-2.4	-2.42

The market's reaction is significantly negative. In addition, the negative abnormal returns are significant for the three days following the announcement. This suggests that semistrong-form efficiency is violated.

CHAPTER 13
LONG-TERM FINANCING: AN INTRODUCTION

CHAPTER HIGHLIGHTS

This chapter describes the characteristics of the basic sources of long-term financing: common stock, preferred stock and long-term debt.

Common Stock

Owners of corporate common stock are called **stockholders** or **shareholders**. They receive stock certificates representing ownership of the shares. Some of the basic features of common stock are discussed below.

Par and No-Par Stock. Shares of stock often have a **par value**, which is typically low relative to the market value of the share. **No-par** stock does not have a par value. The par value per share multiplied by the number of shares issued is called the **dedicated capital**. The par value of a share is an accounting concept which is generally not significant for financial decision-making.

Authorized versus Issued Common Stock. A corporation's articles of incorporation state the maximum number of shares the corporation is authorized to issue. The number of authorized shares can be increased by the board of directors, following a vote of the shareholders. Once shares are authorized, the board of directors can issue the stock at any time without further shareholder approval. There is no legal limit to the number of shares that can be authorized, but some states impose taxes based on the number of authorized shares.

Capital Surplus. The difference between the equity contributed directly to the corporation by the stockholders and the dedicated capital is called the **capital surplus**. If a corporation sells 1000 shares of $1 par value stock for $20 per share, the dedicated capital is $1000 and the capital surplus is $19,000. The dedicated capital cannot be distributed to shareholders, except in the event of the liquidation of the corporation.

Retained Earnings. In any given year, the portion of net income that is not paid as dividends to the shareholders is retained in the business, and is referred to as **retained earnings**. The dedicated capital, capital surplus, and cumulative retained earnings (since initial incorporation) comprise the **common equity** or **book value** of the corporation. The book value is the total amount of financing contributed to the corporation by the stockholders.

Market Value, Book Value, And Replacement Value. The book value per share is total book value divided by the number of shares outstanding. The number of shares outstanding is equal to the number of shares issued less the number repurchased by the corporation. Repurchased stock is called **treasury stock**. If a stock is publicly traded, its market value is generally different from its book value. **Replacement value** is the cost of replacing the existing assets of the firm, at current market prices.

<u>Shareholders' Rights</u>.   Shareholders control the corporation by electing directors who then elect management.   Directors are elected each year at the annual shareholders meeting.   The voting mechanism is either **straight voting** or **cumulative voting**.

With straight voting, each share entitles the shareholder to one vote and each director is elected separately.   For example, if four directors are to be elected and you own 100 shares, you cast 100 votes in each of the four elections.   With cumulative voting, the directors are elected simultaneously and the number of votes a shareholder may cast is equal to the number of shares owned multiplied by the number of directors to be elected. In the above example you could cast all 400 of your votes for a single director if cumulative voting were used. Therefore, cumulative voting improves your chances of electing a specific individual to the board, which is the reason why cumulative voting makes it easier for minority shareholders to achieve representation on the board of directors.

A shareholder may cast his votes in person, at the annual meeting, or by **proxy**.   A proxy grants to another party the authority to vote the shares.   If a group of shareholders is not satisfied with the management of the firm, these shareholders can seek to obtain a sufficient number of proxy votes to elect board members who will replace current management.   A **proxy fight** often results because management also attempts to get as many proxies as possible.

Shareholders also have the right to share proportionately in dividends paid, in distributions following liquidation, and in the purchase of new stock issued by the corporation.   They also have the right to vote on certain important issues, such as mergers.

<u>Dividends</u>.   Corporations, at the discretion of the board of directors, pay cash dividends to shareholders.   The corporation is not legally obligated to declare dividends, and therefore a corporation cannot become bankrupt as a result of its failure to pay dividends.   In contrast, interest payments on debt are a legal obligation of the firm.   Dividends, unlike interest payments, are not tax deductible for the corporation.   Dividends are taxed as ordinary income to the shareholder, unless the shareholder is another corporation.   In this case, only 20% of the dividends received are taxed as income.

<u>Classes of Stock</u>.   Corporations may have different classes of common stock with different voting rights.   The usual reason for multiple classes of stock is to allow one group of shareholders to control the corporation by granting, for example, 60% of the voting rights to one class of stock held by that group.   This class of stock is often held by corporate management or founding shareholders.

Corporate Long-term Debt: the Basics

The distinction between debt and equity is important, although it is not always clear whether a specific obligation is debt or equity.   A debt is a promise to repay **principal** (i.e., the original amount of the loan) plus interest, at a specified time, to the lender, or **creditor**.   The corporation is the **debtor** or **borrower**.   The amount owed to the creditor is a liability of the corporation, although the corporation has the option to legally default at any time and turn over the corporate assets to the lenders.

From a financial point of view, three features distinguish debt from equity.   First, debt does not represent an ownership interest; creditors do not have voting powers in the corporation.   Second, interest paid on a debt is fully deductible as a business expense while stock dividends are considered a return to shareholders on their contributed capital and therefore are not deductible for tax purposes. Thus, compared to dividends, the government provides a tax subsidy on the use of debt. Finally, failure to pay creditors can result in bankruptcy. This possibility represents a cost of issuing debt which does not exist if a firm uses only equity financing.

Is It Debt or Equity? The distinction between debt and equity has obvious legal and tax implications, but it is sometimes unclear whether a given security is debt or equity. For example, suppose a corporation issues a perpetual bond on which it is legally obligated to pay interest only if net income exceeds some specified amount. Whether this security is really debt is a matter which is ultimately determined by courts and taxing authorities. The importance of this determination arises from the tax implications mentioned above, since such a security would appear to be an attempt on the part of the issuing firm to obtain the tax advantages of debt for an equity security.

Basic Features of Long-term Debt. Long-term corporate debt is generally in the form of a bond which has a **principal** or **face value** of $1000 and a par value equal to face value. Annual interest on corporate bonds is generally specified as a **coupon rate** equal to a specified percentage of par value; interest payments are made semi-annually. Principal is repaid to the bondholder on a specified date, called the **maturity date**. Prices are often quoted as a percentage of par value, so a quote of 80 indicates a price of $800.

Different Types of Debt. Typically, corporate debt securities are either **notes, debentures**, or **bonds**. Strictly speaking, a bond is secured by a mortgage on specific property, whereas a debenture is unsecured; however the word 'bond' is often used generically. **Long-term** (or **funded**) **debt** is payable more than one year from the date it is issued. A note is a debt security with a maturity that is usually less than seven years.

Repayment. The process of repaying long-term debt by making regular installments is called **amortization**. When the debt is fully repaid, it is **extinguished**. Often the corporation amortizes a loan by making annual deposits to a **sinking fund** which is then used to buy back the bonds.

Typically, a corporation has the option to repurchase a bond, after a specified number of years, at a specified price, regardless of the market price. Such debt is said to be **callable**, and the **call price** is the amount the firm pays to the bondholder when calling a bond. The call price is equal to the par value plus some premium.

Seniority. **Seniority** governs priority of payment to creditors in the event of bankruptcy. Some debt is **subordinated**, which means that other creditors must be repaid first in the event of bankruptcy.

Security. **Security** is property which must be sold in the event of a default on the secured debt. Unsecured creditors have a general claim to assets which remain after secured creditors are paid.

Indenture. The **indenture** is the written agreement between the corporation and its bondholders. The indenture sets forth the terms of the loan (i.e., the interest rate, the maturity date, and other features) and identifies all **restrictive covenants** which restrict certain actions on the part of the corporation. A typical restriction limits the dividends that can be paid to stockholders.

Preferred Stock

Preferred stock differs from common stock in that preferred shareholders must be paid a stated dividend before dividends can be paid to common shareholders, and preferred shareholders have preference over common shareholders to the residual value of assets following liquidation of the corporation.

Stated Value. A preferred share normally has a stated liquidating value of $100 per share. A Husky Corporation preferred stock might be identified as '$8 preferred,' indicating a dividend yield equal to 8% of the stated value.

Cumulative and Noncumulative Dividends. A corporation is not legally obligated to pay dividends on preferred stock. If dividends are **cumulative**, then any dividends not paid must be carried forward, and the entire amount must be paid before any dividends on common stock can be paid. Usually, preferred shareholders are granted voting rights if some specified number of dividends have not been paid.

Is Preferred Stock Really Debt? In many ways, preferred stock resembles a perpetual bond. The dividend is fixed, and preferred shareholders receive a stated value in the event of liquidation. In recent years, many preferred issues have also had sinking funds. The preferred dividend, however, is not tax deductible as a business expense. Corporations find preferred stocks an attractive investment because of the 80% dividend exclusion; thus most preferred stock is held by corporations.

The Preferred Stock Puzzle. Although preferred stock has many of the features of debt, the fact that the dividend is not deductible creates a tax disadvantage, relative to debt, for the issuer. To some extent, this disadvantage is offset by the fact that corporate investors are willing to pay a premium for preferred stock because of the 80% dividend exclusion. However, the result of these two tax effects is a net disadvantage to issuers of preferred stock. The question arises, then, as to why a corporation would ever choose to issue any preferred stock. Three reasons are commonly cited. First, the largest issuers of preferred stock are regulated public utilities, and the nature of utility regulation is such that the additional cost is passed on to the consumer. Second, a company with no taxable income does not benefit from the tax-deductibility of debt interest, and therefore is not at a disadvantage when issuing preferred stock. Finally, preferred stock does not subject the issuer to the threat of potential bankruptcy.

Patterns of Long-term Financing

The dominant source of long-term financing is **internal financing** from operating cash flow, which is defined as net income, plus depreciation, minus dividends paid. Internal financing accounts for 70% to 90% of total long-term financing. About 80% of long term financing is used for capital spending. The difference between the uses of long-term financing and internally generated funds has generally been covered primarily by long term debt; net new equity issues account for less than 10% of long-term financing.

CONCEPT TEST

1. The stated value of a share of stock is often $1. This stated value is called the _____ of the stock.

2. If a share of common stock has no stated value, then the stock is _____ stock.

3. The number of shares issued by a corporation multiplied by the par value of each share is called the _____ of the corporation.

4. At any point in time, the amount of stock that can be sold without shareholder approval is limited to the number of _____ shares.

5. The amount of directly contributed equity capital in excess of par value is called the _____.

6. The portion of net income not paid as dividends is called _____.

7. Total common equity or _____ of a firm is the sum of _____, _____, and _____.

8. For a given corporation, the number of shares outstanding is equal to the number of shares _____ less the number _____.

9. Shares that have been repurchased by the issuing firm are called _____.

10. The most important distinction in the corporate voting mechanism concerns whether elections feature _____ voting or _____ voting.

11. If you own 100 shares of stock and you can cast 100 votes in the election for a member of the board of directors, the stock features _____ voting.

12. If you own 100 shares of stock and you can cast 400 votes in the election for a member of the board of directors, the stock features _____ voting.

13. The information in question 12 indicates that the number of directors to be elected is _____.

14. A grant of authority allowing another party to vote your shares is called a _____.

15. When a group other than management solicits authority to vote shares in order to replace management, a _____ occurs.

16. The payment of dividends is at the discretion of a corporation's _____.

17. Dividends received by individuals are, for the most part, taxed as _____.

18. Of the dividends received by a corporation, _____% are not taxed.

19. The three distinctive features of debt are: debt does not represent an _____, interest paid is _____, and unpaid debt is a _____ of the firm.

20. Long-term corporate debt is usually denominated in units of $_____, called the _____ value or _____ value.

21. Long-term debt prices and interest payments are usually quoted as percentages of _____.

22. Interest payments on long-term debt are usually paid _____.

23. Typical debt securities are called _____, _____, and _____.

24. Strictly speaking, a _____ is secured by property, whereas a _____ is not, but the term _____ is used for both.

25. Long-term debt, by definition, is payable more than _____ from the date it is issued.

26. Long-term debt is sometimes called _____ debt.

27. The process of repaying a long-term debt by making installment payments is called _____.

28. When the last installment is made on a long-term debt, the debt is said to be _____.

29. A typical arrangement for installment payments on long-term debt requires the corporation to make annual deposits in a _____.

30. The corporation usually has the right to repurchase debt prior to maturity, at a specified price. Such debt is said to be _____ and the price the corporation must pay is called the _____.

31. Preference in position among lenders regarding repayment is called _____.

32. In the event of default, holders of _____ debt are generally not paid until other specified creditors are paid.

33. If a debt involves a specific attachment to property, it is called _____ debt.

34. The written agreement between the debt issuer and the lender is called the _____.

35. The written agreement between the debt issuer and the lender generally contains _____ that restrict certain activities of the corporation.

36. Holders of preferred stock must be paid a _____ before any cash can be paid to _____.

37. Preferred shares typically have a stated _____ of $100.

38. Dividends payable on preferred stock are either _____ or _____.

39. The major issuers of preferred stock are _____.

40. The major purchasers of preferred stock are _____.

41. The major source of long-term financing for U.S. corporations is _____.

42. The major use of long-term financing for U.S. corporations is _____.

43. The primary source of external financing for U.S. corporations is _____. In general, net new equity issues account for less than _____% of long-term financing.

ANSWERS TO CONCEPT TEST

1. par value
2. no par
3. dedicated capital
4. authorized
5. capital surplus
6. retained earnings
7. book value; dedicated capital;
    capital surplus; cumulative
    retained earnings
8. issued; repurchased
9. treasury stock
10. straight; cumulative
11. straight
12. cumulative
13. four
14. proxy
15. proxy fight
16. board of directors
17. ordinary income
18. 80
19. ownership interest;
    tax-deductible; liability
20. 1000; face; par
21. par value

22. semiannually
23. notes; bonds; debentures
24. bond; debenture; bond
25. 1 year
26. funded
27. amortization
28. extinguished
29. sinking fund
30. callable; call price
31. seniority
32. subordinated
33. secured
34. indenture
35. restrictive covenants
36. stated dividend; common
    shareholders
37. liquidating value
38. cumulative; noncumulative
39. regulated public utilities
40. corporations
41. internal cash flow
42. capital expenditures
43. long-term debt; 10

PROBLEMS AND SOLUTIONS

The December 31, 1986 capital accounts for Times Mirror Company (a Fortune 400 corporation) are shown below (in thousands of dollars). Use this information to solve Problems 1-3.

Shareholders' Equity	
Common Stock	$ 64,490
Additional Paid-in Capital	166,062
Retained Earnings	1,204,271
Less Treasury Stock, at cost	2,354
	$1,432,469

Problem 1

If Times Mirror stock has a $1 par value, how many shares have been sold?

Solution 1

The common stock account is the dedicated capital, so 64,490,000 shares have been sold.

Problem 2

How much (net) financing has Times Mirror obtained through the direct sale of stock?

Solution 2

Common stock ($64,490,000) plus the capital surplus, or additional paid-in capital ($166,062,000), is the total financing obtained ($230,552,000). Therefore, (net) financing is $230,552,000 less the $2,354,000 in repurchased (treasury) stock for a net total of $228,198,000.

Problem 3

Suppose Times Mirror had net income of $250 million and paid dividends of $96 million in 1987, and that Times Mirror stock had been selling for about $90 per share. If Times Mirror were to sell 5 million new shares at that price during the year, what would the year-end capital accounts look like?

Solution 3

The par value is $1, so the common stock account increases by $5000. The balance from the sale of stock goes into the surplus account. Retained earnings increases by ($250 million - $96 million) = $154 million. Therefore, the capital accounts would appear as follows:

Shareholders' Equity		
Common Stock	$	69,490
Additional Paid-in Capital		611,062
Retained Earnings		1,358,271
Less Treasury Stock, at cost		2,354
		$2,036,469

Problem 4

A corporate bond is selling for 90, and pays 8% interest. If you buy it, how much will you pay? How much interest will you receive? When?

Solution 4

Assuming that this is a typical bond, you will pay $900 per bond (90% of a $1000 par value), and you will receive $80 per year, paid in two $40 semi-annual amounts.

Problem 5

You wish to become a director of Mealey Briers Company. There are 1000 shares outstanding and five directors. What is the minimum number of shares you must have to insure being elected, if Mealey Briers has straight voting? Cumulative voting?

Solution 5

If the firm uses straight voting, the directors are elected one at a time, so you will need (1000/2) = 500 shares. If you have fewer than 500 shares, you can be outvoted each time.

If the firm uses cumulative voting, then there is a total of [5(1000)] = 5000 votes to be cast, and the directors are elected simultaneously. Since there are five directors, 1000 votes is certainly sufficient to guarantee that you will win 1 of the 5 positions. You actually need only [(5000/6) + 1] = 834 votes, however, so that 167 shares are sufficient. In general, if n directors are being elected, the necessary minimum you must have is [1/(n + 1)]% of the shares. This example illustrates how cumulative voting encourages minority participation; it takes fewer shares to get a minority director elected when a firm uses cumulative, rather than straight, voting.

CHAPTER 14
CAPITAL STRUCTURE:
BASIC CONCEPTS

CHAPTER HIGHLIGHTS

For a given collection of assets, a firm has almost unlimited flexibility in choosing its capital structure, or the way in which assets are financed. In order to simplify the discussion of capital structure decisions, we consider only common stock and straight debt financing in this chapter. The appropriate objective for capital structure decisions is to maximize the value of the firm's equity. Unfortunately, exactly how this goal can be achieved is an unsettled issue. Many of the factors affecting this decision are well understood and are discussed in this and the next chapter; however, the interplay among these factors is complex and less well understood. In order to comprehend the issues involved in the capital structure decision, it is essential to keep in mind the fact that we are considering whether the way a firm chooses to finance its assets makes any economic difference; that is, we are focusing only on the issue of how a firm finances a given collection of assets. ✳

The Capital-Structure Question and the Pie Theory

Recall that the market value of a firm (V) is, by definition, equal to the sum of the equity value (S) and the debt value (B). The value of the firm can be viewed as a pie, and the firm's capital structure (or, more accurately, its financial structure) is represented by the way in which the pie is sliced; this is the pie model. The slices of the pie are the equity portion and the debt portion. The capital structure questions then become: First, should stockholders be concerned about maximizing the value of the entire firm, rather than maximizing the value of the firm's equity? And, second, what is the ratio of debt to equity (i.e., the financial structure) that maximizes shareholders' interests?

It is the assets of a firm that generate cash flow. The firm's capital structure is a way of packaging those cash flows and selling them in financial markets. In everyday life, we observe how packaging products in such a way as to maximize appeal and usefulness to the consumer adds value to the product. For example, consumers are probably willing to pay more for six 12-ounce cans of beer than they are for one 72-ounce can. Might the same be true of a firm's cash flows? This is the heart of the capital structure issue.

Maximizing Firm Value versus
Maximizing Stockholder Interests

In this section, we address the first of the two questions posed in the previous section. Consider an all-equity firm whose market value is $100,000. This means that the firm's existing assets are valued at $100,000, so that the firm's existing common stock has a total market value of $100,000. The firm's management is considering a financial restructuring, by borrowing $40,000 and then paying the proceeds of the loan to the shareholders in the form of dividends. There are two important points to note here: First, as mentioned earlier, when we discuss capital structure decisions, we assume a given collection of assets, so that in this restructuring example, the existing assets of the firm are not changed. Second, the result of the stated change in financial structure is to replace equity financing with debt financing.

Under what circumstances do the shareholders benefit from the financial restructuring described in the above example? In order to analyze this issue, we first assume that the restructuring does not affect the value of the firm. Under these circumstances, the wealth of the shareholders is unaffected. Shareholders owned a firm worth $100,000 before the restructuring. After the change in financial structure, they own 60% of a firm worth $100,000, or $60,000, plus dividends totaling $40,000. Shareholders are indifferent to the restructuring if the value of the firm is unchanged.

Under what circumstances do shareholders benefit from a financial restructuring? The answer is that they benefit only if the value of the firm increases. If, for example, the restructuring increases the value of the firm to $110,000, the shareholders now own equity in the firm worth ($110,000 - $40,000) = $70,000, plus dividends of $40,000, for a total of $110,000. In other words, the hypothesized increase in the value of the firm accrues to the stockholders. Consequently, maximizing the value of the firm is equivalent to maximizing the value of the shareholders' position.

Note that we have not yet addressed the issue of whether capital structure affects the value of the firm; we have simply noted that, from the shareholders' point of view, if there is a capital structure which maximizes the value of the firm, then it also maximizes the value of the shareholders' position.

Can an Optimal Capital Structure Be Determined?

Modigliani and Miller: Proposition I (No Taxes). In 1958, Modigliani and Miller (MM) showed that, under certain circumstances, the size of the pie is unaffected by the firm's capital structure. The MM derivation of this result is based on the following two assumptions: first, there are no taxes; and, second, investors can borrow on their own account at the same rate that the firm pays on its debt.

Imagine that we have two firms with identical assets. We will use the symbols V, S, and B to stand for the market values of the firm, the stock, and the bonds, respectively, and the subscripts U and L to represent an 'unlevered' (i.e., all equity) and a 'levered' firm. An investor who purchases 10% of the unlevered company pays $.10S_U$ to purchase 10% of the firm's outstanding shares and expects to receive 10% of the firms profits, $.10Y$, where Y represents the firm's profits. Note that since the firm is an all-equity firm, then $.10S_U = .10V_U$. (We refer to this investment as Strategy I.)

Now consider Strategy II. If the investor purchases 10% of the equity of the levered company, he pays $.10S_L$, which is equal to $[.10(V_L - B_L)]$. In this case, the investor receives $[.10(Y - r_BB_L)]$, where r_B is the interest rate on debt and r_BB_L is the firm's total interest payment.

We now show that the investor can duplicate the returns from Strategy II by combining Strategy I with personal borrowing; we call this combination Strategy III. First, the investor borrows $.10B_L$ of debt at the rate r_B. (Note that we are now assuming that the investor can borrow at a rate equal to the firm's interest rate on debt.) Then the investor uses the proceeds of the loan plus his own personal funds to buy 10% of Firm U. Therefore, he invests $[.10(V_U - B_L)]$ of his own funds. His return is 10% of Y less the interest on his debt, or $[.10(Y - r_BB_L)]$.

For both Strategy II and Strategy III, the investor's return is $[.10(Y - r_BB_L)]$. The difference between the two strategies is in the amounts invested; these are $[.10(V_L - B_L)]$ and $[.10(V_U - B_L)]$ for Strategies II and III, respectively. Since the returns for the two strategies are equal, the investments for each must also be equal, which is true only if $V_L = V_U$. An arbitrage opportunity would exist if V_L were not equal to V_U. Consequently, we have demonstrated the well-known **MM Proposition I**, that the firm's financial structure does not affect the value of the firm. That is, the value of the levered firm is equal to the value of the unlevered firm, indicating that debt in the capital structure does not affect the value of the firm. Also, we demonstrated in the previous section that stockholders' wealth is unaffected if the value of the firm does not change; therefore, changes in capital structure do not affect stockholders' wealth.

Financial Leverage and Firm Value

The conclusions of the previous section depend on two key assumptions. The assumption that there are no taxes is discussed in a later section. Here, we address the issue of whether it is possible for individuals to borrow at the same rate that corporations pay on debt. Although it may seem intuitively that this is not a reasonable assumption, in fact it is often true that individuals can borrow at lower rates than those paid by corporations. Corporations frequently borrow using illiquid assets, such as plant and equipment, for collateral. Effective rates for such loans are often higher than the rates individuals pay when they use securities as collateral in a margin account. An individual investor who establishes a margin account with a broker can borrow, from the broker, up to 50% of the value of the securities in the account. The rate for such loans is relatively low because the broker holds liquid collateral whose value is twice the amount of the loan. Furthermore, if the value of the collateral declines significantly, established procedures require that either the investor makes additional cash deposits to his account, or the broker sells the securities in order to repay the loan. Consequently, since the risk to the broker is low, the interest rate on the loan is also low.

Modigliani and Miller: Proposition II (No Taxes)

MM Proposition II establishes a positive relationship between leverage and the expected return on equity, because the risk of a firm's equity increases as the degree of leverage increases.

In order to derive this proposition, we first define the firm's overall cost of capital, r_0, as follows:

$$r_0 = \frac{\text{Expected earnings to be paid to all investors}}{\text{Value of firm}}$$

The numerator of the above expression can be thought of as the sum of the expected earnings to be paid to equityholders plus earnings to be paid to debtholders. The denominator is equal to the value of the firm's equity plus the value of the firm's debt. The above expression can be rewritten as:

$$r_0 = \frac{B}{B+S} \times r_B \; + \; \frac{S}{B+S} \times r_s$$

where B and S are the values of the firm's debt and equity, respectively, r_B is the interest rate on the firm's debt and r_s is the expected return on the firm's equity. (The parameters r_B and r_s are also called the cost of debt and the cost of equity, respectively.) The above equation indicates that the firm's overall cost of capital is a weighted average of the cost of debt and the cost of equity, where the respective weights are the proportions of debt and equity in the firm's capital structure. Solving the above equation for r_s, we have **MM Proposition II (no taxes)**:

$$r_s = r_0 + \frac{B}{S} \, (r_0 - r_B)$$

This relationship indicates that the required return on equity is a linear function of the debt-to-equity ratio. We know from Proposition I that the value of the firm is not affected by changes in the debt-to-equity ratio, so that it must also be true that the firm's overall cost of capital r_0 does not change with changes in the firm's financial structure. Also, if r_0 is greater than r_B, then r_s increases with the debt-equity ratio. Intuitively, this last conclusion results from the fact that additional debt increases the risk of the firm's equity, and consequently increases the required return on equity. These results are demonstrated graphically in Figure 14.1.

MM Proposition II

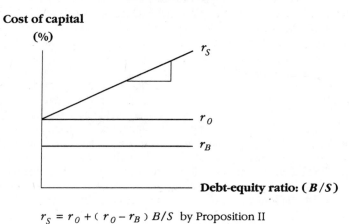

$$r_S = r_0 + (r_0 - r_B)\, B/S \text{ by Proposition II}$$

Figure 14.1

MM: An Interpretation. MM Proposition II states that the cost of equity is given by a straight line with a slope of $(r_0 - r_B)$ and a y-intercept of r_0. As the debt/equity ratio (B/S) increases, the cost of equity (r_s) rises in a linear fashion, but the increased cost of equity is exactly offset by the increased use of cheaper debt. The overall cost of capital (r_0) is the same no matter what the debt/equity ratio is. Since r_0 never changes, and the firm's cash flows never change, the value of the firm is unaffected by the capital structure.

The above conclusions are derived under a set of assumptions which are, to an important extent, inconsistent with the real world. In addition, the conclusion that the debt-equity ratio does not affect value is inconsistent with the behavior of most corporations, whose debt-equity ratios seem to vary with industry characteristics. These observations make it necessary to assess the validity of the MM conclusions under a more realistic set of assumptions. Specifically, in the next section, we consider how the introduction of corporate taxes affects the MM propositions. In the next chapter, we discuss the relevance of bankruptcy costs and other agency costs for these results.

Taxes

As we have seen, a primary difference between debt and equity is that interest is tax-deductible, whereas dividends are not. This tax subsidy on interest increases the attractiveness of debt.

Suppose we are comparing firms U and L again. Earnings before interest and taxes (EBIT) will be the same for both, say $1000. Further suppose that L has issued perpetual bonds in the amount of

$500, on which it pays 10% interest, and that the corporate tax rate is 34%. We can summarize this information as follows:

	Firm U	Firm L
EBIT	$1000	$1000
Interest	0	50
Earnings before taxes (EBT)	1000	950
Taxes (34%)	340	323
Earnings after tax	$660	$627

At this point we can compute the total cash flow to both stockholders and bondholders:

Cash flow to	Firm U	Firm L
Stockholders	$660	$627
Bondholders	0	50
Total cash flow	$660	$677

We see that the total cash flow for L is greater by $17. This occurs because L's tax bill, which is a cash outflow, is $17 less. The interest expense has generated a tax shield equal to the interest payment ($50) multiplied by the corporate tax rate (34%).

Since the debt is perpetual, this same shield will be generated every year forever. The after-tax cash flow to L will be the same $660 that accrues to U, plus the $17 tax shield. Because the tax shield is generated by paying interest, it has the same risk as the firm's debt, so that 10% is the appropriate discount rate. The value of the tax shield is thus:

$$\text{PV} = \frac{\$17}{.10} = \frac{(.34)(.10)(\$500)}{.10} = (.34)(\$500) = \$170$$

In general, the value of the tax shield is $[(T_c)(r_B)(B)/r_B] = T_c B$.

The after-tax cash flow to the stockholders of the unlevered firm is $[\text{EBIT}(1 - T_c)]$. If we assume that all cash flows are perpetual and constant, then the value of the unlevered firm is:

$$V_U = \frac{\text{EBIT}(1 - T_c)}{\rho}$$

where ρ is the appropriate risk-adjusted discount rate for an all-equity firm. **MM Proposition I (Corporate Taxes)** states that the value of a levered firm, V_L, is equal to the value of the unlevered firm plus the value of the tax shield:

$$V_L = \frac{\text{EBIT}(1 - T_c)}{\rho} + \frac{T_c r_B B}{r_B}$$

$$= V_U + T_c B$$

This result demonstrates that, in a world with corporate taxes, the firm has an incentive to increase its debt-equity ratio. A higher debt-equity ratio lowers taxes and increases the total value of the firm.

In fact, the above result indicates that a firm should move as close as possible to an all-debt capital structure.

MM Proposition II (Corporate Taxes) indicates a positive relationship between expected return on equity and the debt-equity ratio:

$$r_s = \rho_0 + \frac{B}{S} \times (1 - T_c) \times (\rho - r_B)$$

In this case, the firm's overall cost of capital decreases as the amount of debt increases, which leads to the conclusion that a capital structure of 100% debt is optimal.

CONCEPT TEST

1. Stockholders benefit from a financial restructuring of the firm only if the value of the firm _____.

2. An all-equity company is referred to as an _____ firm, while a company with debt in its financial structure is referred to as a _____ firm.

3. The mixture of debt and equity that a company chooses to employ is called its _____ or _____.

4. A firm's overall cost of capital is a weighted average of the cost of _____ and the cost of _____.

For Questions 5-9, assume that there are no taxes or bankruptcy costs.

5. The value of the firm is unaffected by its debt/equity ratio. This is a statement of _____.

6. The cost of equity capital is linearly related to the debt/equity ratio with a slope of _____ and a y-intercept of _____.

7. The conclusion stated in Question 6 is a statement of _____.

8. The overall cost of capital _____ as the debt/equity ratio increases.

9. The required return on equity _____ with an increase in the debt-equity ratio because additional debt _____ the risk of the firm's equity.

10. An individual investor can often borrow at a rate equal to, or lower than, the rate at which a corporation can borrow by establishing a _____ with a securities broker.

For Questions 11-15, assume that corporate taxes exist but that there are no bankruptcy costs.

11. The value of a levered firm exceeds the value of an unlevered firm with the same assets. This is a statement of _____.

12. A gain from leverage exists because interest payments generate a _____ .

13. The amount by which the value of a levered firm exceeds the value of an unlevered firm with the same assets is equal to the _____ .

14. The overall cost of capital _____ as the debt/equity ratio increases.

15. MM Proposition II (Corporate Taxes) states that there is a _____ relationship between expected return on equity and the debt-equity ratio.

ANSWERS TO CONCEPT TEST

1. increases
2. unlevered; levered
3. capital structure;
    financial structure
4. debt; equity
5. MM Proposition I
6. $r_0 - r_B$; r_0
7. MM Proposition II
8. stays the same

9. increases; increases
10. margin account
11. MM Proposition I
    (Corporate Taxes)
12. tax shield
13. PV of the tax shield
14. decreases
15. positive

PROBLEMS AND SOLUTIONS

Use the information below to solve Problems 1-6.

Maxlever and Nolever are identical firms in all ways except that Maxlever employs debt in its capital structure and Nolever does not. The EBIT for each firm is $100. The total value of the equity in Maxlever is $400, and the total value of the equity in Nolever is $700. Maxlever's bonds have a market value and a face value of $400. The interest rate is 10% and there are no taxes.

Problem 1

Suppose that an investor purchases 20% of the equity of Maxlever. What is the cost and the return for this investment?

Solution 1

The investment is:

$$(.20)(S_L) = (.20)(V_L - B_L) = (.20)(\$400) = \$80$$

where the subscript L stands for the levered firm, Maxlever. The return for this investment is:

$$(.20)(Y - r_B B_L) = (.20)[\$100 - (.10)(\$400)] = \$12$$

where Y is the firm's EBIT and r_B is the interest rate on the firm's debt.

Problem 2

Explain how the investor can duplicate the cash flow from the investment described in Problem 1 by borrowing and investing in the equity of Nolever.

Solution 2

First, borrow $[(.20)(B_L)] = [(.20)(\$400)] = \$80$ at an interest rate of 10%. Then purchase 20% of the equity in Nolever, at a cost of $[(.20)(V_U)] = [(.20)(\$700)] = \$140$, where the subscript U represents the unlevered firm Nolever. The return from this strategy is

$$(.20)(Y - r_B B_L) = (.20)[\$100 - (.10)(\$400)] = \$12$$

which is the same as the cash flow for Problem 1.

Problem 3

Describe the arbitrage opportunity which exists as a result of the fact that the value of Maxlever is greater than the value of Nolever.

Solution 3

The investor's cash flow is the same for the strategy in Problem 2 as for the strategy in Problem 1. The two strategies differ only in the amount invested; in Problem 1, $80 is invested for a cash flow of $12, while in Problem 2, only ($140 - $80) = $60 is invested for the same cash flow. Consequently, a rational investor would pursue the second strategy, thereby increasing the value of Nolever and decreasing the value of Maxlever. Prices will adjust until V_L is equal to V_U. Note that the investor could be more aggressive about his investment strategy by selling short the equity of Maxlever for $80 at the same time that he borrows and invests in the equity of Nolever. This strategy provides a certain $20 profit since, in equilibrium, the values of the two firms must be equal.

Problem 4

Suppose that the total value of Nolever's equity is $900, rather than $700, and that an investor purchases 20% of the equity of Nolever. What is the cost and the return for this investment?

Solution 4

The cost of purchasing 20% of the equity in Nolever is $[(.20)(V_U)] = [(.20)(\$900)] = \$180$. The cash flow from this investment would be $[(.20)(Y)] = [(.20)(\$100)] = \$20$.

Problem 5

Explain how the investor can duplicate the cash flow from the investment described in Problem 4 by lending and investing in the equity of Maxlever.

Solution 5

We can reproduce the cash flow by first lending $[(.20)(B_L)] = [(.20)(\$400)] = \$80$ at a 10% interest rate. Next, purchase 20% of the equity in Maxlever:

$$(.20)(S_L) = (.20)(V_L - B_L) = (.20)(\$400) = \$80$$

The cash flow from this strategy is:

$$(.20)(Y - r_BB_L) + (.20)(r_BB_L) =$$

$$(.20)[\$100 - (.10)(\$400)] + (.10)(\$80) = \$20.$$

Problem 6

Describe the arbitrage opportunity which exists as a result of the fact that the value of Maxlever is greater than the value of Nolever.

Solution 6

The investor's cash flow is $20 for each of the investment strategies described in Problems 4 and 5. However, the size of the investment is $180 in Problem 4 and only $160 in Problem 5. All rational investors would choose the strategy described in Problem 5, thereby resulting in an increase in the value of Maxlever and a decrease in the value of Nolever. Equilibrium is reached when the values of the two firms are equal. As in Problem 3, the investor can use short selling to produce an arbitrage profit; he can sell short the equity of Nolever for $180 and adopt the strategy of lending and buying Maxlever, as described in Problem 5.

Use the information below to solve Problems 7-10.

The North Company, a major manufacturer of document shredders, has a perpetual expected EBIT of $200. The interest rate is 12%.

Problem 7

Assuming that there are no taxes or other imperfections, what is the value of North if its debt/equity ratio is .25 and its overall cost of capital is 16%? What is the value of the equity? What is the value of the debt?

Solution 7

If there are no taxes, then MM Proposition I holds and North's capital structure is irrelevant, so the value of the firm is $(\$200/.16) = \$1250$.

If the debt/equity ratio is .25, then for every $5 in capital, there is $4 in equity. Thus, North is 80% equity, and the value of the equity is $1000. The value of the debt is $250.

Problem 8

What is the cost of equity capital for North?

Solution 8

The cost of equity capital can be computed using MM Proposition II as:

$$r_s = r_o + \frac{B}{S} (r_o - r_B)$$

$$= .16 + (.25)(.16 - .12) = .17 = 17\%$$

Alternatively, we can compute the equity cash flow as [\$200 - .12(\$250)] = \$170. Since the equity is worth \$1000, the cost of capital is (\$170/\$1000) = .17 = 17%.

Problem 9

Suppose the corporate tax rate is 30%, there are no personal taxes or other imperfections, and North has \$400 in debt outstanding. If the unlevered cost of equity is 20%, what is North's value? What is the value of the equity?

Solution 9

We can use MM Proposition I with taxes to value North. The value of North as an unlevered firm is:

$$EBIT(1 - T_C)/\rho = (\$200)(.70)/.20 = \$700$$

The present value of the tax shield is $T_C B$ = [.30(\$400)] = \$120. The total value is therefore \$820. The value of the equity is (\$820 - \$400) = \$420.

Problem 10

In Problem 9, what is the overall cost of capital?

Solution 10

The debt to equity ratio for North is (\$400/\$420). Using MM Proposition II with taxes, the cost of equity is:

$$.20 + (1 - .30)(.20 - .12)(400/420) = 25.33\%$$

Alternatively, the cash flow to equity is:

$$[\$200 - .12(\$400)](1 - .30) = \$106.40$$

Thus, the return on equity is (\$106.40/\$420) = 25.33%, as previously calculated.

The overall cost of capital is:

$$(\$420/\$820)(.2533) + (\$400/\$820)(.12)(1 - .30) = 17.07\%$$

Use the following information to solve Problems 11-15.

Merrick Motors is an all-equity firm with earnings expected to be $450,000 in perpetuity. The firm has 100,000 shares outstanding. The cost of capital is 15%. MM is considering a major expansion of its facilities which will require an initial outlay of $400,000 and which is expected to produce additional annual earnings of $150,000 per year in perpetuity. Management considers the expansion to have the same risk as the firm's existing assets. Assume throughout that there are no taxes and no costs of bankruptcy.

Problem 11

What is the value of the firm's assets prior to undertaking the proposed expansion? What is the value of the firm's equity? What is the price per share of the firm's stock?

Solution 11

The value of the firm is ($450,000/.15) = $3,000,000. Since MM is an all-equity firm, the value of the firm's equity is also $3,000,000. Price per share is ($3,000,000/100,000) = $30.

Problem 12

Suppose MM plans to finance the expansion by issuing common stock. How many shares of stock must be issued? What is the value of the firm's equity after the new stock issue? What is the price per share of the firm's stock?

Solution 12

The net present value of the expansion is:

$$-\$400,000 + (\$150,000/.15) = \$600,000$$

Therefore, when the firm announces the expansion, the value of the firm increases to ($3,000,000 + $600,000) = $3,600,000. That is, the value of the firm's assets and the value of the equity each increase to $3,600,000. Therefore, price per share increases to ($3,600,000/100,000) = $36. Note that this increase in value occurs immediately following the announcement of the expansion, but before the financing is obtained. In order to obtain $400,000 in equity financing, the firm sells ($400,000/$36) = 11,111 shares of stock. The proceeds of the stock issue are used to acquire the new assets, so that the value of the firm becomes ($3,000,000 + $600,000 + $400,000) = $4,000,000, which is the value of the firm's equity. The price per share is still $36 after the financing; that is, ($4,000,000/111,111) = $36.

Problem 13

Suppose MM plans to finance the expansion by issuing bonds with an interest rate of 10%. What is the value of the firm after the new bond issue? What is the value of the firm's equity? What is the price per share of the firm's stock?

Solution 13

As in Problem 12, the value of the firm increases to $3,600,000 after the announcement of the expansion. When the firm issues $400,000 of new debt, the value of the firm's assets increases to

$4,000,000, but the value of the firm's equity remains at $3,600,000. The value of the firm is the same as under the equity financing arrangement, as indicated by MM Proposition I (No Taxes). The price per share of the firm's stock is $36 after the announcement and before the financing is obtained, and remains at $36 after the financing is obtained.

Problem 14

Calculate the expected yearly income after interest for the equityholders. Use the expected yearly income to calculate the expected return for the equityholders.

Solution 14

Expected yearly income is:

$$\$450,000 + \$150,000 - (.10)(\$400,000) = \$560,000$$

The expected return for the equityholders is ($560,000/$3,600,000) = 15.556%.

Problem 15

Use MM Proposition II (no taxes) to determine the expected return for the equityholders.

Solution 15

MM Proposition II (no taxes) indicates that the return to equityholders (r_s) is:

$$r_s = r_0 + \frac{B}{S} (r_0 - r_B)$$

$$r_s = .15 + \frac{\$400,000}{\$3,600,000} (.15 - .10) = .15556 = 15.556\%$$

CHAPTER 15
CAPITAL STRUCTURE:
LIMITS TO THE USE OF DEBT

CHAPTER HIGHLIGHTS

The MM Propositions of the previous chapter state that a firm can increase its value by increasing leverage, thereby implying that firms should be financed largely by debt. In reality, however, most firms are not highly leveraged. The explanation for this discrepancy lies in the fact that the theory of the previous chapter ignores two important considerations. The first of these factors is the cost of bankruptcy, which increases with increases in debt. The second factor is the differential treatment of interest income and equity distributions in so far as personal income taxes are concerned. In this chapter, we discuss the impact of these two factors on the MM conclusions.

Costs of Financial Distress

Bankruptcy Risk or Bankruptcy Cost? The obligation to pay principal and interest on debt puts pressure on the firm since failure to meet the obligation results in some form of financial distress; the ultimate financial distress is bankruptcy, in which case ownership of the firm's assets is transferred to the bondholders. Costs of financial distress offset the advantages of debt under certain circumstances.

Consider a firm that expects its cash flow to be insufficient to meet debt obligations in the event of a recession. Suppose that, under these circumstances, bondholders expect that the payment they will receive from the firm will be equal to the firm's cash flow. The price bondholders are willing to pay for the bond will be based on the expected value of the cash flow to the bondholders. For example, assume principal plus interest due to bondholders in one year is $100, but that in the event of a recession, the firm's cash flow will be only $50. Then, if the probability of a recession is .50, the expected value of the payment to the bondholders is [(.50)($100) + (.50)($50)] = $75. If bondholders were confident that they would receive $100, they would accept a 10% interest rate and would pay ($100/1.10) = $90.91 for the bond today. However, given the likelihood of bankruptcy, bondholders are willing to pay only ($75/1.10) = $68.18. (Note that we are assuming here that bondholders will accept the same expected rate of return on the risky bond that they would on the guaranteed bond; that is, we are assuming, for the sake of simplicity, that the bondholders are risk-neutral.) Consequently, the promised yield to the bondholders is [($100/$68.18) - 1] = 46.67%.

According to the pie model, the fact that the bondholders reduce the price they are willing to pay for the bonds does not reduce the value of the firm; to this point in the example, we are simply redistributing the firm's cash flow between stockholders and bondholders. However, the costs of bankruptcy further reduce the price bondholders are willing to pay to acquire the firm's bonds, and also reduces the value of the firm. If bondholders expect that payments to attorneys, and other legal expenses in the event of a bankruptcy, will total $20, the expected value of the cash flow to the bondholders is reduced to [(.50)($100) + (.50)($30)] = $65 and the price of the bonds is reduced to ($65/1.10) = $59.09. The reduction in the price of the bonds from $68.18 to $59.09 reflects the fact that, in the event of bankruptcy, $20 of the firm's cash flow will go to parties other than the stockholders and bondholders, thereby reducing the value of the firm. The expected value of the reduction in the firm's cash flow is $[(.50)(\$0) + (.50)(\$20)] = \$10$, which has a present value of $(\$10/1.10) = \$9.09$, which is precisely the amount of the decrease in the value of the bonds: $(\$68.18 - \$59.09) = \$9.09$.

Who pays the cost of financial distress in the above example? The answer is that it is the stockholders, rather than the bondholders. The bondholders lower the price they are willing to pay for the bonds to reflect the costs associated with bankruptcy, so that the stockholders receive less than they otherwise would for the sale of the bonds. Consequently, the value of the firm is reduced by these costs, and stockholders bear the cost associated with bankruptcy.

Description of Costs

Since a firm can incur costs of financial distress even in the absence of a legal bankruptcy, the more appropriate term is financial distress costs rather than bankruptcy costs. In this section, we describe the costs associated with financial distress.

Direct Costs of Financial Distress. The direct costs of financial distress include attorneys' fees, administrative and accounting fees, and, in the event of a trial, fees to expert witnesses. Empirical studies indicate that these costs are generally a relatively small percentage of the market value of the firm. Estimates range from approximately 1% to 3% of the firm's value.

Indirect Costs of Financial Distress. Bankruptcy often results in an impaired ability to conduct business. Customers question the ability of the firm to provide service subsequent to a purchase, and are consequently less likely to buy from a firm in bankruptcy. Although these costs are difficult to estimate, they are thought to be much greater than the direct costs cited above.

The prospect of bankruptcy also provides an incentive for the firm to take larger risks than might otherwise be the case. Suppose that a firm is considering two mutually exclusive projects, each with two possible payoffs, depending on the state of the economy. The low-risk project will result in a total value of the firm equal to $500 or $1000, each with probability .5. The high-risk project will result in total value equal to $300 or $1150, each with probability .5. The expected value for the low-risk project is $[(.5)(\$500) + (.5)(\$1000)] = \$750$ and the expected value for the high-risk project is $[(.5)(\$300) + (.5)(\$1150)] = \$725$. It would appear that the firm would accept the low-risk project since the expected value of the firm is higher under this alternative. However, suppose that the promised payment to debtholders is $400. For the low-risk project, payments to the debtholders will be $400, regardless of the outcome of the project, so that the expected value of the firm's equity is $(\$750 - \$400) = \$350$. For the high-risk project, payments to the debtholders will be either $300 or $400, depending on the outcome of the project. Therefore, the expected value of the firm's equity is $[(.5)(\$0) + (.5)(\$750)] = \$375$. The expected value of the equity is larger for the high-risk project, even though the expected value of the firm is lower, because there is a .5 probability that the debtholders will not receive the full $400 payment. Consequently, stockholders would select the high-risk project. This **incentive to take large risks** arises from the fact that the firm is close to bankruptcy; an all-equity firm, or a firm which is not close to bankruptcy, would select the low-risk project, which has the higher expected value for the firm.

A similar indirect cost of financial distress is the **incentive toward underinvestment**. A firm which is close to bankruptcy might chose not to undertake a positive NPV investment project because the benefit from the project might accrue primarily to the bondholders of the firm. For example, suppose that a firm's cash flow will be insufficient to pay the claims of creditors in the event of a recession;

the claims of creditors are $4000 and the cash flow will be $1000 in a recession. An investment project which is certain to increase cash flow by $3000 provides no benefit to stockholders in a recession. Consequently, stockholders may find that it is not in their best interests to undertake such a project, even if it has a positive net present value.

Stockholders have an incentive to **milk the property** in times of financial distress. In other words, it is in the stockholders' interest to pay extra dividends, thereby reducing the value of the firm which would go to bondholders in the event of bankruptcy.

The three strategies described in this section represent distortions of the investment process which result from the fact that there is a probability of bankruptcy or financial distress. In each case, stockholders take an action which is contrary to the best interests of the bondholders, so it would seem that the cost of these actions is incurred by the bondholders. However, bondholders who are aware of the likelihood of bankruptcy anticipate that stockholders will choose investment strategies which are not in the bondholders' best interests. Consequently, anticipating this possibility, bondholders increase the interest rate required on the firm's bonds. These increased costs are paid by stockholders, who are thereby paying the costs of the strategies described above.

Can Costs of Debt Be Reduced?

Protective covenants and **consolidation of debt** can reduce, but not eliminate, the costs of financial distress described in the previous section.

Protective Covenants. Stockholders agree to protective covenants, incorporated into the loan document (or indenture), in order to reduce the interest rate paid on the debt. **Negative covenants** limit or prohibit certain actions. For example, negative covenants limit the amount of dividends that can be paid, or prohibit mergers, the issue of new debt, or the pledging, sale or lease of certain assets. **Positive covenants** require certain actions on the part of the company, such as maintaining a specified minimum level of working capital or providing financial statements to the lender. Protective covenants should reduce the costs of bankruptcy, thereby increasing the value of the firm.

Consolidation of Debt. One source of the direct costs of financial distress cited above is the conflict among various creditors in the event of bankruptcy. These costs can be reduced if the firm arranges financing with only one lender, or a few lenders. Furthermore, if bondholders also own stock, the conflict between creditors and stockholders can be alleviated.

Integration of Tax Effects and Financial Distress Costs

Financial distress costs are insignificant for a firm with little or no debt. As such a firm adds a small amount of debt to its capital structure, it derives the benefit of the tax shield on debt without incurring significant costs of financial distress. As a firm uses more and more debt, however, the savings in taxes are eventually offset by the increased likelihood that financial distress costs will be incurred. Conceivably, there exists a point short of 100% debt where these two factors exactly offset each other, and the value of the firm is maximized.

If we include the costs of financial distress, then the value of the levered firm could be written as:

$$V_L = V_U + PV(\text{Tax Shield}) - PV(\text{Financial Distress Costs})$$

and an optimum (or target) capital structure exists where the benefit of another dollar in debt is balanced by the increased likelihood of financial distress.

Figure 15.1 summarizes this discussion in terms of the value of the firm. If we begin with no debt, the value of the firm increases as debt is added. The incremental gains from additional debt begin diminishing, however, because of the increased likelihood of financial distress. An optimal capital structure occurs when the present value of the tax saving from an additional dollar of debt (the marginal benefit of leverage) equals the increase in the present value of expected bankruptcy costs (the marginal cost of leverage). At this point, the value of the firm is maximized.

Value of the Firm

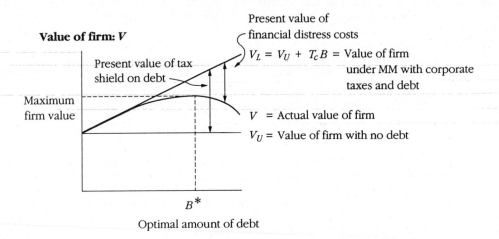

Figure 15.1

Two qualitative conclusions are derived from this analysis: firms with higher tax rates should borrow more, and firms with higher risks of distress (perhaps those with higher operating risks) should borrow less.

Pie Again. We initially viewed the value of the firm as being equal to the value of the stock plus the value of the debt. A way of reconciling much of the discussion in this chapter is to recognize that the pie representing the firm is actually composed of much more than just the debt and equity portions. For example, the government takes a substantial slice in the form of taxes. In the event of bankruptcy, many other parties will take a slice. Therefore, a large number of different types of claims to the firm's cash flow may exist at any time.

All the claims to the firm's cash flow can nonetheless be divided into two groups. The debt and equity are the **marketed claims** and the rest are **nonmarketed claims**. When we speak of the capital structure issue, we are really investigating whether the total value of the marketed claims can be increased by decreasing the size of the nonmarketed claims. For example, the interest tax shield increases the size of the marketed claims by decreasing the size of the nonmarketed government claim. It is important to keep in mind that the size of the pie is constant when we include all the claims. The issue under consideration is how the cash flow from operations is paid out. The optimum capital structure minimizes the 'nibbling' by those who hold nonmarketed claims.

Shirking and Perquisites: A Note on Equity Costs

In this section, we consider a cost of equity which tends to increase the optimal debt-equity ratio. This **agency cost of equity** indicates that a manager-owner of a firm is more likely to shirk and to obtain more perquisites if he owns a smaller portion of the firm.

Imagine that an owner-entrepreneur, who owns 100% of the firm, is seeking to obtain additional financing. If he chooses to obtain the financing in the form of debt, he retains 100% ownership of the firm, but, of course, incurs a fixed debt obligation.   We assume that the owner is highly motivated by the opportunity for financial gain and, since the debt obligation is fixed, the owner is still motivated to expend substantial time working at the business. In other words, the issuing of debt does not change the fact that any financial benefit derived from his work at the business accrues entirely to him, once the fixed debt obligation is met. On the other hand, suppose that the same owner-entrepreneur chooses to sell common stock in order to obtain the required financing. If, for example, he sells a 40% interest in the firm to new owners, his motivation to work is immediately reduced by the fact that 40% of any financial benefit resulting from his expenditure of time and effort goes to the new stockholders of the firm, while he keeps only 60%. Similarly, he is motivated to acquire perquisites, such as a large office or company car, since 40% of the cost of these perquisites is paid by the new stockholders.

The costs associated with the entrepreneur's incentive to shirk and to acquire perquisites are called agency costs, because they result from the manager's role as an agent of the stockholders. The owner-entrepreneur bears these costs if he obtains equity, rather than debt, financing. Consequently, the agency costs of equity tend to reduce equity financing and increase debt financing.

Personal Taxes

A key feature of the U.S. tax code is that interest received from bonds is taxed as ordinary income. The capital gain portion of the return on stocks, however, is not taxed until the gain is realized, i.e., until the stock is sold. Thus, while interest paid receives favorable treatment at the corporate level, it is taxed unfavorably at the personal level. It is possible, then, that the tax saving at the corporate level is offset by increased taxes at the personal level.

To illustrate this scenario, we again consider the example of Firms U and L, introduced in the previous chapter. Suppose that the highest personal tax rate on interest income is 60%. Also, neither U nor L pays dividends; all of the firm's cash flow is reinvested in the firm. Since the capital gains tax can be postponed indefinitely, we assume that the stockholders pay zero personal taxes.

As indicated in the previous chapter, the cash flows after corporate taxes, but before personal taxes, are:

Cash flow to	Firm U	Firm L
Stockholders	$660	$627
Bondholders	0	50
Total cash flow	$660	$677

After personal taxes are paid, the bondholders will have [$50(1 - .60)] = $20 and the after-tax cash flows are:

Cash flow to	Firm U	Firm L
Stockholders	$660	$627
Bondholders	0	20
Total cash flow	$660	$647

In the absence of personal taxes, we found that Firm L has the greater after-tax cash flow. This conclusion has now been reversed! With personal taxes, Firm U has the greater after-tax cash flow and is thus more valuable.

Given these results, we expect that Firm L (and all other leveraged firms) would substitute equity for debt. The supply of bonds would then diminish and the interest rate would decline. As this occurs, bonds become less attractive to investors in the higher tax brackets. As a result, the relevant personal tax bracket on interest income declines as well.

In our example, it is easy to see that if the bondholders were in a 66% tax bracket, then the total cash flow would be the same for Firm U and Firm L. Investors in tax brackets greater than 66% would not hold corporate bonds, preferring instead the lightly-taxed equity. Investors in tax brackets below 66% find the bonds attractive. Investors in the 66% tax bracket are indifferent. At this point, any tax savings at the corporate level are exactly offset at the personal level, so no net tax savings exists. The value of Firm U is equal to the value of Firm L, and capital structure is irrelevant.

The Miller Model. In 1977, Miller demonstrated that the value of the levered firm (V_L) can be expressed in terms of the value of the unlevered firm (V_U) as follows:

$$V_L = V_U + [\ 1 - \frac{(1 - T_c) \times (1 - T_s)}{(1 - T_B)}\ ] \times B$$

where T_s and T_B are the personal tax rates on equity and debt, respectively.

The easiest way to comprehend Miller's model is to picture the optimum capital structure as the one that minimizes total taxes (i.e., corporate and personal) paid. This is accomplished if the entity in the lowest tax bracket pays the tax bill. If the combined corporate and personal equity tax rates exceed the personal rate on interest, more debt is called for, and vice versa. An equilibrium occurs when the combined corporate and personal equity tax rate is equal to the personal tax rate on interest. In this case, capital structure does not matter because total taxes paid will be the same under any mixture of debt and equity.

A striking feature of the new (1986) tax code is that the corporate tax rate (34%) exceeds the highest personal tax rate (33%) for the first time in history. Even if the personal tax rate on equity were zero, the gain from leverage would still be:

$$1 - [(1 - .34)(1 - .00)/(1 - .33)] = .015$$

or .015 cents for every dollar of debt. Thus there currently appears to be some definite benefit to leverage, as suggested by MM, but the gain is probably much smaller than indicated by MM Proposition II with taxes.

How Firms Establish Capital Structure

The results of this and the previous chapter do not provide an exact formula for evaluating the relationship between leverage and firm value. Consequently, it is important to consider evidence from the real world, as well as the theoretical considerations described above, in establishing capital structure policy. In this section, we consider several observed regularities in corporate capital structures. First, most firms do not use a great deal of debt, and many of these firms pay substantial taxes. There would appear to be limits on the ability of firms to exploit the interest tax shield. Second, when firms announce capital structure changes, increases in leverage typically result in immediate (and substantial) increases in firm value, while decreases in leverage tend to result in substantial decreases in firm value. Also, there is little evidence of a substantial bankruptcy risk impact. Finally, firms in similar industries tend to have similar capital structures, but capital structures appear to vary widely across industries. This fact suggests that capital structure is influenced by the nature of a firm's assets.

There is evidence that firms do have target capital structures and adjust their borrowing to move toward a target. Also, firms that are more profitable tend to use less debt and firms with high proportions of intangible assets also tend to use less debt.

The two factors that seem to dominate the capital structure decision are taxes and financial distress costs. If the firm is in a higher tax bracket than its bondholders, then leverage creates a valuable tax shield. If a firm has relatively tangible assets, then its financial distress costs should be low. If a firm has assets such as growth opportunities or research and development, these assets may disappear in bankruptcy, making the costs of financial distress higher.

CONCEPT TEST

1. The _____ costs of financial distress include attorneys' fees, administrative and accounting fees, and fees to expert witnesses.

2. If a firm is close to bankruptcy, the incentive to _____ may result in the acceptance of a high-risk project with a relatively low expected value.

3. A firm close to bankruptcy may chose not to undertake a positive NPV project because of the incentive toward _____.

4. Stockholders have an incentive to _____ in times of financial distress, which means that it is in the stockholders' best interest to pay extra dividends.

5. The indirect costs of financial distress are paid by _____.

6. Two ways to reduce the costs of financial distress are the inclusion of _____ in the bond indenture and _____.

7. _____ covenants limit or prohibit certain actions, while _____ covenants require certain actions on the part of the company.

8. One often discussed limitation to the amount of debt that a firm can employ is _____.

9. If we consider the impact of corporate taxes and the possibility of bankruptcy, the optimum capital structure is the point where the gain from additional _____ is offset by

10. In Question 9, the value of a levered firm is equal to the value of an unlevered firm with the same assets, plus the PV of the _____, less the PV of the _____.

11. The costs associated with an entrepreneur's incentive to shirk and to acquire perquisites when new equity is issued are referred to as the _____ of equity.

12. A key feature of the U.S. tax code is that payments to bondholders, relative to shareholders, are taxed _____ at the personal level.

13. Suppose that corporations are not taxed at all and that there are personal taxes on interest but not on capital gains. In this case, the optimum capital structure is _____.

14. If the firm is viewed as a pie, then the value of the pie can be decomposed into two types of claims: _____ claims and _____ claims.

15. When firms announce increases in leverage, firm value typically _____ and when firms announce decreases in leverage, firm value typically _____.

ANSWERS TO CONCEPT TEST

1. direct
2. take large risks
3. underinvestment
4. milk the property
5. stockholders
6. protective covenants; consolidation of debt
7. negative; positive
8. financial distress costs

9. tax savings; increased risk of bankruptcy
10. tax shield; bankruptcy costs
11. agency cost
12. unfavorably
13. 100% equity
14. marketed; nonmarketed
15. increases; decreases

PROBLEMS AND SOLUTIONS

Use the following information to solve Problems 1-3.

Firms X, Y and Z each expect to be in business for one year and each forecasts cash flows of either $100 or $500 for the year. The probability of each cash flow is .50. Bondholders and stockholders of each firm are risk-neutral and the interest rate is 10 percent. Firm X is an all-equity firm. Firms Y and Z have debt obligations of $50 and $150, respectively, due at the end of the year.

Problem 1

Calculate the value of the equity, the debt and the firm for X, Y and Z.

Solution 1

The expected cash flow to the stockholders of Firm X is $[(.5)(\$100) + (.5)(\$500)] = \$300$ and the value of the equity is $(\$300/1.10) = \$272.73$. Since there is no debt, the value of Firm X is also $272.73.

The cash flow to the stockholders of Firm Y will be either $50 or $450, and the expected cash flow is $[(.5)(\$50) + (.5)(\$450)] = \$250$. The value of the equity is $(\$250/1.10) = \$227.27$. The value of the debt is $(\$50/1.10) = \$45.45$. The value of the firm is $(\$227.27 + \$45.45) = \$272.72$. The value of X is equal to the value of Y, except for a small rounding error. These values must be equal because the two firms simply represent different allocations of the firms' cash flows. In both cases, the value of the firm is the present value of the expected cash flow of $300.

For Firm Z, the possible cash flows to the debtholders are $150 and $100. In the latter case, the firm would be bankrupt. The possible cash flows to the stockholders are $350 and $0. The expected values of the cash flows to the debtholders and the stockholders are $125 and $175, respectively. Note again that the total expected cash flow is still $300, so that the value of the firm must be the same as for Firms X and Y. For Firm Z, the value of the firm's debt is $113.64 and the value of the firm's equity is $159.09, so that the value of the firm is $272.73.

Problem 2

What is the expected return and the promised return for the bondholders of Firm Y? For the bondholders of Firm Z?

Solution 2

For each firm, the expected return for the bondholders is 10%. For Firm Y, the promised return is also 10%, because the bondholders are assured of receiving their $50 payment, and the present value of $45.45 is derived by discounting this payment at a 10% rate. For Firm Y, however, the promised return is greater than the expected return; the promised return is $[(\$150/\$113.64) - 1] = 32\%$, although bondholders know that there is a .50 probability that they will receive only $100.

Problem 3

Suppose that, in the event of bankruptcy, financial distress costs for Firm Z will total $40. What is the value of the debt, the equity and the firm for Z?

Solution 3

The value of the firm's equity is unchanged because the expected cash flow and the discount rate are unaffected by the financial distress costs. (Note that the discount rate is unchanged throughout this problem because we assume that investors are risk-neutral.) The expected cash flow to the bondholders is now $[(.5)(\$150) + (.5)(\$60)] = \$105$ and the value of the bonds is $(\$105/1.10) = \$95.45$. The value of the firm is $(\$159.09 + \$95.45) = \$254.54$. The value of the debt and the value of the firm have each decreased by $18.19. This is equal to (except for a rounding error) the present value of the expected value of the financial distress costs:

$$[(.5)(\$0) + (.5)(\$40)]/1.10 = \$18.18$$

This result indicates that financial distress costs reduce the total of the portions of the 'pie' which go to the stockholders and the bondholders.

Use the following information to solve Problems 4-6.

Nick's Noodles, Inc. is considering two mutually exclusive projects to expand manufacturing capacity. Nick is obligated to make a $500 payment to bondholders next year. The projects will determine the value of the firm as follows:

```
                        PROJECT A
                 Value       Value         Value
Probability      of firm     of stock      of bonds
   .5            $ 2,000     $ 1,500       $   500
   .5            $ 3,000     $ 2,500       $   500
```

```
                        PROJECT B
                 Value       Value         Value
Probability      of firm     of stock      of bonds
   .5            $   100     $     0       $   100
   .5            $ 4,700     $ 4,200       $   500
```

Problem 4

Calculate the expected value of the firm, the stock and the bonds if Nick selects Project A.

Solution 4

The expected value of the firm is [(.5)($2000) + (.5)($3000)] = $2500. The expected value of the firm's stock is [(.5)($1500) + (.5)($2500)] = $2000. The value of the bonds is $500.

Problem 5

Calculate the expected value of the firm, the stock and the bonds if Nick selects Project B.

Solution 5

The expected value of the firm is [(.5)($100) + (.5)($4700)] = $2400. The expected value of the firm's stock is $2100 and the expected value of the bonds is $300.

Problem 6

Which project will Nick accept? If Nick's Noodles were an all-equity firm, which project would be accepted?

Solution 6

The expected value of the firm's stock is greater with Project B than with Project A. Consequently, Nick will choose to undertake Project B. Project B is the high-risk project and, with Project B, there is a .50 probability that the firm will be bankrupt. The possibility of bankruptcy increases the firm's motivation to undertake the high-risk project because the loss in value in the event of bankruptcy is shared by the bondholders. The value of the firm is greater for Project A, so that if the firm were an all-equity firm, Nick would accept Project A, the low-risk project.

Use the following information to solve Problems 7-8.

A firm projects that next year's cash flow will be either $7,000 or $3,000, each with probability .50. Since the firm's obligation to bondholders is $5,000, there is a .50 probability of bankruptcy. The firm is considering a project which is certain to increase cash flows by $2,000, thus allowing the firm to avoid bankruptcy. The cost of the project is $1,200, which will be paid by the firm's existing stockholders.

Problem 7

Will the firm adopt the project?

Solution 7

Without the project, the expected value of the bondholders' claim to the firm's cash flows is $[(.5)(\$5000) + (.5)(\$3000)] = \$4000$ and the expected value of the stockholders' claim is $[(.5)(\$2000) + (.5)(\$0)] = \$1000$. With the project, the bondholders are certain to receive $5000 and the expected value of the stockholder's claim increases to $[(.5)(\$4000) + (.5)(\$0)] = \$2000$. However, the stockholders must invest $1200 in order to increase the expected value by only $1000. Therefore, stockholders will not accept the project.

Problem 8

If the firm were an all-equity firm, would the project be accepted?

Solution 8

The project requires that the stockholders invest $1200 in order to receive a certain $2000 cash flow. Since this is a certain $800 return, in one year, on a $1200 investment, this is clearly a positive NPV investment at any reasonable discount rate. Consequently, the stockholders of the firm would adopt the investment if the firm were an all-equity firm. The results of Problem 7 indicate that there is an incentive toward underinvestment when a firm is close to bankruptcy.

Problem 9

Ms. Kristy is the owner-entrepreneur of a publishing company. The firm is currently valued at $5,000,000 and Kristy plans to expand the firm. Financing for the expansion will be obtained either by borrowing $5,000,000 at a 10% interest rate or by issuing $5,000,000 of stock. Total cash flow to the firm after the expansion will depend to a great extent on the intensity with which Kristy works at the firm. If she works five days per week and takes two months vacation, cash flow will be $1,000,000 per year, but if she works six days per week and takes two weeks vacation, cash flow will be $1,500,000 per year. What is the cash flow to Kristy for each alternative?

Solution 9

If Kristy borrows $5,000,000, the interest expense will be $500,000 per year. Cash flow to Kristy, as 100% owner of the firm, will be ($1,000,000 - $500,000) = $500,000 per year if she works five days per week, or ($1,500,000 - $500,000) = $1,000,000 if she works six days per week. If Kristy issues $5,000,000 of stock in exchange for 50% ownership, her cash flow will be either ($1,000,000/2) = $500,000 or ($1,500,000/2) = $750,000. If Kristy works more intensely, the entire benefit of her additional work accrues to her as long as she is 100% owner of the firm. If she is 50% owner, she derives only half of the benefit of her additional work. In this situation, the equity financing alternative reduces Kristy's incentive to work hard.

Use the information below to solve Problems 10-12. (These problems are a continuation of Problems 7-10 in Chapter 14.)

The North Company has a perpetual expected EBIT of $200 and the interest rate is 12%. If North experiences financial distress in a given year, then EBIT is expected to be $100 in that year.

Problem 10

The probability of financial distress for North depends on the amount of debt North uses. Assuming that the corporate tax rate is 30%, complete the table below. Which of the four capital structures described below is optimal? Use the unlevered equity cost to discount any bankruptcy cost effects.

Amount of debt	Probability of distress	Expected EBIT	Cost of equity	Stock value	Total value
$ 0	.00				$800
200	.10				
400	.30				
600	.50				

Solution 10

In the zero debt case, expected EBIT is $200, the cost of equity is ($140/$800) = 17.5%, and the stock value equals the total value. For the case of $200 debt, the expected EBIT is [.90($200) + .10($100)] = $190. The value of the firm is:

$$V_L = \frac{EBIT(1 - T_C)}{\rho} + \frac{T_C r_B B}{r_B}$$

$$V_L = \frac{$200(1 - .30)}{.175} + \frac{(.30)(.12)($200)}{.12} = $820$$

The cost of equity (by MM Proposition II with taxes) is:

$$r_s = \rho_o + \frac{B}{S} \times (1 - T_C) \times (\rho - r_B) =$$

$$.175 + \frac{\$200}{\$620} \times (1 - .30) \times (.175 - .12) = .1874 = 18.74\%$$

The complete table is:

Amount of debt	Probability of distress	Expected EBIT	Cost of equity	Stock value	Total value
$ 0	.00	$200	17.50%	$800	$800
200	.10	190	18.74	620	820
400	.30	170	21.35	400	800
600	.50	150	30.33	180	780

The $200 debt option is optimal because it maximizes firm value.

Problem 11

Assume that the corporate tax rate is 30%, the effective tax rate on personal income from bonds is 40%, and the effective rate on equity income is zero. North has $500 in debt outstanding. The unlevered cost of capital is 20%. What is the gain from leverage for North?

Solution 11

The Miller Model indicates that the value of the levered firm (V_L) is related to the value of the unlevered firm (V_U) according to the following:

$$V_L = V_U + [1 - \frac{(1 - T_c) \times (1 - T_s)}{(1 - T_B)}] \times B$$

where T_s and T_B are the personal tax rates on equity and debt, respectively. Therefore, the gain from leverage is the second term in the above equation:

$$[1 - \frac{(1 - .30)}{(1 - .40)}] \times \$500 = -\$83.33$$

In this case, leverage reduces the value of the firm because the corporation is in a lower tax bracket than its bondholders; therefore, it is not desirable to shield taxes at the corporate level. North should have an all-equity capital structure.

Problem 12

Suppose that, in Problem 11, the effective tax rate on personal income from bonds is 20%. What is the gain from leverage for North?

Solution 12

The gain from leverage is:

$$[1 - \frac{(1 - .30)}{(1 - .20)}] \times \$500 = \$62.50$$

Leverage increases the value of the firm because the corporation is in a higher tax bracket than its bondholders.

Problem 13

Consider an economy with the following four groups of investors and no others:

Group	Marginal tax rate on bonds	Personal wealth (in millions)
Ivy League professors	50%	$2000
Big 10 professors	40	1000
PAC 10 professors	20	500
Big 8 professors	00	10

Assume that the professors are risk-neutral and that they can earn a 5% tax-free return by investing in foreign bonds. The tax rate on equity income is zero and the corporate tax rate is 40%. Corporations are expected to receive EBIT of $180 million in perpetuity. What is the maximum debt/value ratio in this economy? What is the total corporate tax bill? How much is invested in foreign bonds?

Solution 13

Since all investors are risk-neutral, the return on the untaxed stock is 5%. In a Miller-model equilibrium, the bonds must offer [.05/(1 - .40)] = .08333 = 8.333%. Given the tax rates, Ivy League professors will all hold stock; PAC 10 and Big 8 professors will all hold bonds. The Big 10 professors are indifferent between stocks and bonds since they earn 5% after tax from either investment. The maximum debt-to-value ratio occurs when the Big 10 professors all hold bonds.

If the Big 10 professors all hold bonds, the total amount of debt in the economy is [$1000 + $500 + $10] = $1510. The total interest bill is [($1510)(.08333)] = $125.83. Corporate equity is worth:

$$[(\$180 - \$125.83)(1 - .40)]/.05 = \$650$$

Total corporate value is ($650 + $1510) = $2160, and the debt-to-value ratio is 69.90%. The total corporate tax bill is [($180 - $125.83)(.4)] = $21.67. Total wealth in the economy is $3510. Total corporate value is $2160, so ($3510 - $2160) = $1350 is invested by Ivy League professors in foreign stocks.

Problem 14

Try this one on your own. Based on the information in Problem 13, what is the economy's debt-to-value ratio if Big 10 professors all buy stock?

Solution 14

The total amount of debt will be $510. Total interest will be $42.50. Total corporate value will be unchanged at $2160, because the capital structures are irrelevant. The debt-to-value ratio is 23.6%.

CHAPTER 16
CAPITAL BUDGETING,
THE WEIGHTED AVERAGE COST OF CAPITAL,
AND ADJUSTED PRESENT VALUE

CHAPTER HIGHLIGHTS

In previous chapters, we have discussed the use of the risk-free rate to discount riskless cash flows; in addition, we have indicated that an all-equity firm should use the security market line to determine the appropriate discount rate for risky investment projects. In this chapter, we discuss two alternative procedures for incorporating debt financing into the analysis of capital budgeting problems: the weighted average cost of capital and the adjusted present value.

Determining the Costs of Debt and Equity in the
Weighted Average Cost of Capital (WACC) Formula

In order to calculate the **weighted average cost of capital** (WACC), we first determine the costs of each of the individual sources of financing, that is, the cost of equity and the cost of debt. We discuss these procedures in this section. In the next section, we develop the procedure for computing the weighted average. Then, the WACC is applied to capital budgeting problems.

<u>The Cost of Equity</u>. As discussed in Chapter 9, the expected or required return for a share of stock is indicated by the security market line (SML), and can be determined as follows:

$$E(R) = r_f + \beta[E(R_m) - r_f]$$

Suppose that the market risk premium is 8.6%, the risk-free rate is 5.5%, and that the Pettway Company has a beta of .7. Using the SML, the expected return is:

$$E(R) = .055 + .7(.086) = .1152 = 11.52\%$$

The security market line indicates that the expected return, for an investment with β equal to .7, is 11.52%. Consequently, investors expect this rate of return for an investment in Pettway common stock. In terms of dollar values, it might be said that investors who pay $100 for Pettway common stock at date 0 expect that its stock price plus dividends will be worth [$100(1.1152)] = $111.52 at date 1. From the point of view of the existing stockholders, the sale of $100 of new common stock at date 0 requires a cash flow to the purchaser of the stock of $111.52 at date 1. Although part of the cash flow at date 0 is in the form of capital gains, rather than dividends, the cost of equity capital is the 11.52% return required by the new shareholders. For an all-equity firm, the cost of equity capital is the appropriate discount rate for the NPV analysis of capital budgeting projects.

<u>The Cost of Debt Capital</u>. It is generally assumed that the cost of debt (r_B) is the interest rate that the firm will have to pay on new debt. Since interest is tax-deductible, the after-tax cost of debt is

$[(1 - T_C) \times (r_B)]$, where T_C is the corporate tax rate. However, this approach ignores two significant factors associated with bankruptcy which modify this conclusion. First, a firm might issue a bond with a promised yield of 10%, but the expected return is less than 10% if there is some probability of default. Second, in the event of bankruptcy, some of the costs of bankruptcy are not paid to bondholders; therefore, there is a difference between the expected return to the debtholders and the expected cost to the firm. Although these considerations are difficult, if not impossible, to incorporate into the calculation of the cost of debt, they indicate that, at least theoretically, the cost of new debt is not the same as the promised yield on new debt. On the other hand, it is common practice to use the promised yield as the cost of debt. We follow this convention here, although we recognize the inaccuracy.

The Weighted Average Cost of Capital

For a firm that uses both debt and equity financing, the average cost of capital is the amount the firm expects to pay, to stockholders and bondholders, per dollar of financing obtained. The total after-tax cost of debt is $[(B) \times (r_B) \times (1 - T_C)]$ and the total cost of equity is $[(S) \times (r_S)]$, where B and S are the market values of the firm's debt and equity, respectively, and r_B and r_S are the unit costs of debt and equity, respectively. (Note that no tax adjustment is made for the total cost of equity because dividends are not tax-deductible.) The average cost of capital is the total cost of equity plus the total cost of debt, divided by the total value of the firm's capital. The latter quantity is $(B + S)$, and the average cost of capital for the firm is determined as follows:

$$\text{Average cost of capital} = \frac{\text{Total expected cost of capital}}{\text{Total value of capital}}$$

$$= \frac{Sr_S + [Br_B \times (1 - T_C)]}{S + B}$$

$$= \left(\frac{S}{S + B}\right) r_S + \left(\frac{B}{S + B}\right) r_B \times (1 - T_C)$$

The last expression above indicates that the average cost of capital is a weighted average of the firm's cost of equity and the firm's after-tax cost of debt; the weights are the proportion of the total firm value represented by equity $[S/(S + B)]$ and the proportion represented by debt $\{1 - [S/(S + B)]\}$ $= [B/(S + B)]$.

We have determined previously that Pettway's cost of equity is 11.52%. The yield to maturity on Pettway's debt is 8%. The total market value of Pettway's equity is $240 million, and the value of the debt is $160 million. We can compute the WACC as follows:

Financing components	Market values	Weight	Cost of capital	Weighted average cost of capital
Debt	$160	.40	.0528	.02112
Equity	240	.60	.1152	.06912
	$400	1.00		.09024

Thus Pettway's weighted average cost of capital is 9.024%. [Note that, in the above calculation, the cost of debt is the after-tax cost: $(.08)(1-.34) = .0528$.]

Solving Capital-Budgeting Problems

The net present value criterion requires that we now determine the NPV for an investment, using the appropriate discount rate. The appropriate discount rate to use in computing the NPV depends on the risk of the investment. One type of investment would be an expansion of the firm's existing business. In the case of such **scale-enhancing** projects, the investment is in the same risk class as the firm as a whole, and the appropriate discount rate is the firm's overall required return; that is, the firm's weighted average cost of capital. In general, the WACC is the correct rate to use for projects that are similar in risk to the firm as a whole.

Pettway is considering moving its operations from its current Florida location to Missouri, in order to obtain a more geographically central location. The cash flows from doing so are expected to be $25,000 per year for the next 25 years. The cost of the move is estimated at $175,000. Should Pettway move its operations? The cash flows are in the form of an ordinary annuity. At a discount rate of 9.024%, the present value of the cash flows is $245,087.74. Since the cost of the project is $175,000, the net present value of the move is +$70,087.74. Therefore, Pettway should relocate.

When a proposed investment is in a risk class different from the firm's risk class, we determine the expected return on financial market investments in the same risk class as the proposed investment, and use that rate to discount the cash flows from the new project. We do not use the firm's WACC when the risk of the investment differs from that of the firm. What we require of a new investment is that, given its risk, its return must be at least as great as the return for other investments of similar risk. Thus the project, considered in isolation from the overall firm, must be accepted or rejected.

Suppose that Beranek Corporation is in the low-tech printing business and generally has a low level of risk. Beranek is considering expanding into the much riskier electronic publishing business. What discount rate should Beranek use to evaluate the proposed expansion? The wrong answer is the WACC for Beranek. The correct approach would be to look at the required returns for companies already in the electronic publishing business, that is, companies in a risk class similar to that of the new project. The use of Beranek's WACC would lead to an overestimate of NPV because the discount rate is too low.

Adjusted Present Value

The weighted average cost of capital provides one procedure for incorporating the effects of debt financing in the capital-budgeting decision. Another alternative is the adjusted present value (APV) technique.

The three effects of debt which must be considered in the capital-budgeting problem are: flotation costs, the tax shield from debt, and the effects of subsidized financing. The WACC correctly accounts for the tax shield, but does not incorporate the other two effects. The APV technique can correctly incorporate all three aspects.

The adjusted present value is defined as the net present value of a project, under the assumption that the project is financed entirely with equity, plus the present value of the additional effects of debt.

To illustrate the application of the adjusted present value technique, consider the Brite Lites Production Company, which is evaluating an investment in a new production studio. The cost of the studio is $500,000 and straight-line depreciation will be used over the expected ten-year life of the asset. Incremental cash flow is expected to be $100,000 per year throughout the life of the studio.

The corporate tax rate is 34%, the risk-free rate for debt is 8%, and the cost of unlevered equity is 15%.

The incremental after-tax cash flow is [($100,000)(1 - .34)] = $66,000 per year, and the depreciation tax shield is ($50,000)(.34) = $17,000 per year. Discounting these cash flows at 15% and 8%, respectively, the present value of the annuities is ($331,238.73 + $114,071.38) = $445,310.11. The net present value of the project, assuming it is financed entirely with equity, is:

$$-\$500,000 + \$455,347.65 = -\$54,689.89$$

The negative net present value indicates that, if Brite Lites is an all-equity firm, the studio is not an acceptable project. However, suppose that Brite Lites is able to obtain $300,000 of debt financing (after payment of flotation costs) at an interest rate of 8%; the loan is non-amortizing, so that Brite Lites must pay [(.08)($300,000)] = $24,000 interest each year for ten years, and repay the $300,000 principal at the end of the ten years. We must now consider the effect of the flotation costs and the tax subsidy on the net present value of the project.

With flotation costs of 1.5%, the net amount of the loan is 98.5% of the amount borrowed, so that the total amount borrowed is ($300,000/.985) = $304,568.53, and the flotation costs are ($304,568.53 - $300,000) = $4,568.53. The flotation costs are amortized over the life of the loan, so that the firm will have a tax-deductible expense of $456.85 per year, or a net cash flow of ($456.85)(.34) = $155.33 per year for ten years. Discounted at 8% over the ten-year life of the loan, the present value of the tax deduction is $1,042.28 and the net present value of the flotation cost is (-$4,568.53 + $1,042.28) = -$3,526.25.

The net present value of the tax subsidy is equal to $300,000 (i.e., the amount borrowed at date 0) minus the sum of the present value of the interest payments and the present value of the principal payment. The after-tax cost of the interest payments is [($24,000)(1 - .34)] = $15,840. Discounted at 8%, the present value of the interest payments is $106,287.69, and the present value of the principal payment is [$300,000/(1.08)^{10}] = $138,958.05. The net present value of the loan is:

$$\$300,000 - \$106,287.69 - \$138,958.05 = \$54,754.26$$

The adjusted present value of the studio is:

$$-\$54,689.89 - \$3,526.25 + \$54,754.26 = -\$3,461.88$$

Consequently, Brite Lites should not build the studio even if $300,000 of the cost can be financed with the loan described above. However, another source of benefits associated with financing arises if the firm is able to obtain subsidized financing from a governmental agency. The benefit of such financing can be incorporated into the APV analysis using the techniques indicated in this section. If Brite Lites can obtain subsidized financing with a present value greater than the negative APV indicated above, then the studio project would become acceptable.

APV and Beta

The procedure described in the previous section uses the cost of capital for an all-equity firm to discount the cash flows from a scale-enhancing project. However, the firm performing the evaluation is not an all-equity firm. Therefore, we must develop a procedure for deriving the value of beta for the hypothetical unlevered firm from the beta for the actual levered firm; the cost of equity capital is then determined from the security market line using the beta for the unlevered firm.

No Taxes. We first derive the appropriate beta value under the assumption that there are no corporate taxes. Assume that one individual owns both the debt and equity of the levered firm. The beta value for this individual's portfolio, which is the same as the beta for the levered firm, is equal to the following weighted average:

$$\beta_{Portfolio} = \beta_{Levered\ Firm} = \frac{B}{B + S}(\beta_{Debt}) + \frac{S}{B + S}(\beta_{Equity})$$

where B and S are the market values of the firm's debt and equity, respectively, and β_{Equity} is the beta of the equity for the levered firm. Since the cash flows to the debtholders and the equityholders of the levered firm are equal to the cash flows to the equityholders of the unlevered firm, it is also true that β for the unlevered firm ($\beta_{Unlevered\ Firm}$) is equal to $\beta_{Levered\ Firm}$. Furthermore, if we assume that β_{Debt} is zero, then:

$$\beta_{Unlevered\ Firm} = \frac{S}{B + S}(\beta_{Equity})$$

Corporate Taxes. The above conclusions can be extended to the case where the corporate tax rate is T_C, so that the relationship between $\beta_{Unlevered\ Firm}$ and β_{Equity} is as follows:

$$\beta_{Unlevered\ Firm} = \frac{S}{S + (1 - T_C)B}(\beta_{Equity})$$

This result indicates how the firm should determine the relevant value of beta for the hypothetical all-equity firm (i.e., $\beta_{Unlevered\ Firm}$). Suppose, for example, that Friskey Pet Products is considering a scale-enhancing project. The market values of Friskey's debt and equity are $10 million and $30 million, respectively; regression analysis indicates that β_{Equity} is 1.2 and the firm's debt is riskless. The risk-free rate is 8% and the market risk premium is 8.5%. The corporate tax rate is 34%. $\beta_{Unlevered\ Firm}$ is given by:

$$\beta_{Unlevered\ Firm} = \frac{\$30\ million}{\$30\ million + (1 - .34)\$10\ million} \times 1.2$$

$\beta_{Unlevered\ Firm}$ is equal to .9836. The discount rate is derived from the SML as follows:

$$r_s = r_f + \beta[E(R_m) - r_f] = .08 + (.9836)(.085) = .1636 = 16.36\%$$

The NPV of Friskey's scale-enhancing project is calculated using this discount rate for the hypothetical all-equity firm, and then the effects of debt are determined in order to arrive at the APV.

A Comparison of WACC and APV

The WACC approach to incorporating the effects of debt in capital budgeting requires that the firm determine the costs of equity and debt, and the proportions of equity and debt for the firm as a whole. For a scale-enhancing project, these values are relatively easy to determine, so that the WACC can be used to determine the net present value of the project. However, the WACC approach is difficult to apply to capital budgeting projects which are not scale-enhancing. Consequently, some firms use capital budgeting guidelines which indicate that the WACC approach is used for scale-enhancing projects, while the APV is used for projects which are not scale enhancing. Although it is sometimes difficult to assign a particular project to one or the other of these categories, in general, many projects can be clearly categorized.

The APV approach can appropriately incorporate other aspects of capital budgeting problems associated with debt financing, such as the benefits of subsidized financing and flotation costs. In addition, as will be shown in a subsequent chapter, APV can also be used for lease-versus-buy analysis while WACC cannot.

CONCEPT TEST

1. For a firm that is financed entirely with equity, the appropriate discount rate for the NPV analysis of capital budgeting projects is the _____.

2. If bankruptcy costs can be ignored, then the promised yield on new debt can be used as the _____.

3. If a firm uses both debt and equity financing, then the cost of capital for the firm is called the _____.

4. Projects that have similar systematic risk are said to be in the same _____.

5. If the risk for a project differs from the risk of the firm, then that project should be evaluated by discounting cash flows at a rate equal to the _____ for securities with similar systematic risk.

6. The first step in computing the WACC for a project is to find firms in the same _____ as the proposed investment.

7. Interest paid by a corporation is tax-deductible. This feature of the tax code creates the _____ on debt.

8. The appropriate cost of debt to use in computing the WACC is the _____ cost of debt.

9. The weight applied to the cost of equity in the calculation of the WACC is the _____ that the firm employs in its capital structure.

10. Suppose that a firm uses its WACC to evaluate a project that is substantially riskier than the firm's current operations. The resulting estimate of NPV will be too _____.

11. If a firm uses its WACC to evaluate all projects, then it will be biased toward rejecting _____-risk projects and accepting _____-risk projects.

12. Venkatesh can sell bonds priced to yield 11%. If Venkatesh is in the 50% tax bracket, the after-tax cost of debt is _____.

13. A firm may have to raise financing for a new project. The costs associated with doing so are called _____.

14. The three effects of debt which must be considered in the capital-budgeting problem are: _____, _____, and _____

15. The _____ is defined as the net present value of a project, under the assumption that the project is financed entirely with equity, plus the present value of the additional effects of debt.

16. The _____ correctly accounts for the flotation costs, tax shield and the effects of subsidized financing.

17. The WACC correctly accounts for the _____ but does not account for the other two effects of debt.

18. The _____ approach is difficult to apply to capital-budgeting projects which are not scale-enhancing.

ANSWERS TO CONCEPT TEST

1. cost of equity capital
2. cost of debt capital
3. weighted average cost of capital (WACC)
4. risk class
5. expected return
6. risk class
7. tax subsidy
8. after-tax
9. percentage of equity
10. high

11. low; high
12. 5.5%
13. flotation costs
14. flotation costs, tax shield from debt, subsidized financing
15. adjusted present value
16. adjusted present value
17. tax shield
18. WACC

PROBLEMS AND SOLUTIONS

Use the following information for Problems 1-15:

Margo Corporation is a major producer of lawn care products. Margo stock currently sells for $80 per share; there are 10.5 million shares outstanding. Margo also has debt outstanding with an aggregate market value of $360 million. The bonds issued by Margo are currently yielding 10%, and the risk-free rate is 8%. The market risk premium is 9%, and Margo has an equity beta of 2. The corporate tax rate is 34%. Assume a one-factor model and corresponding SML throughout.

Problem 1

Margo is considering a scale-enhancing project. What is the cost of equity capital for Margo?

Solution 1

The cost of equity can be determined from the SML:

$$E(R) = r_f + \beta[E(R_m) - r_f] =$$

$$8\% + (2)9\% = 26\%$$

Problem 2

What discount rate should Margo use in evaluating the scale-enhancing project identified in Problem 1?

Solution 2

Since the proposed investment is scale-enhancing, the appropriate discount rate is Margo's WACC. The total value of Margo's equity is [(10.5 million)($80)] = $840 million. Since the total value of Margo's debt is $360 million, Margo has a total value of $1.2 billion, of which 70% is equity and 30% is debt. The cost of debt is 10%. The WACC is thus:

$$.7(26\%) + .3(1 - .34)(10\%) = 20.18\%$$

Problem 3

The project under consideration by Margo requires an outlay of $1,000,000 and will increase revenues by $380,000 per year for each of the next five years. The assets will be depreciated on a straight-line basis. Should Margo undertake the project?

Solution 3

After-tax revenues are [($380,000)(1 - .34)] = $250,800 and the depreciation tax shield is [($1,000,000/5)(.34)] = $68,000. These are each five year annuities; after-tax revenues should be discounted at the WACC and the depreciation tax shield should be discounted at the risk-free rate. The present values of the annuities are $747,084.47 and $271,504.28, respectively, so the total present value is $1,018,588.75. The net present value of the project is +$18,588.75, so Margo should undertake the project.

Problem 4

Suppose that Margo decides to use the APV approach to analyze the capital budgeting project. Ignoring taxes, what is the value of beta for Margo if the firm were financed entirely with equity (i.e., what is the value of $\beta_{Unlevered\ Firm}$)?

Solution 4

The value of $\beta_{Unlevered\ Firm}$ is given by:

$$\beta_{Unlevered\ Firm} = \frac{S}{B + S} (\beta_{Equity})$$

or [(840/1200)2] = 1.4.

Problem 5

If taxes are considered, what is the value of $\beta_{\text{Unlevered Firm}}$?

Solution 5

The value is determined as follows:

$$\beta_{\text{Unlevered Firm}} = \frac{S}{S + (1 - T_c)B}\,(\beta_{\text{Equity}})$$

or [$840/($840 + (.66 × $360))](2) = (.7795)(2) = 1.5590.

Problem 6

Calculate the cost of equity capital for Margo under the assumption that Margo is an all-equity firm.

Solution 6

The cost of equity capital is determined from the SML, using the value of β calculated in Problem 5:

$$E(R) = r_f + \beta[E(R_m) - r_f] =$$

$$.08 + (1.5590)(.09) = .22031 = 22.031\%$$

Problem 7

Calculate the net present value of the project described in Problem 3, under the assumption that the project is financed entirely with equity.

Solution 7

The after-tax revenues and depreciation tax shield identified in Problem 3 are now discounted at 22% and 8%, respectively. (Note that we are rounding the cost of equity capital from Problem 6 to the nearest percent.) The present values of the annuities are $718,200.85 and $271,504.28, for a total present value of $989,705.13. The net present value is -$10,294.86. (Note: since this calculation does not yet incorporate the additional effects of debt, we can not yet determine whether the investment is acceptable according to the APV approach.)

Problem 8

Suppose that Margo can borrow $300,000 of the cost of the project at a 10% interest rate, with flotation costs of 1%. Calculate the net present value of the flotation costs for this loan.

Solution 8

The total amount borrowed is ($300,000/.99) = $303,030, so that flotation costs are $3,030. The flotation costs are amortized over the life of the loan; therefore, the firm will have a net cash flow of [($606)(.34)] = $206.04 per year for five years. The present value of this annuity, discounted at the risk-free rate, is $822.66 and the net present value of the flotation costs is (-$3,030 + $822.66) = -$2,207.34.

Problem 9

Calculate the net present value of the loan described in Problem 8. (Assume that the loan is non-amortizing.)

Solution 9

The loan interest payments are [($300,000)(.10)] = $30,000 per year. The after-tax cost of the payments is [($30,000)(1 -.34)] = $19,800. The present values of the interest and principal payments, respectively, are $75,057.58 and $186,276.40. The net present value of the tax subsidy for the loan is:

$$\$300,000 - \$75,057.58 - \$186,276.40 = \$38,666.02$$

Problem 10

Calculate the adjusted present value for the project described in Problem 3.

Solution 10

The adjusted present value of the project is:

$$-\$10,294.86 - \$2,207.34 + \$38,666.02 = \$26,163.82$$

The adjusted present value indicates that the project is acceptable.

Problem 11

Margo is considering expanding into the homebuilding industry. Wildt Corporation is a construction operation that is similar to the one proposed by Margo. Wildt has a required return on equity of 17% and a target total indebtedness ratio (B/B + S) of 40%. Assume that Margo's expansion into the homebuilding industry will be financed entirely with equity. What value of beta would Margo use in evaluating this expansion?

Solution 11

We first determine the equity beta for Wildt. Wildt's required return on equity is 17%, the risk-free rate is 8% and the market risk premium is 9%. Therefore, using the SML from Problem 1, and solving for β, the equity beta is [(.17 - .08)/.09] = 1. Since this value of beta applies to Wildt, a levered firm, we next determine $\beta_{\text{Unlevered Firm}}$ using the following:

$$\beta_{\text{Unlevered Firm}} = \frac{S}{S + (1 - T_c)B} (\beta_{\text{Equity}})$$

The total indebtedness ratio for Wildt is 40%, so for every $.40 in debt, Wildt has $.60 in equity. The relevant value of beta is thus [$.60/($.60 + (.66 × $.40))](1) = .6944.

Problem 12

Use the beta value from Problem 11 to determine the appropriate value of beta for Margo to use in evaluating its expansion into the construction business.

Solution 12

The appropriate value of beta is based on the risk of the construction business, as indicated by the beta value from Problem 11, and Margo's capital structure. Solve for β_{Equity} is the following equation:

$$\beta_{Unlevered\ Firm} = \frac{S}{S + (1 - T_C)B} (\beta_{Equity})$$

where $S = \$840$, $B = \$360$, $T_C = .34$ and $\beta_{Unlevered\ Firm} = .6944$. The value of β_{Equity} is .8908.

Problem 13

Calculate the discount rate Margo should use in its evaluation of the proposed construction operation.

Solution 13

Using $\beta_{Equity} = .8908$ from Problem 12 and the SML from Problem 1, the cost of equity is 16.02%. The appropriate WACC for Margo to use is:

$$.70(16.02\%) + .30(10\%)(.66) = 13.19\%$$

Problem 14

If Margo enters the construction business, it will have to raise $300 million (ignoring issue costs) to finance the operation. The present value of the future cash flows has been estimated at $340 million. Assuming that Margo proceeds with the proposal and that Margo's debt-to-equity ratio will not change, calculate Margo's equity beta **after** the investment.

Solution 14

The new equity beta will be a weighted average of the old equity beta and the equity beta of the construction project. Before the project, Margo's equity was worth $840 million. The value of the new project is $340 million, so the equity will increase by 70% of the $340 million, or $238 million. The total equity value will be ($840 million + $238 million) = $1.078 billion. The beta on the original $840 million is 2 and, on the new equity, .8908. The weighted average beta is:

$$(840/1078)2 + (238/1078).8908 = 1.7551$$

Problem 15

Suppose that Margo's costs of debt and equity are 10% and 20%, respectively. Also, because of recent setbacks, Margo has a substantial accumulated loss; as a result, the firm will not pay taxes anytime in the near future. What is the WACC?

Solution 15

Margo is effectively in a 0% tax bracket. The WACC is thus:

$$.70(20\%) + .30(10\%) = 17\%$$

CHAPTER HIGHLIGHTS

Simple intuition suggests that dividend policy should not matter a great deal. Investors wishing a cash payout from their stock portfolios can simply sell some stock and pay themselves a cash 'dividend.' Investors who do not want a cash dividend can simply reinvest dividends received. As discussed below, however, there are factors at work that complicate this simple argument. That is, financial managers and investors find that there are reasonable arguments in favor of high dividend payout and other factors which support a policy of low dividend payout. In addition, there are those who believe that dividend policy is irrelevant. These conflicting points of view are addressed in detail in this chapter.

Different Types of Dividends

A **dividend** is a cash payment, made to stockholders, from earnings. If the payment is from sources other than current earnings, it is called a **distribution** or a liquidating dividend. Commonly, a corporation pays a **regular cash dividend** four times a year. An **extra cash dividend** may also be paid periodically.

A **stock dividend** is paid in the form of additional shares of stock and is not a true dividend. A 10% stock dividend, for example, increases by 10% the number of shares held by each stockholder. Since the number of shares is increased by 10%, without any change in the total value of the firm, each share is worth correspondingly less. A stock dividend is essentially equivalent to a **stock split**. A share distribution for which the number of shares is increased by more than 25% is considered a stock split, while a smaller distribution is called a stock dividend. Stock splits and stock dividends are, for the most part, just paper transactions which do not change either the total value of the firm or the value of the stockholder's position.

Standard Method of Cash-Dividend Payment

A cash dividend is expressed as either dollars per share (**dividends per share**), a percentage of market price (**dividend yield**), or as a percentage of earnings per share (**dividend payout**). A dividend becomes a liability of the firm once it is declared.

The mechanics of dividend payment involve the following four dates: the **declaration date**, the **date of record**, the **ex-dividend date**, and the **date of payment**. On the declaration date, the board of directors announces the amount of the dividend and the date of record. The dividend is paid to shareholders who are listed in corporate records on the date of record. The dividend checks are mailed to these owners on the date of payment.

If you were to buy the stock the day before the date of record, this fact would not be reflected in the corporation's records, because of processing delays, and the previous owner would be the shareholder of record. To avoid inconsistencies created by such delays, brokerage firms set the ex-dividend date four business days before the record date. Anyone purchasing on or after the ex-dividend date does not receive the dividend. Prior to the ex-dividend date, the stock is said to be trading **cum dividend** (with dividend); subsequently, it trades **ex dividend.**

Suppose a stock pays a $1 dividend and goes ex dividend on Wednesday. If you buy the stock on Tuesday, just before the market closes, you will receive the dividend; if you buy on Wednesday, just as the market opens, you will not. The price of the stock declines overnight by approximately the amount of the dividend. Since dividends are taxed as ordinary income, the price decline is actually closer to the after-tax value of the dividend, rather than the full amount of the dividend.

An Illustration of the Irrelevance of Dividend Policy

The basic argument for dividend irrelevance can be illustrated with a simple numerical example. Consider a corporation with one hundred shares outstanding which will have a certain cash flow of $110 at date 1, and will liquidate for a certain $242 at date 2. If 10% is the required rate of return, then the total value of the firm is:

$$(\$110/1.10) + [\$242/(1.10)^2] = \$300$$

and each share is worth $3.

One possible dividend policy is to pay $110 at date 1 and $242 at date 2. Suppose that, instead, the stockholders prefer a $200 dividend at date 1. In order to pay this, the firm could sell $90 worth of new stock at year's end and pay out a total of $200. What dividend would be paid to the old stockholders at date 2? There is $242 available at date 2. The new stockholders demand a 10% return, so they would have to be paid [$90(1.10)] = $99, leaving $143 for the old stockholders. The present value of the dividends the old stockholders receive is:

$$(\$200/1.10) + [\$143/(1.10)^2] = \$300$$

This result is exactly the same as before. In fact, no matter how the available cash is paid out as dividends, the value is always $300.

The Indifference Proposition. The above example illustrates the fact that, under certain conditions, dividend policy is irrelevant. Modigliani and Miller (MM) have shown this result to be generally applicable if markets are perfect, individuals have homogeneous expectations, and the investment policy of the firm is pre-determined and is unaffected by dividend policy.

Homemade Dividends. Suppose you own ten shares of stock in the company described above, and the firm has decided to pay out $110 and $242 at date 1 and date 2, respectively. You will therefore receive $11 and $24.20. However, you would rather receive $20 and $14.30 respectively. You can sell some shares at the end of the first year in order to get the extra $9. In doing so, you give up [$9(1.10)] = $9.90 at date 2. Thus, you will receive ($24.20 - $9.90) = $14.30, effectively creating a new dividend policy or **homemade dividend.**

It is important to keep in mind that we are not saying that dividends per se are irrelevant. Instead, we are saying that the decision to pay dividends now or later is irrelevant. It is also important to note that it is assumed here that dividend policy does not affect investment policy. That is, we assume that the firm accepts all positive NPV investment opportunities prior to making the dividend decision.

Taxes

The irrelevance of dividend policy established in the previous section is based on the assumptions of no taxes, no transactions costs, and no uncertainty. Clearly, these assumptions are inconsistent with reality. The current section is devoted to a discussion of the manner in which existing tax laws affect the earlier conclusions.

Firms without Sufficient Cash to Pay a Dividend. The simplest case to evaluate is that of a firm that does not have sufficient cash available with which to pay a dividend. Such a firm would have to obtain financing in order to pay a dividend. Suppose that a corporation issues $1,000 of common stock in order to pay $1,000 in dividends to its existing stockholders. If the existing stockholders are in the 28% marginal tax bracket, their net proceeds would be $720 after taxes. The firm will have sold common stock worth $1,000 so that existing stockholders will receive dividends worth $720. From the stockholders' point of view, this is a negative NPV transaction because they have sold part ownership of their company worth $1,000 and have received a benefit of only $720. Furthermore, the costs of issuing new stock further exacerbate the situation because the firm would have to issue more than $1,000 of common stock in order to both cover these costs and pay the $1,000 dividend. It is also possible that the issue of new common stock would put downward pressure on the price of the firm's outstanding stock. These considerations lead us to the conclusion that a corporation should not issue stock in order to pay a dividend. A similar evaluation applies to a policy of using debt to finance the payment of common stock dividends.

A counter-argument to the above recommendation is sometimes offered in the case of a company which has paid a regular dividend for many years but which is currently unable to continue the payment without additional financing. The stockholders' preference for continued dividend stability might outweigh the adverse consequences noted above, but empirical evidence seems to indicate that companies rarely issue common stock to finance a dividend payment.

Firms with Sufficient Cash to Pay a Dividend. Suppose that a firm has adopted all available capital-budgeting projects with positive net present value and still has $1,000 in cash. Should such a firm pay the $1,000 in dividends to its shareholders, in spite of the tax implications and transactions costs noted above? Consider the alternatives to a dividend payment: (1) select additional capital-budgeting projects; (2) repurchase shares of common stock; (3) acquire other companies; and, (4) purchase financial assets.

Any additional capital-budgeting projects have negative NPV, so that the first alternative to payment of dividends is unacceptable. In spite of this fact, some managers follow this course of action, to the detriment of the stockholders. The repurchase of shares might be preferable to dividend payment for some stockholders because taxes are lower for share repurchase; only the capital gain is taxable to the shareholder. However, this alternative is infrequently used because of IRS regulations restricting share repurchase as an alternative to dividend payment. The acquisition of another company is generally not profitable to the acquiring company. In part, this results from the fact that the acquiring company often pays a substantial premium above market value for the acquisition. As in the case of alternative (1) above, however, managers often undertake such acquisitions in spite of the cost to the stockholders.

The firm's purchase of financial assets is, under certain circumstances, advantageous to the stockholders. In the absence of taxes, this would not be the case since either the stockholder, or the firm on behalf of the stockholder, could invest in Treasury bills, for example, and receive the same future return, free of taxes. However, given the current corporate tax rate of 34% and the marginal 28% tax rate for individuals, stockholders prefer the payment of current dividends. If stockholders receive dividends today, they pay 28% taxes on both the dividends and the Treasury bill interest income. On the other hand, if the firm retains cash and invests in Treasury bills, interest income is taxed at the 34% corporate rate and then future dividends paid from the proceeds of the T-bill interest are taxed at the 28% rate. Clearly, the former alternative is preferable, but this conclusion results only from the fact that the corporate income tax rate exceeds the individual tax rate.

Consider a firm with $10 extra cash. Suppose the corporation is in the 30% bracket and shareholders are in the 20% bracket. If the $10 is paid as a dividend now, the shareholders will have $8 after tax. If they invest this $8 at a 10% pre-tax rate (8% after tax), then they will have $11.75 in five years. If the corporation invests the money at a 10% pre-tax rate (7% after tax), it will grow to $14.03 in five years. This $14.03 can then be paid out, and the shareholders will net $11.22 after tax. In this example, the shareholders are better off if the corporation pays the $10 dividend today.

Expected Return, Dividends, and Personal Taxes

Suppose that capital gains are not taxed, but dividends are taxed at 30%. The common stock of firm A, which does not pay dividends, sells for $20 a share today and is expected to sell for $22 in one year. The expected after-tax return on A is 10% and comes in the form of a $2 capital gain. Firm B is identical to Firm A, except that the stock of firm B is expected to pay a $2 dividend and to sell for $20 at the end of the year. What will firm B common stock sell for today? The after-tax dividend is $1.40 and the required rate of return is 10% (since B has the same risk as A). The price today is thus ($21.40/1.10) = $19.45. An investor who buys a share of firm B common stock for $19.45 receives an after tax return of 10% and a pre-tax return of [($22 - $19.45)/$19.45] = 13.1%. The pre-tax return for a high-dividend stock is higher than that of a low dividend stock in order to compensate for the taxes.

Under current tax law, dividends and capital gains are taxed at the same rate. Nonetheless, capital gains taxes are still postponed until a gain is actually realized, so the present value of the capital gains tax is less. Therefore, the conclusions from the previous example should still be relevant, although to a lesser extent than indicated in the example.

Empirical Evidence. A number of studies have investigated whether firms with higher dividend yields do have higher pre-tax returns, but the evidence is mixed. In one well-known series of studies, Litzenberger and Ramaswamy concluded that there is a positive relationship between dividend yields and expected returns. This finding suggests that a low dividend payout is the preferred strategy because firms with higher dividend yields have higher costs of equity capital. Other studies find no connection between expected return and dividend yields.

Real World Factors Favoring a High-Dividend Policy

Some have argued that a high dividend payout policy is preferable because of the **desire for current income** and the **resolution of uncertainty**.

Desire for Current Income. Some investors, including many on fixed incomes, undoubtedly desire current income. These investors might conceivably pay a premium for stocks with high dividends. Selling a portion of the stock each period in order to produce current income may be undesirable because of brokerage fees, among other reasons. However, a mutual fund could very easily provide this service by regularly selling its holdings of low-dividend stocks in order to pay dividends to its stockholders.

Uncertainty Resolution. A dollar received in the form of a dividend has a known value, while a dollar reinvested by the corporation has an uncertain future value. Therefore, it has been argued that the cash dividend reduces the risk of owning the stock. However, it is inappropriate to conclude that dividend policy affects the risk of the firm's future cash flows.

A Resolution of Real World Factors?

A general consensus exists on the important factors in dividend policy. Tax effects and flotation costs favor a low payout, whereas the desire for current income favors a high payout. Although the issue has been studied extensively, it is not possible to determine which of these factors dominates, so the policy question is unresolved. As explained below, the evidence is not easy to interpret.

Information Content of Dividends. It is generally established that stock prices increase following an announcement of a dividend increase. This fact seems to be an argument in favor of a high dividend payout. However, financial actions by the firm are sometimes regarded as a way of signaling future prospects to the financial markets. Firms resist cutting dividends, so an announcement of an increase indicates that the firm expects future cash flow to be sufficient to support a higher level of dividends. This is a positive signal, and the stock price increases. It is difficult to separate this information content of the announcement from the dividend itself.

The Clientele Effect. Some investors prefer high dividend payouts while others prefer low payouts. Different firms may end up catering to one group (or clientele) or the other. As long as both groups are satisfied, there is no gain to the corporation from changing its dividend policy because doing so just attracts a different clientele. This is called the **clientele effect**. A natural type of clientele is based on tax brackets. Evidence suggests that investors in low tax brackets tend to hold high payout stocks, and investors in high brackets hold low payout stocks.

CONCEPT TEST

1. Strictly speaking, a cash payment to shareholders which is not paid out of current earnings is called a _____.

2. Most public companies pay _____ dividends _____ times a year.

3. A dividend paid in the form of additional shares of stock is called a _____.

4. If a distribution of shares of stock increases the number of outstanding shares by less than _____%, it is called a _____.

5. Instead of paying cash dividends, a corporation can distribute money to its shareholders by means of a stock _____.

6. A cash dividend expressed as dollars per share is called _____.

7. A cash dividend expressed as a percentage of market price is called the _____.

8. A cash dividend expressed as a percentage of earnings per share is called the _____.

9. The mechanics of dividend payment involve _____ dates.

10. Chronologically, the first significant date in the process of paying a dividend is the _____ date.

11. The second significant date in the process of paying a dividend is the _____ date.

12. The third significant date in the process of paying a dividend is the _____ date.

13. The last significant date in the process of paying a dividend is the _____ date.

14. A dividend becomes a liability of the firm on the _____ date.

15. Suppose you own a share of stock. If you sell it on the ex-dividend date, will you receive the dividend payment?

16. If you buy a share of stock two days before the date of record, will you receive the dividend payment?

17. Typically, a stock goes _____ four days before the record date .

18. If you buy a share of stock before the record date and you receive the dividend, the stock must have been selling _____.

19. A stock is selling for $100 at the close of trading on the last with-dividend date. The dividend is $2. If there are no taxes, then the opening price the next day will be about $_____.

20. In the previous question, suppose that there are no capital gains taxes and that dividends are taxed at a 30% rate. The opening price would be about $_____.

21. A stockholder who is dissatisfied with the dividend policy of the firm can, by buying or selling shares of stock, substitute _____ dividends for the firm's dividends.

22. True or false: Dividends may be irrelevant.

23. True or false: Dividend policy may be irrelevant.

24. A firm should consider immediately paying out extra cash to stockholders if the corporate tax rate is _____ than stockholder tax rates.

25. _____ are an example of a tax-paying group that may have a preference for high dividends.

26. The _____ associated with new equity sales result in a preference for a low dividend payout.

27. Two factors which are often cited as arguments favoring a high dividend payout are the desire that shareholders may have for _____ and the _____.

28. Stock prices often react to announcements of changes in dividends. This reaction may stem from the _____ of dividends.

29. The _____ argument states that different groups of investors have different preferences regarding the level of dividends. One natural basis for the existence of such groups is differing _____.

ANSWERS TO CONCEPT TEST

1. distribution
2. regular cash; four
3. stock dividend
4. 25; stock dividend
5. repurchase
6. dividends per share
7. dividend yield
8. dividend payout
9. four
10. declaration
11. ex-dividend
12. record
13. payment
14. declaration
15. yes

16. no
17. ex-dividend
18. cum dividend
19. 98
20. 98.60
21. homemade
22. false
23. true
24. higher
25. corporations
26. flotation costs
27. current income; resolution of uncertainty
28. information content
29. clientele effect; tax rates

PROBLEMS AND SOLUTIONS

Use the following information to solve Problems 1-5.

The balance sheet for Reebop Corporation is shown below, in market value terms. There are 100 shares outstanding.

Assets		Liabilities	
Cash	$100	Equity	$1000
Fixed assets	900		

Problem 1

Reebop has declared a dividend of $.50 per share. The stock goes ex-dividend tomorrow. What is the price of the stock today? What will its price be tomorrow? (Assume no taxes.)

Solution 1

Since the balance sheet shows market values, the stock is worth $10 per share today (cum dividend). The ex-dividend price will be $9.50. Notice that once the dividend is paid, Reebop has $50 less cash, so the total equity is worth $950, or $9.50 per share.

Problem 2

Reebop has declared a 20% stock dividend. The stock goes ex-dividend tomorrow. What will the ex-dividend price be?

Solution 2

After the stock dividend is paid, 120 shares will be outstanding. The total value of the shares is still $1000; that is, the total market value of the equity is unchanged. Therefore, the per share value is ($1000/120) = $8.33. Notice that this is not 20% less than the old price; rather the old price is 120% of the new price: [$8.33(1.20)] = $10.

Problem 3

Instead of paying a cash dividend, Reebop has announced that it is going to repurchase $50 of stock. What is the effect of this repurchase? Ignoring taxes, show how this repurchase is effectively the same as a $.50 dividend per share.

Solution 3

Reebop will purchase 5 shares, leaving 95 outstanding. The total equity value will be $950, so that the market price is still $10 per share.

Consider an investor who owns 20 shares. With the cash dividend, this investor receives $10 in cash and has 20 shares (each worth $9.50), for a total value of $200. Using the $10, the investor could purchase 1.053 more shares and have 21.053 shares worth $9.50 each. With the repurchase, the investor has 20 shares worth $10 each, if she does not sell any shares. Alternatively, she could just sell one share for $10. As a result, she would have 19 shares (each worth $10), and $10 in cash, for a total of $200 again.

Problem 4

Suppose that capital gains are not taxed, but dividends are taxed at a 40% rate, and that taxes are withheld at the time the dividend is paid. If Reebop is going to pay a $.60 dividend per share, what is the ex-dividend price?

Solution 4

The price will decrease by the after-tax amount of the dividend, or [$.60(1 - .40)] = $.36. The ex-dividend price will be $9.64.

Problem 5

Suppose that, in problem 4, capital gains are taxed at a 20% rate. What is the ex-dividend price?

Solution 5

This problem is somewhat more difficult. Consider the following scenario: suppose you buy a share just before the stock goes ex-dividend, and then sell immediately thereafter. You will have an after-tax dividend of $.36 and a capital loss of D, the decline in the stock price. Since this loss is tax deductible, your after-tax loss is [D × (1 - .20)]. You will be indifferent with regard to buying the share with the dividend only if $.36 = [D × (.80)]. In this scenario, the price decrease will be ($.36/.80) = $.45.

In reality, capital gains are not taxed until the gain (or loss) is realized, so the size of the price decline would be much more difficult to determine; however, it would probably be less than the amount of the dividend but more than the after-tax value of the dividend.

Problem 6

Dadadas Company is in the same risk class as Old Balance Company. Dadadas has an expected dividend yield over the next year of 10%, while Old Balance pays no dividends. The required return on Old Balance is 20%. Capital gains are not taxed, but dividends are taxed at 40%. What is the required pre-tax return on Dadadas?

Solution 6

The 10% dividend yield is equivalent to a 6% after-tax return. Since the total expected after-tax return is 20%, the expected capital gain is 14%. The after-tax return is thus 'grossed up' to a pre-tax return of (10% + 14%) = 24%.

Problem 7

You own 20 shares of stock in Boing Aircraft. You are certain that you will receive a $.50 per share dividend at date 1. At date 2, Boing will pay a liquidating dividend of $13.80 per share. The required return is 20%. Assuming no taxes, what is the price per share of the common stock? Suppose that you would rather have equal dividends in each of the next two years; how can you accomplish this by using homemade dividends?

Solution 7

The value of your stock is the present value of the dividends, discounted at 20%, or $10 per share. Therefore, the total value of your position is $200. An annuity of $130.91 per year for two years has the same present value. At date 1, your stock will be worth the present value of the liquidating dividend, or $11.50 per share. You will receive $10 in total dividends at date 1. You will have to sell $120.91 worth of stock, or ($120.91/11.5) = 10.514 shares, leaving you with 9.486 shares. At the end of the second year, you will receive [9.486($13.80)] in dividends, for a total of $130.91, thereby accomplishing your goal.

Problem 8

Try this one on your own. Suppose that, in Problem 7, you wanted only $5 at date 1. What is your homemade dividend at date 2?

Solution 8

Your liquidating dividend will be $282, which is $6 greater than it would have been.

CHAPTER HIGHLIGHTS

The sale of securities to the investing public is an essential source of long-term financing for a corporation. To a great extent, the procedures described in this chapter apply to new issues of both debt and equity, but the emphasis is on equity.

The Public Issue

The Securities and Exchange Commission (SEC) is responsible for administering the Securities Act of 1933, which governs new interstate issues of securities, and the Securities Exchange Act of 1934, which governs securities already outstanding.

The Basic Procedure for a New Issue. Once the board of directors approves a new issue, the firm must prepare and file a **registration statement** with the SEC. This statement is a long, detailed financial disclosure. Under **Regulation A**, issues of less than $1.5 million require only an abbreviated statement. This is the 'small-issues' exemption. Debt securities maturing in less than 9 months are also exempt from the requirement to file the registration statement.

The SEC studies the registration statement during a twenty-day waiting period. During this period, the firm may provide potential investors with a preliminary **prospectus**, which contains much of the information in the registration statement. The issue is advertised in the financial press during and after the waiting period. The advertisements are placed by the **underwriters,** or **investment bankers,** who purchase the securities from the issuing firm and sell them to the investing public. The ads are called **tombstones** because they are comprised largely of the names of the investment banking firms which underwrite the issue.

The registration becomes effective in twenty days, unless the SEC issues a 'letter of comment' specifying changes in the registration statement. After the changes are made, another twenty-day waiting period begins. Securities may not be sold during the waiting period. When the registration becomes effective, the security's price is determined and the sale to the public commences. A final prospectus must accompany the delivery of securities or the confirmation of sale, whichever comes first.

Alternative Issue Methods

If an issue is sold to fewer than 35 investors, it is regarded as a private issue; consequently, registration with the SEC is not required. In contrast, a public offering of a new issue may be a **general cash offer** or a **rights offer**. Some equity securities, and almost all debt securities, are sold through a cash offering, which is an offer to sell to the general public. A rights offering is an offer to sell common stock to the firm's existing stockholders. Underwriters are generally employed for cash offers but not necessarily for rights offers.

A company's first public offering of equity securities is called an **initial public offering** (IPO) or **unseasoned new issue**. All IPOs are, by definition, cash offers, as opposed to rights offers, since a purchase of a new issue by the existing owners of a privately held company would not be a public offering. A **seasoned new issue** is a new issue by a company that has previously issued securities.

The Cash Offer

For a cash offer, underwriters formulate the method used to issue the securities, price the securities, and sell the securities to the public. Typically, the underwriter buys the securities from the firm and offers them to the public at a higher price. If the underwriter purchases the entire issue, then the issuing firm receives a fixed price for the securities, and all the risk associated with the sale of the securities is transferred to the underwriter. This procedure is called **firm-commitment underwriting**. The difference between the underwriter's buying price and the price at which the underwriter offers the security to the public is called the **spread**. The underwriter accepts the risk of not being able to sell the securities, in exchange for compensation received in the form of the spread. For large issues, the risk is shared by forming a group of investment bankers, called a **syndicate**, headed by a lead underwriter.

For a **best-efforts offering,** the underwriter does not purchase the securities, but rather acts as an agent and receives a commission for each share sold. The investment banker must make his 'best effort' to sell the shares at the agreed upon offering price, and the issuing firm bears the risk that the securities cannot be sold at that price. This type of underwriting is common for smaller IPOs but is used infrequently otherwise.

The period immediately after the sale is called the aftermarket. The principal underwriter is allowed to buy shares in the aftermarket in order to 'support' or stabilize the price.

Underwriting contracts often contain a **green shoe provision** which allows the syndicate to purchase additional shares at the offering price in order to cover excess demand. This option, which normally expires in about thirty days, is beneficial to the underwriter if the stock price exceeds the initial offering price during this period.

Investment Bankers. Underwriters are at the heart of the new issues market. Their services include providing advice to the issuing firm, underwriting the issue, and marketing the securities. The setting of an appropriate issue price is essential to the investment banker's business. Mispricing affects the issuing firm and the investor, as well as the investment banker's ability to attract underwriting business in the future.

The issuing firm selects an investment banker through either a **competitive offer** or a **negotiated offer**. In a competitive offer, the issuing firm selects the underwriter who submits the highest bid for the securities. A negotiated offer generally involves negotiations between the issuing firm and one underwriter.

The Offering Price. One of the most difficult tasks for an investment banker is the pricing of an IPO. If the price is set too low, the firm's existing shareholders incur an opportunity loss; if it is set too high, the issue fails to sell. New issues are typically underpriced, which is beneficial to new shareholders, but detrimental to existing shareholders. The degree of underpricing varies considerably, but the tendency is greater for smaller issues.

✦

Underpricing: A Possible Explanation. Because of underpricing, the returns from buying new issues are often substantial. Why does underpricing exist? Consider the following analogy. Suppose 1000 used Chevrolets are for sale at $600 each. On average, used Chevys are worth $600, so if you buy all of them, your profit will be zero. However, some are worth more than $600, and some are worth less. Suppose you cannot tell which are which, but car dealers can, and they bid on the good ones. If you try to buy all of the cars, the good ones will be rationed because demand will exceed supply, and you will be able to purchase only a percentage of them. On the other hand, you will get all the bad ones and, on average, you will lose money. As a result of this 'winner's curse,' you will not bid at all unless the price is less than $600. This reasoning is thought to be at least part of the explanation for the fact that new issues are, on average, underpriced; if they were not underpriced, ordinary investors would not buy them.

The Announcement of New Equity and the Value of the Firm

It might seem that firms would arrange new long-term financing after identifying positive NPV projects, and that the announcement of a new issue would be a positive signal to the securities markets which would lead to an increase in share prices. In reality, however, the reverse happens. Superior information in the hands of management may result in the issuing of new shares at a time when they are overvalued. Also, firms needing new equity may be those with excess debt. In either case, an announcement of an equity sale would be a negative signal. After all, if the firm truly has a superior opportunity, it is not beneficial to existing shareholders to share this information by selling new shares of stock. It would be preferable to issue debt and thereby ensure that existing stockholders receive all the benefit.

The Cost of New Issues

The issuer of new securities incurs numerous costs in addition to the spread paid to the underwriter. The costs include other direct costs (such as legal fees), indirect costs (such as management time), abnormal returns (the decrease in value of existing shares), underpricing, and the green shoe option.

Based on actual issuer experience, five conclusions can be drawn: (1) as a percentage of proceeds, costs are much smaller for larger issues; (2) overall, direct costs are higher for best-efforts underwriting, while direct costs are comparable for issues of a given size; (3) underpricing is more extreme with best-efforts underwriting; (4) underpricing exceeds the total direct discount; and (5) the costs of going public are substantial.

Rights

A firm's articles of incorporation may contain a **preemptive right**, which specifies that any new issue of common stock must be first offered to existing stockholders. The preemptive right gives shareholders the opportunity to maintain their percentage ownership of the firm when new securities are sold.

A common stock issue offered to existing shareholders is called a **rights offering**. A shareholder has one right for each share owned. A specified number of rights gives the shareholder the option to buy a new share at a fixed price, called the **subscription price**, during a specified period of time. The rights expire after this time. Shareholders can exercise their rights by purchasing the stock, or they can sell the rights to someone else.

The Mechanics of a Rights Offering. Three issues must be addressed with regard to a rights offering. The financial manager must determine: (1) the subscription price; (2) the number of rights required to purchase a new share; and, (3) the effect of the rights offering on the existing stock price.

Subscription Price. Suppose that MRR Corporation intends to raise $20 million in new equity through a rights offering. The firm's outstanding common stock currently sells for $40 per share; 10 million shares are outstanding.

Number of Rights Needed to Purchase a Share. The subscription price must be set below the market price in order for the rights offering to succeed. If the subscription price for the new issue is set at $20 per share, 1 million new shares will be sold in order to raise the $20 million. Since one new share will be sold for every ten shares outstanding, it will take ten rights to buy one new share. Clearly, there is a mathematical relationship between the subscription price and the number of rights required in order to purchase a new share. If, for example, the subscription price were $10, then 2 million shares would have to be sold, and five rights would be required to buy one share.

Effects of Rights Offering on Price of Stock. The right to buy for $20 a share of stock that is currently selling for $40 has value. In addition, the price per share of the outstanding stock will decrease. In the above example, an investor could buy 10 shares of MRR common stock for $400, receive 10 rights, and exercise the rights to obtain another share for $20. Since anyone can therefore acquire 11 shares for $420, the price per share will fall to ($420/11) = $38.18 following the exercise of the rights. The original 10 shares each carried a right, whereas the new share does not. The difference between the value of one of the original shares and the value of the new share is ($40 - $38.18) = $1.82, which is the value of a right.

For rights offerings, the **holder-of-record date** and the **ex-rights date** are comparable to the corresponding dates for dividend payments. The ex-rights date is four business days prior to the holder-of-record date, so that if a share is sold before the ex-rights date (i.e., 'rights-on' or 'cum rights'), then the purchaser receives the right. On the ex-rights day, the price of the stock decreases by the value of the right. As indicated above, the value of one right is the rights-on price less the ex-rights price. Alternatively, it can be computed as:

$$[(\text{ex-rights price} - \text{subscription price})/N]$$

where N is the number of rights required to buy one new share.

Note that in the above example, the investor can purchase 10 shares before the ex-rights date, for $400, and then use the rights to purchase the additional share for $20, for a cost of $38.18 per share. Alternatively, an investor could purchase shares after the ex-rights date for $38.18 per share. He could also purchase 10 rights for (10 × $1.82) = $18.20, and then use the 10 rights to purchase a share for $20; the total expenditure would then be $38.20 for a share, which differs slightly from the ex-rights price given above due to rounding in these calculations.

Effects on Shareholders. As long as shareholders either exercise or sell their rights, they are not harmed by the rights offering and the subsequent decline in stock price. In the above example, an owner of ten shares who exercises her rights has invested $420 and owns eleven shares worth $420. On the other hand, the investor may choose to sell her rights for (10 × $1.82) = $18.20; she will then own 10 shares worth (10 × $38.18) = $381.80, which, when added to the $18.20 value of the rights, leaves her total wealth unchanged at $400.

The Underwriting Arrangements. A rights offering often involves **standby underwriting**. The underwriter is paid a **standby fee** and agrees to purchase any unsubscribed shares. Only a small portion of a rights offering would normally not be subscribed; furthermore, shareholders are usually given an **oversubscription privilege**, which gives them the option to buy additional shares, at the subscription price, should any be available. Thus it is generally unlikely that the standby underwriter will need to 'take up' any unsold shares.

The New Issues Puzzle

Pure rights offerings (i.e., those without standby underwriting) are less expensive for the issuing firm than other forms of equity offerings; in addition, pure rights offerings permit shareholders to maintain their proportionate ownership of the firm. Despite these advantages of a rights offering, underwritten cash offerings are the dominant form of new equity issues. It is not clear why this anomaly exists. It is sometimes argued that underwriters serve to increase the stock price, but evidence suggests that this is not so. Underwriters provide some insurance as to the amount of financing raised, but this amount is not known until the issue price is set. Since this occurs only about 24 hours prior to the sale of the securities, the value of this insurance is minimal. In addition, the advantages of an underwritten issue include the fact that the proceeds are available sooner, the stock is more widely distributed, and the underwriter offers potentially valuable advice. While these arguments are plausible, none seems persuasive in light of the enormous cost differential.

A recently identified advantage of an underwritten issue arises from the fact that the underwriter may be thought of as 'certifying' the value of the issue. The value of this underwriting function, which is derived from the underwriter's reputation, has not been measured, but this function may explain why underwriters are commonly used.

Shelf Registration

In 1983, the SEC adopted permanently **Rule 415**, which permits a corporation to register an offering it expects to sell within the next two years. This **shelf registration** procedure permits the corporation to sell a portion of the issue any time during the two-year period.

To qualify for shelf registration, a corporation must be rated 'investment' grade, must not have defaulted on its debt or violated the Securities Act in the past three years, and must have equity with a market value in excess of $150 million.

Shelf registration has been controversial. Critics of the procedure have argued that the timeliness and quality of information provided to investors is reduced because of the two-year period. Also, the fact that the corporation can bring a large block of stock to the market at any time may depress market prices because investors perceive this market 'overhang' as a potential supply of stock which would cause price declines in the future. Evidence suggests, however, that neither of these arguments is valid. Nonetheless, shelf registration is not especially common.

Venture Capital

Small, new firms generally do not have access to the public equity markets as a source of equity financing. These firms must often rely on the **venture capital** market for private financing.

Suppliers of Venture Capital. Venture capital is supplied by four categories of investors: (1) wealthy families which provide start-up capital; (2) private partnerships and corporations, which may include institutional investors as well as individuals; (3) venture-capital subsidiaries of large industrial or financial corporations, and; (4) an informal venture-capital market comprised of individual investors.

CONCEPT TEST

1. The _____ administers federal laws and regulations concerning the public sale of securities.

2. With two exceptions, a _____ is required for all public issues.

3. One exception to the requirement described in Question 2 involves issues of _____ in size. This is called the _____ exemption, and it is governed by _____.

4. The two kinds of public issues are _____ and _____.

5. A public issue sold to existing shareholders is a _____.

6. The first public equity issue by a corporation is called an _____ or _____.

7. A _____ is a new issue by a corporation that has previously issued securities.

8. In order to spread the risk of a new issue, underwriters frequently form underwriting _____.

9. The basic compensation in an underwritten cash offer is called the underwriting _____.

10. A _____ is an advertisement listing the names of the underwriters of a new issue.

11. If an underwriter purchases the entire issue from the firm at a fixed price, then this is called _____ underwriting.

12. If the underwriter promises only to attempt to sell the issue, then this is called _____ underwriting.

13. A _____ allows the underwriter to purchase additional shares at the initial price for a period of time subsequent to the offering date.

14. In an auction, it is sometimes remarked that the highest bidder is the one who made the biggest mistake. This is an example of a _____.

15. Following an announcement of a new issue, the value of existing shares is observed to _____ on average.

16. On average, new issue prices appear to be too _____. This tendency is called _____.

17. If a firm's articles of incorporation contain a _____, then a new issue of common stock must first be offered for sale to existing stockholders.

18. In a rights offer, the cost of a new share is called the _____ price.

19. In a rights offer, the ex-rights date is _____ trading days before the _____ date.

20. Prior to the ex-rights date, the shares are said to be selling _____ or _____.

21. After the ex-rights date, the shares are said to be selling _____.

22. If a rights issue is underwritten, the arrangement is usually _____ underwriting, for which the underwriter is paid a _____.

23. The value of one right is the difference between the _____ price and the _____ price.

24. In a rights offering, shareholders are usually given an _____ which enables them to buy additional shares if any are available.

25. The least expensive way to sell securities to the public is a _____.

26. The most common way in which securities are sold to the public is through an _____.

27. SEC _____ allows corporations to register securities that it reasonably expects to sell over the next _____ years. This is called _____.

ANSWERS TO CONCEPT TEST

1. Securities and Exchange Commission (SEC)
2. registration statement
3. less than $1.5 million; small issue; Regulation A
4. general cash offer; rights offer
5. rights offer
6. initial public offer (IPO); unseasoned new issue
7. seasoned new issue
8. syndicates
9. spread
10. tombstone
11. fixed commitment
12. best efforts
13. green shoe option
14. winner's curse
15. decline
16. low; underpricing
17. preemptive right
18. subscription
19. four; holder-of-record
20. rights-on; cum rights
21. ex rights
22. standby; standby fee
23. rights-on; ex-rights
24. oversubscription privilege
25. pure rights offer
26. underwritten cash offer
27. Rule 415; two; shelf registration

PROBLEMS AND SOLUTIONS

Problem 1

Yul Company has just floated an IPO. Under a fixed commitment agreement, Yul received $10 for each of the 1 million shares sold. The initial offering price was $11 per share, and the stock rose to $14 per share in the first few minutes of trading. Yul paid $60,000 in direct legal and other costs. Indirect costs were $40,000. What was the flotation cost as a percentage of funds raised?

Solution 1

Yul received $10 million. The underwriter spread was $1 million total. The direct and indirect costs were $100,000. The stock was underpriced by $3 per share, or $3 million total. Total costs were $4.1 million, so the flotation cost was 41% of the financing obtained.

Problem 2

Firms A and B have announced IPOs; each firm's stock will be sold for $10 per share. One of these issues is undervalued by $1, the other is overvalued by $.50, but you do not know which is which. You plan to buy 100 shares of each firm's stock. If an issue is rationed, you will only get half your order. If you get 100 shares of each firm's stock, what is your profit? What profit do you actually expect?

Solution 2

If you are able to purchase all the shares for which you bid, you earn a profit of $50. However, the undervalued issue will be rationed while the overvalued issue will not be rationed. You should therefore expect to get 50 shares of the former issue, for a profit of $50, and 100 shares of the latter issue, for a loss of $50; therefore, you expect to earn no profit. Notice that, on average, these new issues are underpriced by 2.5% ($.25 per $10). The fact that you expect to make a zero profit illustrates the winner's curse.

Problem 3

Emery Enterprises has announced a rights offer to raise $10 million for a new publishing project. The stock currently sells for $80 per share and there are 2 million shares outstanding. What is the maximum possible subscription price? What is the minimum?

Solution 3

In principle, the minimum subscription price could be arbitrarily small as long as it is not zero, so there is no minimum. This illustrates the fact that a rights offer cannot be underpriced. The maximum is $80, because the issue would not sell at a price higher than the current market value. In practice, a price of $80 would be too high because the market price could fall below this during the offer and the issue would not sell.

Problem 4

Using the information from the previous question, suppose that Emery sets the subscription price at $20 per share. How many shares must be sold? How many rights are required in order to buy one share?

Solution 4

At $20 per share, 500,000 shares must be sold in order to raise $10 million. There are 2 million shares outstanding, so it will take $(2/.5) = 4$ rights to buy one new share.

Problem 5

In the previous question, what is the ex-rights price? What is the value of a right?

Solution 5

Someone who owned no Emery stock could buy four shares for $80 and then exercise the rights to acquire a fifth share for $20. Thus 5 shares can be purchased for $340, or $68 per share. The ex rights price is $68, and the value of one right is ($80 - $68) = $12.

Problem 6

In the previous question, demonstrate the fact that a shareholder with 100 shares, and no desire (or money) to buy additional shares, is not harmed by the rights offer.

Solution 6

Before the rights offer, the 100 shares were worth $8000. After the offer, they are worth $6800. However, the 100 rights were sold for $1200, so the stockholder has $6800 worth of stock and $1200 in cash, for a total of $8000.

Problem 7

Try this one on your own. Refer to the information in Problem 3; suppose that Emery Enterprises had set the subscription price at $50. How many shares must be sold? How many rights are required in order to buy 1 new share?

Solution 7

Emery must sell 200,000 shares. Ten rights are required in order to buy one new share.

Problem 8

Based on your answer to Problem 7, what is the ex-rights price? What is the value of one right?

Solution 8

The ex-rights price is $77.27, so the value of one right is $2.73.

CHAPTER 19
LONG-TERM DEBT

CHAPTER HIGHLIGHTS

Thus far we have treated debt more or less generically; however, there are really many different types of debt with different features. In this chapter, we discuss these features in detail, including the distinction between publicly issued bonds and those forms of long-term debt which are not publicly issued; the latter category includes term loans and private-placement bonds. In addition, we describe and analyze the call feature that is commonly found in corporate debt.

Long-term Debt: A Review

Long-term debt securities are promises to pay principal and interest, usually in the form of semiannual coupon payments, according to a specified payment schedule. The **maturity** of a debt is the length of time a debt remains outstanding. A distinction is generally made between long-term, or funded, debt and short-term, or unfunded, debt; maturities are greater than one year for the former category and less than one year for the latter.

The Public Issue of Bonds

In general, the procedure for selling bonds to the public is the same as that for selling stocks, as described in the previous chapter. The **indenture** is the written agreement between the corporation and a trust company. The trust company is appointed by the corporation to represent the bondholders, and is charged with making sure that the terms of the indenture are followed, managing the sinking fund, and representing the bondholders in the event of a default. An indenture typically describes, in detail, the basic terms of the debt, the property used as security, the protective covenants, the sinking fund provision, and the call provision.

The Basic Terms. Bonds usually have a **face value** (or denomination) of $1000. As discussed in Chapter 5, the market price of a bond depends on the level of interest rates, and changes over time as interest rates change. In the financial community, bond prices are quoted as a percent of face value; therefore, a price quote of 110 indicates that a bond with a $1,000 face value is selling at a price of $1,100. Interest payments are typically indicated as a stated percent of face value, and payments are made semi-annually. A bond with interest payments equal to 8.4% of face value might pay $42 on March 1 and September 1 of each year, until the maturity date. Suppose that you purchase this bond on May 1, and the price is quoted at 90 on that date. The cost of the bond is $900, plus the interest accrued since the last interest payment on March 1. The $42 semi-annual payment amounts to $7 per month. In this case, two months have passed, so the accrued interest is $14, and the total you would have to pay to purchase the bond is $914.

Bonds can be either **registered** bonds or **bearer** bonds. If a bond is registered, the company's appointed registrar mails the interest payment directly to the owner of record. Bearer bonds, as well as some registered bonds, have dated coupons attached; every six months, the bondholder detaches a coupon and mails it to the company, which then makes the interest payment to the bondholder. The ownership of a bearer bond is not recorded with the company and is evidenced only by ownership of the bond certificate. As a result, bearer bonds can be easily lost or stolen; also, there is no direct way for the company to notify bondholders of important events. On the other hand, since bearer bonds can not be easily traced, they may have advantages to some investors!

Security. Debt securities differ in the collateral pledged as security for the payment of debt. **Collateral trust bonds**, for example, are backed by common stock held by the corporation. **Mortgage securities** are secured by a mortgage on real property, usually real estate. The mortgage is described in a legal document called the mortgage-trust indenture or trust deed. An open-end mortgage permits the company to issue additional mortgage bonds on the specified property, while a closed-end mortgage restricts the company's ability to do so. A mortgage may be on a specific piece of property (e.g., a building) or it may be a blanket mortgage which pledges many of the company's assets.

A **debenture** is not secured by specific property. Most of the corporate bonds issued today are debentures, although public utilities and railroads issue primarily mortgage bonds.

Protective Covenants. A **protective covenant** restricts certain actions of the company. A **negative covenant** (such as a dividend restriction) disallows certain actions. A **positive covenant** (such as a requirement that working capital be maintained at a specified minimum level) requires that certain actions be taken by the corporations.

The Sinking Fund. A corporation may repay the face value of a bond at maturity, but most corporate bonds are repaid prior to maturity. For public issues, repayment takes place through the use of a sinking fund and a call provision. A **sinking fund** is an arrangement which requires the corporation to make annual payments to the bond trustee, who then repurchases bonds. Bonds may be either repurchased in the open market or selected by lottery and redeemed at a specified price.

Sinking fund arrangements vary. Most start between five and ten years after the original issue date. Some call for equal annual payments throughout the life of the bond. The amount paid into the sinking fund may be insufficient to redeem the entire issue so that the corporation may have to make a large 'balloon' payment at maturity.

Sinking funds provide additional security to bondholders by providing for the orderly retirement of debt and by serving as an early warning system regarding potential problems. This benefit to bondholders is tempered by the fact that sinking funds give the corporation a valuable option. If rates are high, the corporation can buy bonds in the open market. If rates are low, the corporation can redeem the bonds at the specified price, rather than the higher market price. This feature makes bonds with a sinking fund less attractive to investors.

The Call Provision. A **call provision** allows the company to repurchase, or call, the entire debt issue prior to maturity at a specified price. Almost all debentures are callable. The call price is usually the face value of the bond plus a **call premium**. The call premium might be one year's interest initially and decline every year as maturity approaches. Often, bonds cannot be called for some number of years following issue (a **deferred call**) and are said to be **call-protected** during this period.

Bond Refunding

Bond refunding is the process of calling all or part of a bond issue and replacing it with a new bond issue. Two questions arise regarding callable bonds. First, should the firm issue callable bonds? Second, if a firm has issued callable bonds, when should they be called?

<u>Should Firms Issue Callable Bonds</u>? Call provisions have value to the issuer because the firm has the option to replace a bond issue with bonds paying a lower interest rate, if interest rates decline. On the other hand, bondholders require compensation for the possibility that their bonds may be called away. As a result, a firm must pay a higher interest rate on a callable bond than on a comparable non-callable bond.

Suppose we plan to issue a perpetual bond which pays 9% interest, the current market rate. There is an equal chance that the market interest rate will be either 11.25% or 7.5% one year from now. Thus, if the bond is not callable, its value at the end of the year will be either $800 ($90/.1125) or $1200 ($90/.075). The expected value of the future price is [.5($800) + .5($1200)] = $1000, so that the current price is [($90 + $1000)/1.09] = $1000.

Now suppose the bond described above is callable at $1090, and that it will be called if the interest rate drops to 7.5%. What must the coupon interest payment be in order for the firm to be able to issue the bond at the par value of $1,000? If we let C stand for the coupon, then, at the end of the year, the bondholder will have either $1090 (the call price) or a bond worth (C/.1125), in addition to an interest payment of C dollars. Algebraically:

$$\$1000 = [C + .50(\$1090) + .50(C/.1125)]/1.09$$

Solving for C, we find that the coupon payment must be $100.10. If this coupon were paid on a non-callable bond, the bond would sell for ($100.10/.09) = $1,112.22, so the corporation is paying $112.22 for the call option.

The value of the call provision to the corporation may exceed its cost for four reasons. First, if management has inside information that the interest rate the corporation pays will be lower in the future, then the firm might benefit by issuing callable debt. Second, if the bondholders are in a lower tax bracket than the corporation, then the corporation gains more from the tax-deductibility of the interest payments than the bondholders pay in taxes, resulting in a net benefit to the firm and/or the bondholders. Third, a call provision enables the firm to eliminate protective covenants which restrict the firm's ability to take advantage of positive NPV investment opportunities. Finally, a call provision reduces the sensitivity of a bond's price to changes in interest rates; the decrease in the bond's price volatility can benefit both bondholders and shareholders.

<u>Calling Bonds: When Does It Make Sense</u>? The call policy that maximizes shareholder wealth requires that the firm minimize the value of its callable bonds. This objective is accomplished by calling the bonds and issuing new bonds whenever the market price of the callable bonds exceeds the cost of calling the bonds; the cost is the sum of the call price and costs incurred in calling and refunding.

Bond Ratings

Firms typically pay to have a credit rating assigned to their bonds by either or both of the two largest rating agencies, Moody's Investors Services and Standard & Poor's Corporation (S&P). Bonds are rated according to the likelihood of default and the protection afforded the bondholders in the event of default. The two highest ratings are AAA and AA (S&P) or Aaa and Aa (Moody's). These ratings indicate a very low probability of default. Bonds rated at least BBB (S&P) or Baa (Moody's) are considered investment grade, while lower-rated bonds are referred to as low-grade or high-yield bonds; these are also commonly called 'junk' bonds. A bond that is in default is given a D rating.

Because of their higher risk, bonds with lower ratings have higher interest rates. However, it is unclear whether a bond rating has value, since the rating is simply a reflection of the bond's risk as determined on the basis of publicly available information.

Some Different Types of Bonds

In this section, we discuss the basic features of three kinds of bonds with unusual characteristics: floating-rate bonds, deep-discount bonds, and income bonds.

Floating-Rate Bonds. The coupon interest payments on a **floating-rate** bond are adjusted as interest rates change. This adjustment is based on an interest rate index such as the Treasury bill interest rate or the 30-year Treasury bond rate. The value of the bond depends on the nature of the adjustment mechanism and the frequency of the adjustments. Most 'floaters' have a 'put' provision which gives the holder the option to redeem the bond, at par value; usually, a put provision takes effect following a specified time period after the bond is issued. Another feature of most floaters is a floor-and-ceiling provision, specifying the minimum and maximum coupon rates payable throughout the life of the bond.

For the investor, the primary advantage of floating-rate bonds is that they reduce the inflation risk associated with investment in long-term bonds. Inflation rates have a direct impact on interest rates, so that rising inflation rates, which result in higher interest rates, have a negative impact on bond values. However, for floating-rate bonds, coupon payments increase with increases in interest rates, so that bond values remain relatively constant.

Inflation risk also affects the issuer of a bond; although the coupon payments for a level-coupon bond are fixed in nominal terms, the real cost to the borrower varies with the rate of inflation. Consequently, bond issuers may also find floating-rate debt advantageous because it reduces the variability in the real interest cost. Since the uncertainty affects both the borrower and the lender, it may be advantageous to both parties to write loan agreements that reduce this risk.

Deep-discount Bonds. A **pure-discount bond** is a bond with no annual coupon interest payments; principal and interest are paid at maturity, and the bond is issued at a price below face value. Such bonds are also called **original-issue discount bonds**, **deep-discount bonds**, or **zero-coupon bonds**.

Suppose a corporation issues a 10-year pure-discount bond when the market rate of interest is 10%. The price of the bond is the present value of $1000, to be received in 10 years, discounted at 10%, or $385.54. Over the life of the bond, the issuer pays ($1000 - $385.54) = $614.46 in interest.

Income Bonds. The coupon payment for an **income bond** is dependent on corporate income; that is, the company is obligated to make interest payments only if income is sufficient. Income bonds offer the advantage of the tax deduction for interest expense, without the risk of financial distress; an income bond is not in default when a coupon payment is omitted due to insufficient income. Despite these important advantages, corporations rarely issue income bonds. No adequate explanation of the reason for this inconsistency has been forthcoming.

Direct Placement Compared to Public Issues

More than 50% of all debt is directly placed, either as **term loans** or **private placements**. A term loan is a direct business loan that is normally amortized over a period of one to fifteen years. The major lenders are commercial banks and insurance companies. A private placement is similar to a term loan except for the fact that the maturity is generally longer.

Private placements tend to have higher interest rates than public issues and are also more likely to have restrictive covenants. The benefits of private placements are that they are easier to renegotiate, need not be registered with the SEC, and incur lower distribution costs.

CONCEPT TEST

1. The _____ is the written agreement between the corporation and the trustee.

2. Bonds usually have a _____ value of _____.

3. Bond prices are quoted net of _____.

4. If the coupon interest payment is mailed directly to the owner, the bond must be in _____ form.

5. With a _____ bond, a coupon must be presented before an interest payment is made.

6. If the pledged assets for a secured bond are securities, then these securities are called the _____.

7. If the collateral for a secured bond is real property, then the bond is a _____ security.

8. An unsecured bond is called a _____.

9. A bond indenture contains _____ that limit the firm's activities.

10. An indenture might prohibit the firm from merging with another firm. This is an example of a _____.

11. An indenture might require that the firm supply audited financial statements every quarter. This is an example of a _____.

12. A _____ is an account managed by the bond trustee for the purpose of repaying the bonds prior to maturity.

13. An _____ mortgage permits the company to issue additional mortgage bonds on the specified property, while a _____ mortgage restricts the company's ability to do so.

14. A _____ gives the corporation the option of repurchasing or _____ an entire bond issue at a stated price.

15. If the option described in Question 14 is inactive for the first ten years, then this is a _____ and the bonds are _____ during this period.

16. Replacing all or part of an outstanding bond issue prior to maturity is called bond _____.

17. The two largest bond rating agencies are _____ and _____.

18. The highest bond rating is _____.

19. The lowest bond rating is _____.

20. Bonds rated below BBB are called _____ bonds.

21. Bonds with _____ ratings have higher interest rates.

22. Bonds with adjustable coupons payments are called _____ bonds.

23. Bonds that have no coupon payments are called _____ bonds.

24. Bonds that pay coupon interest payments only when corporate income is above a certain level are called _____ bonds.

25. The primary advantage of bonds with adjustable coupon interest payments is that they reduce the risk associated with _____.

ANSWERS TO CONCEPT TEST

1. indenture
2. face; $1000
3. accrued interest
4. registered
5. bearer
6. collateral
7. mortgage
8. debenture
9. protective covenants
10. negative covenant
11. positive covenant
12. sinking fund
13. open-end; closed-end
14. call provision; calling

15. deferred call; call protected
16. refunding
17. Moody's; Standard & Poor's
18. AAA or Aaa
19. D
20. junk
21. lower
22. floating-rate
23. original-issue deep-discount
    or zero-coupon
    or pure-discount
24. income
25. uncertain future inflation

PROBLEMS AND SOLUTIONS

Problem 1

Timberlake Industries has decided to float a perpetual bond issue. The coupon interest payment will be 8% (the current interest rate). There is an equal chance that, in one year, the market rate of interest will be either 5% or 20%. What will the market value of the bonds be one year from now if they are noncallable? If they are callable at par plus $80?

Solution 1

If the bond is not callable, then, in one year, the bond will be worth either ($80/.05) = $1600 or ($80/.20) = $400. The expected value of the future price is $1000. The present value of the $1000 plus the first $80 coupon interest payment is ($1080/1.08) = $1000, so the bond will sell for par.

If the bond is callable, then either it will be called at $1080 (if rates fall to 5%) or it will sell for $400. The expected value of the future price is [($1080 + $400)/2] = $740. The present value is [($740 + $80)/1.08] = $759.26.

Problem 2

If the Timberlake bond in Problem 1 is callable and sells for par, what is the coupon interest payment (C)?

Solution 2

In one year, the bond will be worth either (C/.20) or it will be called for $1080. If the bond sells for par, then:

$$\$1000 = [C + .5(C/.20) + .5(1080)]/1.08$$

$$\$540 = [C + .5(C/.20)] = 3.5C$$

$$C = \$540/3.5 = \$154.29$$

Problem 3

In problem 2, what is the cost to Timberlake of the call provision?

Solution 3

If the bond had a coupon interest payment of $154.29 and was not callable, then in one year it would be worth either $3085.80 or $771.45. The expected value is $1928.62. The bond would sell for [($1928.62 + $154.29)/1.08] = $1928.62. The cost of the call provision is thus $928.62. The size of this cost stems from the volatility of interest rates in this example.

Problem 4

Hanna Company has issued a 5-year, pure-discount, 12% bond. Assuming that the IRS allows straight-line calculation of the interest, calculate the annual interest deduction available to Hanna. Compare this with the true implicit interest. What is the benefit of the straight-line method?

Solution 4

The bond will sell for [$1000(.56743)] = $567.43. The total interest paid is ($1000 - $567.43) = $432.57. Under the straight-line method, the annual interest deduction is ($432.57/5) = $86.51. The implicit interest in the first year is [$567.43(.12)] = $68.09. With four years remaining to maturity, the bond will sell for [$1000(.63552)] = $635.52. The implicit interest in the second year is thus [$635.52(.12)] = $76.26. The necessary computations can be summarized as:

Year	Bond value	Interest deduction	Implicit interest
0	$567.43	$86.51	$68.09
1	635.52	86.51	76.26
2	711.78	86.51	85.41
3	797.19	86.51	95.66
4	892.86	86.51	107.14
Totals		$432.57	$432.57

Notice that, except for some round-off error, the total interest deducted is the same under either method. The straight-line method allows the corporation to receive the tax benefit early, however, thereby increasing the present value of the tax shield.

CHAPTER HIGHLIGHTS

Options such as the call provision on corporate debt have been described in previous chapters. This chapter concerns the valuation of options in general. In addition, we discuss the fact that corporate securities such as common stock and bonds can be thought of as options; consequently, we can gain additional insight into many financial problems and decisions by viewing them as options.

Options

An **option** gives the owner of the option the right, but not the obligation, to buy or sell a certain asset at a fixed price (called the **striking price** or **exercise price**) during a specified period of time. The act of purchasing or selling the underlying asset is referred to as **exercising** the option. The maturity date of the option is called the **expiration date**. An **American** option can be exercised anytime up to the expiration date. A **European** option can be exercised only on the expiration date. Options on stocks and bonds are traded on several exchanges, the largest of which is the Chicago Board Options Exchange (CBOE).

Call Options

A **call option** gives the owner of the option the right to buy a specified asset. The most common call options are options on stocks and bonds. For example, a call option to buy 100 shares of Times Mirror Publishing for $105 per share, anytime during the next several months, can be purchased through the New York Stock Exchange. If the price of Times Mirror stock rises above $105 during this period, the owner of the call can exercise the option at a profit.

The holder of the option does not receive cash dividends, but the striking price and number of shares specified in the option are adjusted for stock splits and dividends. If Times Mirror declares a 2-for-1 split, for example, then the option holder would have the right to purchase 200 shares at $52.50 each.

The Value of a Call Option At Expiration. Let S_T represent the market value of the underlying common stock on the expiration date, T. Suppose that the expiration date is in one year, so that T=1, and that the exercise price is $100. On the exercise date, the option is said to be 'in the money' if $S_1 > \$100$, and the value of the option is $(S_1 - \$100)$. For example, if S_1 is $120, then the owner of the option can buy the stock for $100, by exercising the option, and then immediately sell the stock for $120, for a $20 gain. If $S_1 < \$100$ on the expiration date, then the option is 'out of the money' and has no value. The call can not have a negative value because the owner of the call is not obligated to exercise the option.

Put Options

A **put option** gives the owner of the option the right, but not the obligation, to sell the underlying asset. You might purchase a put option if you expect the value of the underlying stock to decline.

The Value of a Put Option at Expiration. A put option is 'in the money' if the stock price is less than the exercise price and is 'out of the money' otherwise. If you expect that the price of Times Mirror common stock will decline below $105, then you could buy a put with an exercise price of $105. If the stock price fell to $80, you would 'put it to' the seller of the put, who must then buy, for $105, shares which are worth $80. The value of the put is ($105 - S_1), or $25 in this case; the owner of the put can purchase shares for $80 and then exercise the put, thereby selling the shares for $105, for a $25 profit. If the value of the underlying stock exceeds the exercise price of the put, the option value is zero.

Selling Options

An individual who sells an option is referred to as the **writer** of the option. The writer of a call receives a cash payment from the buyer of the call; the cash payment is referred to as the **call premium**. The writer of the call is obligated to sell the stock at the striking price if the buyer of the option chooses to exercise. Similarly, the writer of a put receives the **put premium** from the buyer of the put and is obligated to buy the stock at the exercise price should the buyer of the put elect to exercise.

The writer of a call with an exercise price of $105 is obligated to sell the underlying stock for $105; if the value of the stock is $120, the writer may be forced to buy the stock in the market for $120 in order to sell to the holder of the option for $105. Thus, the writer incurs a loss of $15, while the holder of the option gains $15. The writer's loss is partially offset by the premium which was initially paid to the writer by the buyer of the option. In the event that the price of the stock is less than the exercise price, the call is not exercised, so that the writer's gain is the premium paid by the buyer of the option.

The above situation is reversed for the writer of a put, who loses the difference between the exercise price and the stock price if the stock price is less than the exercise price. A put option with an exercise price of $105 will be exercised only if the stock price is less than $105; for example, if the stock price is $80, the writer of a put must buy, for $105, a share of stock whose value is $80.

Combinations of Options

Puts and calls are the building blocks for more complicated positions in options. For example, suppose that both a put and a call on TMM stock expire in one year and that both options have a striking price of $105; the price of the stock is $93.

Consider the following strategy: (1) buy a put; (2) sell a call; and (3) buy the stock. What will this portfolio be worth one year from now? The answer seems to depend on the price of the stock at that time. Suppose the stock price is $90 on the expiration date. In this case, you can exercise your put option, for a gain of $15, by buying a share in the market for $90 and then selling it to the writer of the put for $105. The owner of the call option will not exercise the call, and the total value of the portfolio is ($90 + $15) = $105, because you own one share of stock and you have gained $15 by exercising the put. Alternatively, you could simply exercise the put, by selling the share you own, so you would be left with $105 cash.

On the other hand, if, at the end of the year, the stock price is $110, then you will not exercise the put, and it will expire worthless. The owner of the call will exercise it against you; therefore, you will sell for $105 a share of stock that is worth $110. If you purchase the share in the market for $110, you lose $5 when the call is exercised. The value of the portfolio is $110 - $5 = $105. The alternative here is to sell the share you own to the holder of the put for $105, again leaving you with $105 in cash.

Notice that, regardless of the market price of the stock on the expiration date, the value of the portfolio is equal to the exercise price of the options; this is the general result for any value of the stock price on the expiration date. The fact that the value of the portfolio is $105 regardless of the price of the stock on the expiration date indicates that the above portfolio is riskless. Consequently, the cost of establishing this portfolio must be such that the strategy pays the riskless rate of interest; if this were not the case, then the resulting arbitrage opportunity would provide an investor with a return greater than the risk-free rate for an investment which is free of risk.

If the risk-free rate is 10%, then the present value of the $105 exercise price is ($105/1.10) = $95.45. The put premium minus the call premium plus the current stock price must be $95.45, so that the rate of return for this strategy will be 10%. This so-called **put-call parity theorem** is satisfied if, for example, the price of the stock is $93, the put premium is $14.45 and the call premium is $12, so that the cost of initiating this position is ($93 + $14.45 - $12) = $95.45 and the risk-free return is 10%.

Valuing Options

The preceding sections indicate option values immediately prior to expiration; in this section, we begin to determine the present value of an option.

Bounding the Value of a Call. A call that is in the money prior to expiration is worth at least the difference between the value of the stock and the exercise price of the call. Suppose the stock is selling for $80 and the option to buy the stock at $60 is selling for $15. You could buy the option for $15, exercise it by purchasing the stock for another $60, and then sell the stock for a guaranteed profit of $5. Consequently, the price of the call must be at least $20; at a lower price, the existence of arbitrage opportunities would immediately drive the price higher. The call premium will generally exceed the difference between the stock price and the exercise price of the call due to the opportunity for additional profit should the price of the stock increase further prior to the expiration date of the call. At the other extreme, the option cannot be worth more than the stock itself since the option is simply the right to buy the stock.

The Factors Determining Call-Option Values. Five factors determine an option's value. Two of these factors are features of the option contract: the **exercise price** and the **expiration date**. The remaining factors are characteristics of the underlying stock and the financial markets: the **stock price**, the **variability of the underlying asset**, and the **interest rate**.

The value of a call option increases with a decrease in the exercise price and increases with a longer term to expiration. The first of these relationships is clear from the preceding discussion; an option to buy an asset at a lower price has greater value than an option to buy the same asset at a higher price. The longer the term to expiration, the greater the value of the option, since the option with the longer term provides the holder of the option a longer period of time during which to exercise.

The previous discussion also indicates that, for a given exercise price, the value of a call increases with an increase in the value of the underlying stock. It is not immediately apparent, however, that the value of a call increases with an increase in the variability of the underlying asset. Although this result may seem counter-intuitive, imagine that you own a call on a riskless asset which is currently selling for $100 and will yield 10% over the year. What is the value of a call option to buy this asset for $120? Obviously, the value is zero because this asset can never be worth more than $110 during the year. If this asset's value were variable, however, then there would be a possibility that it would sell for more than $120, and the call would have value. The greater the variability, the greater the chance for profit, and consequently, the greater the value of the option.

The purchaser of a call option will potentially pay the exercise price at some future date. The higher the interest rate, the lower the present value of this future amount. Thus, the higher the interest rate, the more the call option is worth.

Factors Determining Put-Option Values. The five factors which determine call-option values also determine put-option values. Two of these factors affect put options in the same way that they affect call-option values: a longer term to expiration and greater variability of the underlying asset both increase put-option values. The effect of the remaining factors on put-option values is the opposite of their effect on call-option values: stock price increases reduce the value of a put; a higher exercise price increases the value of a put; and, an increase in interest rates reduces the value of a put.

An Option-Pricing Formula

In the previous section, we discussed the five factors that influence an option's value; in this section we discuss precise, quantitative option-valuation models. It is useful to first consider some simplified cases before proceeding to the well-known **Black-Scholes option pricing model**.

A Two-state Option Model. To introduce uncertainty, we initially hypothesize a world in which future stock price can take on one of two values; that is, we are presenting a two-state option model. Suppose a share of stock is currently selling for $100, and that the risk-free rate is 10%. Also, we assume that, one year from now (i.e., at date 1) the stock price will be either $105 or $120. A call option with expiration at date 1 has an exercise price of $100. How much is the call worth today?

If you buy a share of stock, then, at date 1, you will have a share of stock whose value is either $105 or $120. If you buy the option today, then you will have either $5 or $20 at date 1. Suppose that, in addition to buying the option today, you also lend the present value of the exercise price, ($100/1.10) = $90.91. At the end of the year, you have $100 from the repayment of the loan and either $5 or $20 from the exercise of the option, for a total of either $105 or $120; that is, the strategy of buying the option and lending $90.91 has the same possible future returns as does the strategy of simply buying the stock. This is the key to option pricing: it is always possible to identify a combination of buying the option and either lending or borrowing which has exactly the same payoff as simply buying the stock. Therefore, we can always determine the value of the option, as long as there are no arbitrage opportunities. In this particular example, the option is worth ($100 - $90.91) = $9.09.

What is remarkable about this result is that we did not have to know the probability that the stock price would be $105 or $120; we had to know only the **possible** prices, not the expected price!

The Black-Scholes Model. Black and Scholes derived a formula for the value of a call for the more general case where there are more than two states. The intuition behind this formula is the same as that described above for the two-state model. The **Black-Scholes call pricing equation** is:

$$C = SN(d_1) - Ee^{-rt} N(d_2)$$

where:

$$d_1 = [\ln(S/E) + (r + .5\sigma^2)t]/(\sigma t^{.5})$$

$$d_2 = d_1 - \sigma t^{.5}$$

$N(d)$ is the probability that a standardized normal variable (often referred to as 'z') is less than or equal to d. For example, if d were 0, there is a 50% probability that 'z' is less than 0, so that $N(d)$ = $N(0)$ = .5. (The cumulative probabilities for a standard normal distribution can be determined from Table A.5 in the Appendix.) S is the current stock price, E is the exercise price of the call, t is the number of years to expiration of the call, r is the continuously compounded risk-free rate, and σ is the annual standard deviation of the continuous return on the stock. The notation ln refers to the natural logarithm, which is most easily determined using a calculator with an [ln] function.

The primary attraction of this equation is that, of the five parameters, only the standard deviation has to be estimated; the other four can be observed directly.

The assumptions underlying this model are:

1.   Short selling is permitted without restriction or penalty.
2.   There are no trading costs or taxes.
3.   The option is European.
4.   The stock pays no dividends before the option expires.
5.   The stock price changes in a continuous fashion; there are no instantaneous jumps in the price.
6.   The market never closes.
7.   The risk-free rate is known and constant over the life of the option.
8.   The stock price has a 'lognormal' distribution; i.e., the log of the stock price has a normal distribution.

Although many of these assumptions are unrealistic, it is possible to modify the model in accordance with a more realistic set of assumptions. For example, if the stock pays no dividends before the expiration date of the option, the holder of an American call is always better off selling the option rather than exercising it, so an American option will not be exercised prior to maturity; therefore, assumption 3 does not pose a problem in applying the model.

Stocks and Bonds as Options

The financial decision-making process can often be reformulated in terms of options. Viewing financial decisions from this perspective often provides insight which is beneficial to the decision maker in understanding and solving a problem. In the remaining sections of this chapter, we analyze three categories of financial problems from this perspective. In this section, we view stocks and bonds as options on the value of the firm.

The Firm Expressed in Terms of Call Options. Suppose that a firm has a single debt issue that is coming due in one year. At that time, the shareholders will have a choice. If the value of the firm (V_1) exceeds the face value of the debt (B_1), then the stockholders will pay off the debt and the stock will be worth $S_1 = (V_1 - B_1)$. By paying off the debt, the stockholders own the assets of the firm.   However, if V_1 is less than B_1, then the stockholders will not exercise their option to acquire the firm's assets, and the bondholders will own the firm. The stock is worth zero in this case. Consequently, the equity in a firm with debt can be viewed as a call option on the assets of the firm.

The bondholders' position can be described as follows: the bondholders own the firm and they have written a call option against the value of the firm, with an exercise price equal to the value of the debt. The value of the bonds is then equal to the value of the firm's assets less the value of the call option held by the stockholders

The Firm Expressed in Terms of Put Options. The positions of the stockholders and bondholders of a firm can also be described in terms of a put option on the value of the firm. In this case, the stockholders' position can be described as follows: the stockholders own the firm; they owe interest and principal to the bondholders; and, they own a put option on the value of the firm. The position of the bondholders is: the bondholders are owed interest and principal by the stockholders; and, the bondholders have sold a put option on the value of the firm to the stockholders.

How can this put option be interpreted? In the event that the value of the firm is less than the face value of the debt at maturity, the stockholders do not have to make up the difference to the bondholders. Instead, they 'put' the assets of the firm to the bondholders. Effectively, the bondholders buy the assets of the firm for more than they are worth. This is exactly what happens when the seller of a put option has that option exercised against her.

A Resolution of the Two Views. The conclusions of this section are consistent with the concept of put-call parity described earlier in the chapter. That is, the put-call parity theorem implies that the relationship between the stockholders' position, described in terms of call options, is equivalent to the stockholders' position, described in terms of put options. Similarly, put-call parity implies that the two descriptions of the bondholders' position are equivalent.

A Note on Loan Guarantees. Regardless of how the risky bonds are viewed, the shareholders right to default is valuable. The option framework is useful in a variety of ways. For example, in 1980, the U.S. government guaranteed the debt of the Chrysler Corporation. Chrysler recovered and was able to repay its debt without any further help. Since the government did not actually have to pay anything to grant this guarantee, it might seem as though the guarantee was 'free.' This is incorrect. The government gave Chrysler's creditors a put option on the taxpayers. This put option, like any other, was valuable.

Capital-Structure Policy and Options

Some differences exist between stock options and the options created when a firm issues securities. First, the underlying assets are the equity in the firm in one case and the assets of the firm in the other. Second, the holders of corporate securities receive cash flows directly from the firm. Third, the holders of corporate securities have the power to change the corporation's dividend policy, capital structure, and investment policy.

Option theory explains a phenomenon we noted in earlier chapters: the incentive that stockholders have to shift the firm into higher risk investments. We know that the value of an option increases when the variability of the rate of return on the underlying asset increases. By substituting high risk assets for lower risk ones, the stockholders increase the variability of the rate of return on the assets of the firm, thereby increasing the value of the option to purchase those assets, or, equivalently, the option to put those assets to the bondholders. The protective covenants that bondholders require of the firm can be viewed as ways of limiting the ability of the stockholders to increase the value of their option.

Investment in Real Projects and Options

Standard textbook treatment of capital budgeting decisions requires the calculation of net present value based on all current and future cash outflows and inflows for a given investment project. However, it is often useful to regard a particular project from the perspective of options theory. For example, suppose that a firm is interested in acquiring and developing a particular location; however, the value of the project is dependent on any of a number of political or economic factors which may not be resolved for some period of time. Consequently, it may be appropriate to acquire the property and to postpone the decision regarding development until a later date. In this context, the decision to acquire the property can be viewed as equivalent to purchasing a call option, and subsequent development costs can be thought of as the exercise price on the option.

CONCEPT TEST

1. If you pay money to acquire the right to buy a specified asset at a fixed price anytime during the next 90 days, you have _____ a _____ option.

2. If you receive money in exchange for the potential obligation to buy a specified asset at a fixed price anytime during the next 90 days, you have _____ a _____ option.

3. If you receive money in exchange for the potential obligation to sell a specified asset at a fixed price anytime during the next 90 days, you have _____ a _____ option.

4. If you pay money to acquire the right to sell a specified asset at a fixed price anytime during the next 90 days, you have _____ a _____ option.

5. The fixed price in an option contract is called the _____ or _____ price.

6. The act of buying or selling an asset under the terms of an option contract is called _____ the option.

7. The maturity date on an option is called the _____ date.

8. An option that can only be exercised on the day it matures is a _____ option.

9. An option that can be exercised anytime up to the day it matures is an _____ option.

10. If the exercise price on a call option is less than the stock price, then the option is said to be _____.

11. If the exercise price on a call option is greater than the stock price, then the option is said to be _____.

12. Another term for selling an option is _____ an option.

13. What is the value of a call option with an exercise price of zero?

14. The five factors affecting an option's value are _____, _____, _____, _____, and _____.

15. Of the five factors which determine a call option's value, only one has an inverse relationship with the option's value. Which one?

16. Of the five factors affecting a put option's value, two have an inverse relationship with the option's value. Which two?

17. The equity in a levered firm can be viewed as a _____ option on the underlying assets of the firm.

18. The formula for valuing call options is called the _____ call option pricing equation.

19. Suppose you purchase the assets of a firm and sell a call option back to the original owner as a part of the deal. What corporate security have you effectively created for yourself?

20. Suppose you are a sole proprietor and thus have unlimited liability for business debts. To protect yourself, you purchase insurance. What corporate security have you effectively created for yourself?

21. If we view the equity in a levered firm as a call option, who owns the assets?

22. The value of risky debt can be viewed as the value of risk-free debt _____ the value of a _____ option.

ANSWERS TO CONCEPT TEST

1. purchased; call
2. sold; put
3. sold; call
4. purchased; put
5. exercise; striking
6. exercising
7. expiration
8. European
9. American
10. in the money
11. out of the money
12. writing
13. the same as the asset value

14. the stock price; the exercise price;
     the time to expiration;
     the risk-free rate;
     the volatility of the underlying asset
15. the exercise price
16. the stock price; the interest rate
17. call
18. Black-Scholes
19. a risky bond
20. levered equity
21. the bondholders
22. less; put

PROBLEMS AND SOLUTIONS

Use the following information about the Shome Corporation to solve Problems 1-5.

The price of Shome Corporation common stock will be either $60 or $80 at the end of the year. A standard call option contract for the purchase of 100 shares of Shome stock has an expiration date in one year. Investors can borrow and lend at 8%.

Problem 1

Suppose the current price of Shome stock is $65 and that the exercise price of the call is $70. What are the possible values of the call contract on the expiration date?

Solution 1

On the expiration date, Shome stock will be worth either $60 per share or $80 per share. If the stock is worth $60 per share, the option to buy at $70 is worthless. If the stock is worth $80 per share, then the call option is worth [($80 - $70)(100)] = $1000.

Problem 2

For the data in Problem 1, what is the current value of the call contract?

Solution 2

If you buy the call, then, at the end of the year, you will have either $0 or $1000, as indicated in Problem 1. We must determine a strategy consisting of borrowing and buying stock that leaves us with the same payoffs as the call. It can be shown that the number of shares per option that must be purchased is equal to the difference between the call payoffs divided by the difference between the stock payoffs. In this case, you must purchase:

$$($1000 - 0)/($8000 - $6000) = .5 \text{ shares per option}$$

or a total of 50 shares.

If you buy 50 shares, you will have either $4000 or $3000 at the end of the year. If we arrange a loan that requires us to repay $3000, the net payoff from borrowing and buying 50 shares of stock is either $1000 or $0, the same as the call option payoffs. At an interest rate of 8%, we can borrow ($3000/1.08) = $2777.78. At $65 per share, 50 shares of stock costs $3250. Therefore, the net investment required to duplicate the call option is ($3250 - $2777.78) = $472.22, which is equal to the value of the call option contract.

Problem 3

Suppose that the option described in Problem 1 has an exercise price of $50. What is the value of the call contract?

Solution 3

If you buy the contract, then your payoff at the end of the year will be either $1000 or $3000. The number of shares of stock required to replicate the call is:

($3000 - $1000)/($8000 - $6000) = 1 per option

The cost of buying 100 shares is $6500. Your payoff from owning 100 shares will be either $6000 or $8000. If you repay $5000 on a loan, then you have replicated the payoffs from the option. Thus, you will borrow ($5000/1.08) = $4629.63. The net cost of replicating the option is ($6500 - $4629.63) = $1870.37, which is equal to the value of the call option contract.

Problem 4

Suppose a call contract for 100 shares of Shome common stock, with an exercise price of $65, sells for $1000. What is the current value of the stock?

Solution 4

The number of shares required in order to replicate the call is ($1500/$2000) = .75 per call, or a total of 75 shares. Your payoff on 75 shares will either be $4500 or $6000. To duplicate the call payoffs, borrow the present value of $4500, or ($4500/1.08) = $4166.67. The total value of the 75 shares is thus ($4166.67 + $1000) = $5166.67 and the current value of the stock is ($5166.67/75) = $68.89 per share.

Problem 5

Calculate the value of the call if the current stock price is $50 and the exercise price is $70.

Solution 5

You need .5 shares per option, or $2500 of common stock. To replicate the call, you borrow the present value of $6000, or $5555.56. The value of the call contract appears to be ($2500 - $5555.56) = -$3055.56; however, since the value of the call cannot be negative, the call is worth zero.

How can the option to buy a share of stock that may be worth $80 for only $70 be worth nothing? The inconsistency here arises from the fact that the current stock price cannot be $50. You can borrow $50 at an 8% interest rate, and buy one share of stock. Under the worst case scenario, the share will be worth $60, but you will have to repay only [($50)(1.08)] = $54 on the loan. As a result, you would earn, at a minimum, a costless, riskless $6. There is an arbitrage opportunity here because the return on the stock is always greater than the riskless 8% interest rate. Therefore, the stock must sell for more than $50 per share.

Problem 6

Kau Corporation, the publisher of Gourmand magazine, is currently selling at $50 per share. Assume that there is no uncertainty and that the continuously compounded interest rate is 10%. What is the value of a call option to buy one share of Kau for $40 in one year?

Solution 6

If there is no uncertainty, then the value of Kau's stock will be ($50e$^{.10}$) = $55.26 in one year. The payoff on the option is thus $15.26. The value of the call is ($15.26e$^{-.10}$) = $13.81.

Problem 7

Calls on Hanna Corporation common stock are currently selling for $10; puts are selling for $8. The exercise price of both options is $80 and the expiration date is in one year. The risk-free rate is 12%. What is the value of Hanna common stock?

Solution 7

We can use the put-call parity theorem to solve this problem. The present value of the exercise price is ($80/1.12) = $71.43. The put-call parity theorem states that the put premium minus the call premium plus the current stock price equals the present value of the exercise price. Therefore, the value of the common stock is the value of x in the following equation:

$$\$8 - \$10 + x = \$71.43$$

so that the value of the common stock is $73.43.

Problem 8

For the data in Problem 7, what is the maximum you can make if you buy the put? If you buy the call?

Solution 8

If you buy the put, the most profitable outcome would result if the stock price decreases to zero. In this case, you earn $80 if you exercise the put on the expiration date. The present value of this $80 is $71.43. In principle, there is no upper limit to what you can make on the call. For either option, the profit is reduced by the premium paid for the option.

Problem 9

Suppose that a stock is 'at the money,' meaning that the current price of the stock is equal to the exercise price of the option. What is the relationship between the value of the call and the value of the put?

Solution 9

From the put-call parity theorem, the call premium minus the put premium is equal to the current stock price minus the present value of the exercise price. If the current stock price is equal to the exercise price, then the current stock price must be greater than the present value of the exercise price; the difference is the exercise price times the risk-free rate, which is equal to the difference between the call premium and the put premium.

Problem 10

In February 1990, a call on Cool Breeze, Inc., common stock, with a September 1990 expiration date sells for $5.45. The exercise price of the call is $60. Treasury bills coming due in September 1990 are priced to pay a yield of 12.6% and Cool Breeze common stock is selling for $55 per share. What is the value of a September 1990 put on Cool Breeze common stock with an exercise price of $60?

Solution 10

Using the put call parity theorem, and seven months to the expiration date, the value of the put is equal to the call premium plus the present value of the exercise price minus the price of the stock. The present value of the exercise price is [$60/1.126$^{(7/12)}$] = $55.99, so that the value of the put is ($5.45 + $55.99 - $55) = $6.44.

Problem 11

Use the Black-Scholes model to determine the price of a six-month call option, given the following information:

$$S = \$80, \ E = \$70, \ r = .10, \ d_1 = .82, \ d_2 = .74$$

Solution 11

We must evaluate the following:

$$C = SN(d_1) - Ee^{-rt} \ N(d_2)$$

$$= (\$80) \ N(.82) - (\$70) \ e^{(-.10 \times .5)} \ N(.74)$$

The value of N(.82) can be determined from Table A-5 in the appendix. The table indicates that .2929 is the probability that d_1 is greater than zero and less than .82. Therefore, the probability that d_1 is less than .82 is equal to .2939 plus the probability that d_1 is less than zero; this latter value is .50, so that N(.82) is (.2939 + .50) = .7939. N(.74) is .7704. The value of the option is $12.21.

Problem 12

Calculate the Black-Scholes price for a 9-month call option given the following:

$$S = \$80, \ E = \$70, \ \sigma = .30, \ r = .10$$

Solution 12

The call option value is determined from the following substitutions:

$$C = SN(d_1) - Ee^{-rt} \ N(d_2)$$

$$= (\$80) \ N(d_1) - (\$70) \ e^{(-.10 \times .75)} \ N(d_2)$$

$$d_1 = [\ln(S/E) + (r + .5\sigma^2)t]/(\sigma t^{.5})$$

$$= [\ln(80/70) + (.10 + (.5)(.3)^2(.75)]/[(.3)(.75)^{.5} = .9325$$

$$d_2 = d_1 - \sigma t^{.5}$$

$$= .9325 - (.3)(.75)^{.5} = .6727$$

$N(d_1)$ is approximately .8245, and $N(d_2)$ is approximately .7494, and the value of the option is $17.29.

Problem 13

Here are some additional problems to be solved using the Black-Scholes model. Try them on your own. The interest rate given is annual. Your answers may differ slightly from those in the solution because of rounding in the 'z' table.

Stock price	Exercise price	Risk-free rate	Maturity	Variance	Call price
$50	$60	8%	6 months	20%	
25	15	6	9 months	30	
50	60	8	6 months	40	
0	10	9	12 months	65	
90	30	7	forever	22	
50	0	8	6 months	44	

Solution 13

Stock price	Exercise price	Risk-free rate	Maturity	Variance	Call price
$50	$60	8%	6 months	20%	$ 3.61
25	15	6	9 months	30	11.18
50	60	8	6 months	40	6.18
0	10	9	12 months	65	0.00
90	30	7	forever	22	90.00
50	0	8	6 months	44	50.00

Use the following information about the Anondezi Company to solve Problems 14-15.

Anondezi Company has a discount bank loan that matures in one year and requires the firm to pay $1000. The current market value of the firm's assets is $1200. The annual variance of the value of the firm's assets is .30 and the annual risk-free interest rate is 6%. Anondezi is considering two mutually exclusive investments. Project A has an NPV of $100, and Project B has an NPV of $150. If Project A is accepted, the firm's variance will increase to .40. If Project B is accepted, the variance will decrease to .25.

Problem 14

What is the market value of the firm's debt and equity before undertaking any investment?

Solution 14

To value the equity of the firm before a project is accepted, we use the Black-Scholes model with a value of $1200, an exercise price of $1000, a variance of 30%, a maturity of one year, and a risk-free rate of 6%. The value of the equity is $381.70, so the value of the debt is ($1200 - $381.70) = $818.30.

Problem 15

What is the value of the firm's assets, debt and equity after accepting Project A? What is the value of the firm's assets, debt and equity after accepting Project B? Which project would the stockholders choose? Why?

Solution 15

With Project A, the value of the assets increases to ($1200 + $100) = $1300. With the new variance of .40, the value of the equity increases to $491.03, and the value of the debt decreases to $808.97.

With Project B, the value of the assets increases to ($1200 + $150) = $1350. With the new variance of .25, the value of the equity increases to $484.61, and the value of the debt increases to $865.39.

The stockholders would choose Project A, even though it has a lower NPV, because it has the greater effect on the value of the equity. The increased variance that results from accepting Project A benefits the stockholders at the expense of the bondholders. With Project B, the reduced variance that results benefits the bondholders.

CHAPTER HIGHLIGHTS

The characteristics of warrants and convertible bonds as financing arrangements are described in this chapter. These instruments are typically a mixture of debt and stock options.

Warrants

A warrant gives the holder the right to buy common stock directly from the company at a fixed price during a specified time period. To the holder, a warrant is essentially a call option, although warrants usually have longer maturities. Warrants are generally issued in combination with privately placed debt, but they are sometimes issued with public debt or new common stock issues. Typically, warrants are attached to the bond with which they are issued; however, some warrants are detachable, which means that the warrants can be sold separately from the bond.

The Difference Between Warrants and Call Options

To the firm, a warrant is substantially different from a call option. A call option sold on the firm's stock is a private transaction between investors, in which the firm is not directly involved. In contrast, a warrant is a security issued by the firm. When a call option is exercised, existing stock merely changes hands, but when a warrant is exercised, the firm must issue new stock.

An example best illustrates the difference between warrants and calls. The Vinson Company, a family corporation, is financed entirely with equity. The firm currently has assets valued at $9000 and has 900 shares outstanding. Elizabeth and Steve Vinson each own 450 shares. Each has decided to sell a call option on 150 shares to Claire Vinson. The call option has an exercise price of $12. If the company prospers, its assets might increase in value to $13,500. In this case, each share is worth $15. Claire will exercise her options by paying a total of $3600 to Steve and Elizabeth and she will acquire a total of 300 shares. At this point, 900 shares are still outstanding and each share is still worth $15. Claire has made a profit of [300($15 - 12)] = $900, but, from the corporation's point of view, no change has taken place; that is, the number of shares outstanding remains the same and no new financing becomes available to the firm.

Now, suppose that Steve and Elizabeth have sold warrants entitling Claire to buy 300 shares at $12 per share. Although the terms of the warrant appear, from Claire's point of view, to be identical to those of the call option, the result of the exercise of the warrant is substantially different. Assume again that the assets increase in value to $13,500 and that the warrants are about to expire. Note that the value of the firm can be thought of as either the value of its assets or the value of its equity, because the firm is financed entirely through equity (that is, the firm has no liabilities). Since both the existing common stock and the warrants represent a claim on the firm's assets, then, prior to the expiration of the warrants, the total value is equal to the value of the common stock plus the value of the warrants. We would like to determine the value of each of these two components.

If Claire exercises her warrants, the firm issues 300 new shares and receives 300($12) = $3600. The firm is now worth ($13,500 + $3,600) = $17,100 and 1200 shares are outstanding. Each share is worth ($17,100/1200) = $14.25. Claire's profit is [300($14.25 - $12)] = $675 because she owns shares worth $14.25 for which she paid only $12. Just before expiration of the warrants, the common stock is worth [($14.25)(900)] = $12,825 and the warrants are worth $675, for a total of $13,500. The reason that the shares are worth $14.25 instead of $15 is that the warrants, which represent a direct claim on the firm's assets and cash flow, have value.

Even though the terms of the call and the warrant appear comparable, the effects of the exercise of these options differ. In the case of the call option, the value of the firm and the value of a share are unaffected by the exercise of the option. Before and after exercise, the firm has 900 shares outstanding, each share is worth $15 and the total value of the firm is $13,500. Claire's profit is $900 since she exercises an option on each of 300 shares, and earns a $3 profit on each share. On the other hand, when Claire exercises the warrant, 300 new shares are issued and the value of the firm increases by the $3600 payment. The exercise of the warrant changes the total number of shares from 900 to 1200; the value of each share is $14.25, rather than $15; the value of the firm is $17,100 rather than $13,500. Since each share is worth $14.25, Claire's profit on the exercise of the warrant is $675, compared to her $900 profit on the exercise of the call.

The exercise of the warrants results in an increase in the number of shares, so that earnings per share will be diluted. Firms with a significant number of warrants, or convertibles, outstanding report EPS in two ways: 'primary' (earnings divided by outstanding shares) and 'fully-diluted' (earnings divided by the number of shares that would be outstanding if all warrants and convertibles are converted to stock).

How the Firm Can Hurt Warrant Holders. If a firm has warrants outstanding, it can reduce the value of those warrants, and provide a net benefit to stockholders, by splitting the stock. If the warrant has a fixed exercise price, then the warrants are worth less. Similarly, a large cash dividend to existing stockholders provides a benefit to the stockholders, at the expense of the warrant owners, because the value of the existing shares is decreased by the dividend. To prevent such actions, warrants are usually protected against both stock dividends and splits by providing for an adjustment in the exercise price in such situations.

Warrant Pricing And The Black-Scholes Model

In the previous section we establish the fact that the gain to the investor is different for a call than for a warrant. Here we summarize this difference mathematically.

The gain from exercising a call option on a single share is the difference between the value of a share and the exercise price of the call. This gain is indicated mathematically as:

$$\frac{\text{Firm's value net of debt}}{\#} - \text{Exercise price}$$

where # indicates the number of shares outstanding, and the first term above is the value of a share.

For a warrant, the value of a share after exercise of the warrant is:

$$\frac{\text{Firm's value net of debt} + (\text{Exercise price} \times \#_w)}{\# + \#_w}$$

where $\#_w$ is the number of warrants. Therefore, the gain from exercising a single warrant is the difference between the above expression for the value of a share and the exercise price. This gain can be written in the following form, which clarifies the relationship between the gain on the exercise of a call and the gain on the exercise of a warrant:

$$\frac{\#}{\# + \#_w} \times \left(\frac{\text{Firm's value net of debt}}{\#} - \text{Exercise price} \right)$$

The expression in parentheses is the gain on the exercise of a call; it is clear from this expression that the gain on a warrant is a fraction of the gain on a call. This result implies that the application of the Black-Scholes model to warrant pricing requires that the value of the warrant be determined by applying the above fraction to the value of an otherwise identical call.

Convertible Bonds

A **convertible bond** is a corporate bond that can be exchanged for a fixed number of shares of the firm's common stock, at the holder's option, at any time prior to the maturity of the bond. A convertible preferred stock is similar to a convertible bond except that it has no maturity date. Convertible bonds are normally protected against stock dividends and splits.

Consider a convertible subordinated debenture with a face value of $1000 and a $50 **conversion price**. The bondholder can exchange this bond for ($1000/$50) = 20 shares of stock; that is, the **conversion ratio** is 20. When a convertible bond is issued, the conversion price typically exceeds the stock price. The difference between the conversion price and the market value of the stock is called the **conversion premium**.

The Value of Convertible Bonds

The value of a convertible bond is related to the following concepts: the straight bond value, the conversion value, and the option value of the convertible.

<u>Straight Bond Value</u>. The **straight bond value** is the price at which the bond would sell if it were not convertible. This is a minimum value for a convertible bond in the sense that, even if the convertibility feature is worthless, the convertible still has value as a bond. A convertible sells at a price only slightly above its straight bond value when the company has performed poorly and the conversion price greatly exceeds the stock price. The straight bond value is the present value of the coupon payments and the maturity value, and is therefore dependent on the appropriate discount rate for bonds with a given risk level.

<u>Conversion Value</u>. The **conversion value** is the value of the bond if it were immediately converted into common stock. That is, conversion value equals the conversion ratio multiplied by the current stock price. The conversion value is another minimum value for a convertible bond since the bond cannot sell for less than its conversion value. If a convertible were to sell for less than its conversion value, an immediate arbitrage profit would be available to any investor who bought the bond, immediately converted to common stock, and then sold the stock. If the firm has performed well, then the convertible bond value depends primarily on the conversion value, because the conversion value is significantly greater than the straight bond value.

Option Value. The value of a convertible bond generally exceeds both the straight bond value and the conversion value because the holder has the right, but not the obligation, to convert; essentially, the bondholder has a call option which has value, thereby increasing the value of the bond.

Consider a firm with five shares of stock and one convertible bond outstanding. The bond is about to mature and the bondholder can convert the bond to one share of stock. If the bondholder does not convert, she will receive the $1000 face value of the bond or the value of the firm (V), whichever is less.

Under what circumstances should the bondholder convert? If she converts, she will own one share out of six, or 1/6 of V. Obviously, she should convert only if 1/6 of V is greater than $1000. For example, if the value of the firm is $9000, she should convert because 1/6 of $9000 is $1500. If the firm is worth $5400, then she should let the bond mature because 1/6 of $5400 is $900, which is less than the $1000 face value of the bond.

A Spurious Reason for Issuing Warrants and Convertibles

A bond that is convertible or has warrants attached pays a lower coupon rate than does an identical straight bond. This interest saving is an apparent advantage to the issuing firm. Also, it is sometimes argued that warrants and convertibles provide the firm with the opportunity to issue stock at a premium over current prices. This argument is based on the fact that the warrant or convertible is usually 'out of the money' initially, so that exercise will take place only if the stock price increases. These arguments seem to indicate that warrants and convertibles are 'no lose' propositions for the issuer. As explained below, this conclusion is incorrect.

The 'Free Lunch' Story. Suppose that we can issue either straight subordinated debentures with a 13% coupon rate or convertible subordinated debentures, with a conversion price of $50, and a 10% coupon rate. The common stock currently sells for $40 per share. If the stock declines in value, then the bonds will not be converted, and we will have succeeded in issuing debt at 10%, rather than 13%.

If the stock price increases, then conversion will occur, but the company will effectively be selling stock for $50 per share, or $10 more than the stock was worth at the time the convertible was issued. It appears that the convertible bond is preferable to either new common stock or straight debt as a source of long-term financing. However, the flaw in the above argument lies in the fact that we are comparing convertible-debt financing with each of the two alternatives only under the circumstances which make convertibles appear more attractive. That is, convertibles are preferable to straight-debt financing when the price of the stock declines, but not when the price increases; convertibles are preferable to common stock financing when the price of the stock increases, but not when the price decreases.

The 'Expensive Lunch' Story. If the stock price declines subsequent to the issuing of the convertibles, the firm would have been better off by issuing common stock when its value was high. In comparison with common stock financing, a valuable opportunity is lost by issuing convertibles if the stock price subsequently declines.

If the stock price subsequently rises, then the bondholders convert and reap some of the benefits of the company's prosperity. The firm's existing stockholders would have been better off if the firm had issued straight debt, so that the gains to shareholders would not be diluted. In comparison with straight-debt financing, the existing stockholders are at a relative disadvantage when the firm issues convertibles and the stock price subsequently increases.

A Reconciliation. Neither of the above analyses is correct. In an efficient market, issuing convertibles (or any other financial instrument) is a zero NPV transaction. Issuing convertibles will generally turn out to be worse than issuing straight-debt and better than issuing stock if the company subsequently prospers. If the company does not fare as well, then the reverse is true. Of course, there is no way of knowing in advance whether stock price will increase or decrease, so it is not possible to determine which financing alternative is preferable.

Why are Warrants and Convertibles Issued?

Studies indicate that convertibles typically are subordinated and unsecured, and that they are often issued by firms with lower bond ratings and by firms that are small and growing.

Matching Cash Flows. Convertibles or bond/warrant financing may make sense for small, risky firms because these alternatives require lower cash outflows for interest payments at a time when the firm may be least able to afford large outlays. Subsequent conversion would be expensive, but it will occur later, when the firm can better afford it. Thus, convertibles and warrants allow a matching of cash flows for these companies.

Risk Synergy. Under certain circumstances, the various risks of a firm are difficult to assess. If the risk turns out to be low, then the option value of convertibles or warrants will be low, but the straight bond value will be high. If the firm turns out to be very risky, then the straight bond value will be low, but the option value will be high. For either scenario, the effects of risk have some tendency to offset each other; however, it is not clear whether warrants or convertibles significantly reduce the investor's need to evaluate risk in order to correctly value the firm's securities.

Agency Costs. Since convertible bonds have both a debt component and an equity component, the issuing of convertibles can serve to mitigate the agency problems which arise between creditors and equity owners. As a result, convertible bond issues often require less security and fewer restrictive covenants. The agency costs associated with convertible bonds are lower as a consequence.

Conversion Policy

As indicated earlier, a convertible bond cannot sell for less than the larger of its conversion value or its straight bond value, and will actually sell for more than these minimum values because of the option feature.   Therefore, the holder of a convertible always finds it advantageous to sell the bond rather than convert it, which means that convertible bonds normally are not converted prior to maturity. On the other hand, the corporation may prefer conversion under certain circumstances. In order to be able to force conversion, corporations almost always issue their convertible bonds with a call provision.

When a convertible is called, the owner may choose to either surrender the bond for the call price or convert the bond. Clearly, if the conversion value exceeds the call price, then the bondholder should convert; otherwise, the bondholder will surrender the bond. If the bond is called when the conversion value is higher than the call price, the call is said to **force conversion**.

From the corporation's point of view, the optimal policy is to call the bond when the conversion value is equal to the call price. In any other case, the firm is giving away more than is necessary, either by paying more than the bonds are worth as stock (if the conversion value is less than the call price) or by giving the bondholders stock that is worth more than the call price (if the conversion value exceeds the stock price). The effect of calling a bond when the conversion value equals the call price is the sale of stock at the prevailing market price.

Studies have shown that firms tend to delay forcing conversion until the conversion value is well in excess of the call price. These findings seem to suggest that the call policies used are not in the shareholders' best interests.

CONCEPT TEST

1. The holder of a _____ has the right to buy common stock from an investor at a fixed price for a specified time period.

2. The holder of a _____ has the right to buy common stock from the corporation at a fixed price for a specified time period.

3. A corporate security (e.g., a bond or preferred stock) that can be exchanged for a fixed number of shares of common stock is said to be _____.

4. Warrants are normally issued in combination with _____.

5. A convertible bond might allow the owner to exchange a $1000 face value bond for shares of common stock at $40. The $40 is the _____.

6. The bond described in the previous question can be exchanged for _____ shares of stock. This figure is called the _____.

7. For the bond described in Question 5, suppose the stock were selling for $60 at the time the bond was issued. The $20 differential is called the _____.

8. The price at which a convertible bond would sell if it did not have the conversion privilege is called the _____.

9. The amount that a convertible bond would be worth if it were immediately exchanged for common stock is its _____.

10. The minimum value of a convertible bond is equal to the maximum of its _____ or its _____.

11. The value of a convertible bond generally exceeds the minimum value indicated in Question 10 by the _____.

12. Is it true that a convertible bond will have a lower coupon rate than an otherwise identical nonconvertible bond?

13. Is it true that issuing convertible bonds is always preferable to issuing otherwise identical nonconvertible bonds?

14. In terms of security, most convertible bonds are _____.

15. Since investors prefer not to convert convertible bonds before maturity, most convertible bonds are _____.

16. If the conversion value is greater than the call price on a convertible bond, the effect of a call is to _____.

17. From the corporation's point of view, the optimal time to call a convertible bond is when the call price _____ the conversion value.

18. In retrospect, a firm would have been better off selling _____ rather than convertible bonds if the stock price has increased significantly.

19. In retrospect, a firm would have been better off selling _____ rather than convertible bonds if the stock price has decreased significantly.

20. In practice, firms tend to call convertible bonds when the conversion value _____ the call price.

21. Would a firm with a high growth rate be more or less likely to issue convertibles than a firm with a low growth rate?

22. Would a firm with highly uncertain future prospects be more or less likely to issue a bond/warrant package than a firm with relatively certain prospects?

23. Would a convertible bond tend to have more or fewer restrictive covenants than an otherwise identical nonconvertible bond?

ANSWERS TO CONCEPT TEST

1. call option
2. warrant
3. convertible
4. privately placed debt
5. conversion price
6. 25; conversion ratio
7. conversion premium
8. straight bond value
9. conversion value
10. straight bond value; conversion value
11. option value
12. yes
13. no
14. subordinated debentures
15. callable
16. force conversion
17. equals
18. straight debt
19. common stock
20. exceeds
21. more
22. more
23. fewer

PROBLEMS AND SOLUTIONS

Problem 1

You have been hired to value a new 30-year callable, convertible bond. The bond has a 6% coupon rate, with interest payable annually. The conversion price is $100 and the stock currently sells for $50.12. The stock price is expected to grow at 10% per year. The bond is callable at $1100, but based on prior experience, it would not be called unless the conversion value was $1300. The required return on this bond is 8%. What value would you assign?

Solution 1

We must first determine when the bond is likely to be called. The conversion ratio is ($1000/$100) = 10, so the bond will be called when the stock price reaches $130 per share. The time required for the stock price to grow from $50.12 to $130 can be determined by solving for n in the following equation:

$$\$130 = \$50.12 \times (1.10)^n$$

The value of n can be most easily determined using a trial-and-error approach or by locating, in the future value tables, the value of n such that $[(1.10)^n] = (\$130/\$50.12) = 2.5938$; thus, we determine that n is approximately 10 years.

If we buy the bond, we expect to receive an annuity of $60 per year, for 10 years, and then to convert to stock worth $1300. The present value of the annuity, discounted at 8%, is $402.60. The present value of the $1300, to be received in ten years, is $602.15. Therefore, the bond is worth $1004.75.

Problem 2

Suppose that the bond described in Problem 1 were not callable. What would its value be? (Assume that the dividend yield on the stock is negligible.)

Solution 2

If the bond is not callable, it will not be converted until maturity. At a growth rate of 10% per year, the stock price is expected to be $874.564 per share in 30 years. Therefore, the conversion value is expected to be $8745.64 at that time. At a discount rate of 8%, the present value of the conversion value is $869.12. The present value of the annuity of $60 per year for 30 years is $675.47. The value of the bond is ($869.12 + $675.47) = $1544.59.

Problem 3

For the bond described in Problem 1, what is the minimum price at which the bond could sell when it is issued? (Assume that comparable nonconvertible bonds are priced to yield 7%.)

Solution 3

The minimum value is the greater of either the straight debt value or the conversion value. The conversion value is $[10(\$50.12)] = \$501.20$. The straight debt value, using a discount rate of 7%, is $875.91. Therefore, the minimum price is the straight debt value of $875.91.

Problem 4

Suppose that the bond described in Problem 1 sells for $900. What is the option value of the bond?

Solution 4

The option value is the difference between the selling price of the bond and the minimum price of $875.91, as determined in Problem 3; therefore, the option value is $24.09.

Problem 5

Consider the convertible bond described in Problem 1; suppose that, ten years after the bond is issued, the price of the firm's common stock increases to $120 per share and that yields for comparable nonconvertible bonds decline to 6%. What is the straight debt value of the bond? What is the conversion value of the bond? Why is the conversion value now the minimum value of the bond?

Solution 5

The straight debt value of the bond is now $1000, and the conversion value is [($120)(10)] = $1200. The bond can not sell for less than its conversion value because such a price would provide an arbitrage opportunity for an investor who bought the bond, converted to common stock, and then sold the common stock for $1200.

Problem 6

A bond with ten detachable warrants has been offered for sale at a price of $1000. The bond matures in 30 years and has an annual coupon payment of $100. Each warrant gives the owner the right to purchase five shares of stock at $15 per share. Ordinary bonds (i.e., bonds without warrants) of similar quality are priced to yield 14%. What is the value of a warrant?

Solution 6

If there were no warrants, the bond would be worth $719.89. The total value of the warrants is ($1000 - $719.89) = $280.11. Since there are ten warrants, each is worth $28.01.

Problem 7

Using the data from Problem 6, determine the maximum current price of the firm's stock.

Solution 7

The straight bond value is $719.89. Each bond enables the owner to buy a total of 50 shares of stock for $15 per share. The minimum value of the warrants is [50(S - $15)]; the solution to Problem 6 indicates that the total value of the warrants is $280.11. Therefore, the current stock price is at most the value of S in the following equation:

$$50(S - \$15) = \$280.11$$

Solving for S, we find that the current stock price is at most S = [$15 + ($280.11/50)] = $20.60.

Use the following information to solve Problems 8-15.

Ringworld Company has 5000 shares of stock outstanding. The market value of Ringworld's assets is $700,000. The market value of outstanding debt is $200,000. Some time ago, Ringworld issued 100 warrants that are now about to expire. Each warrant gives the owner the right to purchase ten shares of stock at a price of $80 per share.

Problem 8

What is the price per share of Ringworld stock?

Solution 8

The total value of the warrants and stock is ($700,000 - $200,000) = $500,000. If all of the warrants are exercised, then the number of shares increases by 1000, to a total of 6000 shares outstanding. The total equity value would be [$500,000 + ($80)(1000)] = $580,000, and the per share price is ($580,000/6000) = $96.6667.

Problem 9

What is the value of one warrant?

Solution 9

The total value of the stock, just before exercise of the warrants, is [($96.6667)(5000)] = $483,333.33. Since the total value of the warrants and stock is $500,000, the value of the warrants is ($500,000 - $483,333.33) = $16,666.67, and the value of one warrant is $166.67.

Problem 10

What is the effective exercise price of the warrants?

Solution 10

The warrantholders will pay a total of $80,000 if they exercise the warrants. They will own 1000 of 6000 shares outstanding, or 1/6 of the equity. Effectively, they pay [(5/6)($80,000)] = $66,666.67. The effective exercise price per share is $66.67. Ignoring the proceeds from the warrant exercise, the value of 1/6 of the equity is $83,333.33. Therefore, the value of the warrants is ($83,333.33 - $66,666.67) = $16,666.67, as calculated above.

Problem 11

What is the profit from exercising one warrant?

Solution 11

The holder of one warrant can purchase ten shares of stock for $80 per share. Each share has a value of $96.6667, so the warrantholder has a profit of $16.6667 per share, or a total profit of [($16.6667)(10)] = $166.67, as indicated in Problem 9. Note that this is an alternative approach to determining the value of a warrant.

Problem 12

Suppose that a call option to buy ten shares of stock in a company comparable to Ringworld has an exercise price of $80. The comparable company is identical to Ringworld, except that it has no warrants outstanding. What is the price of this firm's stock? What is the profit from exercising this call option?

Solution 12

For this identical firm, the stock is worth [($700,000 - $200,000)/5000] = $100 per share. The exercise of a call option does not affect either the number of shares outstanding or the value of the firm, so exercise of the call option results in a profit of [($100 - $80)(10)] = $200.

Problem 13

Let q be the ratio of total shares that can be purchased using warrants to shares currently outstanding for Ringworld. Show numerically that the value of a warrant to buy one share is [1/(1 + q)] of the value of a call option, with an exercise price of $80, on an identical firm that has no warrants outstanding.

Solution 13

In the identical firm, the stock is worth $100 per share. At an $80 exercise price, the payoff on a call option is $20. From Problem 9, the payoff per share on the warrants is $16.67. The ratio q is (1000/5000) = .2, and [1/(1 + q)] = .83333. Using this ratio, the payoff on the warrant is ($20/1.2) = $16.67, which is the solution to Problem 9. Since this ratio is constant, the value of the call option is always (1 + q) times the value of the warrant.

Problem 14

Suppose that Ringworld declares a 4-for-1 stock split. If the warrants are protected, what adjustments would be made?

Solution 14

Each warrant would give the owner the right to buy 40 shares at a price of $20 per share.

Problem 15

Suppose that Ringworld declares a 20% stock dividend. If the warrants are protected, what adjustments would be made?

Solution 15

Each warrant would give the owner the right to buy 20% more shares at a price that is 20% less. The number of shares would thus be 12 and the exercise price would be ($80/1.20) = $66.67.

CHAPTER 22
LEASING

CHAPTER HIGHLIGHTS

Leasing is a method of financing the acquisition of assets. Corporations use both long-term and short-term leasing; the focus of this chapter is long-term leasing of fixed assets, over a period of more than five years. Leasing is the most common method for financing the acquisition of equipment.

Types of Leases

A lease is a contractual agreement between the owner of an asset (the **lessor**) and the user of an asset (the **lessee**). The lessee uses the asset for some period of time and makes periodic lease payments to the lessor.

Operating Leases. The life of an **operating lease** is generally less than the economic life of the asset. Consequently, an operating lease is not fully amortized since the payments over the term of the lease do not cover the entire cost of the asset. Also, under an operating lease, the lessor is generally responsible for maintenance and insurance of the leased asset. Finally, most operating leases contain a cancellation option allowing the lessee to terminate the lease and return the asset to the lessor.

Financial Leases. A **financial lease** differs from an operating lease in three ways: (1) the lease is fully amortized; (2) the lessee is responsible for maintenance and insurance; and (3) the lease is not cancelable. These characteristics imply that default on a financial lease can lead to bankruptcy. In addition, the lessee typically has the right to renew a financial lease.

A **sale and lease-back** is a financial lease of an asset which is initially owned by the lessee, who agrees to simultaneously sell the asset to the lessor and to lease the asset from the lessor.

A **leveraged lease** is a three-sided, tax-motivated deal involving a lessee, a lessor, and a lender. The lessor borrows a substantial fraction of the purchase price from the lender; the lessor receives lease payments from the lessee and makes interest payments to the lender. A leveraged lease gives the lessor the depreciation and other tax benefits associated with ownership. The lessee may benefit because some of the tax benefits may be passed on to the lessee in the form of lower lease payments.

Accounting and Leasing

The Federal Accounting Standards Board (FASB) released the Statement of Financial Accounting Standards No. 13 (FAS 13), "Accounting for Leases," in November 1976. The effect of FAS 13 is to require that all financial, or capital, lease obligations must be 'capitalized' and reported on the balance sheet as a liability; that is, the present value of all future lease payments appears as a liability on the balance sheet. Also, the same amount appears as an asset on the left-hand side of the balance sheet. Operating leases are not capitalized, however. Prior to FAS 13, all leases were **off-balance-sheet financing**, meaning that their existence was not reported on the balance sheet.

For accounting purposes, a lease must be classified as a capital lease if at least one of the following is true:

1. The lease transfers ownership to the lessee by the end of the lease term.
2. The lessee can purchase the asset for less than market value when the lease expires.
3. The lease term is 75% or more of the asset's economic life.
4. The present value of the lease payments is 90% or more of the asset's market value at the start of the lease.

If none of these conditions is met, the lease is an operating lease and only appears in the form of summary information in the footnotes.

Taxes, the IRS, and Leases

A lease has the potential for providing tax advantages, in comparison to a loan, because the lease payments may actually represent a technique for accelerating depreciation deductions. Consequently, the IRS may scrutinize a lease agreement to determine whether its sole purpose is the avoidance of taxes. In general, the following guidelines must be followed if the lease is to be qualified by the IRS:

1. The term must be less than 30 years.
2. The lessee must not have an option to buy the asset at a price below market value.
3. The lease payments must not be much larger early in the life of the lease than towards the end of the lease.
4. The lease payments must provide the lessor with a fair market rate of return.
5. The lease must not limit the lessee's ability to borrow or pay dividends.
6. Renewal options must be reasonable and reflect the asset's market value.

The Cash Flows of Leasing

Suppose we wish to acquire a new personal computer (PC). It costs $5000 and, for simplicity, we assume it is depreciated on a straight-line basis to a value of zero over a three-year period. Because of technological obsolescence, it will be worthless three years from now. Our tax rate is 34%, and we can borrow at 10%. The firm is currently in a taxpaying position. We have the option to lease the PC for three years, at a cost of $2100 per year. The first lease payment would be due in one year. (Usually, the first payment on a lease is due immediately.) Should we lease or buy?

Regardless of whether we lease or buy, the benefits derived from the use of the asset are the same; therefore we need consider only the costs. If we lease the PC, we do not have to pay the $5000 purchase price, which would have to be paid immediately if we purchase. However, we do have to make a tax-deductible payment of $2100 each year. Also, if we lease, we cannot depreciate the asset since we do not own it; therefore, we lose the depreciation tax shield.

We can now summarize the difference between the cash flows associated with leasing rather than buying the asset in this example. By leasing, we save the $5000 outlay for the purchase of the asset today. The after-tax lease payment is:

$$L(1 - T_c) = \$2100(1 - .34) = \$1386$$

where L is the lease payment and T_c is the corporate tax rate. The depreciation tax shield we forfeit by leasing is:

$$T_c(Dep) = (\$5000/3)(.34) = \$567$$

where Dep is the annual depreciation expense. In tabular form, these cash flows are:

Lease vs. buy	0	1	2	3
Cost of equipment	+$5000			
After-tax lease payment		-$1386	-$1386	-$1386
Lost depreciation tax benefit		-$ 567	-$ 567	-$ 567
Total	+$5000	-$1953	-$1953	-$1953

Note that in this approach we are indicating the changes in cash flows associated with leasing rather than purchasing the asset; consequently, the cost of the equipment is viewed as an inflow, since we avoid the outlay for the purchase price, while the lease payments and lost tax benefit are regarded as outflows, since they are costs incurred by leasing rather than purchasing. If the decision was presented in terms of purchasing instead of leasing, then the signs of the cash flows would be reversed; of course, the decision is unaffected by the perspective we adopt.

At this point, we must determine the net present value of the lease alternative, compared to the purchase alternative. However, it is first necessary to determine the appropriate discount rate.

NPV Analysis of the Lease-versus-Buy Decision

Since the cash flows associated with a lease are similar in nature and risk to those associated with a secured loan, a reasonable choice of discount rate is the interest rate the firm pays on secured borrowing. However, there are several additional considerations which must be addressed in identifying the appropriate rate. First, since the cash flows identified in the above analysis are after-tax cash flows, the relevant discount rate is the after-tax rate on the firm's secured loans. Second, the cash flows associated with a lease have different risk levels. The depreciation tax shield is a benefit to the firm only if taxable income is sufficient to derive a benefit from the tax deduction. Therefore, the depreciation tax shield is riskier than the lease payments and should be discounted at a higher rate. In addition, since tax rates change over time, the benefit derived from depreciation tax deductions can change as well. Although the difference in risk level does exist, it may be small enough to ignore in practical applications; therefore, we discount all cash flows at the same after-tax rate.

In the example above, the interest rate at which the firm borrows is 10%. Since we are discounting after-tax cash flows, we use the after-tax borrowing rate of $[.10(1 - .34)] = .066 = 6.6\%$. At this discount rate, the net present value of the lease alternative is $[\$5000 - 1953(2.643614)] = -\$162.98$; since the net present value of the lease alternative is negative, the lease is not a desirable financing arrangement.

lessee's NPV = -162.98

Debt Displacement and Lease Valuation

The analysis of the lease indicates that the alternative to leasing would be for the firm to borrow in order to finance the acquisition of the asset. In this section, we determine the amount of borrowing which is displaced when the firm elects to lease. One way to calculate this debt displacement is to compute the size of an **equivalent loan**; in other words, we determine the size of the loan the firm could obtain and subsequently repay with payments exactly equal to the after-tax cash flows of the lease. For the above example, the equivalent loan is the amount we can borrow today if we agree to after-tax payments of $1953 each year for three years. If the after-tax borrowing rate is 6.6%, then we can borrow the present value of the three-year annuity of $1953 per year, or $5162.98.

What is the difference between leasing and borrowing in this case? If we borrow $5162.98, we can then acquire an asset worth $5000 (just as we do with the lease), but we have $162.98 remaining. Earlier, we determined that the net present value of the lease is -$162.98. The lease has a net present value of negative $162.98 precisely because we could have raised an additional $162.98 by borrowing the money and repaying the loan with the same cash outflows as those associated with the lease.

Another way of viewing the analysis here is to note that the lease provides $5000 in financing, but it displaces $5162.98 in borrowing. Notice that we do not consider the specific borrowing arrangements that might be made. This is because the amount of debt displaced is $5162.98, regardless of the specific financing which might be arranged for buying the asset.

In general, the net present value of a lease is calculated by determining the annual cash flows associated with leasing instead of buying, and discounting these cash flows at the after-tax cost of secured borrowing. If the present value of these cash flows is less than the cost of the asset, then leasing is the preferable alternative.

Does Leasing Ever Pay: The Base Case

To this point, we have evaluated the lease from the lessee's point of view; now we consider the lessor's perspective. The lessor must perform a net present value analysis of the cash flows associated with purchasing the asset and then leasing it to the lessee. The lessor purchases the asset, for $10,000 in this case, and then obtains cash inflows in the form of depreciation tax benefits and lease payments from the lessee. Assuming the same straight-line depreciation and tax rate as indicated above in the analysis of the lessee's decision, the lessor obtains cash inflows identical to the lessee's cash outflows; that is, the lessee's after-tax inflows are $1953 per year for three years. If these cash flows are discounted at the same 6.6% after-tax rate indicated above, then the net present value of the lessor's position is positive $162.98.

The result here can be generalized: if the lessor and lessee are subject to the same tax rates and interest rates, and if there are no transactions costs associated with the lease arrangement, then the sum of the net present values of the lease, from the lessor's and the lessee's perspectives, is exactly equal to zero. Furthermore, if the lease payment is determined such that the cash flows of the two parties are identical in size, but opposite in sign, then the net present values from the two perspectives are also identical in size and opposite in sign. In other words, the lease arrangement is a zero NPV transaction, and it is impossible for both parties to benefit from the lease. Given this result, the question arises as to why leasing exists; we discuss this question in the next section.

Reasons for Leasing

In a perfect market, there is no reason for leasing to exist. This is because leasing, like any other strictly financial arrangement, is simply a zero NPV transaction for all parties. In a perfect market, there are no transaction costs associated with leasing, information is both costless and available to everyone, and everyone is taxed exactly the same way. If these conditions do not hold, however, then leasing may offer some advantages. Many reasons are cited as advantages of leasing instead of buying; some make economic sense and some do not.

Good Reasons for Leasing. Leasing makes sense if taxes can be reduced, damaging uncertainty can be reduced, or transactions costs are lower for leasing than for financing acquisition using debt or equity. Of these considerations, potential tax savings are probably the most important.

Leasing can generate tax benefits to both the lessor and the lessee when the two firms are in different tax brackets. Suppose that, in our previous example, the lessee does not pay taxes. If the lease payment were reduced to $2010 per year, then the net present value of the lease alternative, discounted at the 10% rate for secured borrowing, would be [$5000 - $2010(2.486852)] = $1.43. We ignore the depreciation tax shield since it has no value to the lessee, and we use 10% as the discount rate because it is both the pre-tax and the after-tax cost of borrowing for a lessee who pays no taxes. The lessor (in the 34% tax bracket) receives after-tax annual cash inflows equal to:

$$L(1 - T_c) + T_c(\text{Dep}) = \$2010(.66) + (.34)(\$5000/3) = \$1893.27$$

Discounted at 6.6%, the net present value of the lease for the lessor is [-$5000 + $1893.27(2.643614)] = $5.07; consequently, the lease is beneficial to both parties. The government is the net loser in the transaction because the tax advantage of the depreciation deduction has been taken by the party which most benefits from the deduction, and its value has been shared by both parties.

If the leased property has a **residual value**, then leasing may be a way for the lessee to avoid the uncertainty associated with determining that value. Suppose a firm borrows in order to finance the purchase of an asset, rather than leasing it for three years. The firm intends to pay off the loan at the end of three years by using the proceeds from the sale of the asset. Since the asset's value is uncertain, it may not be possible to accomplish this. Theoretically, at least, the firm can eliminate this uncertainty by pre-selling the asset; that is, by arranging a forward contract today to sell the machine at a fixed price in three years.

A lease accomplishes the same thing as borrowing and forward contracting; it removes uncertainty concerning the residual value. Is there any particular advantage to eliminating this uncertainty? If the lessor is a small company, then it may be true that the leasing company is better diversified, and consequently better able to bear this risk.

An obvious reason for short-term leasing is the reduction of transactions costs. If you are visiting a foreign country, it is undoubtedly less expensive to lease a car for a week than it is to buy and resell within a week. Similar reasoning may apply to long-term leases, but, in general, the arguments are much less convincing in this case.

Bad Reasons for Leasing. Leasing affects accounting statements. An operating lease results in an expense, but, at least in the early years of a lease, this expense is usually less than the combined interest and depreciation charge that would result from buying. Thus, reported income is higher with a lease. Also, an operating lease does not appear as a liability on the balance sheet. As a result, net worth, return on assets, and other accounting measures may look better if a firm leases an asset rather than purchasing it. However, as we have seen earlier, it is unlikely that this kind of 'cooking the books' will fool participants in the financial markets.

It is sometimes argued that leasing provides 100% financing, whereas borrowing requires a down payment. This argument is not particularly convincing, however, because leasing displaces other debt financing which the firm could otherwise acquire.

Some Unanswered Questions

The analysis of this chapter does not address some empirical regularities. For example, firms that use more debt also tend to use more leasing. On the other hand, we argued earlier that debt and leasing are substitutes. This apparent inconsistency is not necessarily troubling because it may simply reflect the fact that firms with substantial debt capacity choose to both lease and borrow more than other firms.

We have noted that leases are offered by both manufacturers and leasing companies; the offsetting effects of taxes explain why these two different categories of lessor exist. For a manufacturer, the depreciable basis of a leased asset is the manufacturing cost, while for a third-party leasing company, it is the sale price. Since the sale price is higher, this difference benefits leasing companies. However, for a manufacturer, the manufacturing profit and associated tax liability can often be deferred when an asset is leased; this provides a benefit to manufacturers.

Some assets are leased more frequently than others. This may occur because, for some assets, ownership provides a greater incentive to minimize maintenance costs. Also, leasing may be a way of circumventing laws against charging a price that is too low.

CONCEPT TEST

1. In a lease arrangement, the owner of the asset is the _____.

2. In a lease arrangement, the user of the asset is the _____.

3. In a lease arrangement, the _____ gets the tax benefit from depreciating the asset.

4. An _____ lease is short-term (usually 3 to 5 years) and is sometimes called a _____ or _____ lease.

5. A _____ lease is long-term and is sometimes called a _____ lease.

6. If a lease can be canceled at the lessee's option, it is probably an _____ lease.

7. If the payments under a lease are sufficient to recover the cost of the asset, then the lease is said to be _____ and is probably a _____ lease.

8. A financial lease originates as either a _____ or a _____.

9. If a firm previously owned a leased asset, then the lease is probably a _____ arrangement.

10. If the lessor borrows a substantial fraction of the purchase price of the asset, then the financial lease is called a _____.

11. The cash flow benefit to the lessee is that the lessee does not pay the _____.

12. For the lessee, the costs associated with leasing are the _____ and the _____.

13. A financial lease is a source of financing much like _____.

14. If the firm has an optimal capital structure, then an indirect cost of leasing is the resulting _____.

15. The appropriate discount rate for valuing a lease is the _____.

16. In a perfect market, there is no particular reason for financial leasing to exist since the lease would be a _____ transaction.

17. If markets are perfect, and the lessor concludes that a lease has an NPV of $100, then the NPV for the lessee is _____.

18. The primary advantage of leasing in an imperfect market is _____.

19. A major reason for short-term leasing is _____.

20. Prior to FAS 13, all leases were _____ financing.

21. A financial lease is likely to be beneficial to all parties when the lessor's tax bracket is _____ than the lessee's.

In Questions 22-24 indicate whether, from an accounting perspective, the lease is a capital lease or an operating lease, and also indicate whether the IRS might view the lease as a loan.

22. You lease a Porsche 911 for six years. At the end of the sixth year, you have the option to purchase the car for $1.

23. You lease a computer with a five-year economic life. The lease term is three years and the present value of the lease payments is 80% of the cost of the computer. You can purchase the computer for its fair market value at the end of the lease.

24. You lease a Boeing 747 for two years at $1 million per year. You can buy it at its fair market value of $200 million when the lease expires. During the lease, you cannot issue additional debt for other purposes.

ANSWERS TO CONCEPT TEST

1. lessor
2. lessee
3. lessor
4. operating; service; maintenance
5. financial; capital
6. operating
7. fully-amortized; financial
8. direct lease; sale and lease-back
9. sale and lease-back
10. leveraged lease
11. purchase price
12. after-tax lease payments;
    lost depreciation benefit

13. secured borrowing
14. debt displacement
15. after-tax cost of secured borrowing
16. zero NPV
17. -$100
18. tax avoidance
19. transactions costs
20. off-balance-sheet
21. higher
22. financial; might be a loan
23. operating; probably a lease
24. operating; might be a loan

PROBLEMS AND SOLUTIONS

Use the following information to solve Problems 1-5.

Lorenzo Airlines and Pizza Delivery Service, Inc., is in desperate need of a new airplane. The purchase price is $150 million. It can be leased for 10 years at $20 million per year. Lorenzo is in the 34% tax bracket and can borrow on a secured basis at 12%. Aircraft are depreciated on a straight-line basis to a zero residual value over 10 years. Since regulations require that planes be permanently grounded after 10 years, the actual residual value is negligible.

Problem 1

What is Lorenzo's after-tax cash outflow from leasing instead of buying?

Solution 1

The after tax cash outflow is:

$$L(1 - T_c) + T_c(Dep) =$$

$$(\$20,000,000)(1 - .34) + .34(15,000,000) = \$18,300,000$$

Problem 2

What is the net present value of the lease? Should Lorenzo lease or buy? What is the value of the lease from the lessor's point of view.

Solution 2

Lorenzo saves the $150 million purchase price by paying $18.3 million per year for ten years. The appropriate discount rate is the after-tax cost of borrowing, which is $[.12(1 - .34)] = .0792$. The NPV of the lease is thus:

$$\$150,000,000 - \$18,300,000(6.7344) = +\$26,761,185$$

Lorenzo should lease instead of buy. The lessor loses $26.761 million on the deal.

Problem 3

What amount of debt is displaced by the lease?

Solution 3

The after-tax cash flows from the lease are $18.3 million. At an interest rate of 7.92%, we can borrow [($18.3 million)(6.7344)] = $123.239 million by agreeing to make these same after-tax payments on a loan. Therefore, the debt displaced is $123.239 million. Notice that this $123.239 million plus the NPV of the lease is equal to the $150 million raised by the lease.

Problem 4

Suppose that Lorenzo has sufficient tax-loss carryforward to avoid paying taxes for ten years, and that the lease payment is $26.1 million. Should the firm lease or buy?

Solution 4

The cost of leasing instead of buying is the $26.1 million lease payment. The discount rate is 12%. The NPV of the lease is thus:

$$\$150,000,000 - \$26,100,000(5.6502) = \$2,529,780$$

Therefore, the firm should lease.

Problem 5

What is the value of the lease described in Problem 4, from the lessor's point of view? (Assume that the lessor is in the 34% tax bracket and can borrow on a secured basis at 12%.)

Solution 5

For the lessor, the cash flows are:

$$\$26,100,000(.66) + (.34)(\$15,000,000) = \$22,326,000$$

At 7.92%, the lessor's NPV is:

$$-\$150,000,000 + \$22,326,000(6.7344) = \$352,214$$

Problem 6

An asset costs $50,000, has a useful life of five years and no salvage value. Assume that the asset will be depreciated on a straight-line basis. The corporate tax rate on ordinary income is 34%. The relevant interest rate for secured debt is 10%. The annual lease payments are $12,500 paid at the end of each of the next five years. What are the annual cash outflows for the lessee?

Solution 6

The annual after-tax cash outflow is:

$$L(1 - T_c) + T_c (Dep) =$$

$$(\$12,500)(1 - .34) + .34(10,000) = \$11,650$$

Problem 7

For the lease described in Problem 6, what is the net present value of the lease for the lessee?

Solution 7

The appropriate discount rate is $[.10(1 - .34)] = .066$. The NPV of the lease is:

$$\$50,000 - \$11,650(4.1445) = \$1,717$$

Problem 8

Suppose that the lease payments described in Problem 6 are paid at the beginning of each year; what is the net present value of the lease for the lessee?

Solution 8

The present value of the after-tax cash flows is now equal to:

$$\$11,650(4.1445)(1.066) = \$51,470$$

The net present value of the lease is ($50,000 - $51,470) = -$1470. Therefore, the lease becomes unacceptable to the lessee due to the increase in the present value of the outflows resulting from the earlier payment.

Problem 9

For the lease described in Problem 6, what lease payment will make the lessee indifferent between leasing and purchasing the asset?

Solution 9

The lessee will be indifferent if the net present value of the lease is zero. Therefore, the lease payment is the value of L which is the solution to the following equation:

$$\$50,000 - (.66L)(4.1445) - (\$3400)(4.1445) = 0$$

The value of L is $13,128. Note that the lessor will also have a net present value of zero for a lease payment of $13,128. If the lease payment is greater than this amount, the lessor will have a positive NPV, while the lessee will have a negative NPV, and the sum of the two will be zero. Similarly, for lease payments below $13,128, the lease has a positive NPV for the lessee and a negative NPV for the lessor. Both the lessor and the lessee can have positive NPV for a given lease only if the two parties have different tax rates and/or different interest rates for secured debt.

Problem 10

Suppose that the lessee in Problem 6 is a smaller, less profitable company than the lessor; as a result, the lessee is in a 20% tax bracket and pays 15% interest on unsecured debt. The lease payment is $14,000 per year, paid at the end of each of the next five years. Calculate the net present value of the lease for the lessee.

Solution 10

The after tax cash outflow is:

$$L(1 - T_c) + T_c(Dep) =$$

$$(\$14,000)(1 - .20) + .20(10,000) = \$13,200$$

The appropriate discount rate is $[.15(1 - .20)] = .12$. The NPV of the lease is:

$$\$50,000 - \$13,200(3.6048) = \$2,417$$

Since the NPV is positive, this lease is acceptable to the lessee. Even though the lease payment here is greater than the lease payment calculated in Problem 9, the lease has a positive NPV here primarily because the relevant discount rate is much greater than in the previous problem. The higher discount rate makes the present value of the lease payments smaller and consequently makes the NPV greater. The lower tax rate also affects the above calculations because it makes the after-tax cost of the lease payments greater but also decreases the after-tax value of the depreciation deduction.

Problem 11

For the lease described in Problems 6 and 10, what is the net present value of the lease for the lessor?

Solution 11

The after tax cash inflow for the lessor is:

$$L(1 - T_c) + T_c(Dep) =$$

$$(\$14,000)(1 - .34) + .34(10,000) = \$12,640$$

The appropriate discount rate for the lessor is 6.6%. For the lessor, the NPV of the lease is:

$$-\$50,000 + \$12,640(4.1445) = \$2,386$$

Problem 12

Referring to the data in Problem 10, what lease payment would make the lessee indifferent regarding whether to accept the lease?

Solution 12

The lease payment is the value of L which makes the net present value of the lease zero, as indicated in the following equation:

$$\$50,000 - (.80L)(3.6048) - (\$2000)(3.6048) = 0$$

The value of L is $14,838.

Note that in this case, the NPV of the lease for the lessor plus the NPV of the lease for the lessee is not equal to zero. The reason is that the tax rates and the relevant interest rates differ for the two parties to the lease. In fact, the lease payment which makes the lessor indifferent is $13,128, as indicated in the solution to Problem 9. Furthermore, we see in Problem 11 that a lease payment of $14,000 provides a positive NPV to the lessor, so that a payment of $14,838 would be more profitable to the lessor.

The lease payment of $14,838 is called the reservation payment of the lessee; this is the maximum lease payment the lessee would pay. The reservation payment of the lessor is $13,128, which is the minimum payment the lessor would accept. A negotiated lease payment would have to be between these two figures.

Use the following information to solve Problems 13-15.

Hurts is a specialty car leasing firm. They only lease out Oddy automobiles, and the automobiles are the firm's primary assets. The business has been accelerating and is a run-away success (so to speak).

The standard lease arrangement calls for the lessee to make seven $2000 payments. The first payment is due at lease inception, and the remaining six are paid at the end of each year. There is no purchase option; the cars are sold wholesale after the end of the lease. Experience suggests that the cars will retain about 50% of their value. Hurts is in the 40% tax bracket and the relevant pre-tax borrowing rate is 10%. Hurts' overall weighted-average cost of capital (WACC) is 14%.

A new Oddy costs $18,000 and is depreciated to zero over a six-year period. The percentage of the original price of the asset which can be depreciated each year is fixed at 20%, 30%, 20%, 10%, 10%, and 10%, respectively over each of the six years.

Problem 13

What are the cash flows to Hurts from leasing one Oddy?

Solution 13

The cash flows (in thousands) are:

	0	1	2	3	4	5	6
Purchase price	-$18						
After-tax lease payment	1.20	1.20	1.20	1.20	1.20	1.20	1.20
Depreciation tax shield		1.44	2.16	1.44	.72	.72	.72
After-tax residual value							5.40
Total	-$16.8	2.64	3.36	2.64	1.92	1.92	7.32

Solution notes: The depreciation tax shield in year 2, for example, is [.30($18,000)(.40)] = $2160. The after-tax residual value is [.50(18,000)(1 - .40)] = $5400. The cars are depreciated to zero over their life, so the 'excess' depreciation must be 'recaptured.'

Problem 14

What is the net present value to Hurts from leasing one Oddy?

Solution 14

The after-tax residual value is riskier than the other cash flows. Since Hurts has Oddy cars as its primary assets, we will assume that the WACC is the appropriate discount rate for the residual value. All other cash flows are discounted at the after-tax cost of borrowing, 6%. The present value of the residual is [$5.4(.4556)] = $2.46. The present value of the other cash flows is [$2.64(.9434) + 3.36(.8900) + 2.64(.8396) + 1.92(.7921) + 1.92(.7473) + 1.92(.7050)] = $12.01 thousand. The total present value is $14.47 thousand, so the net present value is (-$16,800 + $14,470) = -$2,330. Hurts loses about $2,330 on every lease. They must be making it up in volume!

Problem 15

Try this one on your own. What must Hurts charge to break even on the lease?

Solution 15

Hurts needs to charge $2657 to break even.

CHAPTER 23
HEDGING RISK

CHAPTER HIGHLIGHTS

A major emphasis in the study of corporate finance is the measurement of risk and the relationship between risk and return. In our discussion of these topics in earlier chapters, we have viewed the risk inherent in a capital budgeting project, for example, as unchangeable. Our analysis centered on whether the return for a given project was sufficient to compensate for the level of risk. In this chapter we approach risk from a different perspective; that is, we consider the issue of whether it is possible, or worthwhile, to reduce the risk of a project, or of the firm as a whole. Procedures for reducing risk are referred to as **hedging**, which is the process of engaging in transactions in the financial markets in order to reduce risk. The financial instruments used for hedging transactions are forward contracts and futures contracts, which are described in the first two sections of this chapter. Then we discuss hedging of both inventory risk, using agricultural and metallurgical futures contracts, and interest-rate risk, using interest-rate futures contracts.

Forward Contracts

A **forward contract** is an agreement to make an exchange of assets at a future date. Suppose that, on January 1, 1990, Kris and Ken sign an agreement specifying that Ken will, on June 1, 1990, purchase an ounce of silver from Kris, for $10. Ken is said to be buying the forward contract on January 1 and Kris is selling the contract. The seller of a forward contract is also referred to as the **writer** of the contract. On June 1, Ken pays $10 to Kris, and Kris gives Ken the ounce of silver. Kris is said to be **making delivery** of the silver, Ken is taking delivery, and the ounce of silver is the **deliverable instrument**. Note that the forward contract is signed on January 1, but no cash changes hands until June 1.

Clearly, forward contracts are not at all unusual or exotic. Forward contracts need not be signed contracts; verbal agreements to make an exchange at a future date are forward contracts. A forward contract is distinguished from a **cash transaction** by the fact that, in the latter case, the exchange of assets occurs immediately. A forward contract differs from an option because both parties to the forward contract are obligated to perform the terms of the contract.

Futures Contracts

Forward contracts traded on an organized exchange are referred to as **futures contracts**. When a trader in the futures markets buys or sells a futures contract, he contracts with the exchange clearinghouse, rather than with an individual trader. If the transaction between Kris and Ken, described above, took place at a futures exchange, Kris would contract with the clearinghouse to sell an ounce of silver for $10 at the same time that Ken contracts with the clearinghouse to buy an ounce of silver for $10. The characteristics which distinguish a futures contract, traded on an exchange, from a forward contract between two parties are: first, the seller of a futures contract can choose to make delivery on any day during the delivery month; second, there is generally a liquid market for futures contracts because they are standardized contracts traded on an exchange; and, third, the prices of futures contracts are **marked to the market** on a daily basis.

The mark-to-the-market provision of futures contracts means that buyers and sellers stand to gain or lose every day that the price of a futures contract changes. Suppose that, on January 1, Ken buys a futures contract, and Kris sells a futures contract, providing for delivery of one ounce of silver, during the month of June, at a price of $10. This is a June contract and, since it is standardized, there are numerous other traders buying and selling June silver contracts. Between January 1 and June 1, the price of the June silver contract will change numerous times. If, on January 2, the price of the contract increases to $10.05, Ken will have gained $.05 and Kris will have lost $.05. Since this is a futures contract, Kris must pay $.05 to the clearinghouse within 24 hours of the closing of the exchange on January 2. Ken will receive $.05 from the clearinghouse. If, on January 3, the price decreases to $9.90, Ken pays $.15 (i.e., the difference between the January 2 price and the January 3 price) to the clearinghouse and Kris receives $.15. If no further price changes occur between January 3 and June 1, and Kris chooses to make delivery on June 1, then Ken pays $9.90 to Kris on that date. The net price received by Kris is the $10 price of the original contract [(-$.05 + $.15 + $9.90) = $10.00]. Similarly, the net price paid by Ken is also $10.

Note that, in the above example, the net purchase price of the silver is $10, regardless of whether the contract is a forward contract or a futures contract; the two contracts differ with respect to the timing of the payments. This conclusion ignores, however, the present value of the payments. For example, the buyer of a futures contract suffers a loss if the price of the futures contract declines substantially shortly after his purchase of the contract. An immediate price decline requires an immediate cash outlay on the part of the buyer, so that the present value of the outlay is greater than it would be for a forward contract.

The mark-to-the-market provisions of futures contracts are designed to reduce the likelihood of a default by either the buyer or the seller of the contract. For a forward contract, a substantial change in price gives one of the parties incentive to default on the contract. For example, if the market price of an ounce of silver decreases to $6 between January 1 and June 1, then Ken has an incentive to default; he can purchase an ounce of silver in the open market for much less than he would have to pay Kris for an ounce of silver, according to the terms of the forward contract. Similarly, if the price should increase substantially, Kris has an incentive to default on the contract and sell her ounce of silver at the going market price. The incentive to default does not exist with a futures contract because of the mark-to-the-market provision.

If the price of an ounce of silver declines from $10 to $9.90, the buyer of the contact pays $.10 to the clearinghouse. If price continues to decline over time, the buyer continues to make payments to the clearinghouse. If, over a period of time, price declines substantially, the buyer has already realized the loss resulting from the price change. This is in contrast with the forward contract, where the buyer has not realized the loss until the date the agreement is carried out; at that point, the buyer of the forward contract has an incentive to default.

Hedging

Futures contracts can be used to hedge two different positions in an asset: a producer of a commodity can use a **short hedge** to reduce the risk of a decline in the price of the commodity; and, a processor of a commodity can use a **long hedge** to reduce the risk of an increase in the price of the commodity which the processor must purchase.

Consider the case of a soybean farmer who anticipates a harvest of 100,000 bushels of soybeans. The farmer can elect to harvest the soybeans and then sell at the going price after the harvest. Since the price at which he can sell the soybeans is not known in advance, this unhedged position is very risky. On the other hand, in order to reduce risk, the farmer can write, or sell, 20 futures contracts, for 5,000 bushels per contract, with delivery date in September. This position is referred to as a short hedge, because the farmer's position in the futures market is a short position; that is, he is obligated to sell 100,000 bushels of wheat in September. If the futures price is $5 per bushel, the farmer will receive $500,000 for the delivery of the soybeans in September.

A processor must buy soybeans in order to produce soybean oil. A processor who anticipates the purchase of 100,000 bushels of soybeans can maintain an unhedged position and simply buy soybeans at the going price after harvest. Alternatively, the processor can adopt a **long hedge** by purchasing 20 September futures contracts; the processor has taken a long position in the futures market. At a price of $5 per bushel, the processor will pay $500,000 for 100,000 bushels of soybeans to be delivered in September.

Interest-Rate Futures Contracts

Treasury-bond futures contracts are among the most widely traded futures contracts. In this section, we discuss the use of Treasury-bond futures contracts for hedging interest-rate risk.

Pricing of Treasury Bonds. The value of a Treasury bond is the present value of future interest and principal payments. Consider a 20-year, 10-percent coupon bond, with a $1000 face value, purchased on June 1, 1990 (i.e., date 0). The first semi-annual interest payment of ($100/2) = $50 is paid on December 1, 1990 (i.e., date 1) and the present value is given by:

$$P_{TB} = \frac{\$50}{(1 + r_1)} + \frac{\$50}{(1 + r_2)^2} + ... + \frac{\$50}{(1 + r_{39})^{39}} + \frac{\$1050}{(1 + r_{40})^{40}}$$

where P_{TB} is the price of the Treasury bond and r_i is the appropriate semi-annual spot rate.

Pricing of a Forward Contract. Suppose an investor signs a forward contract on June 1, 1990, agreeing to buy a 20-year, 10-percent coupon bond on December 1, 1990. The price of the forward contract as of December 1, 1990 (P_{FC}) must satisfy the following equation:

$$\frac{P_{FC}}{1 + r_1} = \frac{\$50}{(1 + r_2)^2} + \frac{\$50}{(1 + r_3)^3} + ... + \frac{\$50}{(1 + r_{40})^{40}} + \frac{\$1050}{(1 + r_{41})^{41}}$$

The right side of the above equation discounts the future interest and principal payments, which begin at date 2, to date 0. The left side discounts the date 1 price of the forward contract to date 0.

We can now demonstrate the fact that there is an inverse relationship between interest rates and the price of a forward contract by multiplying both sides of the above equation by $(1 + r_1)$. The resulting equation has P_{FC} on the left side and the first term on the right side of the equation is:

$$\frac{\$50 \times (1 + r_1)}{(1 + r_2)^2}$$

Suppose that the term structure of interest rates shifts upwards by a constant amount. Then the term above decreases because the increase in r_2 increases the denominator more than the increase in r_1 increases the numerator; this conclusion results from the fact that $(1 + r_2)$ is squared in the above term while $(1 + r_1)$ is not squared. Comparable results occur for all remaining terms of the equation described above, so that the price of the forward contract decreases with an increase in interest rates.

Futures Contracts. The major differences between forward and futures contracts were described in the second section of this chapter. The characteristics of futures contracts which distinguish them from forward contracts are: futures contracts are traded on exchanges; futures contracts allow the seller to deliver on any date during the delivery month; futures contracts are subject to the mark-to-the-market provision; and, there is a liquid market for futures contracts. These characteristics do not alter the fundamental conclusion that a futures contract is a variant of a forward contract. Consequently, the pricing formula for a forward contract should be regarded as a close approximation for the pricing of a futures contract.

Hedging in Interest Rate Futures. In this section, we consider both long and short hedges of mortgages in the Treasury-bond futures contract. The basic principles of this section are analogous to those described in the section on hedging inventories.

Consider the case of Mildred's Mortgage Banking Company. On July 1, 1990, Mildred makes a commitment to lend $500,000 to homeowners, on October 1, 1990. The loans are 30-year mortgages with a 10-percent interest rate. Mildred intends to sell the mortgages to an insurance company prior to October 1. Suppose that the insurance company buys the mortgages on September 30 for $500,000; Mildred then receives an origination fee, which is typically equal to one percent of the face value of the loans, from the insurance company, so that Mildred's profit on the transaction is $[(.01)(\$500,000)] = \$5,000$.

The above scenario ignores the fact that Mildred may not be able to sell the loans for their face value prior to October 1. If mortgage rates increase between July 1 and October 1, the value of the loans to the insurance company will be less than the $500,000 face value. The decrease in the value of the loans is a loss to Mildred. Of course, if interest rates decline, Mildred will be able to sell the mortgages for more than $500,000. However, if Mildred does not want to be subjected to the interest-rate risk resulting from fluctuations in interest rates, she can adopt a short position in Treasury-bond futures.

Suppose that, on July 1, when Mildred makes the commitment to lend $500,000, she also sells five $100,000 Treasury-bond futures contracts with delivery date in December. The futures contracts obligate Mildred to deliver $500,000 of Treasury bonds. If interest rates increase between July and October then, as noted above, the value of the mortgages Mildred sells to the insurance company decreases. An increase in interest rates will also decrease the value of Treasury bonds and, since Mildred has taken a short position in the futures contract, she will gain from the decrease in the value of the deliverable instrument. Since Mildred is no longer subject to interest rate risk on her mortgage position once she sells the mortgages, she will also net out her futures position at the same time; that is, she will buy five Treasury-bond futures contracts in order to terminate her obligation in the futures market.

While the short hedge described above will reduce Mildred's exposure to interest-rate risk, the risk will not be completely eliminated. The risk would be completely eliminated only if the increase in the value of her futures position were sufficient to exactly offset the decrease in the value of the mortgages. As noted earlier, the price of a Treasury bond futures contract is a function of the present value of the Treasury bond which is deliverable against the contract. Although both Treasury bonds and mortgages are affected by interest rate changes in a similar way, the changes in value are not identical for a number of reasons. Mortgages and Treasury bonds have different maturities and payment streams. A twenty-year Treasury bond pays interest semi-annually and principal at maturity, while a thirty-year mortgage pays both interest and principal on a monthly basis. Mortgages have default risk while Treasury bonds do not. Also, mortgages can be repaid prior to maturity. As a result of these differences, the two instruments do not respond identically to changes in interest rates, so that the changes in the value of the mortgages and the short position in the Treasury bond futures contracts will not be exactly offsetting. However, the short hedge does reduce substantially the risk to which the hedger is subjected since the changes in the value of the mortgages and the Treasury bonds are at least partially offsetting.

The example described here suggests that Mildred can offset some of the interest-rate risk associated with the mortgage commitments by adopting a short hedge in Treasury-bond futures. Suppose that, instead of first making the mortgage commitments and then selling the mortgages, Mildred signs an agreement, before she makes the commitments to the borrowers, to sell $500,000 of 10-percent, 30-year mortgages to an insurance company. With this scenario, Mildred's interest-rate risk is the opposite of that identified in the previous example; now, if interest rates decline prior to her finding borrowers, she will incur a loss because she will have to lend at a rate below 10 percent but she will have to deliver 10-percent mortgages to the insurance company. Consequently, Mildred can hedge this risk with a long position in the Treasury-bond futures contract; that is, Mildred will buy five $100,000 Treasury-bond futures contracts.

Duration Hedging

In the previous section, we noted that changes in interest rates affect Treasury bonds and mortgages differently. In part, these differential effects are related to the timing and size of the payments associated with each instrument. In this section, we introduce the concept of duration to explain these effects.

The Case of Zero-Coupon Bonds. We first consider the relationship between maturity and interest-rate risk by studying the example of two zero-coupon bonds with different maturities. Assume that the interest rate for one-year and ten-year zero coupon bonds is 10 percent, and that both bonds have a maturity value of $1,000. The value of the one-year bond is:

$$PV = \frac{\$1,000}{(1.10)} = \$909.09$$

Similarly, the value of the ten-year bond is:

$$PV = \frac{\$1,000}{(1.10)^{10}} = \$385.54$$

Clearly, there is an inverse relationship between value and interest rates for both bonds. The issue here, however, is the size of the price change associated with a given change in the level of interest rates. For example, if one-year and ten-year rates each increase from 10% to 14%, the prices of the bonds decrease to $877.19 and $269.74, respectively. For the one-year bond, the decrease of $31.90 represents a 3.51% decrease in value, while the $115.80 decrease in value of the ten-year bond is a 30.04% decrease. The long-term bond is subject to much greater price volatility for a given change in interest rates; similar results can be easily demonstrated for a decrease in interest rates. The greater price volatility for the long-term bond arises from the compounding of interest over a longer period of time; this is demonstrated mathematically by noting that, in the denominator of the present value calculation for the long-term bond, the factor (1+r) is raised to the tenth power, so that relatively small changes in r are magnified by the compounding process.

The Case of Two Bonds with the Same Maturity but with Different Coupons. In order to demonstrate the relationship between coupon rates and price volatility, consider two 10-year bonds with $1,000 maturity value, one with a coupon rate of 5% and the other with a coupon rate of 10%. If the interest rate for each bond is 10 percent, then the values of the bonds are given by:

$$PV_1 = \frac{\$\,50}{(1.10)} + \frac{\$\,50}{(1.10)^2} + ... + \frac{\$\,50}{(1.10)^9} + \frac{\$1050}{(1.10)^{10}}$$

$$PV_2 = \frac{\$100}{(1.10)} + \frac{\$100}{(1.10)^2} + ... + \frac{\$100}{(1.10)^9} + \frac{\$1100}{(1.10)^{10}}$$

where PV_1 and PV_2 are the present values of the 5% and 10%-coupon bonds, respectively. PV_1 is $692.77 and PV_2 is $1,000. If interest rates increase to 14%, then the values of the two bonds decline to $530.55 and $791.36, respectively. In percentage terms, the decreases are 23.42% and 20.86%, indicating that the low-coupon bond has the larger percentage decrease in value for a given increase in interest rates; again, comparable results can be demonstrated for a decrease in interest rates.

Duration. The two preceding examples demonstrate that price volatility is positively related to maturity and inversely related to coupon rate. Both of these relationships are summarized by the concept of **duration**.

To understand the general premise of duration, think of the ten-year, 10%-coupon bond described above as a series of ten zero-coupon bonds: the first zero-coupon bond pays $100 at maturity, in one year; the second zero-coupon bond pays $100 in two years, and so on; the tenth zero-coupon bond pays $1100 at maturity in ten years. The duration of the ten-year, 10%-coupon bond is the weighted average of the maturities of the ten hypothetical zero-coupon bonds described above, with the weights based on the present value of each of the ten zero-coupon bonds.

Specifically, we calculate the duration of the ten-year, 10%-coupon bond as follows:

1. Calculate the present value of each of the ten annual payments, using the ten percent discount rate originally specified in the example.

Year	Payment	Present Value
1	$ 100	$ 90.909
2	100	82.645
3	100	75.131
4	100	68.301
5	100	62.092
6	100	56.447
7	100	51.316
8	100	46.651
9	100	42.410
10	1100	424.098
		$1000.000

2. Express the present value of each payment in relative terms. That is, express each of the above present values as a percent of the present value of the bond.

Year	Payment	Present Value	Relative Value
1	$ 100	$ 90.909	.090909
2	100	82.645	.082645
3	100	75.131	.075131
4	100	68.301	.068301
5	100	62.092	.062092
6	100	56.447	.056447
7	100	51.316	.051316
8	100	46.651	.046651
9	100	42.410	.042410
10	1100	424.098	.424098
		$1000.000	1.000000

3. Weight the maturity of each payment by its relative value.

Year		Relative Value	
1	x	.090909 =	.090909
2	x	.082645 =	.165290
3	x	.075131 =	.225393
4	x	.068301 =	.273204
5	x	.062092 =	.310460
6	x	.056447 =	.338682
7	x	.051316 =	.359212
8	x	.046651 =	.373208
9	x	.042410 =	.381690
10	x	.424098 =	4.240980
			6.759028

The duration of the bond is 6.759 years, which indicates that the sensitivity of the bond's price to interest rate fluctuations is equivalent to that of a zero-coupon bond with 6.759 years to maturity.

Matching Liabilities with Assets. Financial institutions frequently use the concept of duration in order to **immunize** against interest-rate risk. That is, if a bank, for example, matches the duration of its liabilities with the duration of its assets, it is said to be immune to interest-rate risk in the sense that changes in interest rates will affect both the bank's liabilities and its assets to the same extent. Consequently, the value of the bank's equity is left unchanged.

Consider a bank with the following market-value balance sheet:

Duration	Assets	Market Value
1 year	Short-term loans	$ 500,000
2 years	Industrial loans	$ 350,000
15 years	Mortgage loans	$ 150,000
		$ 1,000,000

Duration	Liabilities	Market Value
0	Checking Accounts	$ 400,000
1 year	Certificates of Deposit	$ 300,000
10 years	Long-term financing	$ 100,000
	Equity	$ 200,000
		$ 1,000,000

The duration of the bank's assets is determined by calculating the weighted-average of the duration of each asset, where the weights are the percentages of the bank's total assets:

$$(1 \text{ year} \times .50) + (2 \text{ years} \times .35) + (15 \text{ years} \times .15) = 3.450 \text{ years}$$

Similarly, the duration of the bank's liabilities is:

$$(0 \text{ year} \times .50) + (2 \text{ years} \times .375) + (15 \text{ years} \times .125) = 2.625 \text{ years}$$

[Note that for the calculation of the duration for the bank's liabilities, the weights used are the percentages of the bank's total liabilities (i.e., $800,000), rather than the liabilities plus equity.]

These results indicate that the bank's assets are substantially more sensitive to changes in interest rates than are the bank's liabilities. Consequently, an increase in interest rates would decrease the value of the assets more than it would decrease the value of the liabilities, resulting in a decrease in shareholders' equity. To immunize against such consequences, the bank can increase the duration of its liabilities and/or decrease the duration of its assets in such a way that:

$$(\text{Duration of assets}) \times (\text{Market value of assets}) =$$

$$(\text{Duration of liabilities}) \times (\text{Market value of liabilities})$$

For example, suppose that the bank decides to decrease the duration of its assets. The duration of the assets must then be reduced to:

$$(\text{Duration of liabilities}) \times \frac{\text{Market value of liabilities}}{\text{Market value of assets}}$$

or $[(2.625 \text{ years}) \times (\$800,000/\$1,000,000)] = 2.10$ years. This would require reduced emphasis on mortgage loans and increased emphasis on short-term and industrial loans.

CONCEPT TEST

1. Procedures for reducing risk are referred to as _____.

2. The financial instruments used for hedging are _____ and _____.

3. A _____ is an agreement to make an exchange of assets at a future date.

4. The seller of a forward contract is referred to as the _____ of the contract.

5. A cash transaction differs from a forward contract in that the exchange of assets occurs _____ for the cash transaction.

6. The difference between a forward contract and an option is that, in the case of the forward contract, the participants are _____ the terms of the contract.

7. When a trader buys or sells a futures contract, he contracts with the exchange _____, rather than with an individual trader.

8. Forward contracts traded on an organized exchange are referred to as _____.

9. The _____ provisions of futures contracts are designed to reduce the likelihood of a default by either the buyer or the seller of the contract.

10. A producer of a commodity can use a _____ to reduce the risk of a decline in the price of the commodity.

11. A processor of a commodity can use a _____ to reduce the risk of an increase in the price of the commodity which the processor must purchase.

12. Long-term bonds are subject to _____ price volatility for a given change in interest rates than are short-term bonds.

13. The greater price volatility for a long-term bond arises from the _____ over a longer period of time.

14. Price volatility is _____ related to maturity and _____ to coupon rate.

15. Financial institutions frequently use the concept of duration in order to _____ against interest rate risk.

ANSWERS TO CONCEPT TEST

1. hedging
2. forward contracts;
   futures contracts
3. forward contract
4. writer
5. immediately
6. obligated to perform
7. clearinghouse

8. futures contracts
9. mark-to-the-market
10. short hedge
11. long hedge
12. greater
13. compounding of interest
14. positively; inversely
15. immunize

PROBLEMS AND SOLUTIONS

Problem 1

Find the price of a Treasury bond with a 10%-coupon rate, a $1000 maturity value and five years to maturity, using the following expected semiannual spot rates:

Time from Today	Semiannual Rate
6 months	0.050
12 months	0.055
18 months	0.058
24 months	0.060
30 months	0.060
36 months	0.060
42 months	0.062
48 months	0.063
54 months	0.065
60 months	0.065
66 months	0.065

Solution 1

The bond described here pays semiannual coupon interest payments of $[(.10)(\$1000)/2] = \$50$. The present value of the bond is found by discounting each of the future payments at the appropriate spot rate. For example, the present value of the first interest payment is $(\$50/1.050) = \$47.619$; the present value of the second payment is $[\$50/(1.055)^2] = \$44.923$. The complete calculation is shown in the following table:

Time from Today	Semiannual Rate	Payment	Present Value
6 months	0.050	$ 50	$ 47.619
12 months	0.055	50	44.923
18 months	0.058	50	42.219
24 months	0.060	50	39.605
30 months	0.060	50	37.363
36 months	0.060	50	35.248
42 months	0.062	50	32.817
48 months	0.063	50	30.669
54 months	0.065	50	28.368
60 months	0.065	$1,050	$ 559.362

Present value = $ 898.193

Problem 2

Suppose you sign a contract today specifying that a five-year Treasury bond, as described in Problem 1, will be delivered to you in six months. If you pay for the bond today, what is the price you would pay? (Note that this is not a forward contract because you pay for the bond today, rather than on the delivery date. Also note that the bond to be delivered has a five-year maturity on the delivery date.)

Solution 2

The first interest payment for the five-year bond will be paid one year from today. The present value of this payment, discounted at the 12-month spot rate from Problem 1, is $[\$50/(1.055)^2] = \$44.923$. The complete calculation is indicated in the table below:

Time from Today	Semiannual Rate	Payment	Present Value
12 months	0.055	$ 50	$ 44.923
18 months	0.058	50	42.219
24 months	0.060	50	39.605
30 months	0.060	50	37.363
36 months	0.060	50	35.248
42 months	0.062	50	32.817
48 months	0.063	50	30.669
54 months	0.065	50	28.368
60 months	0.065	50	26.636
66 months	0.065	$1,050	$ 525.223

Present value = $ 843.071

Therefore, you would pay $843.07 today for a Treasury bond to be delivered to you six months from today. At that time, the bond will have five years to maturity.

Problem 3

Suppose that the contract in Problem 2 is a forward contract, so that payment for the Treasury bond will be made six months from today, when the bond is delivered, rather than today. What is the price of the forward contract, to be paid in six months?

Solution 3

The price to be paid (P_{FC}) is equal to the present value calculated in Problem 2, times one plus the six-month spot rate: [($843.07)(1.05)] = $885.22. This calculation reflects the fact that, rather than paying for the bond today, the forward contract specifies payment in six months; therefore, the size of the payment must include interest over the next six months.

Problem 4

Suppose that, for the bond described in Problem 1, all semiannual rates increased by 10 basis points. (A basis point is one one-hundredth of a percentage point, or .01% = .0001.) What is the value of the bond described in Problem 1?

Solution 4

Each of the semiannual interest rates increases by .10% = .0010. Therefore, the present value of the first interest payment is [$50/(1.051)] = $47.574; the present value of the second payment is [$50/(1.056)^2] = $44.838. The present value of the bond is $891.51. As we expect, the present value of the bond decreases with the increase in interest rates.

Problem 5

Suppose that, as in Problem 2, you sign a contract today specifying that a five-year Treasury bond will be delivered to you in six months. If you pay for the bond today, and interest rates have increased by 10 basis points, what is the price you would pay?

Solution 5

The present value of the first interest payment, to be received in 12 months, is [$50/(1.056)^2] = $44.838. The present value of the bond is $836.02. As a result of the increase in interest rates, the present value of the bond has decreased from the value calculated in Problem 2.

Problem 6

Suppose that the contract in Problem 5 is a forward contract, with delivery of a five-year Treasury bond six months from today. What is the price of the forward contract, to be paid in six months?

Solution 6

P_{FC} is equal to the present value calculated in Problem 5 times one plus the six-month spot rate: [($836.02)(1.051)] = $878.66. Note that, as a result of the increase in the spot rates specified in Problem 4, the price of the forward contract has decreased from $885.22, as calculated in Problem 3, to $878.66 .

Problem 7

Suppose that the spot rates indicated in Problem 1 decrease by 10 basis points. What is the present value of a five-year Treasury bond, with a 10% coupon rate, to be delivered six months from today, if the bond is paid for today? What is the price of a forward contract to purchase the Treasury bond six months from today?

Solution 7

If the Treasury bond is paid for today, the price is $850.20. The price of the forward contract, to be paid six months from today, is $891.86. The decrease in spot rates results in an increase in the price of the forward contract, compared to the value indicated in Problem 3.

Problem 8

Melissa's Mortgage Banking Company has made a commitment to lend $500,000 in mortgage loans. The terms of the loans specify a thirty-year loan with a 10% interest rate and annual payments of principal and interest. The market rate for thirty-year mortgages is also 10%. Melissa will make the loans six months from today. What are the annual mortgage payments on the loans? If the loans are paid monthly, what are the monthly payments?

Solution 8

Using the present value annuity factor for a thirty-year annuity, at 10% interest, the annual payments are ($500,000/9.426914) = $53,039.63. Monthly payments are $4,387.86.

Problem 9

Suppose that, when Melissa makes the loans described in Problem 8, she immediately sells the loans to an insurance company. If the interest rate for 30-year mortgages has increased to 11% at that time, at what price will Melissa be able to sell the mortgages? If the interest rate has declined to 9%, at what price will Melissa sell the mortgages? (Assume that the mortgages specify annual payments of principal and interest.)

Solution 9

When the insurance company buys the mortgages from Melissa, the insurance company is buying a thirty-year annuity, with annual payments of $53,039.63. At a discount rate of 11%, the present value of these payments is [($53,039.63)(8.693793)] = $461,115.56. Therefore, if the interest rate increases from 10% to 11% during the six-month period, Melissa will lose $38,884.44. On the other hand, if the interest rate for thirty-year mortgages declines to 9%, then the present value of the mortgages will increase to $544,910.75, and Melissa will gain $44,910.75.

Problem 10

In order to hedge against the interest-rate risk indicated in Problem 9, Melissa decides to sell five $100,000 Treasury bond futures contracts which specify delivery of Treasury bonds with an 8%-coupon rate and a twenty-year maturity. The delivery date of the contracts is in six months, at the same time that Melissa will extend the mortgage loans. If the interest rate for long-term Treasury bonds is currently 9%, what is the price of the futures contract? [Assume that all relevant semiannual spot rates are equal to (.090/2) = .045.]

Solution 10

The first coupon interest payment for the Treasury bond is $40, to be paid one year from today, and the maturity value plus the last interest payment, or $1040, will be paid 20.5 years from today. We can discount all of these payments, at the 4.5% semiannual rate, to today, and then multiply the present value by 1.045 to find the price of the futures contract six months from today. However, since all the semiannual spot rates are identical, we need only determine the present value of the Treasury bond, as of date 1, with payments beginning as of date 2. The present value of the Treasury bond is $907.99. (Although this calculation is based on the valuation of a forward contract, it is a reasonable approximation for the value of a futures contract.) The futures contract calls for delivery of $100,000 face-value of Treasury bonds, so the price of the futures contract is [(100)($907.99)] = $90,799. Since Melissa will sell five contracts, the price is [(5)($90,799)] = $453,995.

Problem 11

Suppose that Melissa sells the five futures contracts today and that, six months from today, interest rates for twenty-year Treasury bonds have increased to 10%. What is the price of the futures contract on that date.

Solution 11

The present value of a $1000 Treasury bond with an 8%-coupon rate and twenty years to maturity is $828.41. The price of the futures contract is [(5)(100)($828.41)] = $414,205.

Problem 12

Suppose that Melissa makes the commitment on the mortgage loans described in Problem 8 and sells the five Treasury-bond futures contracts described in Problem 10; furthermore, in the next six months, interest rates on thirty-year mortgages increase from 10% to 11% and yields on twenty-year Treasury bonds increase from 9% to 10%. What is the effect on Melissa's position?

Solution 12

The increase in mortgage rates results in a loss in the value of the mortgage commitments of $38,884.44. Since Melissa has sold the futures contracts, the decrease in the price of the futures contract represents a gain of $39,790. Therefore, the net gain is $905.56. Note that by hedging, Melissa has avoided a loss in the value of the loan commitments equal to $38,884.44, and has also gained $905.56.

Problem 13

Three zero-coupon bonds each have a maturity value of $1,000 and are priced to yield 8%. The maturities of the three bonds are 2 years, 5 years and 15 years, respectively. Calculate the current price of each bond.

Solution 13

The present value of the two-year bond is $[1000/(1.08)^2] = \$857.33$. The present value of the five-year bond is $[\$1000/(1.08)^5] = \$680.58$, and the present value of the fifteen-year bond is $[\$1000/(1.08)^{15}] = \$315.24$.

Problem 14

Suppose that the yields for the three bonds described in Problem 13 increase to 9%. Which of the three bonds has the greatest percentage change in price?

Solution 14

The present values are now: $841.68, $649.93 and $274.54, for the two-year, five-year and fifteen-year bonds, respectively. The percentage decreases in price are: 1.825%, 4.504%, and 12.911%. As expected, the bond with the longest maturity also has the greatest percentage decrease in price.

Problem 15

Calculate the duration for a ten-year bond, with a $1000 face value and a 12%-coupon rate, selling at par. Assume that the bond pays annual interest.

Solution 15

Since the bond is selling at face value, its yield is equal to its coupon rate. To find the duration, we first calculate the present value of each interest payment, then express these present values as a percentage of the price of the bond. The resulting weights are multiplied by the 'maturity' of each payment to find the duration. The calculations are demonstrated in the following table:

Year	Payment	Present Value	Relative Value
1	$ 120	$ 107.143	.107143
2	120	95.663	.095663
3	120	85.414	.085414
4	120	76.262	.076262
5	120	68.091	.068091
6	120	60.796	.060796
7	120	54.282	.054282
8	120	48.466	.048466
9	120	43.273	.043273
10	1120	360.610	.360610
		$1000.000	1.000000

We now multiply the relative values in the last column times the year; the sum of these products indicates that the duration is 6.328 years.

CHAPTER 24
CORPORATE FINANCIAL MODELS AND LONG-TERM PLANNING

CHAPTER HIGHLIGHTS

This chapter is primarily concerned with long-term financial planning and financial planning models. The guidelines established as part of the financial planning process should identify the firm's financial goals, analyze the difference between the firm's current status and the established goals, and identify the actions required to achieve the financial goals. Large corporations tend to use an overall growth rate in sales as a major planning component. As this chapter describes, explicit links exist among potential growth, investment decisions and financing decisions.

What is Corporate Financial Planning?

A financial plan identifies the method for achieving financial goals. The plan has two dimensions: a time frame and a level of aggregation. A long-term plan usually covers two to five years; the short-run is generally considered to be the next 12 months.

Creation of a financial plan typically involves a process of combining smaller capital-budgeting decisions into much larger projects. This process is called **aggregation**.

Financial plans often require alternative sets of assumptions. For example, a firm might require that each of its divisions prepare alternative plans under different assumptions regarding the state of the economy and the firm's prospects; these might include a best case, most likely case, and worst case set of assumptions.

The planning process is useful in several ways. First, a financial plan makes explicit the linkage between proposed investment or growth and the financing required to implement the proposals. Second, a plan allows the firm to evaluate different investment and financing options, and their long-run impact on profitability, cash flow, and value. Third, a financial plan establishes whether some courses of action are feasible and consistent with corporate objectives of maximizing shareholder wealth. Finally, a financial plan lends itself to the identification and evaluation of possible future events; this process helps the firm to avoid unpleasant surprises and to prepare contingency plans.

A Financial Planning Model: The Ingredients

The exact form and level of detail in a financial plan varies from firm to firm. The common elements of a financial plan are:

1. **The sales forecast.** A sales forecast is a universal requirement for financial planning.
2. **Pro forma statements.** These are projected accounting statements.
3. **Asset requirements.** The financial plan describes projected capital expenditures and working capital needs.

4. **Financial requirements.** This part of the plan details the way in which needed financing will be obtained. Debt policy and dividend policy are also included here.
5. **The plug.** The projected growth rates in sales, assets and financial requirements are generally not compatible without some adjustment. This financial 'plug' variable might be new debt or equity, or both.
6. **Economic assumptions.** Assumptions about industry sales, interest rates, and the general state of the economy are necessary in order to generate projected financial statements.

Suppose the Amber Corporation forecasts a 20% increase in sales. The most recent income statement is:

```
Sales        $1,000
Costs         - 800
Net income    $200
Dividends     $100
```

Assuming that costs remain at 80% of sales, and the dividend payout ratio remains at 50%, a pro forma income statement can be prepared:

```
Sales        $1,200
Costs         - 960
Net income    $240
Dividends     $120
```

The most recent balance sheet is:

Current assets	$ 800	Current liabilities	$ 600
Fixed assets	3600	Long-term debt	1520
		Equity	2280
Total	$4400		$4400

Amber plans no new long-term borrowing. All current asset and current liability accounts, and fixed assets are assumed to be proportional to sales. For example, current assets were 80% of sales ($800/$1000). If sales rise to $1200, then current assets would be projected at [.80($1200)] = $960. Based on the projected net income, retained earnings will rise by $120, so ending equity will be ($2280 + $120) = $2400. An initial pro forma balance sheet would thus appear as follows:

Current assets	$ 960	Current liabilities	$ 720
Fixed assets	4320	Long-term debt	1520
		Equity	2400
Total	$5280		$4640
Funds needed			640
	$5280		$5280

As indicated by the pro forma balance sheet, Amber has external funds needed (EFN) of $640. This is a result of the increase in assets required to support the higher sales level. Since no new long-term borrowing is planned (perhaps due to restrictive covenants), new common stock must be issued; that is, new equity is the financial 'plug' variable. If Amber does not wish to obtain new equity financing, then growth will have to be scaled back, or some other action (such as a dividend reduction) must be taken. These considerations illustrate the interconnection among growth, asset acquisition, and financing.

The above procedure for determining EFN can be summarized by the following formula:

$$EFN = \frac{Assets}{Sales} \times \Delta S - \frac{Debt}{Sales} \times \Delta S - [p(Projected\ Sales)(1-d)]$$

where ΔS is the dollar change in sales, p is the net profit margin, d is the dividend payout ratio and Debt refers to debts such as accounts payable that vary spontaneously with sales. For Amber, EFN is:

$$EFN = \frac{4400}{1000} \times (200) - \frac{600}{1000} \times (200) - \frac{200}{1000} \times (1200) \times (1-.5)$$

$$= (4.4)200 - (.6)200 - (.2)(1200)(1-.5) = \$640$$

as previously calculated.

To complete the financial plan, the inputs must be altered to examine how the plan changes under different assumptions. This is called a **sensitivity analysis**. For example, the model for Amber Corporation assumes that fixed assets are proportional to sales; suppose instead that Amber has sufficient unused capacity to support a 20% increase in sales with no new plant and equipment. In this case, current assets would still rise by $160, to $960, but fixed assets would remain at $3600 and total assets would be $4560. EFN would then be:

$$EFN = 160 - (.6)(200) - (.2)(1200)(1-.5) = -\$80$$

Note that the -$80 value for EFN represents an $80 **surplus**. Compare this result to the $640 deficit previously calculated! Operating at less than full capacity has a significant impact on EFN.

What Determines Growth?

The use of sales growth as an explicit corporate goal is quite common. However, this may not be consistent with the net present value approach, depending on how growth is achieved. In general, growth should be a consequence of decisions which are consistent with the net present value criterion, rather than a goal in itself. We also know that firms are generally reluctant to issue new equity. If the firm is unwilling to issue new equity and desires to maintain a fixed debt/equity ratio and dividend payout, then, as illustrated below, growth cannot be an externally supplied goal.

To illustrate the linkage between growth and financial policy, we make the following assumptions for Amber Corp.:

1. Assets grow in proportion to sales.
2. Net income is a constant percentage of sales.
3. The dividend-payout policy and debt/equity ratio are fixed.
4. No new stock will be issued.

By definition, the change in assets must equal the change in debt plus the change in equity. As a consequence, only one growth rate is consistent with the four assumptions above; this is the firm's **sustainable growth rate**.

The firm's sustainable growth rate ($\Delta S/S_0$) is given by:

$$\frac{\Delta S}{S_0} = \frac{p(1 - d)(1 + L)}{T - [p(1 - d)(1 + L)]}$$

where L is the debt/equity ratio, T is the ratio of total assets/sales, S_0 is the sales level this year, ΔS is the dollar change in sales, p is the net profit margin, and d is the dividend payout ratio. If we now assume that Amber will take on new debt in order to maintain its present debt/equity ratio of L = [($600 + $1520)/$2280] = .93, then the sustainable growth rate is:

$$\frac{\Delta S}{S_0} = g = \frac{.2(1 - .5)(1 + .93)}{4.4 - [.2(1 - .5)(1 + .93)]} = .046 = 4.6\%$$

If management desires a higher growth rate, then one of the stated assumptions must be modified. This example illustrates the use of a financial planning model for reconciling potentially conflicting goals.

Some Caveats of Financial Planning Models

Financial planning models do not identify optimal financial policies. In addition, the assumptions of the financial planning models we have discussed are too simple to accurately represent reality. Financial planning models are useful for pointing out inconsistencies, but they offer very little guidance concerning the resolution of these inconsistencies.

CONCEPT TEST

1. The two dimensions of financial planning are the _____ and the _____.

2. The process of combining smaller investment proposals into a single larger asset requirement is called _____.

3. All financial plans require a _____.

4. Projected future accounting statements are called _____ statements.

5. A financial plan usually addresses projected capital spending or _____.

6. A financial plan usually addresses dividend and debt policy, or, more generally, _____.

7. In order to reconcile the various financial statements in a financial plan, a _____ variable must be designated.

8. A financial plan must include a set of _____ such as projected interest rates.

9. Financial planning models frequently assume that most variables are proportional to _____.

10. In contrast to the goal of maximization of shareholder wealth, many corporations use an explicit _____ as a goal.

11. Assume a firm's assets and net income are proportional to sales, its debt and dividend policy are fixed, and it will not issue new equity. In this case, the plug variable is _____.

12. The plug variable in question 11 is called the firm's _____.

13. The time horizon considered by most short-term financial plans is _____.

14. The time horizon considered by most long-term financial plans is _____.

15. Amber Corporation has a return on equity of 16% and pays out 30% of net income in the form of dividends. Its approximate growth rate is _____.

ANSWERS TO CONCEPT TEST

1. timo dimension; level of aggregation
2. aggregation
3. sales forecast
4. pro forma
5. asset requirements
6. financing requirements
7. plug
8. economic assumptions
9. sales
10. growth rate
11. growth
12. sustainable growth rate
13. 12 months
14. 2 to 5 years
15. $(.16)(1 - .3) = 11.2\%$

PROBLEMS AND SOLUTIONS

Use the following information for Dworkin Company to solve Problems 1-5. All the financial statements are from the most recent reporting period.

Income statement

Sales	$2000
Cost of sales	1100
Depreciation	400
Interest	300
Tax (34%)	68
Net income	$ 132
Dividends	44

Balance sheet

Current assets	$500	Current liabilities	$165
Net fixed assets	1150	Long-term debt	535
		Equity	950
Total	$1650		$1650

Problem 1

Dworkin forecasts that sales next year will be $2200. Calculate EFN.

Solution 1

The asset/sales ratio is ($1650/$2000) = .825. Profit margin is 6.6%, and the payout ratio is 1/3. Current liabilities will vary spontaneously with sales; however, the amount of long-term debt is under management control and generally does not vary spontaneously. EFN is calculated as follows:

$$EFN = \frac{Assets}{Sales} \times \Delta S - \frac{Debt}{Sales} \times \Delta S - [p(Projected\ Sales)(1 - d)]$$

$$= (.825)(\$200) - (.1)(\$200) - (.066)(\$2200)(1 - 1/3) = \$48.20$$

Problem 2

Assume that Dworkin has sufficient excess capacity to support a sales level of $2100 with no new fixed assets. Calculate EFN for projected sales of $2200.

Solution 2

At the full capacity sales level of $2100, current assets would be [($500/$2000)($2100)] = $525, and fixed assets would be $1150. Total assets would thus be $1675. The asset/sales ratio at full capacity is ($1675/$2100) = .7976, so EFN would be:

$$EFN = [25 + (.7976)\$100] - (.1)(\$200) - (.066)(\$2200)(1 - 1/3) = -\$12.04$$

Problem 3

Dworkin believes that an industry slowdown is possible over the next year. In this case, sales growth will be 5%. Calculate EFN and interpret your answer.

Solution 3

In this case, sales will increase by $100. EFN is:

$$EFN = (.825)(\$100) - (.1)(\$100) - (.066)(\$2100)(1 - 1/3) = -\$19.90$$

A negative value for EFN indicates that Dworkin will have a surplus for the year; no external financing will be required.

Problem 4

Assuming that Dworkin is operating at full capacity, what is the maximum sales increase possible before external financing is required?

Solution 4

Denote the maximum sales level as ($2000 + x). We can solve for x by setting EFN equal to zero:

$$EFN = (.825)(x) - (.1)(x) - (.066)(\$2000 + x)(1 - 1/3) = 0$$

Solving for x, we get a sales level of \$2129.22. This implies that sales could grow by 6.46% before any new financing is required. This is not the maximum sustainable growth rate, however, because the debt/equity ratio will decline in this case. This happens because retained earnings increases while borrowing remains unchanged. (See Problem 5.)

Problem 5

Assume that no new equity will be sold, the dividend payout is fixed, and the debt/equity ratio is fixed; what is Dworkin's maximum sustainable growth rate? In answering, assume that the debt/equity ratio is based only on long-term debt and that total assets is defined as net fixed assets plus net working capital.

Solution 5

The debt/equity ratio (L) is (\$700/\$950) = .7368. The asset/sales ratio is .825. The maximum sustainable growth rate is:

$$\frac{\Delta S}{S_0} = \frac{p(1 - d)(1 + L)}{T - [p(1 - d)(1 + L)]}$$

$$= [.066(2/3)(1.7368)]/[.825 - (.066)(2/3)(1.7368)] = 10.21\%$$

The most recent financial statements for Corwin, Inc. are shown below. Use this information to solve Problems 6-8.

Income statement

Sales	\$6130
Costs	5330
Tax (34%)	272
Net income	\$ 528
Dividends	0

Balance sheet

Net working capital	\$2,590	Long-term debt	\$3,530
Net fixed assets	8,000	Equity	7,060
Total	\$10,590		\$10,590

Problem 6

Prepare a pro forma income statement, balance sheet, and sources and uses statement for Corwin, assuming that sales grow by 20%. New long-term debt is the plug variable. Depreciation (included in costs on the income statement) is 10% of beginning fixed assets.

Solution 6

Assuming all items are proportional to sales, the pro forma income statement and balance sheet are:

Income statement

Sales	$7356
Costs	6396
Tax (34%)	326
Net income	$ 634
Dividends	0

Balance sheet

Net working capital	$3,108	Long-term debt	$5,014
Net fixed assets	9,600	Equity	$7,694
Total	$12,708		$12,708

Depreciation is [.10($8000)] = $800. The sources and uses statement is:

Sources and uses

Sources

Net income	$ 634
Depreciation	800
Operating cash flow	$1434
Borrowing	$1484
New stock issued	0
Total sources	$2918

Uses

Increases in NWC	$ 518
Capital spending	2400
Dividends	0
Total uses	$2918

Solution note: Net capital spending rose by $1600. There was $800 in depreciation during the year, so gross capital spending was $2400.

Problem 7

Solve Problem 6 assuming that Corwin is operating its plant and equipment at only 70% of capacity, and that long-term debt does not change. Use new equity as the plug variable. How do you interpret your answer?

Solution 7

At 70% of capacity, sales were $6130, so $6130 = (.7)(Full capacity sales). Full capacity sales are thus $8757. If sales increase by 20%, no new fixed assets will be needed. The pro forma income statement is unchanged from Problem 6. The balance sheet would look like:

<u>Balance sheet</u>

Net working capital	$3,108	Long-term debt	$3,530
Net fixed assets	7,200	Equity	6,778
Total	$10,308		$10,308

Depreciation is again $800. The sources and uses would be:

<u>Sources and uses</u>

Sources

Net income	$ 634
Depreciation	800
Operating cash flow	$1434
Borrowing	$ 0
New stock issued	-916
Total sources	$ 518

Uses

Increases in NWC	$ 518
Capital spending	0
Dividends	0
Total uses	$ 518

Solution note: No new assets were purchased and depreciation was $800, so fixed assets declined by $800. Beginning equity was $7060, and retained earnings were $634, for a total of $7694. Ending equity (the plug variable) is $6778, so $7694 - $6778 = $916 in common stock was repurchased.

Problem 8

Try this one on your own. Assume that Corwin is operating at full capacity, no dividends will be paid, no new equity will be sold, and the debt/equity ratio remains constant; what is its maximum sustainable growth rate?

Solution 8

The maximum growth rate that can be sustained is 8.09%.

CHAPTER HIGHLIGHTS

This chapter introduces the fundamentals of short-term financial management. Short-term financial management is generally understood to be the analysis of those decisions involving cash flows which occur within a year or less. These decisions affect current assets and/or current liabilities. Some examples of short-term financial decisions are questions such as: How much inventory should be kept on hand? How much cash should be kept on hand? Should goods be sold on credit?

Tracing Cash and Net Working Capital

Current assets are defined as cash and other assets that are expected to be converted to cash within one year. The four major categories of current assets are: cash, marketable securities, accounts receivable, and inventory. Current assets appear on the balance sheet in the order described here, which reflects accounting **liquidity**, the ease and time involved in converting the assets to cash.

Current liabilities are short-term obligations which require payment within one year. The three major categories are: accounts payable; accrued wages and taxes, and other expenses payable; and, notes payable.

Defining Cash in Terms of Other Elements

Net working capital (NWC) is defined as cash plus other current assets, less current liabilities. Given this definition, we can write the balance sheet identity as follows:

$$NWC + Fixed\ assets = Long\text{-}term\ debt + Equity$$

The firm's cash level is thus:

$$Cash = Long\text{-}term\ debt + Equity - NWC\ (excluding\ cash) - Fixed\ assets$$

This equation clearly indicates those actions which increase cash (e.g., increasing long-term debt and equity) and those which decrease cash (e.g., increasing fixed assets or net working capital).

The Sources and Uses of Cash Statement. The sources and uses of cash statement is based on the above equation, and the fact that net income plus depreciation increases cash, while dividend payments decrease cash.

The beginning and ending balance sheets for Fogler Company are shown below. Over the period, Fogler had net income of $1000. A total of $600 in depreciation was deducted as an expense, and a dividend of $400 was paid.

	Beginning	Ending
Cash	$200	$200
Marketable securities	100	150
Accounts receivable	400	300
Inventory	600	700
Total current assets	$1300	$1350
Fixed assets	$10,000	$12,000
Total assets	$11,300	$13,350
Accounts payable	$200	$250
Notes payable	500	600
Accrued expenses payable	100	80
Taxes payable	200	220
Total current liabilities	$1000	$1150
Long-term debt	$2300	$3600
Equity	$8000	$8600
Total liabilities and equity	$11,300	$13,350

Fogler's cash balance is unchanged over the year. However, cash inflows (sources of cash) and cash outflows (uses of cash) occurred during the year. For example, inventory increased by $100; a net increase in inventory requires that cash be used. Similarly, accounts payable increased by $50; this means that Fogler effectively borrowed an additional $50 (on a net basis) from its suppliers, a source of cash. Overall, net working capital decreased by ($300 - $200) = $100.

We can trace the movement of cash by preparing a sources and uses of cash statement as follows:

Sources of cash

Cash flow from operations

Net income	$1000
Depreciation	600

New long-term borrowing	$1300

Decrease in net working capital

Increase in accounts payable	50
Increase in notes payable	100
Increase in accrued expenses	-20
Increase in taxes payable	20
	$3050

Uses of cash

Increase in net fixed assets	$2600

```
Dividends                                        400

Increase in net working capital

Increase in inventory                            100
Increase in accounts receivable                 -100
Increase in marketable securities                 50
                                               $3050

Change in cash balance                         $   0
```

As this statement indicates, cash was generated and used in a variety of ways. Since sources of cash are equal to uses of cash, the cash balance was unchanged.

The Operating Cycle and the Cash Cycle

A typical manufacturing firm's **short-run operating activities** might consist of the following sequence of events and decisions:

Events	Decisions
1. Buying raw materials	1. How much inventory to order?
2. Paying cash for purchases	2. To borrow, or draw down cash balance?
3. Manufacturing the product	3. What choice of production technology?
4. Selling the product	4. To offer cash terms or credit terms to customers?
5. Collecting cash	5. How to collect cash?

These activities create cash inflows and outflows that are both unsynchronized and uncertain.

Short-term operating activities and cash flows can be represented by a **cash-flow time line** (see Figure 25.1). This time line consists of an **operating cycle** and a **cash cycle**. The length of the operating cycle is equal to the sum of the inventory turnover period (i.e., the time required to order, produce, and sell a product) and the accounts receivable turnover period (i.e., the time required to collect cash from a sale).

The accounts payable turnover period is the length of time that the firm can delay payment on its purchases. The cash cycle is the difference between the operating cycle and the accounts payable turnover. A cash cycle of 30 days means that inflows occur 30 days after outflows. This mismatch suggests the need for short-term financing, which can be provided either by borrowing or by maintaining a liquid reserve of marketable securities. Alternatively, the cash cycle can be shortened by changing the inventory, accounts receivable or accounts payable periods.

Some Aspects of Short-term Financial Policy

A firm's short-term financial policy has two dimensions: the size of the investment in current assets, and the financing of current assets. A flexible current asset policy requires maintaining a relatively high ratio of current assets to sales, while a restrictive policy implies a relatively low ratio. A flexible financing policy employs relatively less short-term debt and more long-term debt; a restrictive financing policy requires that current assets are financed primarily by short-term debt.

The Operating Cycle and the Cash Cycle

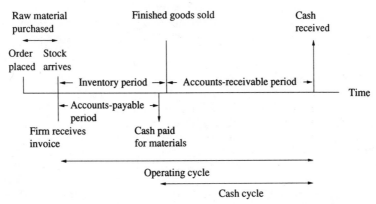

The *operating cycle* is the time period from placement of the order until the receipt of cash. (Sometimes the operating cycle does not include the time from placement of the order until arrival of the stock.) The *cash cycle* is the time period from when cash is paid out to when cash is received.

Figure 25.1

The Size of the Firm's Investment in Current Assets. A flexible current asset policy implies that the firm maintains relatively high levels of cash and inventories, and grants liberal credit terms which result in relatively high levels of accounts receivable; restrictive policies mean that the firm maintains relatively low levels of current assets. In order to determine the optimal levels of current assets, the costs and benefits associated with each policy must be identified.

A flexible policy requires greater initial cash outflows in order to purchase inventory, finance credit sales, and maintain high levels of cash and marketable securities. Future cash inflows, however, should be higher for a flexible policy. The higher level of inventory associated with a flexible policy reduces the likelihood of inventory 'stockouts,' so that sales are stimulated. Similarly, liberal credit policies also stimulate sales. In addition, the larger cash balances associated with a flexible policy ensure that bills can be paid promptly, thereby increasing discounts taken on accounts payable and reducing borrowing costs required in order to meet expenditures.

The costs associated with managing current assets can be classified as costs that increase with the level of investment (i.e., **carrying costs**) and those that decrease with the level of investment (i.e., **shortage costs**). Carrying costs are the opportunity costs of investment in current assets. For example, if the firm holds idle cash, it forgoes the opportunity to earn interest on the investment of that cash. Similarly, investment in inventory implies an opportunity cost for the firm. The two kinds of shortage costs are trading (or order) costs and costs related to safety reserves. Trading or order costs arise when the firm runs out of cash or inventory and must consequently incur the cost of restocking. Costs related to safety reserves include loss of: sales, customer goodwill, or production time when a stock out (or 'cash out') occurs.

The optimal investment in current assets is the level that minimizes the sum of the carrying costs and the shortage costs.

Alternative Financing Policies for Current Assets. For a given level of current assets, different financing policies are feasible. Under ideal circumstances, short-term assets are financed by short-term debts with maturity equal to the life of the assets. Net working capital would always be zero, and short-term assets are perfectly matched with short-term liabilities. For example, inventory is purchased with a bank loan, the inventory is sold, and the proceeds of the sale are used immediately to repay the debt. Current assets and current liabilities simultaneously decline to zero, and the process is then repeated.

In the real world, firms almost always require a permanent investment in current assets. This permanent investment is generally a result of growth in sales, seasonal variation, and unpredictable fluctuations. To finance the permanent component of working capital, a firm could use long-term debt in an amount which always exceeds the firm's total asset requirement. The alternative to this flexible strategy is a restrictive strategy which involves the use of permanent short-term borrowing to finance any deficit.

Which is Best? There is no definitive answer to the question: "How much short-term borrowing is optimal?" Several factors must be considered. First, firms with flexible policies are generally less likely to experience financial distress since this policy implies less concern with meeting short-term obligations. Second, most firms hedge interest-rate risk by matching debt maturities with asset maturities; a policy of financing long-term assets with short-term debt, for example, is inherently risky since frequent refinancing is needed, and short-term interest rates are more volatile than long-term rates. Finally, short-term interest rates tend to be lower than long-term rates. This implies that, on average, borrowing long-term is costlier.

Cash Budgeting

The **cash budget** is a forecast of estimated cash inflows and outflows over a period of time; the cash budget is the primary tool of short-run financial planning.

Suppose that Fogler Company has estimated sales for the next four quarters as follows:

	Q1	Q2	Q3	Q4
Sales	$200	$300	$250	$400

Accounts receivable at the beginning of the year are $120. Fogler has a 45-day collection period. This means that half (45/90) of the sales in a given quarter will be collected during the current quarter and half during the following quarter. In the first quarter, cash collections would be the beginning receivables of $120 plus half of sales, or $220 total. Ending receivables for a given quarter would be half of sales during the quarter. Fogler's cash collections are thus:

	Q1	Q2	Q3	Q4
Beginning receivables	$120	$100	$150	$125
Sales	200	300	250	400
Cash collections	220	250	275	325
Ending receivables	100	150	125	200

Cash Outflow. Fogler's cash outflows consist of payments to suppliers, wages and other expenses, capital expenditures, and long-term financing payments (dividends, interest, and principal paid).

Fogler's purchases from suppliers during a quarter are equal to 60% of next quarter's forecast sales. Fogler's payments to suppliers are equal to the previous period's purchases. In the most recent quarter, Fogler's purchases are [(.60)($200)] = $120, which will be paid during the first quarter (Q1).

Wages, taxes, and other expenses are 20% of sales; interest and dividends are $20 per quarter. A capital expenditure of $100 is planned in the second quarter. The cash outflows are thus:

	Q1	Q2	Q3	Q4
Payment of accounts	$120	$180	$150	$240
Wages, taxes, other expenses	40	60	50	80
Capital expenditures	0	100	0	0
Long-term financing expenses (interest and dividends)	20	20	20	20
Total	$180	$360	$220	$340

The Cash Balance. The forecast **net cash balance** is the difference between cash collections and cash outflows, plus the cash balance at the beginning of the period. Fogler maintains a $10 minimum cash balance to guard against unforeseen contingencies and forecasting errors. The net cash balance is determined as follows:

	Q1	Q2	Q3	Q4
Total cash receipts	$220	$250	$275	$325
Total cash disbursements	180	360	220	340
Net cash flow	40	-110	55	- 15
Cumulative excess cash balance	40	- 70	- 15	- 30
Minimum cash balance	10	10	10	10
Cumulative finance surplus (deficit)	$30	-$80	-$25	- $40

Beginning in the second quarter, Fogler has a cash shortfall. It occurs because of the seasonal pattern of sales (which are higher toward the end of the year), the delay in collections, and the planned capital expenditure.

The Short-term Financial Plan

Fogler must finance the cash shortfall beginning in the second quarter. Two options are secured and unsecured bank borrowing.

Unsecured Loans. Short-term borrowing used to cover a temporary cash deficit most often takes the form of an unsecured short-term bank loan. Such loans are usually arranged as either a noncommitted or a committed line of credit. A noncommitted line of credit is an informal agreement allowing the firm to borrow without submitting the usual paperwork. The interest rate is usually stated as a specified number of percentage points above the prime rate. A committed line of credit is a formal legal agreement specifying that the bank will lend up to a specified amount to the firm; the firm pays a fee, equal to approximately 0.25 percent of the total committed funds. The interest rate is often based on a market rate, such as the London Interbank Offering Rate (LIBOR), or on the bank's cost of funds.

A line of credit arrangement often requires that the firm keep some amount of money on deposit in a low-interest (or zero-interest) account. This **compensating balance** serves to increase the effective rate on the loan because interest on the loan is paid on the full amount borrowed, even though some portion of the loan is not available to the borrower.

Secured Loans. Secured short-term loans usually require either accounts receivable or inventories as security for the loan. With **accounts receivable financing**, accounts are either 'assigned' or 'factored.' If receivables are factored, they are sold to the lender, who assumes the risk of default on the part of the borrower's customer. Under assignment, the lender has a lien on receivables, and the borrower is responsible for bad accounts.

Inventory loans involve either a blanket inventory lien (a lien on all of the borrower's inventory), a trust receipt (the borrower holds inventory 'in trust' for the lender), or field warehouse financing (a public warehouse company controls the inventory for the lender).

Other Sources. **Commercial paper** consists of short-term notes issued by large, highly-rated firms; maturities are short, generally less than 270 days. Commercial paper is a direct obligation of the firm and is often backed by a bank line of credit.

A **banker's acceptance** is a promise by a bank to pay an amount at some specified future date. It is created when a seller sends a bill to a customer. The customer's bank 'accepts' the bill, making it an obligation of the bank.

CONCEPT TEST

1. Current assets are expected to _____ within _____.

2. Current assets appear on the balance sheet in order of their _____.

3. Of the current assets, _____ is typically the least liquid.

4. Other than cash, the most liquid current asset is typically _____.

5. Money owed to a firm by its customers is a current asset called _____.

6. Money owed by the firm to its suppliers is a current liability called _____.

7. Short-term bank borrowing is a current liability often called _____.

8. Short-term finance is concerned with the firm's _____ activities.

In Questions 9-13, indicate whether the action will increase cash (a source) or decrease cash (a use), all other things equal.

9. Fixed assets rise.

10. New equity is sold.

11. New long-term debt is sold.

12. Accounts payable increase.

13. Accounts receivable increase.

14. The cash flow time line consists of an _____ cycle and a _____ cycle.

15. The length of the operating cycle is equal to the sum of the _____ turnover period and the _____ turnover period.

16. The time required to order, produce, and sell a product is the _____ turnover period.

17. The time required to collect the cash receipt from a sale is the _____ turnover period.

18. The length of time the firm is able to delay payment on its purchases is the _____ turnover period.

19. The cash cycle is the difference between the _____ cycle and the _____ period.

20. A firm keeps large amounts of cash and inventory on hand. Its current asset policy is considered _____.

21. A firm finances short-term assets exclusively with short-term debt. Its short-term financial policy is considered _____.

22. Costs that rise with the level of investment in current assets are called _____ costs.

23. Costs that decline with the level of investment in current assets are called _____ costs.

24. The costs identified in Question 23 can be classified as either _____ costs or costs related to _____.

25. The primary tool of short-term planning is the _____.

26. A _____ loan is the most common means of covering a temporary cash deficit.

27. The loan identified in Question 26 is often arranged through a _____.

28. A banking arrangement often requires the firm to keep money on deposit in a low-interest or non-interest paying account. This requirement is called a _____

29. The security on a secured short-term loan is usually either _____ or _____.

30. Short-term notes issued by large, highly-rated corporations are called _____.

ANSWERS TO CONCEPT TEST

1. convert to cash; 12 months
2. accounting liquidity
3. inventory
4. marketable securities
5. accounts receivable
6. accounts payable
7. notes payable
8. short-run operating
9. decrease
10. increase
11. increase
12. increase
13. decrease
14. operating; cash
15. inventory; accounts receivable

16. inventory
17. accounts receivable
18. accounts payable
19. operating; accounts payable
20. flexible
21. restrictive
22. carrying
23. shortage
24. trading (or order); safety reserves
25. cash budget
26. short-term unsecured
27. line of credit
28. compensating balance
29. accounts receivable; inventory
30. commercial paper

PROBLEMS AND SOLUTIONS

Problem 1

Over the course of the year, Bleys Company had the following events occur:

1. Net income was $100
2. Depreciation was $30
3. Accounts payable rose by $20
4. A $10 dividend was paid
5. Inventories were increased by $120
6. Short-term bank borrowing rose by $80
7. Accounts receivable rose by $30

Prepare a statement showing the sources and uses of cash.

Solution 1

We can prepare the statements as follows:

```
              Sources of cash

Cash flow from operations

Net income                              $100
Depreciation                              30

Decrease in net working capital

Increase in accounts payable              20
Increase in notes payable                 80
                                        ─────
                                        $230
```

<u>Uses of cash</u>

Dividends	10
Increase in net working capital	
Increase in inventory	120
Increase in accounts receivable	30
	$ 160
Change in cash balance	$ 70

Use the following selected information from Oberon Corporation's financial statements to solve Problems 2-6.

	<u>Beginning</u>	<u>Ending</u>
Inventory	$1000	$1400
Accounts receivable	1800	2100
Accounts payable	900	1100
Sales (all credit):	$30,000	
Cost of goods sold:	16,000	

Problem 2

Calculate the inventory turnover period.

Solution 2

The inventory turnover period is the average length of time required to order, produce and sell a product. For Oberon, cost of goods sold was $16,000. Average inventory during the year was [($1000 + 1400)/2] = $1200, so Oberon 'turned over' its inventory ($16,000/$1200) = 13.33 times during the year. There are 365 days in a year, so inventory turned over every (365/13.33) = 27.38 days, on average.

Problem 3

Calculate the accounts receivable turnover period.

Solution 3

Average receivables were $1950. Credit sales were $30,000, so receivables turned over ($30,000/$1950) = 15.38 times during the year, or every (365/15.38) = 23.73 days, on average.

Problem 4

Calculate the accounts payable deferral period.

Solution 4

Average payables were $1000. Cost of goods sold was $16,000, so payables turned over 16 times during the year, or every (365/16) = 22.81 days, on average.

Problem 5

Calculate the operating cycle.

Solution 5

The operating cycle is the sum of the inventory period and the accounts receivables period. Using the results from Problems 2 and 3, the operating cycle is (27.38 + 23.73) = 51.11 days.

Problem 6

Calculate the cash cycle.

Solution 6

The cash cycle is the operating cycle less the accounts payable deferral period. Using the results from Problems 4 and 5, the cash cycle is (51.11 - 22.81) = 28.30 days.

Use the following information on Osiris Company to solve Problems 7-9.

Osiris has estimated sales for the next four quarters as:

	Q1	Q2	Q3	Q4
Sales	$510	$870	$450	$600

Accounts receivable at the beginning of the year were $210. Osiris has a 60-day collection period. Osiris' purchases from suppliers in a quarter are equal to 50% of the next quarter's forecast sales. Projected sales for the year following the current one are uniformly 10% higher than the current year's forecast sales. The payables deferral period is 45 days. Wages, taxes, and other expenses are one-third of sales, and interest and dividends are $10 per quarter. No capital expenditures are planned. Osiris is required to maintain a $20 minimum compensating balance.

Problem 7

Calculate Osiris' projected cash collections.

Solution 7

With a 60-day collection period, Osiris collects 1/3 (30/90) of sales in the quarter in which they occur; 2/3 are collected the following quarter. Cash collections are thus:

	Q1	Q2	Q3	Q4
Beginning receivables	$210	$340	$580	$300
Sales	510	870	450	600
Cash collections	380	630	730	500
Ending receivables	340	580	300	400

Problem 8

Calculate Osiris's projected cash outflows.

Solution 8

With a 45-day deferral period, half of purchases from suppliers are paid in the quarter in which they are ordered and half are deferred one quarter. Projected sales in the first quarter of the next year are [$510(1.10)] = $561. The projected cash outflows are:

	Q1	Q2	Q3	Q4
Payment of accounts	$345	$330	$263	$290
Wages, taxes, other expenses	170	290	150	200
Long-term financing expenses (interest and dividends)	10	10	10	10
Total	$525	$630	$423	$500

Problem 9

Calculate the net cash balance and cumulative financing surplus (or deficit) for Osiris. What do you observe?

Solution 9

The net cash balance is:

	Q1	Q2	Q3	Q4
Total cash receipts	$380	$630	$730	$500
Total cash disbursements	525	630	423	500
Net cash flow	-145	0	307	0
Cumulative excess cash balance	-145	-145	162	162
Minimum cash balance	20	20	20	20
Cumulative finance surplus (deficit)	-$165	-$165	$142	$142

Osiris has a highly seasonal sales pattern. Because purchases are made in advance and collections are deferred, Osiris will have an ongoing pattern of short-term deficits followed by surpluses.

Some selected items from Isis Company's beginning and ending balance sheets and income statement are shown below. Use this information to solve Problems 10 - 15.

	Beginning	Ending
Accounts receivable	$800	$900
Inventory	600	700
Accounts payable	200	250

Credit sales:	$10,000
Cost of goods sold:	6,000

Problem 10

Calculate the inventory turnover period, the accounts receivable turnover period and the operating cycle for Isis.

Solution 10

The inventory turnover period is 39.54 days, the accounts receivable turnover period is 31.04 days and the operating cycle is 70.58 days.

Problem 11

Calculate the accounts payable deferral period and the cash cycle for Isis.

Solution 11

The accounts payable deferral period is 13.69 days and the cash cycle is 56.89 days.

Problem 12

Suppose that Isis is able to reduce its inventory turnover period from 39.54 days to 30 days. How will this affect the firm's short-term financing requirements?

Solution 12

An inventory turnover period of 30 days is equivalent to inventory turnover of (365/30) = 12.17 times per year. With cost of goods sold equal to $6,000 per year, the average level of inventory which would be required is the value of x in the following equation:

$$\$6000/x = 12.17$$

The solution to the above equation is $493.01, which is a reduction of ($650 - $493.01) = $156.99 in the level of inventory; consequently, the firm will require, on average, $156.99 less short-term financing with this reduction in the inventory turnover period.

Problem 13

Suppose that Isis is able to reduce its accounts receivable turnover period from 31.04 days to 25 days. How will this affect its short-term financing requirements?

Solution 13

An accounts receivable turnover period of 25 days is equivalent to accounts receivable turnover of 14.60 times per year. The average level of accounts receivable is determined by solving for x in the following equation:

$$\$10,000/x = 14.60$$

Therefore, the new level of accounts receivable is $684.93, which represents a reduction of ($850 - $684.93) = $165.07 in the average level of accounts receivable and, consequently, in the average amount of short-term financing required by the firm.

Problem 14

Suppose that Isis is able to extend its accounts payable deferral period to 18 days, from the current 13.69 days. How will this affect the firm's short-term financing requirements?

Solution 14

An accounts payable deferral period of 18 days is equivalent to accounts payable turnover of (365/18) = 20.28 times per year. The average level of accounts payable which results from this increase is indicated by the value of x in the following equation:

$$\$6000/x = 20.28$$

The new level of accounts payable increases to $295.86, which is an increase of ($295.86 - $225) = $70.86 in the level of accounts payable and consequently a decrease in the amount of short-term financing required from other sources.

Problem 15

Given the changes presented in Problems 12 - 14, what is the new operating cycle? What is the new cash cycle?

Solution 15

The operating cycle is 55 days and the cash cycle is 37 days. We have indicated a reduction in the cash cycle here and a resulting reduction in short-term financing requirements as calculated in Problems 12 - 14; however, it is important to realize that changes such as those suggested above cannot be achieved without incurring related costs. Therefore, the benefit associated with reductions in financing requirements must be weighed against costs such as potential loss of sales due to reduction in credit period.

CHAPTER HIGHLIGHTS

Corporations must hold cash because cash balances provide the liquidity necessary for efficient operations. Holding cash, however, means foregoing the return that could be earned by investing in marketable securities. Cash management involves evaluating the tradeoff between the benefits of liquidity and the opportunity cost of foregone interest. Effective cash management requires that financial managers address three basic concerns. First, how much cash should the firm keep on hand? Second, how should the firm manage cash collection and disbursement? Third, how should 'excess' cash be invested?

Reasons for Holding Cash

There are essentially two reasons for holding cash. A certain amount of cash is required in order to satisfy the **transactions motive**; that is, cash is required for regular disbursements and collections. This requirement arises because cash inflows and outflows are not perfectly matched, so some amount of cash is needed as a buffer.

Cash is also held in the form of compensating balances. A compensating balance is a minimum deposit required by a commercial bank as compensation for bank services. Compensating balance requirements together with the minimum necessary transactions balance establish a minimum total cash requirement.

Determining the Target Cash Balance

If a firm keeps its cash balances too low, then it incurs the trading costs resulting from frequent buying and selling of marketable securities. If the balance is too high, the firm incurs the opportunity cost of foregone interest on marketable securities. The **target cash balance** minimizes the sum of the trading costs and the opportunity cost.

<u>The Baumol Model</u>. The Baumol model is the simplest formal approach to establishing a target cash balance. To illustrate the use of the model, consider the following illustration:

$T = \$240 = $ the total cash needed for transactions over a period (e.g., a year)
$F = \ \ \$1 = $ the fixed cost of making a securities trade to replenish cash balances
$K = \ \ 10\% = $ the interest rate on marketable securities (i.e., the opportunity cost)
$C = \ \ \$10 = $ the beginning cash balance.

We assume that the cash balance is initially at C and declines to zero over the period. When the balance reaches zero, it is replenished. The average cash balance over the period is thus $[(C+0)/2]$ = $(\$10/2) = \$5$. The total opportunity cost is $[(C/2)K] = [\$5(.10)] = \$.50$.

The number of times that the cash balance is replenished during the year is equal to (T/C) = ($240/10) = 24 times. The total trading cost for the year is [(T/C)F] = [(24)$1] = $24. Figure 26.1 illustrates the characteristic 'sawtooth' pattern of the Baumol model.

The Baumol Model

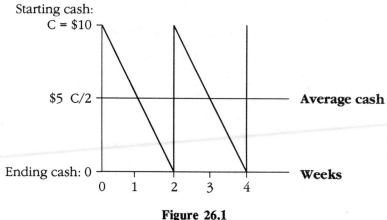

Figure 26.1

The Baumol model identifies the cash balance (C*) which minimizes the sum of the two costs:

$$C^* = (2FT/K)^{.5}$$

For our example, the target cash balance is

$$[2(\$1)(\$240)/.10]^{.5} = (4800)^{.5} = \$69.28$$

The Baumol model is simple to apply, but it has several deficiencies: it assumes a constant rate of cash disbursement, it does not allow for a safety buffer, and it assumes that the firm has no cash receipts during the period. To the extent that these assumptions are inconsistent with reality, the model may not be applicable for a particular firm.

The Miller-Orr Model. The Baumol model assumes certainty in the firm's cash flows; the Miller-Orr model allows for cash flow variability. The essence of the Miller-Orr model is that the firm sets a lower limit, L, on cash holdings, based on the likelihood of a cash shortfall and the firm's willingness to tolerate the risk of a shortfall; then an upper limit, H, and a target balance, Z, are determined by applying the model. When the cash balance reaches H, the firm returns to its target balance by investing (H-Z) dollars in marketable securities. When the balance declines to L, the firm sells (L-Z) dollars of marketable securities in order to increase the cash balance to Z. As long as the firm's cash balance is between L and H, no transactions are made.

Given L, the values of Z and H which minimize expected total cost (Z* and H*, respectively) are determined as follows:

$$Z^* = [(3F\sigma^2)/(4K)]^{1/3} + L$$

$$H^* = 3Z^* - 2L$$

where F is the cost per transaction of buying and selling marketable securities, σ^2 is the variance of the firm's net daily cash flow, and K is the daily interest rate on marketable securities.

The average cash balance is determined as follows:

$$\text{Average cash balance} = (4Z - L)/3$$

Suppose that daily variance of cash flows is $4, the daily interest rate is .02% (.0002), and that management has determined that a lower limit of $10 is desirable. Using the other data from the Baumol model example above, we calculate Z^*, H^*, and the average cash balance as:

$$Z^* = [(3)(\$1)(\$4)/(4)(.0002)]^{1/3} + \$10 = \$34.66$$

$$H^* = 3(\$34.66) - 2(\$10) = \$83.99$$

$$\text{Average cash balance} = [4(\$34.66) - \$10]/3 = \$42.88.$$

The Miller-Orr Model

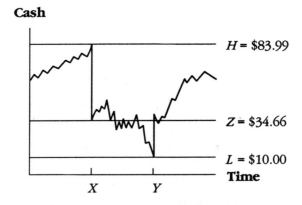

Figure 26.2

Figure 26.2 illustrates the application of the Miller-Orr model in this example. The firm's cash balance fluctuates between $10 and $83.99. If the balance reaches $10 (point Y), we sell ($34.66 - $10) = $24.66 in securities in order to restore the balance to $34.66. If the balance reaches $83.99 (point X), we buy ($83.99 - $34.66) = $49.33 in securities, again restoring the balance to $34.66.

Other Factors Influencing the Target Cash Balance. An alternative to selling securities, in order to raise cash, is to borrow. The interest rate at which the firm borrows is generally higher than the foregone interest on marketable securities. Also, a firm maintaining a low cash balance is more likely to have to borrow the greater is its cash flow variability and the lower is its investment in marketable securities. A simple rule of thumb is to adjust the cash balance until the probability of borrowing equals the extra cost of borrowing relative to the cost of selling securities.

For large firms, the cost of buying and selling Treasury bills is almost certainly less than the interest that can be earned on T-bills, even for an overnight investment. As a result, the primary reasons for such firms to hold cash relate to compensating balance requirements. A large firm may have thousands of accounts so that it may not be worthwhile to manage them all on a daily basis.

Managing the Collection and Disbursement of Cash

The amount of cash on a firm's financial statements ('book' or 'ledger' cash) is not the same as its bank balance ('bank' or 'collected bank' cash). The difference between bank and book cash is called **float**.

Checks written by the firm reduce book cash immediately but do not affect bank cash until the check is actually presented to the firm's bank for payment. This difference in the balances is called **disbursement float**. Checks received, on the other hand, increase book cash but do not increase bank cash until payment is actually received by the bank. In this case, the difference is called **collection float**.

For example, suppose you have $100 on deposit in a checking account. You write a check for $100 to pay for supplies. Once you write the check, you show a balance of zero on your books (i.e., in your check book), but the bank shows a balance of $100 during the time that the check is **clearing**. You have a positive disbursement float of $100 during that time.

If you also deposit a $200 paycheck, then you show an increase in your bank balance of $200, but your bank cash does not increase by $200 until the check clears. This difference is a negative collection float equal to -$200.

Your **net float** is the sum of the collection and disbursement floats, or -$100. In this case, you show $200 book cash, but the bank shows $100 bank cash, so that the net discrepancy, or the net float, is negative (-$100). This negative net float is a disadvantage since, if you were to write another check for $150, the bank balance would not be sufficient to cover the check even though your book cash is sufficient. For this reason, the financial manager has to be more concerned with bank cash than book cash.

Float management involves speeding up collections and delaying disbursements. Float can be broken down into three parts: mail float (the time in the mail), in-house processing float (the time between the receipt and deposit of a check), and availability float (the time required to clear the check through the banking system).

Float measurement depends on the dollar amount and the time delay involved. Suppose your parents mail you a check for $500 from another state. It takes five days in the mail and one day for you to get to the bank in order to deposit the check in your account. The bank holds out of state checks for three days before crediting your account. The total float is [$500(5 + 1 + 3)] = $4500.

The cost of float is the opportunity cost resulting from not being able to use the money. In order to determine this cost, we must first determine the average daily float; this can be determined from the total float defined above. Suppose, for example, that we receive two checks every month: one check is for $2000 and is delayed a total of 15 days; the other is for $3000 and is delayed 5 days.

The total float is [$2000(15) + $3000(5)] = $45,000. The average daily float, assuming a 30-day month, is ($45,000/30) = $1500.

Alternatively, the average daily float can be derived by first calculating the weighted average delay. For the above example, total receipts for the month are $5000. The weighted average delay is thus:

$$($2000/$5000)(15) + ($3000/$5000)(5) = 9 \text{ days}$$

Average daily receipts are ($5000/30) = $166.67. Since this amount is delayed 9 days, on average, then the average daily float is [$166.67(9)] = $1500, as before.

At a .02% daily cost of debt, the present value of the delayed cash flow is:

$$PV = $166.67/[1 + .0002(9)] = $166.37$$

The cost of the float is thus ($166.67 - $166.37) = $.30 per day, or about [$.30(365)] = $109.50 per year.

Accelerating Collections. Techniques to accelerate collections include lockboxes, concentration banking, and wire transfers.

A **lockbox** is the most common approach used to accelerate collections. A firm arranges for customers to mail payments to a post office box maintained by a local bank. The bank collects the checks from the post office box several times a day, and deposits them in the firm's account. Lockboxes reduce mailing time, because customers mail payment to a local post office rather than to company headquarters; use of lockboxes also eliminates the time the corporation would spend processing checks prior to making the deposit.

With a **concentration banking** system, a firm's sales offices are used to receive and process checks. Since customer payments are then deposited in local banks, this process speeds up check-clearing because customer's checks also tend to be drawn on local banks. In addition, mailing time is reduced because checks are mailed to local sales offices. Surplus funds are subsequently transferred to the firm's main bank. Concentration banking is often combined with lockboxes.

The fastest (and most expensive) way to transfer funds to the firm's main bank is a **wire transfer** (an electronic funds transfer). Fedwire (operated by the Federal Reserve) and CHIPS (Clearing House Interbank Payments System) are the two services available; the cost is about $10 per transfer (split between the sending and receiving banks).

Delaying Disbursements. There are three common approaches to delaying disbursements. The first is to make payments from as far away as possible. For example, pay California suppliers with checks drawn on a New York bank. The second is to postmark a payment, but delay mailing it. The third is to mail checks from remote post offices.

Zero-Balance Accounts. A **zero-balance account** has a zero balance until a check is presented for payment. At that time, the exact amount needed is transferred into the account from a master account located at the same bank.

Drafts. A check is drawn on a bank while a draft is drawn on the issuer (the firm) and cannot be paid until it is presented to, and accepted by, the issuer. The issuer then deposits the required amount in order to cover payment of the draft. The use of drafts slows up payments and allows the firm to keep a lower cash balance.

Ethical and Legal Questions. It is often possible for firms to draw on and invest uncollected funds. A systematic policy of exploiting the float is potentially quite profitable, though it presents ethical and legal questions.

Investing Idle Cash

Idle cash can be invested in short term securities (i.e., securities with a maturity of less than one year). The market for these securities is called the money market. Most large firms do their own investing in money markct securities. Smaller firms often rely on money market mutual funds, some of which specialize in corporate cash management. These funds buy money market instruments and manage them for a fee. Banks also offer sweep accounts, in which all excess funds available at the end of the day are invested for the firm.

Temporary cash surpluses help finance seasonal or cyclical activities, planned expenditures, and unanticipated contingencies.

Seasonal or Cyclical Activities. Some firms, such as retailers, have a predictable seasonal cash flow pattern. These firms regularly invest in marketable securities during periods of surplus cash flows and sell securities, or obtain bank loans, during deficit periods.

Planned Expenditures. Firms frequently accumulate cash in anticipation of a large expenditure on a new plant, for example. Stocks and bonds might be sold and the proceeds temporarily invested. The proceeds are then drawn down as construction progresses.

Characteristics of Short-term Securities. Most firms limit their investments in money-market securities to those with maturity of 90 days or less. This strategy virtually eliminates **interest-rate risk**, which is the change in the value of an asset resulting from changes in interest rates. Firms also restrict their short-term investments to highly-rated securities with little or no **default risk**; that is, these securities have a very low probability that interest and principal will not be paid when due. Firms also prefer to invest in securities which are highly **marketable**, or liquid, meaning that they can be quickly sold without loss of value. Finally, a firm must consider the different **degrees of tax exemption** which exist for different securities. Securities issued by state and local governments are exempt from federal taxes, and dividends on common and preferred stock paid to corporate investors are 80% exempt from federal taxes.

Different Types of Money-Market Securities. Treasury bills are direct obligations of the U.S. government. They are issued with maturities of 90 and 180 days (at a weekly auction) and 270 and 360 days (at monthly auctions). Other U.S. Treasury debt matures in more than a year. In all cases, the interest paid on U.S. Treasury securities is exempt from state and local taxes.

Federal agency securities are issued by corporations and agencies created by the federal government. The Government National Mortgage Association (GNMA or 'Ginnie Mae') is an example. These securities pay higher interest rates, but are less marketable, than Treasury securities.

State and local governments and agencies also issue short-term debt. This debt has greater default risk than Treasury debt and is also less marketable. The interest is exempt from federal taxes; as a result, the pre-tax yields are lower.

Commercial paper is short-term, unsecured debt issued by businesses, with maturities ranging from a few weeks to 270 days. Since there is no active secondary market for commercial paper, marketability is low. Default risk varies with the issuer's strength.

Certificates of deposit (CDs) are time deposits in banks. There is an active market for 3-month, 6-month, 9-month and 12-month CDs.

Repurchase agreements are transactions involving the purchase of an instrument (usually Treasury securities) and a simultaneous agreement to sell it back at a higher price in the future.

Other money-market instruments include Eurodollar CDs and banker's acceptances.

CONCEPT TEST

1. Cash that is held for reasons related to normal collection and disbursement activities satisfies the _____ motive.

2. A compensating balance is cash held in a bank account as compensation for _____.

3. The costs that tend to increase as a firm increases its cash balances are the opportunity costs of _____.

4. The costs that tend to decrease as a firm increases its cash balances are the _____ resulting from the buying and selling of securities.

5. The _____ minimizes the sum of the costs in Questions 3 and 4.

6. The simplest formal model of cash management is the _____ model.

7. The _____ model involves the establishment of minimum, maximum, and target cash balances.

8. Checks written by a firm cause a decrease in _____, but no immediate change in _____.

9. Checks received by a firm cause an increase in _____, but no immediate change in _____.

10. The difference between book and bank cash is called _____.

11. Checks written by a firm generate _____ float.

12. Checks received by a firm generate _____ float.

13. The sum of the quantities described in Questions 11 and 12 is the _____.

14. The time a check spends in the postal system is the _____.

15. The time it takes the receiver of a check to process and deposit the check is the _____.

16. The time required to clear a check through the banking system is the _____.

17. The most widely used device for speeding up cash collections is the _____.

18. _____ is a system for getting cash to a firm's main bank more quickly.

19. The fastest way to move cash to the firm's main bank from another bank is a _____.

20. A _____ involves the transfer of funds into the account whenever a check is presented for payment.

21. A _____ is similar to a check except that it is drawn on the issuer instead of a bank.

22. The market for short-term securities is called the _____.

23. The least risky, most liquid short-term security is a _____.

24. An advantage of short-term securities issued by state and local governments or agencies is their exemption from _____.

25. _____ are actively-traded bank time deposits.

ANSWERS TO CONCEPT TEST

1. transactions motive
2. bank services
3. foregone interest
4. trading costs
5. target cash balance
6. Baumol
7. Miller-Orr
8. book cash; bank cash
9. book cash; bank cash
10. float
11. disbursement
12. collection
13. net float
14. mail float
15. in-house processing float
16. availability float
17. lockbox
18. concentration banking
19. wire transfer
20. zero balance account (ZBA)
21. draft
22. money market
23. Treasury bill
24. federal taxes
25. certificates of deposit (CDs)

PROBLEMS AND SOLUTIONS

Problem 1

Given the following information, use the Baumol model to calculate the target cash balance:

```
Annual interest rate:           12%
Fixed order cost:               $100
Total cash needed:              $240,000
```

Solution 1

The target cash balance is:

$$C^* = (2FT/K)^5 =$$

$$[2(\$100)(\$240,000)/.12]^5 = \$20,000$$

Problem 2

Calculate the opportunity cost, the trading costs, and the total cost for holding the target cash balance determined in Problem 1.

Solution 2

The average cash balance will be ($20,000/2) = $10,000, so the opportunity cost is [$10,000(.12)] = $1200. There will be ($240,000/$20,000) = 12 orders during the year, so the order cost is also $1200. The total cost is $2400. The fact that the opportunity cost and the order cost are equal is not coincidental; the fact that this must always be true for the target cash balance identified by the Baumol model is apparent from the mathematical derivation of the model.

Problem 3

Using the data given in Problem 1, calculate the opportunity cost, the trading costs and the total cost assuming that a $15,000 cash balance is held. Calculate the costs assuming that a $25,000 cash balance is held.

Solution 3

If a $15,000 balance is held, the opportunity, trading, and total costs are $900, $1600, and $2500, respectively. For a $25,000 balance, the costs are $1500, $960, and $2460, respectively. Note that the total costs for both the $15,000 and $25,000 balances are higher than the total costs for the $20,000 balance, as derived in Problem 2. This result is, of course, to be expected since the Baumol model identifies the cash balance which minimizes these costs.

Problem 4

Suppose that the fixed order cost (F) is $100, the interest rate is .03% daily, and the standard deviation of daily net cash flows is $50. Management has set a lower limit (L) of $200 on cash holdings. Calculate the target cash balance and upper limit using the Miller-Orr model.

Solution 4

The variance of the daily cash flows is $(50)^2 = 2500$. The target cash balance and upper limit are thus:

$$Z^* = [(3F\sigma^2)/(4K)]^{1/3} + L =$$

$$[(3)(\$100)(2500))/(4)(.0003)]^{1/3} + \$200 =$$

$$\$855 + \$200 = \$1055$$

$$H^* = 3Z^* - 2L =$$

$$3(\$1055) - 2(\$200) = \$2765.$$

Problem 5

On a typical business day, a firm writes checks totaling $1000. On average, these checks clear in 10 days. Simultaneously, the firm receives $1300. On average, the cash is available in 5 days. Calculate the disbursement float, the collection float, and the net float. Interpret your answer.

Solution 5

The disbursement float is $[10(\$1000)] = \$10,000$. The collection float is $[-5(\$1300)] = -\$6500$. The net float is $[\$10,000 + (-\$6500)] = \$3500$. At any time, the firm typically has uncashed checks outstanding of $10,000 and uncollected receipts of $6500. Thus the firm's book cash is typically $3500 less than its bank cash, indicating a positive net float.

Problem 6

A real estate firm receives 100 rental checks a month. Of these, 70 are for $300 and 30 are for $200. The $300 checks are delayed 4 days on average; the $200 checks are delayed 5 days on average. Calculate the average daily collection float, and interpret your answer.

Solution 6

The total float during the month is $[70(\$300)4 + 30(\$200)5] = \$114,000$. The average daily float is $(\$114,000/30) = \$3800$. On an average day, the firm has $3800 in the mail or otherwise uncollected.

Problem 7

Using the data from Problem 6, calculate the weighted average delay. Use the weighted average delay to calculate the average daily float.

Solution 7

Total monthly collections are [70($300) + 30($200)] = $27,000. The weighted average delay is [($21,000/$27,000)4 + ($6000/$27,000)5] = 4.2222 days. Average daily receipts are ($27,000/30) = $900. The average daily float is [4.2222($900)] = $3800, as previously calculated in Problem 6.

Problem 8

Suppose that the interest rate for Problem 7 is 12% per year. Calculate the cost of the float.

Solution 8

We first calculate the daily interest rate: r = (.12/365) = .0003288 = .03288% per day. The interest rate for 4.2222 days is (.0003288 × 4.2222) = .0013883 = .13883%. Daily receipts are $900, and the average delay is 4.2222 days. The total cost of the float is:

$$\$900 - [\$900/(1.0013883)] = \$900 - \$898.7523 = \$1.2477$$

Problem 9

In Problem 8, what would the firm pay to eliminate the float? What would the firm pay to reduce float by one day?

Solution 9

The float costs $1.2477 per day. The daily interest rate is .03288%. If the firm were to eliminate the float, it would be $1.2477 better off every day for the foreseeable future. The present value of this perpetuity is ($1.2477/.0003288) = $3794.71. If we ignore the interest for 4.2222 days, then the firm would pay up to [4.2222($900)] = $3800.

If the float were 3.2222 days, then, following the procedure of Problem 8, the cost of the float would be $.9525 per day. Therefore, the firm saves about $.2952 per day forever. The present value of this perpetuity is $897.78. If we ignore the interest for one day, the firm would pay $900.

Problem 10

Your firm has an average receipt size of $100. A bank has approached you concerning a lockbox service that will decrease your collection float by three days. Your firm typically receives 10,000 checks per day. The daily interest rate is .02%. What would the annual savings be if the service is adopted?

Solution 10

Average daily collections are [$100(10,000)] = $1 million. Accelerating collections by three days frees [3($1 million)] = $3 million (ignoring three days interest). Investing this generates [$3,000,000(.0002)] = $600 interest per day. The annual saving is thus [$600(365)] = $219,000.

Problem 11

The bank's fees for the lockbox service described in Problem 10 are: a fixed annual fee of $5,000 and a variable fee of $0.05 per transaction. Should the lockbox service be adopted?

Solution 11

The bank's total fee would be [$5000 + (.05)(10,000)(365)] = $187,500. Net earnings for the lockbox service would be ($219,000 - $187,500) = $31,500. Therefore, the service should be adopted.

Problem 12

Suppose that, in addition to the fixed annual fee and the variable fee described in Problem 11, the bank requires that the firm maintain a compensating balance of $500,000. Should the lockbox service be adopted?

Solution 12

The cost of the compensating balance can be deducted from the results in Problems 10 and 11 in either of two ways. First, the $500,000 can be viewed as a reduction in the $3 million available cash calculated in Problem 10, so that the annual saving is [($2.5 million)(.0002)(365)] = $182,500. Since this annual saving is $5,000 less than the bank's fees calculated in Problem 11, the lockbox service would not be adopted. The second approach is to calculate the opportunity cost of the $500,000 as follows: [($500,000)(.0002)(365)] = $36,500. Adding this opportunity cost to the $187,500 in bank fees gives a total cost of $224,000 for the lockbox service, which exceeds the $219,000 annual savings.

Problem 13

Given the bank fees identified in Problem 11, what compensating balance would leave the firm indifferent as to whether it adopts the lockbox service?

Solution 13

The firm will be indifferent if the cost of the lockbox service (including the opportunity cost of the compensating balance) is exactly equal to the annual savings calculated in Problem 10. Therefore, the compensating balance which would leave the firm indifferent is the solution for x in the following equation:

$$\$187,500 + (x)(.0002)(365) = \$219,000$$

The solution for x is $431,506.84. Given this figure, the bank might then negotiate the size of the compensating balance with the bank. The firm would adopt the lockbox service only if the bank agreed to accept a compensating balance significantly below this figure. Otherwise, the lockbox service has little or no value to the firm.

Problem 14

A company has all of its collections handled by a bank located in the same city as its home office. The bank requires a compensating balance of $100,000 and handles collections of $750,000 per day. The firm is considering a concentration banking system which would require total compensating balances of $450,000, but which would accelerate collections by two days. The Treasury bill rate is 6%. Should the company implement the new system?

Solution 14

The concentration banking system would provide an additional [($750,000)(2)] = $1,500,000 which can be invested, but an additional $350,000 would be tied up in compensating balances. The net result would be that $1,150,000 can be invested at a 6% annual rate, providing net savings of $69,000. Therefore, the concentration banking system should be implemented.

Problem 15

Try this one on your own. Your firm mails out 15,000 checks, with a total value of $500,000, during a typical day. You have determined that if the checks were mailed from Outer Mongolia, mail time would be increased by three days, on average. It would cost an extra $.10 per check in postage and handling, however. The daily interest rate is .00015. Should you do it?

Solution 15

The firm could increase its disbursement float by $1.5 million. Investing this amount generates $225 per day. The extra cost would be $1,500 per day. The firm should not adopt the plan.

APPENDIX

ADJUSTABLE-RATE PREFERRED STOCK, AUCTION-RATE PREFERRED STOCK, AND FLOATING-RATE CERTIFICATES OF DEPOSIT

Firms normally restrict investments of temporarily idle cash to money market instruments because of their low interest-rate risk and default risk. Three relatively new and nontraditional financial instruments are now in use.

Adjustable-Rate Preferred Stock. Adjustable-rate preferred stock (ARPS) is similar to ordinary preferred stock, except that the dividend is adjusted every quarter, based on a fixed spread over or under the highest of the 90-day T-bill rate, the 10-year T-note rate, or the 20-year T-bond rate. Most ARPS has upper and lower limits on dividend payments. A major advantage of an ARPS for a corporate investor is the fact that the dividend payment is 80% exempt from federal taxes.

The adjustment of the dividend eliminates some, but not all, of the price risk of preferred stock. There are three major categories of risk in the ARPS market. First, these securities have been issued mostly by banks, so that their value has fluctuated with changes in the strength of the banking industry. Second, the market for ARPS is limited, so that lack of liquidity could present a problem to the cash manager. Third, changes in the tax code could potentially have significant impact on the value of an ARPS.

Auction-Rate Preferred Stock. Auction-rate preferred stock differs from adjustable-rate preferred stock primarily in the way the dividend is adjusted. For the auction-rate preferred, bidders submit an offer for some number of shares, and they specify the dividend yield they require. The lowest bid dividend yield that results in all the stock being sold is the yield for the next 49 days, at which time a new auction takes place. This type of auction is called a 'Dutch auction.'

The 49-day reset period and the use of an auction reduce somewhat the risk of this type of stock relative to the risk of ARPS. However, both securities have the same kinds of risk. In addition, there is some risk that an auction will fail. This has yet to happen, but if it did, the dividend yield would be set by a pre-determined fixed formula.

Floating-Rate Certificates of Deposit. A floating-rate certificate of deposit (FRCD) is a debt instrument with a coupon interest payment or interest rate that is adjusted periodically. The interest rate for an FRCD is usually set at a specified spread above or below some well-known market rate. The reset period varies from monthly to semiannually, depending on the specific instrument. An FRCD may have a call feature or a put feature. The former gives the issuer the option to buy back the security from the holder, while the latter gives the holder of the FRCD the option to sell it back to the issuer at a fixed price.

CHAPTER 27
CREDIT MANAGEMENT

CHAPTER HIGHLIGHTS

A firm may require cash on or before delivery in payment for its products, or it may decide to extend credit to its customers. If credit is extended, then the firm must establish a **credit policy**, which involves three distinct components: the **terms of the sale**, **credit analysis**, and **collection policy**.

Terms of the Sale

The terms of sale involve the following three aspects: the credit period, the cash discount, and the type of credit instrument. For example, terms might be quoted as 5/20, net 60. This means that a customer can take a 5% discount from the stated sale price if payment is made within 20 days of the **invoice** date (usually the shipping date or date of sale); otherwise, the full amount of the sale is due within 60 days.

Different industries use different terms. For example, a firm with seasonal sales might offer terms of 2/10, net 30, June 1 dating, which specifies that the invoice date is June 1, regardless of the actual shipping date. Customers take a 2% discount when paying before June 10; otherwise, the full amount is due June 30.

Credit Period. The credit period is the maximum time the customer has to make payment. In setting the credit period, the firm must consider the probability that the customer will not pay, the size of the account, and the extent to which the goods are perishable. Credit terms are generally more restrictive under any of the following circumstances: payment by the customer is considered relatively more risky; the account sizes are small; or, the goods are perishable so that they have low collateral value. A longer credit period is, in effect, a reduction in the price paid by the purchaser; consequently, a longer credit period generally results in an increase in sales.

Cash Discounts. Cash discounts serve to speed up collections because they provide customers with an incentive to pay earlier. Equally important is the fact that a discount is effectively a way to charge higher prices to credit customers.

Suppose we have a customer who routinely places a $100 order every month and pays the entire amount 30 days later. This customer has offered to pay within 10 days of the invoice date in exchange for a 2% discount. Assume that our cost of debt is .03% per day. The present value of our current policy is:

$$\$100/[1 + 30(.0003)] = \$99.12$$

The present value of the new policy is:

$$[\$100(1 - .02)]/[(1 + 10(.0003)] = \$97.71$$

Since the present value is $1.41 less with the new policy, the preferred alternative is not offering the discount.

The analysis of the above problem ignores the possibility of side effects resulting from the credit decision. For example, a general change in credit policy allowing a 2% discount for all customers who pay within ten days would be likely to increase sales. If, in addition, the resulting higher level of sales also implied changes in the firm's cost structure, these additional factors must be taken into account in the present value analysis.

Credit Instruments. A credit instrument is the evidence of indebtedness. Most credit is offered on **open account**, which means that the credit instrument is the invoice. The customer signs the invoice when the goods are received. Alternatively, the selling firm may require a **promissory note**, which is a basic IOU. Use of a promissory note is not common, but it might be required by the seller when the order is large, there is no cash discount, and the customer is a poor credit risk.

A **commercial draft** is a demand for payment sent to a customer's bank, along with the shipping documents. The buyer signs the draft before goods can be shipped to the buyer. If the draft requires immediate payment, it is called a **sight draft**. Otherwise, if the bank 'accepts' the draft for future payment, it is called a **banker's acceptance** because the bank accepts responsibility for making payment. The banker's acceptance is then sent back to the seller of the goods, who can then sell this acceptance (at a discount) or keep it until payment is made.

A firm can also use a conditional sales contract as a credit instrument. In this case, the firm retains title to the goods until payment is completed, and payment is often made in installments.

The Decision to Grant Credit: Risk and Information

The decision regarding whether to grant credit depends on four considerations. First, revenues are delayed if credit is granted. Second, the firm incurs immediate costs if credit is granted. Third, there is some probability of nonpayment. Finally, the decision to grant credit depends on the firm's cost of debt.

Consider the following information:

	Refuse credit	Grant credit
Price per unit	$ 10	$ 11
Cost per unit	$ 5	$ 5
Quantity sold	100	120
Probability of payment	1.0	0.9

The credit period is one month, and the cost of debt is 1% per month. Notice that we have assumed that the firm can charge a higher price if it grants credit. Should credit be granted?

If credit is refused, then the net present value of the decision is simply the immediate cash flow from the sale: NPV = [($10 - $5)100] = $500.

If credit is granted, then the firm will be owed [($11)(120)] = $1320 in one month. Of this, only 90% will actually be collected, so the firm expects to receive [(.90)($1320)] = $1188, and the present value is ($1188/1.01) = $1176.24. The costs are [($5)(120)] = $600, so the net present value is ($1176.24 - $600) = $576.24. This is $76.24 greater than the net present value for the strategy of refusing credit; therefore, credit should be granted.

The Value of New Information About Credit Risk. Suppose that we can run a credit check on a customer for $.60, and that the credit check enables us to determine with complete accuracy which customers will pay when granted credit and which customers will not pay. In the example above, assume that each customer buys one unit, so the cost of checking every customer is [($.60)(120)] = $72. Of the 120 customers, we know that 10%, or 12 customers, will default. Each default costs us $5, because our cost per unit is $5; therefore, identifying these customers ahead of time saves us [($5)(12)] = $60. In this case, the net present value of checking is ($60 - $72) = -$12, so that the credit check is not worthwhile.

Future Sales. Our analysis thus far has ignored the fact that granting credit in the current period may lead to future sales. Also, for the purpose of subsequent sales, we can identify customers who will default as those who default on the initial purchase, and then deny them credit in the future. These two factors increase the value of extending credit.

Optimal Credit Policy

The discussion to this point has focused on whether a firm should grant or deny credit. However, an additional issue which must be considered is the determination of the optimal amount of credit to be granted. In performing this analysis, the firm must consider two categories of costs: the carrying costs associated with granting credit and making the corresponding investment in accounts receivables, and the opportunity costs which result from a refusal to grant credit. The carrying costs include the required return on the investment in receivables, losses from bad debts, and the costs of managing credit. The opportunity costs are the foregone profits from the lost sales which result if we refuse to grant credit. The optimal amount of credit minimizes the sum of the carrying costs plus the opportunity costs.

The optimal credit policy question is similar to the issue of optimal capital structure in the sense that no policy is better than any other in perfect financial markets. However, for imperfect financial markets, taxes, bankruptcy costs and agency costs are important determinants of an optimal policy. For example, firms in high tax-brackets would find it relatively more advantageous to borrow money in order to extend credit because their after-tax borrowing cost is lower. In general, firms with excess capacity, low variable operating costs, high tax-brackets, and repeat customers should have more liberal credit policies.

Credit Analysis

Credit analysis is the process of estimating the probability that a customer will not pay. The firm must first gather relevant information, and then determine the creditworthiness of the customer.

Credit Information. Useful information can be obtained from financial statements, banks, the customer's payment history with the firm, and credit reports on the customer's payment history with other firms. Credit reports can be purchased from a variety of sources, including Dun and Bradstreet, the largest such firm.

<u>Credit Scoring</u>. The traditional **credit scoring** guidelines are the 'five C's' of credit: character (willingness to pay), capacity (ability to pay), capital (financial reserves), collateral, and conditions (general business conditions). These criteria are applied in a subjective manner in determining creditworthiness.

Statistical procedures, called credit-scoring models, are used by some firms to forecast the probability that a customer will default. A variety of customer characteristics are analyzed to determine the relationship between these characteristics and the probability of default. Credit is extended if the score is sufficiently high to indicate that the customer is likely to pay. The characteristics which may be used in credit-scoring models have, to some extent, become a matter of government regulation due to the possibility that credit might be denied on the basis of characteristics such as ethnic background, age or sex.

Collection Policy

Collection policy refers to the process of obtaining payment of overdue accounts.

<u>Average Collection Period</u>. Suppose we offer terms of 2/10, net 30. Our experience has been that half our customers take the discount and pay on day 10, while half do not take the discount and pay on day 30. In this case, the **average collection period** (ACP) is [.50(10 days) + .50(30 days)] = 20 days. This figure is also called 'days sales outstanding.' If we have **average daily sales** of $1000, then, assuming sales occur uniformly throughout the year, our average investment in accounts receivable is [(20 days)($1000)] = $20,000.

<u>Aging Schedule</u>. An **aging schedule** is a tool commonly used to monitor payments. If our terms are 2/10, net 30, then the aging schedule might look like:

Age of account	Percentage of total value of accounts receivable
0 - 10 days	40%
11 - 30 days	40%
31 - 50 days	10%
Over 50 days	10%

Since our terms require payment within 30 days, 80% of our receivables are currently on time, but 20% of our receivables are late. If this pattern is not typical or appropriate for our firm, then it is a signal that collection efforts should be intensified. Firms with seasonal sales find that the ACP changes during the year, and different aging schedules are typical at different times of the year.

<u>Collection Effort</u>. Collection effort generally involves a series of steps such as: (1) sending a delinquency letter, (2) calling the customer, (3) hiring a collection agency, and (4) initiating legal action.

<u>Factoring</u>. **Factoring** is the sale of accounts receivable to a financial institution known as a factor. The customer sends payment directly to the factor and the factor accepts the risk of default on the part of the customer. The factor typically provides the following services: (1) collection, (2) insurance against nonpayment, and (3) loans against receivables. The factor charges a fee based on the invoice amount; the fee varies, but 1% or so is typical.

CONCEPT TEST

1. The three components of credit policy are the _____, _____, and _____.

2. The conditions under which a firm proposes to grant credit are called the _____.

3. Determining the likelihood that a customer will default is part of the process of _____.

4. The potential problem of actually obtaining the payment from a credit sale is related to the firm's _____.

5. If a firm grants credit, the terms of the sale usually specify the _____, the _____, and the _____.

6. If a firm offers terms of 3/30, net 90, then the full amount of the invoice is due in _____ days from the _____ date.

7. For the terms described in Question 6, a customer can take a _____ discount if payment is made in _____ days.

8. The credit period generally depends on the _____, the _____, and the _____.

For Questions 9-12, indicate which firm is likely to have a longer credit period.

9. Firm A sells milk; firm B sells machine tools.

10. Firm A retails clothing; firm B wholesales to clothing manufacturers.

11. Firm A specializes in products for homeowners; firm B specializes in products for renters.

12. Firm A sells and installs central air conditioning systems; firm B sells window air conditioners.

13. Most credit is offered on _____.

14. In Question 13, the credit instrument is the _____.

15. In some instances, such as a large order from a high-risk customer, the credit instrument may take the form of a _____.

16. If a seller sends the shipping documents to the seller's bank, along with a demand for payment, then the demand for payment is called a _____.

17. In Question 16, the credit instrument is called a _____ if the payment is due immediately.

18. The carrying costs of accounts receivable include the firm's _____ on receivables, the _____, and the costs of _____.

19. The opportunity cost of not granting credit results from _____.

20. What are the 'five C's' of credit?

21. Suppose that a firm typically receives payment in 20 days after a sale. This 20 day period is called the _____.

22. A tabulation of receivables based on the length of time they have been outstanding is called an _____.

23. The sale of a firm's receivables to a financial institution is called _____.

ANSWERS TO CONCEPT TEST

1. terms of sale; credit analysis; collection policy
2. terms of sale
3. credit analysis
4. collection policy
5. credit period; cash discount; type of credit instrument
6. 90 days; invoice
7. 3%; 30
8. risk of payment; account size; perishability of goods
9. firm B
10. firm B
11. firm A
12. firm A
13. open account
14. invoice
15. promissory note
16. commercial draft
17. sight draft
18. required return; bad debt losses; credit management
19. foregone or lost sales
20. character, capacity, capital, collateral, conditions
21. average collection period (ACP)
22. aging schedule
23. factoring

PROBLEMS AND SOLUTIONS

Problem 1

Pournelle Company currently has a credit policy of "in God we trust, everybody else pays cash." It is considering altering this policy and has estimated the following data:

	Refuse credit	Grant credit
Price per unit	$25	$27
Cost per unit	$15	$16
Quantity sold	3000	3200
Probability of payment	1.00	0.95

The credit period will be 60 days, and the cost of debt is 1.25% per month. Should Pournelle change its credit policy?

Solution 1

If the company does not grant credit, the cash flows are [($25 - $15)3000] = $30,000. If credit is granted, the cash inflow is expected to be [$27(3200)(.95)] = $82,080.   The present value is: [$82,080/(1.0125)^2] = $80,065.84. The costs are [3200($16)] = $51,200, so the net present value is ($80,065.84 - $51,200) = $28,865.84. Since the net present value of the alternative is $30,000, credit should not be extended.

Problem 2

For the data in Problem 1, what does the sale price have to be in order for Pournelle to breakeven?

Solution 2

For Pournelle to grant credit and still have the same net present value from its credit policy, the net present value of this policy must be $30,000. Therefore, S is the sale price in the following equation:

$$[S(3200)(.95)/(1.0125)^2] - \$51,200 = \$30,000$$

Solving for S, we find that the sale price would have to be $27.38 per unit in order to break even.

Problem 3

Suppose that the Pournelle Company in Problem 1 could sell its product for $28 if credit were granted; assuming that all other data are unchanged from Problem 1, what is the net present value of the decision to grant credit?

Solution 3

The cash flows and net present value for the decision to refuse credit are the same as in Problem 1, so that the net present value of this alternative is $30,000. The present value of the decision to grant credit is now [($28)(3200)(.95)/(1.0125)^2] = $83,031.25 and the net present value is ($83,031.25 - $51,200) = $31,831.25. As we would expect, given the result from Problem 2, it is now beneficial for Pournelle to extend credit.

Problem 4

For the data given in Problem 3, calculate the carrying costs associated with granting credit and the opportunity costs which result from the refusal to grant credit.

Solution 4

By granting credit, the firm incurs three kinds of carrying costs: the required return on the investment in receivables, losses from bad debts, and the costs of managing credit. The required return on the investment in receivables is the difference between the total revenue collected and the present value of that revenue, discounted for two months. Total revenue is [(.95)($28)(3200)] = $85,120, so that the required return is:

$$(\$85,120) - [(85,120)/(1.0125^2)] = \$2088.75$$

Losses from bad debts are $[(.05)(3200)(\$28)] = \$4480$. The firm's costs of managing credit are equal to $[(\$16 - \$15)(3200)] = \$3200$. (We assume here that the increase in per unit cost exactly offsets the cost of managing credit.)

The opportunity costs resulting from the refusal to grant credit are equal to the difference between the revenue for the policy of granting credit and revenue for the policy of refusing credit:

$$[(\$28 - \$15)(3200)] - [(\$25 - \$15)(3000)] = \$11,600$$

The net result for the policy of granting credit is an increase in profit of $11,600, less additional costs of ($2088.75 + $4480 + $3200) = $9768.75, for a net gain of $1831.25. This is exactly equal to the difference in net present values in Problem 3. The solution here is simply an alternative way of viewing the previous calculations.

Problem 5

Suppose that the Pournelle Company, as described in Problems 1 and 3, considers extending additional credit, so that the relevant data become: price per unit is $29; cost per unit is $17, number of units sold is 3300, probability of payment is .90, average collection period is 90 days. Should credit be further extended?

Solution 5

We can analyze this problem be calculating the carrying costs and opportunity costs for this extension of credit in relation to the decision to grant credit presented in Problems 3 and 4. Total revenue is $[(.90)(\$29)(3300)] = \$86,130$, so that the required return on the investment in receivables is:

$$(\$86,130) - [(\$86,130)/(1.0125^2)] = \$2113.54$$

Losses from bad debts are $[(.10)(3300)(\$29)] = \$9570$. The firm's costs of managing credit are equal to $[(\$17 - \$15)(3300)] = \$6600$. The total of these carrying costs is $18,283.54, which is an increase of ($18,283.54 - $9,768.75) = $8,514.79 compared to the initial extension of credit. The opportunity costs resulting from the refusal to grant credit are equal to:

$$[(\$29 - \$15)(3300)] - [(\$25 - \$15)(3000)] = \$16,200$$

This is an increase of ($16,200 - $11,600) = $4600 over the initial credit decision. The net result for the extension of additional credit is an increase in profit of $4600, and an increase of $8514.79 in costs, so that the additional extension of credit should not be offered.

The optimal credit policy for Pournelle is a moderate extension of credit. In general, additional credit should be extended as long as the opportunity cost associated with the refusal to grant additional credit is greater than the additional carrying costs incurred when extending additional credit.

Problem 6

Suppose that, in Problem 1, we can obtain a credit report for $.25 per customer. Assuming that each customer buys one unit and that the credit report identifies all customers who would not pay, should credit be extended?

Solution 6

If we eliminate sales to those who would default, we will sell [.95(3200)] = 3040 units. The cash inflow will be [$27(3040)] = $82,080 and the present value is $80,065.84, as before. The costs, however, are [3040($16) + 3040($.25)] = $49,400. The net present value is now $30,665.84, so credit should be extended and the credit reports should be purchased.

Problem 7

Icarus Company (a well-known 'high flyer') manufactures suntan lotion. Its credit terms are 5/20, net 40. Historically, 80% of its customers take the discount. What is the average collection period?

Solution 7

The average collection period is [.80(20 days) + .20(40 days)] = 24 days.

Problem 8

In Problem 7, Icarus sells 5000 cases of suntan lotion each month, at a price of $15 per case. What is its average balance sheet amount in accounts receivable?

Solution 8

Icarus has average daily sales of [$15(5000)/30] = $2500. With an average collection period of 24 days, receivables average [($2500)(24)] = $60,000.

Problem 9

Daedulus Company has annual credit sales of $2 million. The average collection period is 30 days. Production costs are 80% of sales. What is Daedulus's average investment (i.e., its actual cost, as opposed to the balance sheet amount) in receivables?

Solution 9

Annual costs are $1.6 million, or $4444.44 per day. With an average collection period of 30 days, Daedulus has $133,333.33 in costs tied up in receivables.

Problem 10

A firm offers terms of 2/10, net 30. What effective annual interest rate does the firm earn when a customer does not take the discount?

Solution 10

Suppose the product costs $100. The firm receives $98 if the discount is taken. If the discount is not taken, then the firm receives $2, or ($2/$98) = 2.04%, more. This 2.04% is earned by extending (30 - 10) = 20 additional days credit. There are approximately (360/20)= 18 such periods per year. The annualized interest rate is a hefty $[(1.0204)^{18} - 1] = .43836 = 43.836\%$. The calculation here does not depend on the cost of the product since the 2.04% figure derived above would apply regardless of purchase price.

The annualized effective rate when foregoing a discount is often determined as follows:

$$[d/(1 - d)] \times [360/(\text{net period - discount period})]$$

where d is the discount expressed as a percent of the invoice price. However, this approach does not consider the effect of compounding in determining the annual rate. For the terms of 2/10, net 30, this alternative approach indicates that the annualized effective rate is 36.735%, rather than 43.836% as derived previously.

Note that the interest rate the firm earns is the same as the interest rate the customer pays by not taking the discount. Consequently, from the customer's point of view it is generally not reasonable to pay an interest rate in excess of that which would be paid by financing the purchase through an alternative source.

Problem 11

For each of the following credit terms, use the formula presented in Problem 10 to determine the annualized effective rate:

3/15, net 60; 1.5/20, net 45; 1/10, net 40

Solution 11

For terms of 3/15, net 60, d is .03, and the annualized effective rate is:

$$[.03/(1 - .03)] \times [360/(60 - 15)] = .24742 = 24.742\%$$

For terms of 1.5/20, net 45, d is .015, and the annualized effective rate is:

$$[.015/(1 - .015)] \times [360/(45 - 20)] = .21929 = 21.929\%$$

For terms of 1/10, net 40, the annualized effective rate is 12.121%.

Problem 12

For each of the credit terms identified in Problem 11, determine whether a firm should take the discount or pay the net amount of the invoice. Assume that the firm would have to borrow from a bank at a 15% annual interest rate in order to take advantage of the discount.

Solution 12

For terms of 3/15, net 60, the firm would have to borrow 97% of the invoice amount in order to take advantage of the discount. Interest on the loan would then accumulate at the rate of 1.5% per month, or approximately 2.25% for 45 days, at which time we assume that the firm would repay the bank loan. Let x represent the net amount, so that the bank loan is .97x and interest plus principal of $[(.97x)(1.0225)] = .9918x$ is repaid to the bank after 45 days. Since this is less than the net amount of the invoice, the firm is better off borrowing from the bank than paying the net amount. In general, if the annualized effective rate is greater than the rate at which the firm borrows, the firm is better off borrowing from the bank in order to take advantage of the discount. Therefore, for terms of 1.5/20, net 45, the firm should borrow in order to take the discount, but for terms of 1/10, net 40, the firm should pay the net amount.

Problem 13

The Kneebopper Corporation has an average collection period of 50 days. Its average investment in receivables is $3 million. What are the firm's annual credit sales?

Solution 13

Average daily sales equals accounts receivable divided by average collection period: ($3 million/50) = $60,000 per day. Annual sales are thus $[\$60,000(360)] = \$21.6$ million.

Problem 14

Krishna, Inc., has collected the following information:

```
Annual credit sales        $270,000
Collection period (days)        120
Terms                        net 90
Interest rate (monthly)          1%
```

Krishna is contemplating offering customers terms of 2/30, net 60. Krishna anticipates that 50% of its customers will take the discount, while the remainder will pay in 90 days. Therefore, the collection period will fall to 60 days. Should the new terms be offered?

Solution 14

Under the current policy, average daily sales are ($270,000/360) = $750. On average, this amount is collected in three months, so the present value is $[\$750/(1.01)^4] = \$720.74$.

Under the new policy, $375 of daily credit sales will be collected 30 days after the sale; since a 2% discount will be taken, $367.50 will actually be received by the company. The present value is thus $[(\$367.50/1.01) + (\$375/1.01^3)] = \$727.83$. The new terms should be offered.

Problem 15

Brahma Company is considering extending credit to a new customer. Based on past experience, there is a 50% chance that the customer will default. The item costs $100 to manufacture and sells for $200. Payment is due in 30 days and the monthly interest rate is 1.5%.

If the customer does pay, then she will place another order, and the probability of payment in 30 days is 100%. Should Brahma grant credit? (Assume that the sale will be lost if Brahma does not grant credit.)

Solution 15

If Brahma grants credit, the expected value of future payments is $[(.50)(\$200)] = \$100$, expected in 30 days. If this were a one-time sale, the net present value would be:

$$[(\$100/1.015) - \$100] = -\$1.48$$

However, if payment is made, Brahma will make another sale. Therefore, there is a 50% chance of an additional sale. The net present value of this second sale is:

$$[.50(\$200)/(1.015)^2] - [.50(\$100)/1.015] = \$47.81$$

The net present value of extending credit is $46.33. This example illustrates the importance of considering repeat business when analyzing the credit-granting decision.

CHAPTER HIGHLIGHTS

In principle, the decision to acquire another firm is a capital budgeting decision much like any other. However, since the net present value of such an acquisition is difficult to measure, the subject of mergers and acquisitions warrants specific attention.

Mergers differ from ordinary investment decisions in at least five ways. First, the value of a merger may depend on benefits, referred to as synergies, which are often difficult to measure. Second, the accounting, tax, and legal aspects of a merger are frequently complex. Third, mergers often involve issues of corporate control; for example, the major issues in mergers and acquisitions are often related to the underlying conflict between managers and shareholders. Fourth, mergers affect not only the value of the firm, but also the relative value of the firm's stocks and bonds. Finally, mergers are often 'unfriendly' transactions because management and/or stockholders of the sought-after firm do not want the firm to be acquired.

The Basic Forms of Acquisitions

The legal mechanism used by one firm to acquire another takes one of the following forms: (1) merger or consolidation, (2) stock acquisition, or (3) asset acquisition.

Merger or Consolidation. A **merger** is the absorption of one firm by another, so that the acquiring firm retains its identity while the acquired firm ceases to exist. In a **consolidation**, an entirely new firm is created. The stockholders of each of the two firms involved in a consolidation exchange their shares for shares of the new firm. Since the differences between mergers and consolidations are generally insignificant for our purposes, we will use the general term merger to refer to both of these forms of reorganization.

The primary advantage of a merger is its legal simplicity; for example, in contrast to an acquisition of assets, it is not necessary to transfer title to each individual asset. A disadvantage of a merger is the fact that the shareholders of each firm must vote to approve a merger. Usually a two-thirds majority is required for approval.

Acquisition of Stock. Another way to acquire a firm is to buy the target firm's voting stock directly from stockholders. This is generally accomplished through a process called a **tender offer**. This means that the acquiring firm makes an offer, directly to the shareholders of a firm, to buy the firm's common stock.

A stock acquisition does not require a stockholder vote for approval; those wishing to keep their stock simply do not 'tender' their shares to the acquiring firm, and they thereby retain their ownership interest in the target firm. A stock acquisition bypasses both the board of directors and the management of the sought-after firm. This is an important feature of a tender offer because the management of the target firm is frequently opposed to the acquisition. However, management's resistance can make this form of acquisition quite expensive. Often, a minority of shareholders choose not to sell their shares, so that the firm is not completely absorbed. Complete absorption requires a merger. Many stock acquisitions are subsequently completed as a formal merger.

Acquisition of Assets. A firm can buy another firm by simply purchasing the assets of the target firm. This procedure involves a costly legal transfer of title to the assets and must be approved by the shareholders of the selling firm.

A Classification Scheme. Acquisitions can be classified as **horizontal**, **vertical**, or **conglomerate**. A horizontal acquisition occurs if the two firms compete in the same product market. A vertical acquisition is a reorganization of firms at different stages of the production process. Conglomerate acquisitions involve firms in unrelated lines of business.

A Note on Takeovers. A **takeover** is the transfer of control of a firm from one group to another. The acquiring firm, referred to as the **bidder**, makes an **offer** to pay cash or securities in order to acquire the target firm. A takeover can occur by **acquisition** (as described above), a **proxy contest**, or a **going-private transaction**.

In a proxy contest, a group of dissident shareholders seeks to obtain enough proxies from the firm's existing shareholders in order to gain control of the board of directors. In a going-private transaction, a small group of investors buys all of the firm's common stock. The stock is then delisted, so that it no longer trades on a stock exchange.

The Tax Forms of Acquisition

The acquisition of one firm by another may or may not be a taxable transaction. The primary issue in determining the tax status is whether the shareholders of the acquired firm have sold their shares, resulting in a realized, taxable capital gain, or exchanged their shares for new shares of equal value. The former is a **taxable acquisition**, while the latter is a **tax-free acquisition**.

For a taxable acquisition, the shareholders of the acquired firm have a realized, taxable capital gain equal to the difference between the price they receive for their shares and the initial purchase price of their stock. In addition, the acquiring firm may elect to 'write-up' the value of the assets acquired, based on the cost of the acquisition. This has the advantage of increasing the firm's subsequent depreciation expenses; however, the firm must also treat the acquisition price of the assets as currently taxable income. Since the latter effect is immediate, while the former takes place over several years, the acquiring firm generally does not elect to write-up the value of the assets. Since assets are therefore not written-up for either a taxable or a tax-free acquisition, the only significant consequence is the difference in the tax implications for the stockholders of the acquired company.

Accounting for Acquisitions

For accounting purposes, an acquisition is treated as either a purchase or a pooling of interests.

The Purchase Method. The **purchase method** of accounting for an acquisition requires that the assets of the acquired firm are reported at fair market value on the financial statements of the acquiring firm. Furthermore, the difference between the purchase price and the fair market value of the acquired assets is identified as 'goodwill' on the balance sheet of the acquiring firm. The goodwill is amortized over a period of years, but this amortization is not a tax-deductible expense.

Pooling of Interests. With a **pooling of interests**, the balance sheets of the two firms are simply combined. Asset values are not adjusted to market value and, therefore, no goodwill is created. This accounting treatment of an acquisition is generally used when at least 90 percent of the voting common stock of the acquired firm is exchanged for voting stock in the combined firm; otherwise, the purchase method is used.

Purchase or Pooling of Interests: A Comparison. Income reported to stockholders subsequent to the acquisition is lower for the purchase method because of the amortization of goodwill and the write-up of asset values which result in higher depreciation expenses. However, neither of these considerations has any effect on the firm's taxable income. Therefore, these alternative accounting treatments do not have any consequences for cash flow or net present value determinations.

Determining the Synergy from an Acquisition

If firm A (with value V_A) is acquiring firm B (with value V_B), then the acquisition is beneficial to the stockholders of firm A if:

$$V_{AB} > V_A + V_B$$

where V_{AB} is the value of the combined firm.

The synergy from such an acquisition is defined as follows:

$$Synergy = V_{AB} - (V_A + V_B)$$

If A and B are public companies, then their values as separate companies can be observed in the marketplace. Synergy exists when the cash flow for the combined firm is greater than the sum of the cash flows for the two firms as separate entities. The gain from the merger is the present value of this difference in cash flows.

Source of Synergy From Acquisitions

The discussion of the incremental cash flows in capital budgeting indicates that the synergy from an acquisition results from one or more of the following: (1) revenue enhancement, (2) cost reduction, (3) lower taxes, or (4) lower cost of capital.

Revenue Enhancement. Increased revenues may result from marketing gains, strategic benefits, and market power. Marketing gains are produced by more effective advertising, an improved distribution network, and a more balanced product mix. Strategic benefits are the opportunities presented by options to enter and exploit new lines of business. Finally, a merger may reduce competition, and thereby increase market power, allowing the company to increase prices and to obtain monopoly profits. Such mergers, of course, may run afoul of antitrust legislation; furthermore, there is little evidence that market power has been a major motivation for acquisitions.

Cost Reductions. A larger firm may be able to operate more efficiently than two smaller firms. Horizontal mergers, for example, may generate 'economies of scale,' meaning that the average production cost decreases following the merger. A vertical merger may allow a firm to save, for example, by more closely coordinating production and distribution; vertical mergers may also give rise to transfer of technology among different products. Economies may also be achieved when firms have complementary resources. This might occur when one firm has excess production capacity and another has insufficient capacity. Acquisitions may also serve to eliminate inefficient management.

Tax Gains. Tax gains resulting from a merger may arise because of unused tax losses, debt capacity or surplus funds. A profitable firm may find it advantageous to acquire a firm that has **net operating losses** (NOL). The profitable firm can then immediately use these losses to reduce taxes on current income. This gain is limited, however, because a firm with NOL can 'carry back' losses for three years and 'carry forward' losses for up to fifteen years. That is, since the firm with NOL can apply current losses against past, as well as future, profits, the benefit of an acquisition must be greater than the tax benefit the acquired firm could derive from its own losses. In addition, the IRS may disallow the tax credit if the primary purpose of the acquisition is to avoid taxes.

A merger produces some diversification benefit, which reduces the likelihood and cost of financial distress for the merged firm. As a result, the merged firm may be able to increase its debt capacity, which can produce significant tax savings.

A firm with surplus funds may have motivation for acquiring another firm. The alternatives for a firm with surplus funds are the distribution of surplus funds as a dividend or the repurchase of some of the firm's outstanding shares. Both of these alternatives increase shareholders' income taxes, however. With an acquisition, no income taxes are paid by the shareholders of the acquiring firm.

The Cost of Debt Capital. The cost of debt can often be reduced when two firms merge because the costs of issuing securities are inversely related to the size of the issue.

Calculating the Value of the Firm after an Acquisition

The procedure for valuing an acquisition depends on the source of the synergies resulting from the acquisition; different sources of synergy have different risks and consequently should be discounted at different rates. Tax gains can be estimated fairly precisely and should be discounted at the cost of debt capital to reflect this relative certainty. Cost reductions arising from operating efficiencies can also be determined with some confidence. Since these savings have ordinary business risks, they should be discounted at the overall cost of capital. Gains from a strategic advantage are not easy to estimate and are probably highly uncertain; therefore, a relatively high discount rate would be appropriate.

Avoiding Mistakes. Since the valuation of the benefits from an acquisition is more difficult than the valuation of a standard capital-budgeting project, the analyst must be aware of the sources of potential errors. First, when possible, market values should be used to establish the value of an opportunity. For example, it is not necessary to 'estimate' the value of a publicly traded firm as a separate entity because its value can be directly observed in the market. Second, only cash flows that are incremental to the acquisition are relevant; the value of a target firm as a separate entity already reflects the value of its existing cash flows. Third, the discount rate used should reflect the risk associated with the incremental cash flows. The acquiring firm, for example, should not use its own cost of capital to value the cash flows of a firm to be acquired. Finally, acquisition generally involves significant fees and costs which are incremental expenses and therefore should not be ignored.

A Cost to Stockholders from Reduction in Risk

The variability of both cash flows and firm value is usually less for a merged firm than for each of the firms separately. As a result, there may be circumstances under which one or the other of the separate firms would have defaulted on its debt, but the combined firm will not. Consequently, the firm's debt is less risky and the cost of borrowing may decline. This **coinsurance effect** represents a mutual guarantee of each firm's debt by the other firm after the merger.

In a merger where there is no synergy, the bondholders benefit from the coinsurance effect at the expense of the stockholders. Under these circumstances, the value of the combination is the same as the sum of the individual values, but the value of the bonds increases as a result of the reduction in risk. Hence, if the bonds increase in value, then the value of the stock must decrease. These results apply for mergers without synergy. For synergistic mergers, stockholders may benefit in spite of the coinsurance effect; the extent to which stockholders benefit depends on the amount of synergy present.

How Can Shareholders Reduce Their Losses from the Coinsurance Effect? The coinsurance effect can be neutralized to some extent if the acquiring firm retires debt before the announcement of the merger and then issues new debt subsequent to the merger. Also, additional new borrowing after the merger can benefit stockholders. Additional borrowing is possible because the combined firm generally has greater debt capacity as a result of the coinsurance effect. By borrowing more, the combined firm obtains increased value, from a reduction in taxes, which is beneficial to the stockholders.

Two "Bad" Reasons for Mergers

Earnings Growth. Firm A has decided to acquire Firm B through an exchange of stock. Both firms are 100% equity. The following is some pre-merger information:

	Firm A	Firm B
Total earnings	$100	$200
Shares outstanding	200	500
Price per share	$ 10	$ 2

Firm B has a market value of [($2)(500)] = $1000. To acquire Firm B, Firm A will have to give ($1000/$10) = 100 shares to the shareholders of Firm B. The combined firm will thus have 300 shares outstanding.

Before the merger, earnings per share (EPS) for Firm A are $.50. After the merger, the combined firm will have $300 in earnings and 300 shares, so EPS will be $1 per share, a 100% growth! Of course, no real change has occurred. Firm A has a higher value per share than does Firm B, so B's 500 shares are replaced with 100 shares of A. Naturally, EPS rises, but this increase has no cash flow consequences, and, as a result, no impact on value.

Diversification. Diversification is often cited as a benefit in mergers. However, diversification by itself does not create value because the shareholders of the acquiring firm can accomplish the same result as that accomplished by the merger by purchasing stock in the target firm.

To understand that a merger does not provide a diversification benefit to the stockholders of the acquiring firm, recall that variability of return consists of unsystematic and systematic components. Systematic variability, which is common to all firms, cannot be eliminated by any form of diversification, including merger. Unsystematic variability, which is specific to a particular firm, can be reduced by diversification. However, an individual stockholder can achieve this diversification very inexpensively by purchasing shares of stock in different companies. Diversification by merger can produce benefits for the stockholders of the acquiring firm under the following circumstances: if unsystematic risk is reduced at lower cost by an acquisition than by an individual investor's own portfolio diversification; and, if diversification increases debt capacity by reducing risk.

The NPV of a Merger

As noted earlier, an acquisition should be regarded as equivalent to a capital-budgeting project, and its evaluation is based on net present value analysis. This analysis is somewhat complicated when the acquisition is made in exchange for stock instead of cash. The simpler case of an acquisition for cash is discussed first.

Cash. Suppose that Firms A and B are worth $200 and $100, respectively, as separate firms, and that the combined firm will be worth $380. Firm B has indicated that it is willing to be acquired for $150 cash. Should Firm A proceed with the acquisition? The value of Firm A after the acquisition is equal to the value of the combined firm less the cash paid for Firm B, or ($380 - $150) = $230. The net present value of the acquisition is ($230 - $200) = $30, so that the acquisition is beneficial to the stockholders of Firm A.

Suppose that, before the merger, Firm A had twenty shares outstanding, selling for ($200/20) = $10 per share. After the merger, the value of Firm A stock will rise to [($380 - $150)/20] = $11.50 per share. The increase of $1.50 per share is the net present value of $30 on a per share basis, or ($30/20) = $1.50 per share gain.

The net present value of the acquisition can also be regarded as the difference between the synergy and the premium of the merger. The synergy is equal to the value of the combined firm less the total value of the two separate firms, or [$380 - ($200 + $100)] = $80. The premium is the difference between the purchase price and the market value of the acquired firm: ($150 - $100) = $50. Therefore, the net present value is ($80 - $50) = $30, as indicated earlier.

Common Stock. Suppose that, in the previous example, Firm A pays the $150 acquisition cost by giving 15 shares of stock to the stockholders of Firm B. The cost appears to be $150 in this case, because each share of Firm A is worth $10 prior to the merger; however, this is an underestimate of the actual cost. After the merger, the firm is worth $380 and 35 shares are outstanding. The value per share is ($380/35) = $10.857, so that the actual cost of the acquisition is [(15)($10.857)] = $162.86.

Note that the $10.857 per share value in this case is less than the $11.50 value indicated above for a cash acquisition. The difference arises from the fact that a portion of the $30 net present value goes to the new stockholders. The 15 new shares of Firm A stock are each worth ($10.857 - $10) = $.857 more than the pre-merger value of Firm A stock, for a total of [(15)($.857)] = $12.86 to the former stockholders of Firm B. That is, as indicated above, the stockholders of Firm B actually receive $162.86 in this merger.

When common stock is used as the consideration, or payment, the cost of the merger is equal to the percentage of the new firm that is owned by the previous shareholders of the acquired firm, multiplied by the value of the new firm. In this example, the Firm B shareholders own [(15 shares)/(20 + 15) shares] = 42.857% of the new firm. The value of the new firm is $380, so the true cost of the merger is [(.42857)($380)] = $162.86

In a cash merger, the benefits of the merger go entirely to the stockholders of the acquiring firm. When a merger is financed by an exchange of stock, the benefits are shared by the stockholders of both the acquiring and the acquired firm.

How many shares of Firm A stock should the Firm B stockholders receive so that they actually receive the $150 price they are willing to accept? In order for the Firm B stockholders to receive $150, they must receive stock which has a total value equal to ($150/$380) = .39474 = 39.474% of the merged firm. Therefore, the new shares issued must represent 39.474% of the outstanding shares of the merged firm. This value is determined by solving for x in the following equation:

$$[x/(20 + x)] = .39474$$

The number of new shares which should be issued to the stockholders of Firm B is 13.0437. The total number of shares outstanding will then be (20 + 13.0437) = 33.0437 and the price per share will be ($380/33.0437) = $11.50. Since the stockholders of Firm B receive 13.0437 shares worth $11.50, they receive a total of [(13.0437)($11.50)] = $150.

Cash versus Common Stock. The decision as to whether an acquisition should be financed with cash or stock depends on three factors. First, if the management of the acquiring firm believes that its stock is overvalued, then a stock acquisition may be the less costly alternative. Second, a cash acquisition is usually a taxable transaction; this consideration may result in a higher price for the target firm. Third, the use of stock means that the shareholders of the acquired firm will share in any gains from the merger; on the other hand, if the merger is unsuccessful, then the acquired firm's shareholders will share in the loss.

Defensive Tactics

Management of a target firm frequently resists takeover attempts. This resistance may enable stockholders to subsequently receive a higher price for their shares. On the other hand, management resistance to a takeover may be based largely, if not exclusively, on management's desire to protect its own interests. The defensive tactics commonly used by the management of a target firm in order to resist takeovers are described in this section.

The Corporate Charter. The firm's charter can be amended to make acquisition more difficult for the acquiring firm. For example, the charter can be amended to require that an 80% majority of stockholders must vote to approve a merger. Such a 'super majority' provision is in contrast to the usual two-thirds majority required for approval of a merger. Another strategy is the 'staggering' of the election of board members so that only a few board members are elected at any one time. This makes it more difficult to change the membership of the board quickly.

Repurchase Standstill Agreements. A standstill agreement specifies that the bidding firm will limit its holdings in the target firm. Such agreements often precede a targeted repurchase; under this arrangement, the target firm buys back its own stock from the bidder. Since this repurchase is usually at a premium above market price, the premium is viewed by critics as a bribe, and is frequently termed 'greenmail.'

Exclusionary Self-Tenders. In an exclusionary self-tender, the target firm offers to buy back its own stock, at a premium, from all stockholders except the bidder. By excluding the bidder, the firm effectively transfers wealth to other stockholders by reducing the value of the bidder's stock.

Going Private and Leveraged Buyouts. A privately-owned firm is not subject to unfriendly takeovers. A publicly-traded firm 'goes private' when a group, which usually includes the existing management, buys all of the firm's publicly held stock and takes it off the market. Such transactions frequently take the form of **leveraged buyouts** (LBOs), which means that management arranges a large amount of debt financing to obtain some or all of the needed funds.

Since a leveraged buyout generally requires the payment of a premium above market value for the acquisition of the firm's stock, the transaction is profitable to the acquirer only if the synergy created is greater than this premium. The two potential forms of synergy cited for LBOs are: first, the increased tax deduction which results from the high debt level; and, second, the increased incentive on the part of managers who become owners of the firm. Empirical evidence regarding the extent to which synergy exists for LBOs is inconclusive.

Other Devices and Jargon of Corporate Takeovers. A **golden parachute** is compensation paid to top management in the event of a takeover. The **crown jewels** are major assets that a firm sells when faced with an unfriendly takeover; the sale of these assets makes the firm less attractive as a takeover target. A **poison pill** is a tactic used to make a firm an unattractive (i.e., very expensive) target. An example would be a provision giving shareholders the right to buy shares in the merged firm at a bargain price, thereby making the acquisition less profitable.

Some Evidence on Acquisitions

The impact of acquisitions on shareholder wealth has been a controversial topic which has been extensively studied. Some empirical evidence regarding this issue is considered here.

Do Acquisitions Benefit Shareholders? There is little doubt that the shareholders of the acquired firm benefit substantially from an acquisition. Abnormal returns for these shareholders have been shown to be approximately 20% in the case of mergers and 30% for tender offers. Tender offers are typically made when a proposed friendly merger is rejected by the management of the target firm. Subsequent tender offers must generally be at a higher price, resulting in the larger abnormal returns.

The gains to the shareholders of acquiring firms are difficult to measure. The best evidence suggests that these shareholders gain little, if anything, from an acquisition, and, in fact, losses in value subsequent to merger announcements are not unusual. Some studies indicate that abnormal returns to shareholders of the acquiring firm average approximately four percent for tender offers and zero for mergers, while other studies indicate significant losses. These results seem to suggest that overvaluation of the target firm by the bidding firm is common. An alternative explanation of the evidence is that management is simply not pursuing the best interests of the shareholders in such cases.

CONCEPT TEST

1. The three basic procedures a firm can use to acquire another firm are: _____, acquisition of _____, and acquisition of _____

2. The complete absorption of one firm by another is called a _____.

3. If an entirely new firm is created by an acquisition, then the event is called a _____.

4. If two firms that compete in the same product market merge, the acquisition is said to be _____.

5. If a firm were to merge with its major supplier, the acquisition would be _____.

6. A _____ acquisition involves two firms in completely unrelated lines of business.

7. In an acquisition, the firm attempting the takeover is called the _____. The other firm is called the _____.

8. Takeovers can occur by _____, _____, or _____.

9. A _____ occurs when a dissident shareholder group solicits proxies in an attempt to gain control of a firm.

10. If the shareholders in an acquired firm receive shares of stock as compensation, the acquisition would normally be _____.

11. A _____ is a general transfer of control from one group to another.

12. An advantage of a cash acquisition is the fact that the assets of the acquired firm can be _____.

13. A disadvantage of a cash acquisition is the fact that the shareholders of the acquired firm are generally obligated to pay _____.

14. The _____ method of accounting reports the assets of the acquired firm at fair market value on the balance sheet.

15. The _____ method of accounting reports the balance sheet of the acquired firm as the total of the balance sheets of the acquired and the acquiring firm.

16. For the procedure described in Question 14, the difference between the purchase price and the fair market value would be reported on the balance sheet as _____.

17. Revenue enhancing benefits from mergers may come from _____, _____, and _____.

18. If a merger reduces the average production cost for a product, then an _____ is said to exist.

19. Net operating losses, debt capacity, and surplus funds are all possible sources of _____ in a merger.

20. When two leveraged firms merge, the new firm may have a lower cost of debt and a higher debt capacity because of the _____.

21. If an acquisition has a positive NPV, then, all other things equal, the cost of the acquisition will be higher if _____ is used to pay for the acquisition.

22. An amendment to the corporate charter requiring, for example, that 80% of the stockholders must approve a merger is called a _____ provision.

23. With a _____ agreement, a target firm agrees to buy back its own stock, at a premium, from the bidder, in exchange for the bidder's terminating the takeover attempt.

24. With an _____, a target firm offers to buy its own stock, at a premium, from all stockholders except the bidding firm.

25. Going-private transactions are frequently arranged by existing management with the help of outside investors. Such transactions frequently take the form of a _____.

26. In an unfriendly takeover, the bidding firm can bypass existing management and acquire the stock by using a _____.

27. A _____ refers to compensation paid to top management in the event of a takeover.

28. A _____ refers to a defensive tactic designed to make a firm an unattractive target for acquisition.

29. The _____ are major assets that a target firm sells or threatens to sell in an effort to fend off a takeover.

30. Empirical evidence suggests that the shareholders of _____ firms benefit substantially from takeovers, whereas the shareholders of _____ do not benefit.

ANSWERS TO CONCEPT TEST

1. merger or consolidation; stock; assets
2. merger
3. consolidation
4. horizontal
5. vertical
6. conglomerate
7. bidder; target
8. acquisition; proxy contest; going private
9. proxy contest
10. a tax-free acquisition
11. takeover
12. written up
13. capital gains taxes
14. purchase
15. pooling of interests
16. goodwill
17. marketing gains; strategic benefits; market power
18. economy of scale
19. tax gains
20. coinsurance effect
21. stock
22. super majority
23. repurchase standstill
24. exclusionary self-tender
25. leveraged buyout
26. tender offer
27. golden parachute
28. poison pill
29. crown jewels
30. acquired; acquiring

PROBLEMS AND SOLUTIONS

Use the following information to solve Problems 1-9. Assume that Firms A and B have no debt outstanding.

	Firm A	Firm B
Total earnings	$3500	$1400
Shares outstanding	700	350
Price per share	$ 50	$ 20

Problem 1

Firm A is considering the acquisition of Firm B. Firm A has estimated that the value of the combined firm will be $43,000. Firm B has indicated that it would accept a cash purchase offer of $22 per share. Should Firm A proceed with the acquisition?

Solution 1

At $22 per share, Firm A is paying [($22)(350)] = $7700 to acquire Firm B. The value of Firm A after the acquisition is equal to the value of the combined firm less the cash paid for Firm B, or ($43,000 - $7,700) = $35,300. The net present value of the acquisition is ($35,300 - $35,000) = $300, so that the acquisition is beneficial to the stockholders of Firm A. Firm A should proceed with the acquisition.

Problem 2

For the data of Problem 1, what is the synergy from the merger? What is the premium paid for the acquisition? Use the synergy and the premium to determine the net present value of the acquisition.

Solution 2

The synergy is equal to the value of the combined firm less the total value of the two separate firms:

$$\$43,000 - [(\$50)(700) + (\$20)(350)] = \$1,000$$

The premium is the difference between the purchase price and the market value of the acquired firm:

$$(\$22)(350) - (\$20)(350) = \$700$$

Therefore, the net present value is the synergy minus the premium, or ($1000 - $700) = $300, as indicated in Problem 1.

Problem 3

For the data of Problem 1, what is the price of Firm A's stock after the merger?

Solution 3

The net present value of the merger is $300, so the stock will increase in value by ($300/700) = $.43 per share. The stock price will be $50.43. Alternatively, Firm A is worth $35,000 prior to the merger. After the merger, it is worth [$35,000 + ($8000 - $7700)] = $35,300. The per share value is thus ($35,300/700) = $50.43, as previously calculated.

Problem 4

For the data of Problem 1, what is the net present value of the merger if Firm A pays for the acquisition with common stock, based on the current market prices?

Solution 4

At current values, Firm A will exchange one of its shares for every 2.5 shares of Firm B [($50/$20) = 2.5]. In total, Firm B stockholders will receive (350/2.5) = 140 shares. The combined firm will thus have 840 shares outstanding, of which (140/840) = (1/6) are held by the former shareholders of Firm B. The combined firm is worth $43,000, so the cost of the merger is [(1/6)($43,000)] = $7166.67. The net present value is ($8000 - $7166.67) = $833.33.

Problem 5

For the data of Problem 4, what is the post-merger price if Firm A pays for the acquisition with stock based on a price of $22 per share for Firm B? What is the cost of the merger? What is the net present value of the merger?

Solution 5

Firm A will have to give ($22/$50) = .44 shares of its stock for every share of B, or [(.44)(350)] = 154 shares. [Note that this result is also equal to the cash price of the acquisition divided by the current market value of a share of Firm A stock: ($7700/$50) =154.] The new firm will have a total of 854 shares outstanding. The combined firm is worth $43,000, so the per share value is ($43,000/854) = $50.3513. The cost of the merger is [(154/854)($43,000)] = $7754.10, so the net present value is $245.90. [Note that the cost of the merger is also equal to the per share value of the merged firm times the number of shares received by the stockholders of Firm B: ($50.3513)(154) = $7754.10.]

Problem 6

For the data of Problem 5, what is the synergy from the merger? What is the premium paid for the acquisition? Use the synergy and the premium to determine the net present value of the acquisition. Why is the net present value lower for the acquisition through exchange of stock in Problem 5 compared to the acquisition for cash in Problem 1?

Solution 6

The synergy is $1000, as indicated in Problem 2. The premium is the difference between the purchase price and the market value of the acquired firm:

$$(\$7754.10) - [(\$20)(350)] = \$754.10$$

The net present value is the synergy minus the premium, or ($1000 - $754.10) = $245.90. This NPV is $54.10 less than the $300 NPV of the acquisition for cash. The stockholders of Firm B receive [(154/854)($300)] = $54.10 of the net present value when the acquisition is paid for with an exchange of stock. This difference can also be viewed as the increment in the value of the shares of Firm A which is given to the stockholders of Firm B; that is, [($50.3513 - $50)(154)] = $54.10.

Problem 7

Problem 1 indicates that the shareholders of Firm B are willing to accept $7700 for the acquisition. How many shares of Firm A stock should Firm B stockholders receive so that they actually receive the $7700 price?

Solution 7

In order for the Firm B stockholders to receive $7700, they must receive stock which has a total value equal to ($7700/$43,000) = .17907 = 17.907% of the merged firm. Therefore, the new shares issued must represent 17.907% of the outstanding shares of the merged firm. This value is determined by solving for x in the following equation:

$$[x/(700 + x)] = .17907$$

The number of new shares which should be issued to the stockholders of Firm B is 152.691, so that the total number of shares outstanding will then be (700 + 152.691) = 852.691. The price per share will be ($43,000/852.691) = $50.4286. The stockholders of Firm B receive 152.691 shares worth $50.4286, for a total value of [(152.69)($50.4286)] = $7700.

Problem 8

Assume that Firm A acquires Firm B in exchange for stock valued at $21 per share. How will this affect earnings per share for Firm A?

Solution 8

The new firm will have total earnings of $4900. At $21 per share, Firm A will have to give [($21/$50)(350)] = 147 shares to the shareholders of Firm B, so that the new firm will have 847 shares outstanding. Thus, EPS will be ($4900/847) = $5.785 per share; this is an increase of $.785 from the pre-merger level of $5 per share.

Problem 9

For the data of Problem 8, what is the price per share of the new firm if the market is 'fooled' by this earnings growth? What will the price/earnings ratio be if the market is not 'fooled?'

Solution 9

Before the merger, A had a P/E ratio of ($50/$5) = 10. If the market is fooled, in the sense that this P/E ratio is unchanged after the merger, the stock will rise in value to [(10)($5.785)] = $57.85.

If the market is not fooled, then the P/E ratio will fall to ($43,000/$4900) = 8.776, and the price per share will be [(8.776)($5.785)] = $50.77. This result is also equal to the value of the firm divided by the number of shares: ($43,000/847) = $50.77.

Problem 10

Blizzard Manufacturing, producer of snow-removal equipment, is analyzing the possible acquisition of Max Motors, manufacturer of engine components. Blizzard forecasts that the purchase would result in incremental after-tax cash flows of $10,000 per year for the foreseeable future. The current market values of Blizzard and Max are $500,000 and $200,000, respectively. The relevant opportunity cost of capital for the incremental cash flows is 20 percent. What is the synergy from the merger?

Solution 10

The synergy is the present value of the perpetual annuity of $10,000 per year: ($10,000/.20) = $50,000. Therefore, Max's value to Blizzard is ($200,000 + $50,000) = $250,000.

Problem 11

Suppose that, for the data of Problem 10, Blizzard is considering an offer of $220,000 cash for the acquisition of Max Motors. What is the premium of the merger? What is the net present value of the merger?

Solution 11

The premium is ($220,000 - $200,000) = $20,000. The net present value is the synergy minus the premium, or ($50,000 - $20,000) = $30,000. The net present value can also be determined as the difference between the value of the acquisition and the cost: ($250,000 - $220,000) = $30,000.

Problem 12

As an alternative to the $220,000 offer described in Problem 11, Blizzard is considering offering 25 percent of its stock to the stockholders of Max Motors. What is the net present value of this offer?

Solution 12

Twenty-five percent of the combined company is worth [(.25)($250,000 + $500,000)] = $187,500. The net present value of this acquisition would be ($250,000 - $187,500) = $62,500. Blizzard would prefer to acquire Max Motors for 25 percent of the firm's stock rather than the $220,000 cash offer described in Problem 11.

Use the following information to solve Problems 13 and 14.

Kau Vineyards ($ in thousands)			
Current assets	$ 100	Current liabilities	$ 60
Fixed assets	900	Long-term debt	200
		Equity	740
Total	$ 1000		$ 1000

Hilliard Vineyards ($ in thousands)			
Current assets	$ 200	Current liabilities	$ 140
Fixed assets	600	Long-term debt	100
		Equity	560
Total	$ 800		$ 800

Problem 13

Assume that the balance sheets above are in terms of book values. Construct the balance sheet for Kau assuming that Kau purchases Hilliard and the pooling of interests method of accounting is used.

Solution 13

With a pooling of interests, the balance sheets are added together, so the new balance sheet appears as follows:

Kau Vineyards ($ in thousands)			
Current assets	$ 300	Current liabilities	$ 200
Fixed assets	1500	Long-term debt	300
		Equity	1300
Total	$ 1800		$ 1800

Problem 14

Suppose that the fair market value of Hilliard's fixed assets is $900, in contrast to the $600 book value shown. Kau pays $1200 for Hilliard and raises the needed funds through an issue of long-term debt. Construct the balance sheet assuming that the purchase method of accounting is used.

Solution 14

Hilliard's fair market value is $900 plus $200 in current assets, or $1100 total. The $100 premium paid ($1200 - $1100) is goodwill. Kau's fixed assets would be $900 (the book value of Kau's pre-merger fixed assets) plus $900 (the market value of Hilliard's assets), or $1800 total. The balance sheet appears as follows:

Kau Vineyards ($ in thousands)			
Current assets	$ 300	Current liabilities	$ 200
Fixed assets	1800	Long-term debt	1260
Goodwill	100	Equity	740
Total	$ 2200		$ 2200

Solution note: Hilliard's assets are $1100. Assuming that the current liabilities and long-term debt are shown at market value, the equity in Hilliard is worth ($1100 - $140 - $100) = $860. Kau pays a $100 premium, so the total amount of debt that Kau must raise is $960. The total long-term debt after the merger is ($960 + $100 + $200) = $1260, as shown.

Problem 15

Firm A manufactures umbrellas. Firm B manufactures suntan lotion. The values of the two firms depend on the weather and are shown below:

Weather	Probability	Value of A	Value of B
Rainy	.5	$100	$50
Sunny	.5	60	90
Expected value		$80	$70

Each firm has debt outstanding with a face value of $66. Calculate the value of the equity and the value of the debt for each weather condition, and the expected values of the equity and the debt.

Solution 15

The bonds are worth either $66 or the value of the firm, whichever is less. The stock is worth either zero or the value of the firm less $66, whichever is more. Thus:

Weather	Probability	Firm A		Firm B	
		Stock	Debt	Stock	Debt
Rainy	.5	$34	$66	$0	$50
Sunny	.5	0	60	24	66
Expected values		$17	$63	$12	$58

Notice that the value of Firm A is ($17 + $63) = $80, and the value of Firm B is ($12 + $58) = $70.

Problem 16

Firms A and B have proposed a merger. There is no synergy. How would the stockholders view this proposal? Why?

Solution 16

Before the merger, the total value of the stock in the two firms is ($17 + $12) = $29. The total value of the bonds is ($63 + $58) = $121. Since there is no synergy, the value of the merged firm will be $150. The values of the equity and debt are shown below:

Weather	Probability	Firm Value	Debt Value	Equity Value
Rainy	.5	$150	$132	$18
Sunny	.5	150	132	18
Expected value		$150	$132	$18

This problem illustrates the coinsurance effect. The merged firm has a certain value of $150. The bonds are worth $11 more ($132 - $121) than before the merger, and, as a result, the equity is worth $11 less than before the merger.

CHAPTER HIGHLIGHTS

The basic principles of corporate finance apply to international corporations just as they do to domestic corporations; that is, international corporations seek to invest in positive NPV projects and to arrange financing that creates value for shareholders. However, application of these principles in international finance is complicated by differences in foreign exchange, accounting methods, tax rates and government intervention.

Terminology

As in all specialized subject areas, international finance has a unique vocabulary. Some of the most important terms are defined in this section.

1. **American Depository Receipt** (ADR): a security issued in the United States, representing a share of a foreign company's stock.
2. **Belgian Dentist:** a stereotype of an investor who purchases Eurobonds (see below) because the income derived from these anonymous-bearer bonds is untraceable.
3. **Cross rate:** exchange rate between two non-U.S. currencies.
4. **European Currency Unit** (ECU): a basket of ten European currencies intended to serve as the monetary unit for the European Monetary System (EMS).
5. **Eurobond:** a bond issue denominated in a particular currency, sold simultaneously in several European countries, issued in bearer form.
6. **Eurocurrency:** money deposited in financial institutions outside the country whose currency is involved. Eurodollars, the most important Eurocurrency, are dollars deposited in banks outside the U.S.
7. **Foreign bonds:** bonds issued by foreign borrowers in another country and denominated in the currency of the country where issued.
8. **Gilts:** British and Irish government securities.
9. **London Interbank Offered Rate** (LIBOR): the rate on overnight Eurodollar loans between major international banks. Interest rates on short-term debt of corporate and government borrowers are frequently based on this rate.
10. **Swaps:** a currency swap is an agreement to exchange currencies; an interest rate swap is an exchange of a debt with a floating-rate payment for a debt with a fixed-rate payment (or vice versa).

Foreign Exchange Markets and Exchange Rates

The foreign exchange market is the world's largest financial market. It is strictly an over-the-counter market, consisting of a worldwide telecommunications network among traders in major commercial and investment banks around the world. Most of the trading takes place in a small number of major currencies, including the U.S. dollar, West German deutschemark, British pound sterling, Japanese yen, Swiss franc and French franc.

Exchange Rates. An exchange rate is the price of one country's currency expressed in terms of another's. In practice, almost all exchange rates are quoted in terms of U.S. dollars. Thus the French franc (FF) might be quoted at FF 10, indicating that it takes ten francs to buy one dollar. A quote of units of foreign currency per dollar is called an indirect (or European) quote. A rate can also be quoted in terms of the number of dollars required to buy one unit of foreign currency: for example, .1 dollar to buy 1 franc. This is a direct, or American, quote.

The quoting of all exchange rates in dollars reduces the number of possible cross-currency quotes; it eliminates, for example, the need to quote an exchange rate for British pounds in terms of French francs. In addition, it makes **triangular arbitrage** more difficult. Suppose the following exchange rates existed:

```
French francs /German D-marks: 5
French francs /U.S. dollars:   10
German D-marks/U.S. dollars:    3
```

You could convert $1 into three marks. Next, convert three marks to 15 francs and then convert the francs to dollars; at the exchange rate of 10 francs to the dollar, you will have $1.50, or a 50% risk-free return! This outcome is, of course, impossible in an efficient market; quoting exchange rates in dollars reduces the likelihood of such inconsistencies.

Types of Transactions. Three kinds of transactions exist in the foreign exchange market. **Spot trades** involve agreement on the exchange rate today, called the **spot-exchange rate**, for settlement in two business days. **Forward trades** involve agreement today on an exchange rate for settlement in the more distant future. The exchange rate in this case is the **forward-exchange rate**, and settlement is typically one to fifty-two weeks in the future. A **swap** is an agreement to sell/purchase currencies today and later repurchase/resell the same currencies. The difference between the two exchange rates in a swap is called the **swap rate**.

The Law of One Price and Purchasing Power Parity

The **law of one price** (LOP) states that a particular commodity will have the same price regardless of the country in which it is purchased. For example, suppose that a gallon of gasoline sells for two dollars in the U.S. and for 30 French francs (30 FF) in France. If the exchange rate is 10FF per dollar, then you could purchase a gallon of gasoline in the U.S. for $2, sell the gasoline in France for 30FF, and then exchange the 30 francs for $3. The profit for the transaction is $1. According to the law of one price, the above scenario could not continue to exist; the stated prices and/or exchange rate would adjust in such a way as to eliminate the arbitrage profit for this transaction. This profit is eliminated if:

$$P^{US}(t) = S_{FF}(t) \, P^{FF}(t)$$

where $P^{US}(t)$ is the current price of gasoline in the U.S., $P^{FF}(t)$ is the current price of gasoline in France, and $S_{FF}(t)$ is the spot exchange rate (i.e., the number of dollars required to purchase one franc). If, for example, the prices remain the same, then, in order for the LOP to prevail, $S_{FF}(t)$ must equal (1/15). In general, the law of one price implies that both prices and exchange rates will adjust in circumstances such as those described above. For instance, the profit opportunity indicated in the example would result in both increased demand for gasoline in the U.S. and increased supply in France, so that price would increase in the U.S. and decrease in France. In addition, the demand for francs would decrease and the demand for dollars would increase, thereby reducing the exchange rate.

The above argument is strictly accurate only if there are no shipping or other transactions costs, no barriers to trade, and commodities are identical in both countries. Clearly, these conditions are rarely met, so that, in general, we do not expect the LOP to apply precisely.

The LOP implies **purchasing power parity** (PPP), which means that exchange rates and prices adjust in such a way that a 'market basket' of goods costs the same regardless of the country in which the items are purchased. A related concept is **relative purchasing power parity** (RPPP); according to RPPP, the rate of change in the exchange rate between two countries depends on the relative inflation rates in the two countries.

Let $S_{FF}(t)$ be the exchange rate quoted as dollars per franc ($/FF) at time t; then RPPP can be stated as follows:

$$\frac{P^{US}(t+1)}{P^{US}(t)} = \frac{S_{FF}(t+1)}{S_{FF}(t)} \times \frac{P^{FF}(t+1)}{P^{FF}(t)}$$

The term on the left side of the equation is (1 + the U.S. inflation rate), which can be written (1 + Π_{US}); similarly, the last term is (1 + the French inflation rate), or (1 + Π_{FF}), so that RPPP can be written:

$$\frac{1 + \Pi_{US}}{1 + \Pi_{FF}} = \frac{S_{FF}(t+1)}{S_{FF}(t)}$$

Suppose the inflation rates over the next year in the United States and France are forecast to be 5% and 9%, respectively. If the current exchange rate is .1 dollar per franc, then RPPP indicates that the exchange rate in one year $S_{FF}(t+1)$ = [.1(1.05/1.09)] = .09633. This result can also be derived from the following relationship: the rate of change in the exchange rate is approximately equal to the difference in the inflation rates, (Π_{US} - Π_{FF}). Therefore, (Π_{US} - Π_{FF}) = (.05 - .09) = -.04, and $S_{FF}(t+1)$ = (.1)[1 + (-.04)] = .096. It takes fewer dollars to buy 1 franc because the higher inflation rate in France makes the franc worth relatively less.

Interest Rates and Exchange Rates: Interest Rate Parity

Suppose that the current, or spot, exchange rate is FF 10 = $1, and that the rate at which you can exchange francs for dollars in 90 days (i.e., the 90-day forward rate) is FF 10.2 = $1. Since it takes more francs to buy $1 in the future than it does now, then the franc is less valuable in the forward market than in the spot market. Therefore, the franc is said to be selling at a **discount** in the forward exchange market. If the forward exchange rate were FF 9.8, then the franc would be selling at a **premium** in the forward exchange market.

The **interest rate parity theorem** (IRP) indicates that the relationship between the spot and forward exchange rates is a function of the relationship between foreign and domestic interest rates. Let S(0) be the spot exchange rate, expressed in dollars per franc ($/FF), and F(0,1) be the similarly quoted forward rate for contracts maturing one period in the future. If we define i_{US} and i_F to be the risk-free interest rates in the United States and France, respectively, over the forward period, then the IRP theorem specifies that:

$$\frac{1 + i_{US}}{1 + i_F} = \frac{F(0,1)}{S(0)}$$

If the current exchange rate, S(0), is .1 dollar per franc, and the 90-day risk-free rates are 2% in the United States and 2.2% in France, then, the forward rate, F(0,1), equals (1.02/1.022)(.1) = .0998.

The IRP theorem is an outcome which results from the fact that arbitrage opportunities do not exist in an efficient market. Suppose that, in the above example, a trader were to invest $1 at the 2% risk-free rate available in the U.S. He would then have [($1)(1.02)] = $1.02 at the end of 90 days. Alternatively, if the trader were to exchange the dollar for francs at the spot rate, he would have 10 FF which could be invested at 2.2%, producing a return of [(10FF)(1.022)] = 10.22 FF after 90 days. The trader can sell the francs forward at the rate F(0,1) = .0998, thereby exchanging the 10.22 FF for [(10.22)(.0998)] = $1.02. Either investment strategy produces the same result at the end of ninety days, indicating the parity of the risk-free rate in the U.S. and the so-called covered foreign exchange rate.

The Forward-Discount and Expected-Spot Rates. If traders are unconcerned about the risk of changes in exchange rates, then the forward rate, F(0,1), must be equal to the market consensus expectation regarding the future spot rate, E[S(1)]. Equivalently, the forward premium or discount must equal the expected change in the spot exchange rate.

Exchange-Rate Risk. Firms dealing in international trade are subject to exchange-rate risk because they both make payments in foreign currencies and receive foreign currencies in payments. Suppose the current exchange rate is FF 10 = $1 and that a company has receivables of 10 million francs to be collected in 90 days. At the current exchange rate, the firm will be able to exchange 10 million francs for 1 million dollars. If, however, the exchange rate in 90 days is FF 12.5 = $1, then the firm will actually receive only ($10 million/12.5) = $800,000. The firm's exchange-rate risk is the uncertainty associated with the dollar-value of the future payment in the foreign currency.

The forward market provides a means for hedging exchange-rate risk. Suppose that, in the example above, the 90-day forward rate is FF 10.2 = $1. The firm can eliminate exchange-rate risk by purchasing a forward contract and promising to deliver francs for dollars. At the FF 10.2 = $1 forward exchange rate, the firm will be certain to receive ($10 million/10.2) = $980,392 90 days from now. Hedging is generally considered advantageous because, in an efficient market, exchange-rate speculation is a zero NPV activity, and the costs of hedging are generally quite low.

International Capital Budgeting

Suppose we are considering building a factory in Slobovia. The factory is a 3-year project and will cost 100 slobs (SL 100) to build and will produce after-tax cash flows of SL 40 per year. The current exchange rate is SL 2 = $1, or $.50 = SL 1. The appropriate cost of capital for **dollar** cash flows is 10%.

Foreign Exchange Conversion. To calculate the net present value, we convert the SL cash flows to dollar flows, and discount the dollar cash flows at 10%. This calculation requires that we know the future exchange rates. Suppose the one-year risk-free rates for the United States and Slobovia are quoted at 5% and 3%, respectively, and the United States inflation forecast is 3%.

Assuming that the forward rate is equal to the expected spot rate, the IRP theorem specifies that:

$$[1 + i_{US}]/[1 + i_{SL}] = F(0,1)/S(0) = E[S(1)]/S(0)$$

According to RPPP:

$$[1 + \Pi_{US}]/[1 + \Pi_{SL}] = E[S(1)]/S(0)$$

Taken together, IRP and RPPP indicate that:

$$[1 + \Pi_{US}]/[1 + \Pi_{SL}] = [1 + i_{US}]/[1 + i_{SL}]$$

Using this result, we can estimate the Slobovian inflation rate, Π_{SL}, as follows:

$$1.03/[1 + \Pi_{SL}] = 1.05/1.03$$

$$[1 + \Pi_{SL}] = 1.03(1.03/1.05) = 1.0104$$

Therefore, the Slobovian inflation rate is approximately 1%.

We can now use the RPPP result to estimate the expected spot exchange rate in one year, $E[S(1)]$:

$$E[S(1)]/(.5) = 1.03/1.01$$

$$E[S(1)] = (1.03/1.01)(.5) = .5099$$

Assuming no change in the inflation forecasts, we can derive the expected exchange rate in two years using the same procedure:

$$E[S(2)]/E[S(1)] = E[S(2)]/.5099 = 1.03/1.01$$

$$E[S(2)] = .5200$$

Notice that $E[S(2)]$ can also be written as:

$$E[S(2)] = E[S(1)](1.03/1.01) = S(0)(1.03/1.01)^2$$

In general, the expected spot rate in t periods is:

$$E[S(t)] = S(0)(1.03/1.01)^t$$

For example, $E[S(3)]$ in this case is:

$$E[S(3)] = .50(1.03/1.01)^3 = .5303$$

We can now convert the cash flows from slobs to dollars:

Year	Cash flows (SL)	Exchange rate	Cash flows ($)
0	SL -100	.5000	$ -50.00
1	40	.5099	20.40
2	40	.5200	20.80
3	40	.5303	21.21

Using the 10% discount rate, the net present value is $1.67.

Unremitted Cash Flows. The example above assumes that the cash flows from the project are remitted to the United States as they are earned. However, in reality, this assumption is frequently not appropriate. First, foreign countries often place limitations on the ability of international firms to remit cash flows. Second, the issue of remittance is affected by foreign taxes. For example, tax incentives may make it advantageous for an international firm to reinvest foreign cash flows in the foreign country. Total taxes paid by a multinational firm may be affected by the timing of remittances. Therefore, the timing of remittances may affect the net present value of a foreign investment.

The Cost of Capital for International Firms. The cost of capital for international investments may differ from that of domestic investments for two reasons. First, a firm may use a higher cost of capital to reflect increased political risk, such as the risk of expropriation, and remittance controls for international investments. On the other hand, international diversification may be beneficial to a firm's stockholders. The firm may be able to diversify in ways that the individual shareholders cannot, perhaps by investing in countries that do not have capital markets. This benefit would reduce the cost of capital.

International Financial Decisions

The cash required to finance a foreign investment can be raised either domestically, or in the country where the project is located, or in a third country. The decision among these three alternatives depends on relative interest rates and the desirability of hedging exchange-rate risk. An international firm which obtains financing in the United States is subject to exchange-rate risk. This risk can be hedged in the forward markets only to a limited extent, because forward contracts generally have maturities of one year or less. Exchange-rate risk can be more effectively hedged by obtaining financing in the country where the investment is to be made. The risk reduction occurs because changes in the value of the investment will be partially offset by changes in the value of the liabilities. Financing might also be obtained in a third country, because of lower interest rates. However, this alternative must be based on real, rather than nominal, rates; also, exchange-rate risk must be considered for this alternative.

Short-Term and Medium-Term Financing. U.S. international firms can borrow from U.S. banks or they can borrow from foreign banks (**Eurobanks**) in the Eurocurrency market. The interest rate on a Eurocurrency loan usually floats at a fixed margin above the LIBOR. Such loans typically have maturities up to ten years, with semiannual adjustments in the interest rate.

International Bond Markets. International bonds are classified as either foreign bonds or Eurobonds.

Foreign bonds are issued in a country other than the borrowing firm's home country, and are denominated in the currency of the country where they are issued. Many foreign bond issues are registered. They are often nicknamed for the country where they are issued; Yankee bonds, for example, are dollar-denominated bonds issued in the United States by a foreign company.

Eurobonds are denominated in a particular currency and are issued simultaneously in several countries. Most are bearer bonds, making them attractive to 'Belgian dentists.' Eurobonds are usually underwritten in a way that is similar to the underwriting procedure for a domestic bond issue, with the exception that the underwriting syndicate is international.

International Capital Structure

Whether capital structures vary from country to country is a matter of some debate. Some studies suggest that companies in Japan and Germany are more highly levered than are companies in the United States and the United Kingdom. Other studies indicate little difference exists in capital structure, on a market value basis, after controlling for industry differences.

Reporting Foreign Operations

When a U.S. firm prepares its financial statements, the information on foreign operations must be translated into dollars. The major issues which arise from this process are: first, the determination of the appropriate exchange rate; and, second, accounting for gains and losses from foreign-currency translation. Financial Accounting Standards Board Statement Number 52 requires that all assets and liabilities be translated at current, rather than historical, exchange rates. Gains and losses from exchange rate fluctuations are carried as a separate item on the balance sheet and are not recognized on the income statement.

CONCEPT TEST

1. A security issued in the United States which represents a share of stock in a foreign firm is called an _____.

2. A 'Belgian dentist' purchases Eurobonds because they are in _____.

3. A _____ is the exchange rate for two non-U.S. currencies.

4. Bonds denominated in a particular currency and simultaneously issued in several countries are called _____.

5. A _____ is money deposited in financial institutions outside of the country whose currency is involved.

6. Dollars on deposit in a London bank are called _____.

7. A _____ is a basket of 10 European currencies intended to serve as a monetary unit for the EMS.

8. A U.S. firm issues pound-denominated bonds in England. Such bonds are generically called _____.

9. A British government security is called a _____.

10. The overnight interest rate banks charge each other on Eurodollar loans is the _____.

11. A currency _____ refers to an exchange of one currency for another.

12. The _____ is the world's largest financial market.

13. The price of one country's currency expressed in terms of another's is called the _____.

14. _____ is a means of profiting from inconsistencies in exchange rates by converting currencies.

15. Foreign exchange trades that are settled in two business days are called _____ trades and take place at the _____ rate.

16. Foreign exchange trades that settled in sixty days are called _____ trades and take place at the _____ rate.

17. The _____ states that a particular commodity has the same price regardless of the country in which it is selling.

18. An implication of the concept identified in Question 17 is that the price of a 'market basket' of goods is the same in all countries and currencies. This is called _____.

19. _____ states that the relative inflation rates in two countries determine the rate of change in the exchange rate.

20. The _____ theorem states that the difference between the spot and forward exchange rates depends on relative interest rates.

21. If it takes more dollars to buy a foreign currency in the forward market than in the spot market, the foreign currency is said to be selling at a _____ in the forward market.

22. The uncertainty associated with changes in the value of future cash flows resulting from changes in exchange rates is called _____.

23. The cost of capital for international investments may be increased because of _____.

24. The cost of capital for international investments may be decreased because of gains from _____.

25. Current accounting rules require that all balance sheet items must be translated into dollars at the _____ exchange rate.

ANSWERS TO CONCEPT TEST

1. American Depository Receipt (ADR)
2. bearer form
3. cross rate
4. Eurobonds
5. Eurocurrency
6. Eurodollars
7. European Currency Unit (ECU)
8. foreign bonds
9. gilt
10. London Interbank Offer Rate (LIBOR)
11. swap
12. foreign exchange market
13. exchange rate
14. triangular arbitrage
15. spot; spot
16. forward; forward
17. law of one price (LOP)
18. purchasing power parity (PPP)
19. relative purchasing power parity (RPPP)
20. interest rate parity
21. premium
22. exchange-rate risk
23. political risk
24. diversification
25. current

PROBLEMS AND SOLUTIONS

Problem 1

You can exchange 4 stellars for 1 dollar. What is the direct exchange rate? What is the indirect exchange rate?

Solution 1

The direct (or American) rate is quoted as dollars per unit of foreign currency, so the direct rate is .25 dollar = 1 stellar. The indirect (or European) rate is units of foreign currency per dollar, or 4 stellars = 1 dollar.

Problem 2

The direct exchange rate for Mongolian dollars is .10. How many Mongolian dollars do you receive in exchange for 1 U.S. dollar?

Solution 2

Each Mongolian dollar costs .10 U.S. dollar, so you receive 10 in exchange for one U.S. dollar.

Problem 3

The direct exchange rate for German marks is .50. The direct exchange rate for British pounds is 1.5. If you have 1 mark, how many pounds can you buy? (That is, what is the cross rate?)

Solution 3

Your one mark will buy .50 dollar. With .50 dollar, you can buy 1/3 of a pound. The cross rate is 3 marks = 1 pound.

Problem 4

Suppose that, for the data in Problem 3, the cross rate is 3.3 marks = 1 pound, rather than the calculated result of 3 marks = 1 pound. Describe the triangular arbitrage opportunity which would exist under these circumstances.

Solution 4

Use the one mark to purchase .50 dollar and then exchange the .50 dollar for 1/3 pound. At the cross rate of 3.3 marks = 1 pound, 1/3 pound can be exchanged for 1.1 mark, or an arbitrage profit of 10%.

Problem 5

Suppose that, for the data in Problem 3, the cross rate is 2.7 marks = 1 pound. Describe the triangular arbitrage opportunity which would exist under these circumstances.

Solution 5

Exchange one mark for (1/2.7) = .37037 pounds and then purchase [(.37037)(1.5)] = .55556 dollar. At the exchange rate of .50 dollar = one mark, .55556 dollar can be exchanged for [(.55556)(2)] = 1.1111 marks. This result represents an arbitrage profit of 11.11%.

Problem 6

An ounce of silver costs 5 dollars in the U.S. or 800 yen in Japan. The exchange rate is 150 yen = 1 dollar. Is this an equilibrium situation? Suppose that a trader has $500 available. Can the trader make an arbitrage profit?

Solution 6

The trader can purchase ($500/$5) = 100 ounces of silver in the U.S. This can then be sold for [(100)(800 yen)] = 80,000 yen in Japan. At the exchange rate of 150 yen = 1 dollar, the trader can exchange 80,000 yen for (80,000/150) = $533.33, so that the arbitrage profit is $33.33. This is not an equilibrium situation because the demand for silver in the U.S. will cause the dollar price of silver to increase and the supply of silver will decrease the price in Japan. Also, the exchange rate will increase due to the increased demand for dollars and the decreased demand for yen.

Problem 7

Suppose that, for the data in Problem 6, the price of silver in Japan is 700 yen per ounce. Describe the arbitrage profit opportunity for a trader with $500 available.

Solution 7

In this situation, the trader can exchange \$500 for [(500)(150)] = 75,000 yen. With 75,000 yen, the trader can then purchase (75,000/700) = 107.1429 ounces of silver in Japan. He can sell the silver for [(\$5)(107.1429)] = \$535.71, for an arbitrage profit of \$35.71.

Problem 8

Suppose that, for the data in Problem 6, the price of silver in the U.S. and Japan remains constant, but the exchange rate adjusts in accordance with the law of one price. What is the equilibrium exchange rate?

Solution 8

According to the law of one price, the stated prices and/or exchange rate adjust in such a way as to eliminate the arbitrage profit. This profit is eliminated if:

$$P^{US}(t) = S_Y(t)\ P^Y(t)$$

where $P^{US}(t)$ and $P^Y(t)$ are the price of silver, in dollars and yen, respectively, and $S_Y(t)$ is the exchange rate for dollars in terms of yen. The equilibrium exchange rate is the value of $S_Y(t)$ in the following equation:

$$5 = [S_Y(t)] \times 800$$

Therefore, the equilibrium exchange rate is 160 yen = 1 dollar.

Problem 9

The direct spot exchange rate for marks is .50 and the 90-day forward rate is .51. Is the mark selling at a premium or discount?

Solution 9

It takes more dollars (\$.51 compared to \$.50) to buy a mark forward than it does to buy a mark today. Therefore the mark is selling at a premium.

Problem 10

Suppose that, in Problem 9, the U.S. 90-day risk-free rate is 3%. What is the German risk-free rate, i_G?

Solution 10

From the interest rate parity theorem:

$$1.03/(1 + i_G) = .51/.50$$

Therefore, the German risk-free rate is .9804%, or approximately 1%.

Problem 11

Suppose the Swiss inflation rate is forecast to be 2% during the coming year and the United States rate over the same period will be 5%. The current exchange rate is SF 1 = $ 1.50. What is the expected spot exchange rate in one year?

Solution 11

From relative purchasing power parity:

$$(1.05/1.02) = E[S(1)]/1.5$$

Therefore, $E[S(1)] = 1.544$.

Solution note: You must be careful here to use the exchange rate expressed as dollars per unit of foreign currency. It costs $1.50 to buy a Swiss franc today. The difference between the U.S. and the Swiss inflation rates is 3%, so the price of a Swiss franc will rise by approximately 3%: $[(\$1.50)(1.03)] = \$1.545$.

Problem 12

The current yen/dollar exchange rate is 150. The risk-free interest rate in Japan is 6% and in the United States is 8%. What is the expected spot exchange rate in one year?

Solution 12

The current exchange rate, expressed as dollars per yen, is $(\$1/150) = \$.006667$. Based on IRP:

$$(1.08/1.06) = F(0,1)/(.006667)$$

Therefore, the forward rate is $.0067925, or 147.22 yen per dollar. This result is based on the assumption that the forward rate is equal to the expected spot rate.

Problem 13

Suppose that, for the data in Problem 12, the U.S. inflation rate is expected to be 4%. What is the expected spot exchange rate in five years, $E[S(5)]$?

Solution 13

Using the IRP and RPPP, the Japanese inflation rate, Π_J, can be determined as follows:

$$(1.08/1.06) = (1.04/[1 + \Pi_J])$$

$$\Pi_J = 2.074\%$$

Using RPPP, the expected spot exchange rate in five years is:

$$E[S(5)] = (.006667)(1.04/1.02074)^5 = .00732$$

This is equivalent to approximately 137 yen per dollar.

Use the following information to solve Problems 14 and 15.

You have been asked to evaluate a proposed investment in the country of Westfield. Westfield's home currency is the Sar, abbreviated SA. The current exchange rate is 1 Sar = $2. The inflation rate in Westfield is expected to be 10% higher than in the United States; that is, $\Pi_W/\Pi_{US} = 1.10$.

The project will cost SA 1000 and is expected to generate SA 300 per year for three years. The project will then be sold for an estimated SA 400. The appropriate discount rate for dollar flows of this risk level is 12%.

Problem 14

What is the expected exchange rate at the end of the project's life?

Solution 14

The current exchange rate is $.50. This is expected to decline by (1/1.10) = .9091 per year. In three years, the exchange rate is expected to be:

$$.50(.9091)^3 = \$.376.$$

Problem 15

Try this one on your own. What is the net present value of the proposed investment, in dollars? In Sars?

Solution 15

The cash flows and exchange rates are:

Year	Cash flows (SA)	Exchange rate	Cash flows ($)
0	SA -1000	.50000	$ -500.00
1	300	.45454	136.36
2	300	.41322	123.97
3	700	.37566	262.96

At a 12% discount rate, the NPV in dollars is -$92.25. The NPV in Sars is -184.50 Sars.

Appendix: Mathematical Tables

Table A.1 Present value of $1 to be received after T periods $= 1/(1 + r)^T$

					Interest rate				
Period	1%	2%	3%	4%	5%	6%	7%	8%	9%
1	0.9901	0.9804	0.9709	0.9615	0.9524	0.9434	0.9346	0.9259	0.9174
2	0.9803	0.9612	0.9426	0.9246	0.9070	0.8900	0.8734	0.8573	0.8417
3	0.9706	0.9423	0.9151	0.8890	0.8638	0.8396	0.8163	0.7938	0.7722
4	0.9610	0.9238	0.8885	0.8548	0.8227	0.7921	0.7629	0.7350	0.7084
5	0.9515	0.9057	0.8626	0.8219	0.7835	0.7473	0.7130	0.6806	0.6499
6	0.9420	0.8880	0.8375	0.7903	0.7462	0.7050	0.6663	0.6302	0.5963
7	0.9327	0.8706	0.8131	0.7599	0.7107	0.6651	0.6227	0.5835	0.5470
8	0.9235	0.8535	0.7894	0.7307	0.6768	0.6274	0.5820	0.5403	0.5019
9	0.9143	0.8368	0.7664	0.7026	0.6446	0.5919	0.5439	0.5002	0.4604
10	0.9053	0.8203	0.7441	0.6756	0.6139	0.5584	0.5083	0.4632	0.4224
11	0.8963	0.8043	0.7224	0.6496	0.5847	0.5268	0.4751	0.4289	0.3875
12	0.8874	0.7885	0.7014	0.6246	0.5568	0.4970	0.4440	0.3971	0.3555
13	0.8787	0.7730	0.6810	0.6006	0.5303	0.4688	0.4150	0.3677	0.3262
14	0.8700	0.7579	0.6611	0.5775	0.5051	0.4423	0.3878	0.3405	0.2992
15	0.8613	0.7430	0.6419	0.5553	0.4810	0.4173	0.3624	0.3152	0.2745
16	0.8528	0.7284	0.6232	0.5339	0.4581	0.3936	0.3387	0.2919	0.2519
17	0.8444	0.7142	0.6050	0.5134	0.4363	0.3714	0.3166	0.2703	0.2311
18	0.8360	0.7002	0.5874	0.4936	0.4155	0.3503	0.2959	0.2502	0.2120
19	0.8277	0.6864	0.5703	0.4746	0.3957	0.3305	0.2765	0.2317	0.1945
20	0.8195	0.6730	0.5537	0.4564	0.3769	0.3118	0.2584	0.2145	0.1784
21	0.8114	0.6598	0.5375	0.4388	0.3589	0.2942	0.2415	0.1987	0.1637
22	0.8034	0.6468	0.5219	0.4220	0.3418	0.2775	0.2257	0.1839	0.1502
23	0.7954	0.6342	0.5067	0.4057	0.3256	0.2618	0.2109	0.1703	0.1378
24	0.7876	0.6217	0.4919	0.3901	0.3101	0.2470	0.1971	0.1577	0.1264
25	0.7798	0.6095	0.4776	0.3751	0.2953	0.2330	0.1842	0.1460	0.1160
30	0.7419	0.5521	0.4120	0.3083	0.2314	0.1741	0.1314	0.0994	0.0754
40	0.6717	0.4529	0.3066	0.2083	0.1420	0.0972	0.0668	0.0460	0.0318
50	0.6080	0.3715	0.2281	0.1407	0.0872	0.0543	0.0339	0.0213	0.0134

*The factor is zero to four decimal places.

					Interest rate					
10%	12%	14%	15%	16%	18%	20%	24%	28%	32%	36%
0.9091	0.8229	0.8772	0.8696	0.8621	0.8475	0.8333	0.8065	0.7813	0.7576	0.7353
0.8264	0.7972	0.7695	0.7561	0.7432	0.7182	0.6944	0.6504	0.6104	0.5739	0.5407
0.7513	0.7118	0.6750	0.6575	0.6407	0.6086	0.5787	0.5245	0.4768	0.4348	0.3975
0.6830	0.6355	0.5921	0.5718	0.5523	0.5158	0.4823	0.4230	0.3725	0.3294	0.2923
0.6209	0.5674	0.5194	0.4972	0.4761	0.4371	0.4019	0.3411	0.2910	0.2495	0.2149
0.5645	0.5066	0.4556	0.4323	0.4104	0.3704	0.3349	0.2751	0.2274	0.1890	0.1580
0.5132	0.4523	0.3996	0.3759	0.3538	0.3139	0.2791	0.2218	0.1776	0.1432	0.1162
0.4665	0.4039	0.3506	0.3269	0.3050	0.2660	0.2326	0.1789	0.1388	0.1085	0.0854
0.4241	0.3606	0.3075	0.2843	0.2630	0.2255	0.1938	0.1443	0.1084	0.0822	0.0628
0.3855	0.3220	0.2697	0.2472	0.2267	0.1911	0.1615	0.1164	0.0847	0.0623	0.0462
0.3505	0.2875	0.2366	0.2149	0.1954	0.1619	0.1346	0.0938	0.0662	0.0472	0.0340
0.3186	0.2567	0.2076	0.1869	0.1685	0.1372	0.1122	0.0757	0.0517	0.0357	0.0250
0.2897	0.2292	0.1821	0.1625	0.1452	0.1163	0.0935	0.0610	0.0404	0.0271	0.0184
0.2633	0.2046	0.1597	0.1413	0.1252	0.0985	0.0779	0.0492	0.0316	0.0205	0.0135
0.2394	0.1827	0.1401	0.1229	0.1079	0.0835	0.0649	0.0397	0.0247	0.0155	0.0099
0.2176	0.1631	0.1229	0.1069	0.0930	0.0708	0.0541	0.0320	0.0193	0.0118	0.0073
0.1978	0.1456	0.1078	0.0929	0.0802	0.0600	0.0451	0.0258	0.0150	0.0089	0.0054
0.1799	0.1300	0.0946	0.0808	0.0691	0.0508	0.0376	0.0208	0.0118	0.0068	0.0039
0.1635	0.1161	0.0829	0.0703	0.0596	0.0431	0.0313	0.0168	0.0092	0.0051	0.0029
0.1486	0.1037	0.0728	0.0611	0.0514	0.0365	0.0261	0.0135	0.0072	0.0039	0.0021
0.1351	0.0926	0.0638	0.0531	0.0443	0.0309	0.0217	0.0109	0.0056	0.0029	0.0016
0.1228	0.0826	0.0560	0.0462	0.0382	0.0262	0.0181	0.0088	0.0044	0.0022	0.0012
0.1117	0.0738	0.0491	0.0402	0.0329	0.0222	0.0151	0.0071	0.0034	0.0017	0.0008
0.1015	0.0659	0.0431	0.0349	0.0284	0.0188	0.0126	0.0057	0.0027	0.0013	0.0006
0.0923	0.0588	0.0378	0.0304	0.0245	0.0160	0.0105	0.0046	0.0021	0.0010	0.0005
0.0573	0.0334	0.0196	0.0151	0.0116	0.0070	0.0042	0.0016	0.0006	0.0002	0.0001
0.0221	0.0107	0.0053	0.0037	0.0026	0.0013	0.0007	0.0002	0.0001	*	*
0.0085	0.0035	0.0014	0.0009	0.0006	0.0003	0.0001	*	*	*	*

Table A.2   Present value of an annuity of $1 per period for T periods = $[1 - 1/(1 + r)^T] \div r$

	Interest rate								
Number of periods	1%	2%	3%	4%	5%	6%	7%	8%	9%
1	0.9901	0.9804	0.9709	0.9615	0.9524	0.9434	0.9346	0.9259	0.9174
2	1.9704	1.9416	1.9135	1.8861	1.8594	1.8334	1.8080	1.7833	1.7591
3	2.9410	2.8839	2.8286	2.7751	2.7232	2.6730	2.6243	2.5771	2.5313
4	3.9020	3.8077	3.7171	3.6299	3.5460	3.4651	3.3872	3.3121	3.2397
5	4.8534	4.7135	4.5797	4.4518	4.3295	4.2124	4.1002	3.9927	3.8897
6	5.7955	5.6014	5.4172	5.2421	5.0757	4.9173	4.7665	4.6229	4.4859
7	6.7282	6.4720	6.2303	6.0021	5.7864	5.5824	5.3893	5.2064	5.0330
8	7.6517	7.3255	7.0197	6.7327	6.4632	6.2098	5.9713	5.7466	5.5348
9	8.5660	8.1622	7.7861	7.4353	7.1078	6.8017	6.5152	6.2469	5.9952
10	9.4713	8.9826	8.5302	8.1109	7.7217	7.3601	7.0236	6.7101	6.4177
11	10.3676	9.7868	9.2526	8.7605	8.3064	7.8869	7.4987	7.1390	6.8052
12	11.2551	10.5753	9.9540	9.3851	8.8633	8.3838	7.9427	7.5361	7.1607
13	12.1337	11.3484	10.6350	9.9856	9.3936	8.8527	8.3577	7.9038	7.4869
14	13.0037	12.1062	11.2961	10.5631	9.8986	9.2950	8.7455	8.2442	7.7862
15	13.8651	12.8493	11.9379	11.1184	10.3797	9.7122	9.1079	8.5595	8.0607
16	14.7179	13.5777	12.5611	11.6523	10.8378	10.1059	9.4466	8.8514	8.3126
17	15.5623	14.2919	13.1661	12.1657	11.2741	10.4773	9.7632	9.1216	8.5436
18	16.3983	14.9920	13.7535	12.6593	11.6896	10.8276	10.0591	9.3719	8.7556
19	17.2260	15.6785	14.3238	13.1339	12.0853	11.1581	10.3356	9.6036	8.9501
20	18.0456	16.3514	14.8775	13.5903	12.4622	11.4699	10.5940	9.8181	9.1285
21	18.8570	17.0112	15.4150	14.0292	12.8212	11.7641	10.8355	10.0168	9.2922
22	19.6604	17.6580	15.9369	14.4511	13.1630	12.0416	11.0612	10.2007	9.4424
23	20.4558	18.2922	16.4436	14.8568	13.4886	12.3034	11.2722	10.3741	9.5802
24	21.2434	18.9139	16.9355	15.2470	13.7986	12.5504	11.4693	10.5288	9.7066
25	22.0232	19.5235	17.4131	15.6221	14.0939	12.7834	11.6536	10.6748	9.8226
30	25.8077	22.3965	19.6004	17.2920	15.3725	13.7648	12.4090	11.2578	10.2737
40	32.8347	27.3555	23.1148	19.7928	17.1591	15.0463	13.3317	11.9246	10.7574
50	39.1961	31.4236	25.7298	21.4822	18.2559	15.7619	13.8007	12.2335	10.9617

					Interest rate				
10%	12%	14%	15%	16%	18%	20%	24%	28%	32%
0.9091	0.8929	0.8772	0.8696	0.8621	0.8475	0.8333	0.8065	0.7813	0.7576
1.7355	1.6901	1.6467	1.6257	1.6052	1.5656	1.5278	1.4568	1.3916	1.3315
2.4869	2.4018	2.3216	2.2832	2.2459	2.1743	2.1065	1.9813	1.8684	1.7663
3.1699	3.0373	2.9137	2.8550	2.7982	2.6901	2.5887	2.4043	2.2410	2.0957
3.7908	3.6048	3.4331	3.3522	3.2743	3.1272	2.9906	2.7454	2.5320	2.3452
4.3553	4.1114	3.8887	3.7845	3.6847	3.4976	3.3255	3.0205	2.7594	2.5342
4.8684	4.5638	4.2883	4.1604	4.0386	3.8115	3.6046	3.2423	2.9370	2.6775
5.3349	4.9676	4.6389	4.4873	4.3436	4.0776	3.8372	3.4212	3.0758	2.7860
5.7590	5.3282	4.9464	4.7716	4.6065	4.3030	4.0310	3.5655	3.1842	2.8681
6.1446	5.6502	5.2161	5.0188	4.8332	4.4941	4.1925	3.6819	3.2689	2.9304
6.4951	5.9377	5.4527	5.2337	5.0286	4.6560	4.3271	3.7757	3.3351	2.9776
6.8137	6.1944	5.6603	5.4206	5.1971	4.7932	4.4392	3.8514	3.3868	3.0133
7.1034	6.4235	5.8424	5.5831	5.3423	4.9095	4.5327	3.9124	3.4272	3.0404
7.3667	6.6282	6.0021	5.7245	5.4675	5.0081	4.6106	3.9616	3.4587	3.0609
7.6061	6.8109	6.1422	5.8474	5.5755	5.0916	4.6755	4.0013	3.4834	3.0764
7.8237	6.9740	6.2651	5.9542	5.6685	5.1624	4.7296	4.0333	3.5026	3.0882
8.0216	7.1196	6.3729	6.0472	5.7487	5.2223	4.7746	4.0591	3.5177	3.0971
8.2014	7.2497	6.4674	6.1280	5.8178	5.2732	4.8122	4.0799	3.5294	3.1039
8.3649	7.3658	6.5504	6.1982	5.8775	5.3162	4.8435	4.0967	3.5386	3.1090
8.5136	7.4694	6.6231	6.2593	5.9288	5.3527	4.8696	4.1103	3.5458	3.1129
8.6487	7.5620	6.6870	6.3125	5.9731	5.3837	4.8913	4.1212	3.5514	3.1158
8.7715	7.6446	6.7429	6.3587	6.0113	5.4099	4.9094	4.1300	3.5558	3.1180
8.8832	7.7184	6.7921	6.3988	6.0442	5.4321	4.9245	4.1371	3.5592	3.1197
8.9847	7.7843	6.8351	6.4338	6.0726	5.4509	4.9371	4.1428	3.5619	3.1210
9.0770	7.8431	6.8729	6.4641	6.0971	5.4669	4.9476	4.1474	3.5640	3.1220
9.4269	8.0552	7.0027	6.5660	6.1772	5.5168	4.9789	4.1601	3.5693	3.1242
9.7791	8.2438	7.1050	6.6418	6.2335	5.5482	4.9966	4.1659	3.5712	3.1250
9.9148	8.3045	7.1327	6.6605	6.2463	5.5541	4.9995	4.1666	3.5714	3.1250

Appendix A

Table A.3 Future value of $1 at the end of T periods $= (1 + r)^T$

Period	Interest rate								
	1%	2%	3%	4%	5%	6%	7%	8%	9%
1	1.0100	1.0200	1.0300	1.0400	1.0500	1.0600	1.0700	1.0800	1.0900
2	1.0201	1.0404	1.0609	1.0816	1.1025	1.1236	1.1449	1.1664	1.1881
3	1.0303	1.0612	1.0927	1.1249	1.1576	1.1910	1.2250	1.2597	1.2950
4	1.0406	1.0824	1.1255	1.1699	1.2155	1.2625	1.3108	1.3605	1.4116
5	1.0510	1.1041	1.1593	1.2167	1.2763	1.3382	1.4026	1.4693	1.5386
6	1.0615	1.1262	1.1941	1.2653	1.3401	1.4185	1.5007	1.5869	1.6771
7	1.0721	1.1487	1.2299	1.3159	1.4071	1.5036	1.6058	1.7138	1.8280
8	1.0829	1.1717	1.2668	1.3686	1.4775	1.5938	1.7182	1.8509	1.9926
9	1.0937	1.1951	1.3048	1.4233	1.5513	1.6895	1.8385	1.9990	2.1719
10	1.1046	1.2190	1.3439	1.4802	1.6289	1.7908	1.9672	2.1589	2.3674
11	1.1157	1.2434	1.3842	1.5395	1.7103	1.8983	2.1049	2.3316	2.5804
12	1.1268	1.2682	1.4258	1.6010	1.7959	2.0122	2.2522	2.5182	2.8127
13	1.1381	1.2936	1.4685	1.6651	1.8856	2.1329	2.4098	2.7196	3.0658
14	1.1495	1.3195	1.5126	1.7317	1.9799	2.2609	2.5785	2.9372	3.3417
15	1.1610	1.3459	1.5580	1.8009	1.0789	2.3966	2.7590	3.1722	3.6425
16	1.1726	1.3728	1.6047	1.8730	2.1829	2.5404	2.9522	3.4259	3.9703
17	1.1843	1.4002	1.6528	1.9479	2.2920	2.6928	3.1588	3.7000	4.3276
18	1.1961	1.4282	1.7024	2.0258	2.4066	2.8543	3.3799	3.9960	4.7171
19	1.2081	1.4568	1.7535	2.1068	2.5270	3.0256	3.6165	4.3157	5.1417
20	1.2202	1.4859	1.8061	2.1911	2.6533	3.2071	3.8697	4.6610	5.6044
21	1.2324	1.5157	1.8603	2.2788	2.7860	3.3996	4.1406	5.0338	6.1088
22	1.2447	1.5460	1.9161	2.3699	2.9253	3.6035	4.4304	5.4365	6.6586
23	1.2572	1.5769	1.9736	2.4647	3.0715	3.8197	4.7405	5.8715	7.2579
24	1.2697	1.6084	2.0328	2.5633	3.2251	4.0489	5.0724	6.3412	7.9111
25	1.2824	1.6406	2.0938	2.6658	3.3864	4.2919	5.4274	6.8485	8.6231
30	1.3478	1.8114	2.4273	3.2434	4.3219	5.7435	7.6123	10.063	13.268
40	1.4889	2.2080	3.2620	4.8010	7.0400	10.286	14.974	21.725	31.409
50	1.6446	2.6916	4.3839	7.1067	11.467	18.420	29.457	46.902	74.358
60	1.8167	3.2810	5.8916	10.520	18.679	32.988	57.946	101.26	176.03

*FVIF < 99,999.

					Interest rate					
10%	12%	14%	15%	16%	18%	20%	24%	28%	32%	36%
1.1000	1.1200	1.1400	1.1500	1.1600	1.1800	1.2000	1.2400	1.2800	1.3200	1.3600
1.2100	1.2544	1.2996	1.3225	1.3456	1.3924	1.4400	1.5376	1.6384	1.7424	1.8496
1.3310	1.4049	1.4815	1.5209	1.5609	1.6430	1.7280	1.9066	2.0972	2.3000	2.5155
1.4641	1.5735	1.6890	1.7490	1.8106	1.9388	2.0736	2.3642	2.6844	3.0360	3.4210
1.6105	1.7623	1.9254	2.0114	2.1003	2.2878	2.4883	2.9316	3.4360	4.0075	4.6526
1.7716	1.9738	2.1950	2.3131	2.4364	2.6996	2.9860	3.6352	4.3980	5.2899	6.3275
1.9487	2.2107	2.5023	2.6600	2.8262	3.1855	3.5832	4.5077	5.6295	6.9826	8.6054
2.1436	2.4760	2.8526	3.0590	3.2784	3.7589	4.2998	5.5895	7.2058	9.2170	11.703
2.3579	2.7731	3.2519	3.5179	3.8030	4.4355	5.1598	6.9310	9.2234	12.166	15.917
2.5937	3.1058	3.7072	4.0456	4.4114	5.2338	6.1917	8.5944	11.806	16.060	21.647
2.8531	3.4785	4.2262	4.6524	5.1173	6.1759	7.4301	10.657	15.112	21.199	29.439
3.1384	3.8960	4.8179	5.3503	5.9360	7.2876	8.9161	13.215	19.343	27.983	40.037
3.4523	4.3635	5.4924	6.1528	6.8858	8.5994	10.699	16.386	24.759	36.937	54.451
3.7975	4.8871	6.2613	7.0757	7.9875	10.147	12.839	20.319	31.691	48.757	74.053
4.1772	5.4736	7.1379	8.1371	9.2655	11.974	15.407	25.196	40.565	64.359	100.71
4.5950	6.1304	8.1372	9.3576	10.748	14.129	18.488	31.243	51.923	84.954	136.97
5.0545	6.8660	9.2765	10.761	12.468	16.672	22.186	38.741	66.461	112.14	186.28
5.5599	7.6900	10.575	12.375	14.463	19.673	26.623	48.039	85.071	148.02	253.34
6.1159	8.6128	12.056	14.232	16.777	23.214	31.948	59.568	108.89	195.39	344.54
6.7275	9.6463	13.743	16.367	19.461	27.393	38.338	73.864	139.38	257.92	468.57
7.4002	10.804	15.668	18.822	22.574	32.324	46.005	91.592	178.41	340.45	637.26
8.1403	12.100	17.861	21.645	26.186	38.142	55.206	113.57	228.36	449.39	866.67
8.9543	13.552	20.362	24.891	30.376	45.008	66.247	140.83	292.30	593.20	1178.7
9.8497	15.179	23.212	28.625	35.236	53.109	79.497	174.63	374.14	783.02	1603.0
10.835	17.000	26.462	32.919	40.874	62.669	95.396	216.54	478.90	1033.6	2180.1
17.449	29.960	50.950	66.212	85.850	143.37	237.38	634.82	1645.5	4142.1	10143.
45.259	93.051	188.88	267.86	378.72	750.38	1469.8	5455.9	19427.	66521.	*
117.39	289.00	700.23	1083.7	1670.7	3927.4	9100.4	46890.	*	*	*
304.48	897.60	2595.9	4384.0	7370.2	20555.	56348.	*	*	*	*

A8   Appendix A

Table A.4   Sum of annuity of $1 per period for T periods = $\{[1 + r)^T - 1]/r\}$

Number of periods	Interest rate								
	1%	2%	3%	4%	5%	6%	7%	8%	9%
1	1.0000	1.0000	1.0000	1.0000	1.0000	1.0000	1.0000	1.0000	1.0000
2	2.0100	2.0200	2.0300	2.0400	2.0500	2.0600	2.0700	2.0800	2.0900
3	3.0301	3.0604	3.0909	3.1216	3.1525	3.1836	3.2149	3.2464	3.2781
4	4.0604	4.1216	4.1836	4.2465	4.3101	4.3746	4.4399	4.5061	4.5731
5	5.1010	5.2040	5.3091	5.4163	5.5256	5.6371	5.7507	5.8666	5.9847
6	6.1520	6.3081	6.4684	6.6330	6.8019	6.9753	7.1533	7.3359	7.5233
7	7.2135	7.4343	7.6625	7.8983	8.1420	8.3938	8.6540	8.9228	9.2004
8	8.2857	8.5830	8.8932	9.2142	9.5491	9.8975	10.260	10.637	11.028
9	9.3685	9.7546	10.159	10.583	11.027	11.491	11.978	12.488	13.021
10	10.462	10.950	11.464	12.006	12.578	13.181	13.816	14.487	15.193
11	11.567	12.169	12.808	13.486	14.207	14.972	15.784	16.645	17.560
12	12.683	13.412	14.192	15.026	15.917	16.870	17.888	18.977	20.141
13	13.809	14.680	15.618	16.627	17.713	18.882	20.141	21.495	22.953
14	14.947	15.974	17.086	18.292	19.599	21.015	22.550	24.215	26.019
15	16.097	17.293	18.599	20.024	21.579	23.276	25.129	27.152	29.361
16	17.258	18.639	20.157	21.825	23.657	25.673	27.888	30.324	33.003
17	18.430	20.012	21.762	23.698	25.840	28.213	30.840	33.750	36.974
18	19.615	21.412	23.414	25.645	28.132	30.906	33.999	37.450	41.301
19	20.811	22.841	25.117	27.671	30.539	33.760	37.379	41.446	46.018
20	22.019	24.297	26.870	29.778	33.066	36.786	40.995	45.762	51.160
21	23.239	25.783	28.676	31.969	35.719	39.993	44.865	50.423	56.765
22	24.472	27.299	30.537	34.248	38.505	43.392	49.006	55.457	62.873
23	25.716	28.845	32.453	36.618	41.430	46.996	53.436	60.893	69.532
24	26.973	30.422	34.426	39.083	44.502	50.816	58.177	66.765	76.790
25	28.243	32.030	36.459	41.646	47.727	54.865	63.249	73.106	84.701
30	34.785	40.568	47.575	56.085	66.439	79.058	94.461	113.28	136.31
40	48.886	60.402	75.401	95.026	120.80	154.76	199.64	259.06	337.88
50	64.463	84.579	112.80	152.67	209.35	290.34	406.53	573.77	815.08
60	81.670	114.05	163.05	237.99	353.58	533.13	813.52	1253.2	1944.8

*FVIFA < 99,999.

					Interest rate					
10%	12%	14%	15%	16%	18%	20%	24%	28%	32%	36%
1.0000	1.0000	1.0000	1.0000	1.0000	1.0000	1.0000	1.0000	1.0000	1.0000	1.0000
2.1000	2.1200	2.1400	2.1500	2.1600	2.1800	2.2000	2.2400	2.2800	2.3200	2.3600
3.3100	3.3744	3.4396	3.4725	3.5056	3.5724	3.6400	3.7776	3.9184	4.0624	4.2096
4.6410	4.7793	4.9211	4.9934	5.0665	5.2154	5.3680	5.6842	6.0156	6.3624	6.7251
6.1051	6.3528	6.6101	6.7424	6.8771	7.1542	7.4416	8.0484	8.6999	9.3983	10.146
7.7156	8.1152	8.5355	8.7537	8.9775	9.4420	9.9299	10.980	12.136	13.406	14.799
9.4872	10.089	10.730	11.067	11.414	12.142	12.916	14.615	16.534	18.696	21.126
11.436	12.300	13.233	13.727	14.240	15.327	16.499	19.123	22.163	25.678	29.732
13.579	14.776	16.085	16.786	17.519	19.086	20.799	24.712	29.369	34.895	41.435
15.937	17.549	19.337	20.304	21.321	23.521	25.959	31.643	38.593	47.062	57.352
18.531	20.655	23.045	24.349	25.733	28.755	32.150	40.238	50.398	63.122	78.998
21.384	24.133	27.271	29.002	30.850	34.931	39.581	50.895	65.510	84.320	108.44
24.523	28.029	32.089	34.352	36.786	42.219	48.497	64.110	84.853	112.30	148.47
27.975	32.393	37.581	40.505	43.672	50.818	59.196	80.496	109.61	149.24	202.93
31.772	37.280	43.842	47.580	51.660	60.965	72.035	100.82	141.30	198.00	276.98
35.950	42.753	50.980	55.717	60.925	72.939	87.442	126.01	181.87	262.36	377.69
40.545	48.884	59.118	65.075	71.673	87.068	105.93	157.25	233.79	347.31	514.66
45.599	55.750	68.394	75.836	84.141	103.74	128.12	195.99	300.25	459.45	700.94
51.159	63.440	78.969	88.212	98.603	123.41	154.74	244.03	385.32	607.47	954.28
57.275	72.052	91.025	102.44	115.38	146.63	186.69	303.60	494.21	802.86	1298.8
64.002	81.699	104.77	118.81	134.84	174.02	225.03	377.46	633.59	1060.8	1767.4
71.403	92.503	120.44	137.63	157.41	206.34	271.03	469.06	812.00	1401.2	2404.7
79.543	104.60	138.30	159.28	183.60	244.49	326.24	582.63	1040.4	1850.6	3271.3
88.497	118.16	158.66	184.17	213.98	289.49	392.48	723.46	1332.7	2443.8	4450.0
98.347	133.33	181.87	212.79	249.21	342.60	471.98	898.09	1706.8	3226.8	6053.0
164.49	241.33	356.79	434.75	530.31	790.95	1181.9	2640.9	5873.2	12941.	28172.3
442.59	767.09	1342.0	1779.1	2360.8	4163.2	7343.9	22729.	69377.	*	*
1163.9	2400.0	4994.5	7217.7	10436.	21813.	45497.	*	*	*	*
3034.8	7471.6	18535.	29220.	46058.	*	*	*	*	*	*

Table A.5 Future value of $1 with a continuously compounded rate r for T periods: Values of e^{rT}

Period (T)	Continuously compounded rate (r) 1%	2%	3%	4%	5%	6%	7%	8%	9%	10%
1	1.0101	1.0202	1.0305	1.0408	1.0513	1.0618	1.0725	1.0833	1.0942	1.1052
2	1.0202	1.0408	1.0618	1.0833	1.1052	1.1275	1.1503	1.1735	1.1972	1.2214
3	1.0305	1.0618	1.0942	1.1275	1.1618	1.1972	1.2337	1.2712	1.3100	1.3499
4	1.0408	1.0833	1.1275	1.1735	1.2214	1.2712	1.3231	1.3771	1.4333	1.4918
5	1.0513	1.1052	1.1618	1.2214	1.2840	1.3499	1.4191	1.4918	1.5683	1.6487
6	1.0618	1.1275	1.1972	1.2712	1.3499	1.4333	1.5220	1.6161	1.7160	1.8221
7	1.0725	1.1503	1.2337	1.3231	1.4191	1.5220	1.6323	1.7507	1.8776	2.0138
8	1.0833	1.1735	1.2712	1.3771	1.4918	1.6161	1.7507	1.8965	2.0544	2.2255
9	1.0942	1.1972	1.3100	1.4333	1.5683	1.7160	1.8776	2.0544	2.2479	2.4596
10	1.1052	1.2214	1.3499	1.4918	1.6487	1.8221	2.0138	2.2255	2.4596	2.7183
11	1.1163	1.2461	1.3910	1.5527	1.7333	1.9348	2.1598	2.4109	2.6912	3.0042
12	1.1275	1.2712	1.4333	1.6161	1.8221	2.0544	2.3164	2.6117	2.9447	3.3201
13	1.1388	1.2969	1.4770	1.6820	1.9155	2.1815	2.4843	2.8292	3.2220	3.6693
14	1.1503	1.3231	1.5220	1.7507	2.0138	2.3164	2.6645	3.0649	3.5254	4.0552
15	1.1618	1.3499	1.5683	1.8221	2.1170	2.4596	2.8577	3.3201	3.8574	4.4817
16	1.1735	1.3771	1.6161	1.8965	2.2255	2.6117	3.0649	3.5966	4.2207	4.9530
17	1.1853	1.4049	1.6653	1.9739	2.3396	2.7732	3.2871	3.8962	4.6182	5.4739
18	1.1972	1.4333	1.7160	2.0544	2.4596	2.9447	3.5254	4.2207	5.0531	6.0496
19	1.2092	1.4623	1.7683	2.1383	2.5857	3.1268	3.7810	4.5722	5.5290	6.6859
20	1.2214	1.4918	1.8221	2.2255	2.7183	3.3201	4.0552	4.9530	6.0496	7.3891
21	1.2337	1.5220	1.8776	2.3164	2.8577	3.5254	4.3492	5.3656	6.6194	8.1662
22	1.2461	1.5527	1.9348	2.4109	3.0042	3.7434	4.6646	5.8124	7.2427	9.0250
23	1.2586	1.5841	1.9937	2.5093	3.1582	3.9749	5.0028	6.2965	7.9248	9.9742
24	1.2712	1.6161	2.0544	2.6117	3.3201	4.2207	5.3656	6.8210	8.6711	11.0232
25	1.2840	1.6487	2.1170	2.7183	3.4903	4.4817	5.7546	7.3891	9.4877	12.1825
30	1.3499	1.8221	2.4596	3.3204	4.4817	6.0496	8.1662	11.0232	14.8797	20.0855
35	1.4191	2.0138	2.8577	4.0552	5.7546	8.1662	11.5883	16.4446	23.3361	33.1155
40	1.4918	2.2255	3.3201	4.9530	7.3891	11.0232	16.4446	24.5235	36.5982	54.5982
45	1.5683	2.4596	3.8574	6.0496	9.4877	14.8797	23.3361	36.5982	57.3975	90.0171
50	1.6487	2.7183	4.4817	7.3891	12.1825	20.0855	33.1155	54.5982	90.0171	148.4132
55	1.7333	3.0042	5.2070	9.0250	15.6426	27.1126	46.9931	81.4509	141.1750	244.6919
60	1.8221	3.3201	6.0496	11.0232	20.0855	36.5982	66.6863	121.5104	221.4064	403.4288

					Continuously compounded rate (r)					
11%	12%	13%	14%	15%	16%	17%	18%	19%	20%	21%
1.1163	1.1275	1.1388	1.1503	1.1618	1.1735	1.1853	1.1972	1.2092	1.2214	1.2337
1.2461	1.2712	1.2969	1.3231	1.3499	1.3771	1.4049	1.4333	1.4623	1.4918	1.5220
1.3910	1.4333	1.4770	1.5220	1.5683	1.6161	1.6653	1.7160	1.7683	1.8221	1.8776
1.5527	1.6161	1.6820	1.7507	1.8221	1.8965	1.9739	2.0544	2.1383	2.2255	2.3164
1.7333	1.8221	1.9155	2.0138	2.1170	2.2255	2.3396	2.4596	2.5857	2.7183	2.8577
1.9348	2.0544	2.1815	2.3164	2.4596	2.6117	2.7732	2.9447	3.1268	3.3201	3.5254
2.1598	2.3164	2.4843	2.6645	2.8577	3.0649	3.2871	3.5254	3.7810	4.0552	4.3492
2.4109	2.6117	2.8292	3.0649	3.3201	3.5966	3.8962	4.2207	4.5722	4.9530	5.3656
2.6912	2.9447	3.2220	3.5254	3.8574	4.2207	4.6182	5.0531	5.5290	6.0496	6.6194
3.0042	3.3201	3.6693	4.0552	4.4817	4.9530	5.4739	6.0496	6.6859	7.3891	8.1662
3.3535	3.7434	4.1787	4.6646	5.2070	5.8124	6.4883	7.2427	8.0849	9.0250	10.0744
3.7434	6.2207	4.7588	5.3656	6.0496	6.8210	7.6906	8.6711	9.7767	11.0232	12.4286
4.1787	4.7588	5.4195	6.1719	7.0287	8.0045	9.1157	10.3812	11.8224	13.4637	15.3329
4.6646	5.3656	6.1719	7.0993	8.1662	9.3933	10.8049	12.4286	14.2963	16.4446	18.9158
5.2070	6.0496	7.0287	8.1662	9.4877	11.0232	12.8071	14.8797	17.2878	20.0855	23.3361
5.8124	6.8210	8.0045	9.3933	11.0232	12.9358	15.1803	17.8143	20.9052	24.5325	28.7892
6.4883	7.6906	9.1157	10.8049	12.8071	15.1803	17.9933	21.3276	25.2797	29.9641	35.5166
7.2427	8.6711	10.3812	12.4286	14.8797	17.8143	21.3276	25.5337	30.5694	36.5982	43.8160
8.0849	9.7767	11.8224	14.2963	17.2878	20.9052	25.2797	30.5694	36.9661	44.7012	54.0549
9.0250	11.0232	13.4637	16.4446	20.0855	24.5325	29.9641	36.5982	44.7012	54.5982	66.6863
10.0744	12.4286	15.3329	18.9158	23.3361	28.7892	35.5166	43.8160	54.0549	66.6863	82.2695
11.2459	14.0132	17.4615	21.7584	27.1126	33.7844	42.0980	52.4573	65.3659	81.4509	101.4940
12.5535	15.7998	19.8857	25.0281	31.5004	39.6464	49.8990	62.8028	79.0436	99.4843	125.2110
14.0132	17.8143	22.6464	28.7892	36.5982	46.5255	59.1455	75.1886	95.5835	121.5104	154.4700
15.6426	20.0855	25.7903	33.1155	42.5211	54.5982	70.1054	90.0171	115.5843	148.4132	190.5663
27.1126	36.5982	49.4024	66.6863	90.0171	121.5104	164.0219	221.4064	298.8674	403.4288	544.5719
46.9931	66.6863	94.6324	134.2898	190.5663	270.4264	383.7533	544.5719	772.7843	1096.633	1556.197
81.4509	121.5104	181.2722	270.4264	403.4288	601.8450	897.8473	1339.431	1998.196	2980.958	4447.067
141.1750	221.4064	347.2344	544.5719	854.0588	1339.431	2100.646	3294.468	5166.754	8103.084	12708.17
244.6919	403.4288	665.1416	1096.633	1808.042	2980.958	4914.769	8103.084	13359.73	22026.47	36315.50
424.1130	735.0952	1274.106	2208.348	3827.626	6634.244	11498.82	19930.37	34544.37	59874.14	103777.0
735.0952	1339.431	2440.602	4447.067	8103.084	14764.78	26903.19	49020.80	89321.72	162754.8	296558.6

Table A.5, continued   Future value of $1 with a continuously compounded rate r for T periods: Values of e^{rT}

Period (T)	Continuously compounded rate (r)						
	22%	23%	24%	25%	26%	27%	28%
1	1.2461	1.2586	1.2712	1.2840	1.2969	1.3100	1.3231
2	1.5527	1.5841	1.6161	1.6487	1.6820	1.7160	1.7507
3	1.9348	1.9937	2.0544	2.1170	2.1815	2.2479	2.3164
4	2.4109	2.5093	2.6117	2.7183	2.8292	2.9447	3.0649
5	3.0042	3.1582	3.3201	3.4903	3.6693	3.8574	4.0552
6	3.7434	3.9749	4.2207	4.4817	4.7588	5.0531	5.3656
7	4.6646	5.0028	5.3656	5.7546	6.1719	6.6194	7.0993
8	5.8124	6.2965	6.8210	7.3891	8.0045	8.6711	9.3933
9	7.2427	7.9248	8.6711	9.4877	10.3812	11.3589	12.4286
10	9.0250	9.9742	11.0232	12.1825	13.4637	14.8797	16.4446
11	11.2459	12.5535	14.0132	15.6426	17.4615	19.4919	21.7584
12	14.0132	15.7998	17.8143	20.0855	22.6464	25.5337	28.7892
13	17.4615	19.8857	22.6464	25.7903	29.3708	33.4483	38.0918
14	21.7584	25.0281	28.7892	33.1155	38.0918	43.8160	50.4004
15	27.1126	31.5004	36.5982	42.5211	49.4024	57.3975	66.6863
16	33.7844	39.6464	46.5255	54.5982	64.0715	75.1886	88.2347
17	42.0980	49.8990	59.1455	70.1054	83.0963	98.4944	116.7459
18	52.4573	62.8028	75.1886	90.0171	107.7701	129.0242	154.4700
19	65.3659	79.0436	95.5835	115.5843	139.7702	169.0171	204.3839
20	81.4509	99.4843	121.5104	148.4132	181.2722	221.4064	270.4264
21	101.4940	125.2110	154.4700	190.5663	235.0974	290.0345	357.8092
22	126.4694	157.5905	196.3699	244.6919	304.9049	379.9349	473.4281
23	157.5905	198.3434	249.6350	314.1907	395.4404	497.7013	626.4068
24	196.3699	249.6350	317.3483	403.4288	512.8585	651.9709	828.8175
25	244.6919	314.1907	403.4288	518.0128	665.1416	854.0588	1096.633
30	735.0952	992.2747	1339.431	1808.042	2440.602	3294.468	4447.067
35	2208.348	3133.795	4447.067	6310.688	8955.293	12708.17	18033.74
40	6634.244	9897.129	14764.78	22026.47	32859.63	49020.80	73130.44
45	19930.37	31257.04	49020.80	76879.92	120571.7	189094.1	296558.6
50	59874.14	98715.77	162754.8	268337.3	442413.4	729416.4	1202604
55	179871.9	311763.4	540364.9	936589.2	1623346	2813669	4876801
60	540364.9	984609.1	1794075	3269017	5956538	10853520	19776403

Table A.6 Present value of $1 with a continuous discount rate r for T periods: Values of e^{-rT}

Period (T)	Continuous discount rate (r)						
	1%	2%	3%	4%	5%	6%	7%
1	0.9900	0.9802	0.9704	0.9608	0.9512	0.9418	0.9324
2	0.9802	0.9608	0.9418	0.9231	0.9048	0.8869	0.8694
3	0.9704	0.9418	0.9139	0.8869	0.8607	0.8353	0.8106
4	0.9608	0.9231	0.8869	0.8521	0.8187	0.7866	0.7558
5	0.9512	0.9048	0.8607	0.8187	0.7788	0.7408	0.7047
6	0.9418	0.8869	0.8353	0.7866	0.7408	0.6977	0.6570
7	0.9324	0.8694	0.8106	0.7558	0.7047	0.6570	0.6126
8	0.9231	0.8521	0.7866	0.7261	0.6703	0.6188	0.5712
9	0.9139	0.8353	0.7634	0.6977	0.6376	0.5827	0.5326
10	0.9048	0.8187	0.7408	0.6703	0.6065	0.5488	0.4966
11	0.8958	0.8025	0.7189	0.6440	0.5769	0.5169	0.4630
12	0.8869	0.7866	0.6977	0.6188	0.5488	0.4868	0.4317
13	0.8781	0.7711	0.6771	0.5945	0.5220	0.4584	0.4025
14	0.8694	0.7558	0.6570	0.5712	0.4966	0.4317	0.3753
15	0.8607	0.7408	0.6376	0.5488	0.4724	0.4066	0.3499
16	0.8521	0.7261	0.6188	0.5273	0.4493	0.3829	0.3263
17	0.8437	0.7118	0.6005	0.5066	0.4274	0.3606	0.3042
18	0.8353	0.6977	0.5827	0.4868	0.4066	0.3396	0.2837
19	0.8270	0.6839	0.5655	0.4677	0.3867	0.3198	0.2645
20	0.8187	0.6703	0.5488	0.4493	0.3679	0.3012	0.2466
21	0.8106	0.6570	0.5326	0.4317	0.3499	0.2837	0.2299
22	0.8025	0.6440	0.5169	0.4148	0.3329	0.2671	0.2144
23	0.7945	0.6313	0.5016	0.3985	0.3166	0.2516	0.1999
24	0.7866	0.6188	0.4868	0.3829	0.3012	0.2369	0.1864
25	0.7788	0.6065	0.4724	0.3679	0.2865	0.2231	0.1738
30	0.7408	0.5488	0.4066	0.3012	0.2231	0.1653	0.1225
35	0.7047	0.4966	0.3499	0.2466	0.1738	0.1225	0.0863
40	0.6703	0.4493	0.3012	0.2019	0.1353	0.0907	0.0608
45	0.6376	0.4066	0.2592	0.1653	0.1054	0.0672	0.0429
50	0.6065	0.3679	0.2231	0.1353	0.0821	0.0498	0.0302
55	0.5769	0.3329	0.1920	0.1108	0.0639	0.0369	0.0213
60	0.5488	0.3012	0.1653	0.0907	0.0498	0.0273	0.0150

Table A.6, continued   Present value of $1 with a continuous discount rate r for T periods: Values of e^{-rT}

Period (T)	Continuous discount rate (r)									
	8%	9%	10%	11%	12%	13%	14%	15%	16%	17%
1	0.9231	0.9139	0.9048	0.8958	0.8869	0.8781	0.8694	0.8607	0.8521	0.8437
2	0.8521	0.8353	0.8187	0.8025	0.7866	0.7711	0.7558	0.7408	0.7261	0.7118
3	0.7866	0.7634	0.7408	0.7189	0.6977	0.6771	0.6570	0.6376	0.6188	0.6005
4	0.7261	0.6977	0.6703	0.6440	0.6188	0.5945	0.5712	0.5488	0.5273	0.5066
5	0.6703	0.6376	0.6065	0.5769	0.5488	0.5220	0.4966	0.4724	0.4493	0.4274
6	0.6188	0.5827	0.5488	0.5169	0.4868	0.4584	0.4317	0.4066	0.3829	0.3606
7	0.5712	0.5326	0.4966	0.4630	0.4317	0.4025	0.3753	0.3499	0.3263	0.3042
8	0.5273	0.4868	0.4493	0.4148	0.3829	0.3535	0.3263	0.3012	0.2780	0.2567
9	0.4868	0.4449	0.4066	0.3716	0.3396	0.3104	0.2837	0.2592	0.2369	0.2165
10	0.4493	0.4066	0.3679	0.3329	0.3012	0.2725	0.2466	0.2231	0.2019	0.1827
11	0.4148	0.3716	0.3329	0.2982	0.2671	0.2393	0.2144	0.1920	0.1720	0.1541
12	0.3829	0.3396	0.3012	0.2671	0.2369	0.2101	0.1864	0.1653	0.1466	0.1300
13	0.3535	0.3104	0.2725	0.2393	0.2101	0.1845	0.1620	0.1423	0.1249	0.1097
14	0.3263	0.2837	0.2466	0.2144	0.1864	0.1620	0.1409	0.1225	0.1065	0.0926
15	0.3012	0.2592	0.2231	0.1920	0.1653	0.1423	0.1225	0.1054	0.0907	0.0781
16	0.2780	0.2369	0.2019	0.1720	0.1466	0.1249	0.1065	0.0907	0.0773	0.0659
17	0.2567	0.2165	0.1827	0.1541	0.1300	0.1097	0.0926	0.0781	0.0659	0.0556
18	0.2369	0.1979	0.1653	0.1381	0.1153	0.0963	0.0805	0.0672	0.0561	0.0469
19	0.2187	0.1809	0.1496	0.1237	0.1023	0.0846	0.0699	0.0578	0.0478	0.0396
20	0.2019	0.1653	0.1353	0.1108	0.0907	0.0743	0.0608	0.0498	0.0408	0.0334
21	0.1864	0.1511	0.1225	0.0993	0.0805	0.0652	0.0529	0.0429	0.0347	0.0282
22	0.1720	0.1381	0.1108	0.0889	0.0714	0.0573	0.0460	0.0369	0.0296	0.0238
23	0.1588	0.1262	0.1003	0.0797	0.0633	0.0503	0.0400	0.0317	0.0252	0.0200
24	0.1466	0.1153	0.0907	0.0714	0.0561	0.0442	0.0347	0.0273	0.0215	0.0169
25	0.1353	0.1054	0.0821	0.0639	0.0498	0.0388	0.0302	0.0235	0.0183	0.0143
30	0.0907	0.0672	0.0498	0.0369	0.0273	0.0202	0.0150	0.0111	0.0082	0.0061
35	0.0608	0.0429	0.0302	0.0213	0.0150	0.0106	0.0074	0.0052	0.0037	0.0026
40	0.0408	0.0273	0.0183	0.0123	0.0082	0.0055	0.0037	0.0025	0.0017	0.0011
45	0.0273	0.0174	0.0111	0.0071	0.0045	0.0029	0.0018	0.0012	0.0007	0.0005
50	0.0183	0.0111	0.0067	0.0041	0.0025	0.0015	0.0009	0.0006	0.0003	0.0002
55	0.0123	0.0071	0.0041	0.0024	0.0014	0.0008	0.0005	0.0003	0.0002	0.0001
60	0.0082	0.0045	0.0025	0.0014	0.0007	0.0004	0.0002	0.0001	0.0001	0.0000

					Continuous discount rate (r)					
18%	19%	20%	21%	22%	23%	24%	25%	26%	27%	28%
0.8353	0.8270	0.8187	0.8106	0.8025	0.7945	0.7866	0.7788	0.7711	0.7634	0.7558
0.6977	0.6839	0.6703	0.6570	0.6440	0.6313	0.6188	0.6065	0.5945	0.5827	0.5712
0.5827	0.5655	0.5488	0.5326	0.5169	0.5016	0.4868	0.4724	0.4584	0.4449	0.4317
0.4868	0.4677	0.4493	0.4317	0.4148	0.3985	0.3829	0.3679	0.3535	0.3396	0.3263
0.4066	0.3867	0.3679	0.3499	0.3329	0.3166	0.3012	0.2865	0.2725	0.2592	0.2466
0.3396	0.3198	0.3012	0.2837	0.2671	0.2516	0.2369	0.2231	0.2101	0.1979	0.1864
0.2837	0.2645	0.2466	0.2299	0.2144	0.1999	0.1864	0.1738	0.1620	0.1511	0.1409
0.2369	0.2187	0.2019	0.1864	0.1720	0.1588	0.1466	0.1353	0.1249	0.1153	0.1065
0.1979	0.1809	0.1653	0.1511	0.1381	0.1262	0.1153	0.1054	0.0963	0.0880	0.0805
0.1653	0.1496	0.1353	0.1225	0.1108	0.1003	0.0907	0.0821	0.0743	0.0672	0.0608
0.1381	0.1237	0.1108	0.0993	0.0889	0.0797	0.0714	0.0639	0.0573	0.0513	0.0460
0.1153	0.1023	0.0907	0.0805	0.0714	0.0633	0.0561	0.0498	0.0442	0.0392	0.0347
0.0963	0.0846	0.0743	0.0652	0.0573	0.0503	0.0442	0.0388	0.0340	0.0299	0.0263
0.0805	0.0699	0.0608	0.0529	0.0460	0.0400	0.0347	0.0302	0.0263	0.0228	0.0198
0.0672	0.0578	0.0498	0.0429	0.0369	0.0317	0.0273	0.0235	0.0202	0.0174	0.0150
0.0561	0.0478	0.0408	0.0347	0.0296	0.0252	0.0215	0.0183	0.0156	0.0133	0.0113
0.0469	0.0396	0.0334	0.0282	0.0238	0.0200	0.0169	0.0143	0.0120	0.0102	0.0086
0.0392	0.0327	0.0273	0.0228	0.0191	0.0159	0.0133	0.0111	0.0093	0.0078	0.0065
0.0327	0.0271	0.0224	0.0185	0.0153	0.0127	0.0105	0.0087	0.0072	0.0059	0.0049
0.0273	0.0224	0.0183	0.0150	0.0123	0.0101	0.0082	0.0067	0.0055	0.0045	0.0037
0.0228	0.0185	0.0150	0.0122	0.0099	0.0080	0.0065	0.0052	0.0043	0.0034	0.0028
0.0191	0.0153	0.0123	0.0099	0.0079	0.0063	0.0051	0.0041	0.0033	0.0026	0.0021
0.0159	0.0127	0.0101	0.0080	0.0063	0.0050	0.0040	0.0032	0.0025	0.0020	0.0016
0.0133	0.0105	0.0082	0.0065	0.0051	0.0040	0.0032	0.0025	0.0019	0.0015	0.0012
0.0111	0.0087	0.0067	0.0052	0.0041	0.0032	0.0025	0.0019	0.0015	0.0012	0.0009
0.0045	0.0033	0.0025	0.0018	0.0014	0.0010	0.0007	0.0006	0.0004	0.0003	0.0002
0.0018	0.0013	0.0009	0.0006	0.0005	0.0003	0.0002	0.0002	0.0001	0.0001	0.0001
0.0007	0.0005	0.0003	0.0002	0.0002	0.0001	0.0001	0.0000	0.0000	0.0000	0.0000
0.0003	0.0002	0.0001	0.0001	0.0001	0.0000	0.0000	0.0000	0.0000	0.0000	0.0000
0.0001	0.0001	0.0000	0.0000	0.0000	0.0000	0.0000	0.0000	0.0000	0.0000	0.0000
0.0001	0.0000	0.0000	0.0000	0.0000	0.0000	0.0000	0.0000	0.0000	0.0000	0.0000
0.0000	0.0000	0.0000	0.0000	0.0000	0.0000	0.0000	0.0000	0.0000	0.0000	0.0000

Table A.6, continued	Present value of $1 with a continuous discount rate r for T periods: Values of e^{-rT}

Period (T)	Continuous discount rate (r)						
	29%	30%	31%	32%	33%	34%	35%
1	0.7483	0.7408	0.7334	0.7261	0.7189	0.7188	0.7047
2	0.5599	0.5488	0.5379	0.5273	0.5169	0.5066	0.4966
3	0.4190	0.4066	0.3946	0.3829	0.3716	0.3606	0.3499
4	0.3135	0.3012	0.2894	0.2780	0.2671	0.2567	0.2466
5	0.2346	0.2231	0.2122	0.2019	0.1920	0.1827	0.1738
6	0.1755	0.1653	0.1557	0.1466	0.1381	0.1300	0.1225
7	0.1313	0.1225	0.1142	0.1065	0.0993	0.0926	0.0863
8	0.0983	0.0907	0.0837	0.0773	0.0714	0.0659	0.0608
9	0.0735	0.0672	0.0614	0.0561	0.0513	0.0469	0.0429
10	0.0550	0.0498	0.0450	0.0408	0.0369	0.0334	0.0302
11	0.0412	0.0369	0.0330	0.0296	0.0265	0.0238	0.0213
12	0.0308	0.0273	0.0242	0.0215	0.0191	0.0169	0.0150
13	0.0231	0.0202	0.0178	0.0156	0.0137	0.0120	0.0106
14	0.0172	0.0150	0.0130	0.0113	0.0099	0.0086	0.0074
15	0.0129	0.0111	0.0096	0.0082	0.0071	0.0061	0.0052
16	0.0097	0.0082	0.0070	0.0060	0.0051	0.0043	0.0037
17	0.0072	0.0061	0.0051	0.0043	0.0037	0.0031	0.0026
18	0.0054	0.0045	0.0038	0.0032	0.0026	0.0022	0.0018
19	0.0040	0.0033	0.0028	0.0023	0.0019	0.0016	0.0013
20	0.0030	0.0025	0.0020	0.0017	0.0014	0.0011	0.0009
21	0.0023	0.0018	0.0015	0.0012	0.0010	0.0008	0.0006
22	0.0017	0.0014	0.0011	0.0009	0.0007	0.0006	0.0005
23	0.0013	0.0010	0.0008	0.0006	0.0005	0.0004	0.0003
24	0.0009	0.0007	0.0006	0.0005	0.0004	0.0003	0.0002
25	0.0007	0.0006	0.0004	0.0003	0.0003	0.0002	0.0002
30	0.0002	0.0001	0.0001	0.0001	0.0001	0.0000	0.0000
35	0.0000	0.0000	0.0000	0.0000	0.0000	0.0000	0.0000
40	0.0000	0.0000	0.0000	0.0000	0.0000	0.0000	0.0000
45	0.0000	0.0000	0.0000	0.0000	0.0000	0.0000	0.0000
50	0.0000	0.0000	0.0000	0.0000	0.0000	0.0000	0.0000
55	0.0000	0.0000	0.0000	0.0000	0.0000	0.0000	0.0000
60	0.0000	0.0000	0.0000	0.0000	0.0000	0.0000	0.0000